PLAUTUS

WITH AN ENGLISH TRANSLATION BY

PAUL NIXON

DEAN OF BOWDOIN COLLEGE, MAINE

IN FIVE VOLUMES

I

AMPHITRYON
THE COMEDY OF ASSES
THE POT OF GOLD
THE TWO BACCHISES
THE CAPTIVES

CAMBRIDGE, MASSACHUSETTS
HARVARD UNIVERSITY PRESS
LONDON
WILLIAM HEINEMANN LTD
MCMLXI

First printed 1916
Reprinted 1921. 1928. 1936, 1950
1956, 1961

PRINTED IN GREAT BRITAIN

CONTENTS

THE GREEK ORIGINALS OF THE PLAYS
IN THIS VOLUME

In this and each succeeding volume a summary
will be given of the consensus of opinion [1] regarding
the Greek originals of the plays in the volume and
regarding the time of presentation in Rome of
Plautus's adaptations. It may be that some general
readers will be glad to have even so condensed an
account of these matters as will be offered them.

The original of the *Amphitruo* is not now thought
to have been a work of the Middle Comedy but of
the New Comedy, very possibly Philemon's Νὺξ
μακρά. A clue to the Greek play's date is found
in the description of Amphitryon's battle with the
Teloboians,[2] a battle fought after the manner of
those of the Diadochi who came into prominence at
the death of Alexander the Great. The date of
the Plautine adaptation of this play, as in the case
of the *Asinaria*, *Aulularia*, *Bacchides*,[3] and *Captivi*, is
quite uncertain, beyond the fact that it no doubt
belongs, like almost all of his extant work, to the

---

[1] See especially Hueffner, *De Plauti Comoediarum Exemplis Atticis*, Göttingen, 1894; Legrand, *Daos*, Paris, 1910, English translation by James Loeb under title *The New Greek Comedy*, William Heinemann, 1916; Leo, *Plautinische Forschungen*, Berlin, 1912.

[2] *Amph.* 203 *seq.*

[3] Produced later than the *Epidicus*. Cf. *Bacch.* 214.

THE GREEK ORIGINALS

last two decades of his life, 204–184 B.C. The *Amphitruo* is one of the five [1] plays in the first two volumes whose scene is not laid in Athens.

The ʼΟναγός of a certain Demophilus,[2] otherwise unknown to us, was the original of the *Asinaria*. The assertion of Libanus that he is his master's Salus [3] is thought to be a fling at the honours decreed certain of the Diadochi, who were called, while still alive, Σωτῆρες. This possibility, together with the fact that the Pellaean [4] merchant and the Rhodian [5] Periphanes travel to Athens—northern Greece and the Aegaean therefore being pacified and Athens at peace with Macedon—would indicate that the ʼΟναγός was written while Demetrius Poliorcetes controlled Macedon, 294–288 B.C.

Very slender evidence connects the *Aulularia* with some unknown play of Menander's in which a miser is represented δεδιὼς μή τι τῶν ἔνδον ὁ καπνὸς οἴχοιτο φέρων. Euclio's distress [6] at seeing any smoke escape from his house seems at least to suggest that Plautus may have borrowed the *Aulularia* from Menander. The allusion to *praefectum mulierum*,[7] rather than *censorem*, would seem to show that in the original γυναικονόμον had been written: this would prove the Greek play to have been presented while Demetrius of Phalerum was in power at Athens (317–307 B.C.), where he introduced this detested office, which was done away with by 307 B.C.

---

[1] *Amphitruo*, Thebes; *Captivi*, Aetolia; *Cistellaria*, Sicyon; *Curculio*, Epidaurus (the Caria first referred to in v. 67 was a Greek town, not the state in Asia Minor); *Menaechmi*, Epidamnus.
[2] *Asin.* Prol. 10–11. [3] *Asin.* 713. [4] *Asin.* 334.
[5] *Asin.* 499. [6] *Aulul.* 299–301. [7] *Aulul.* 504.

Ritschl [1] has shown clearly enough that the original of the *Bacchides* was Menander's Δὶς ἐξαπατῶν. The fact that Athens, Samos, and Ephesus are at peace, that the Aegaean is not swept by hostile fleets, that one can travel freely between Athens and Phocis, together with the allusion to Demetrius,[2] lead one to believe that the Δὶς ἐξαπατῶν was written either between the years 316–307 or 298–296 B.C.

The original of the *Captivi* is quite unknown, while the war between the Aetolians and Eleans gives the only clue to the date of this original. Hueffner [3] considers it probable that the war was that between Aristodemus and Alexander, and the Greek play was produced shortly after 314 B.C. Others [4] assume that the scene of the play would not be Aetolia unless Aetolia had become an important state, and that the war was therefore one of the third century B.C.

---

[1] Ritschl, *Parerga*, pp. 405 *seq.* Cf. Menander, *Fragments*, 125, 126.

[2] *Bacch.* 912.   [3] Hueffner, *op. cit.* pp. 41–42.

[4] Cf. Legrand, *op. cit.* p. 18.

INTRODUCTION

LITTLE is known of the life of Titus Maccius
Plautus. He was born about 255 B.C. at Sarsina,
in Umbria; it is said that he went to Rome at an
early age, worked at a theatre, saved some money,
lost it in a mercantile venture, returned to Rome
penniless, got employment in a mill and wrote,
during his leisure hours, three plays. These three
plays were followed by many more than the
twenty extant, most of them written, it would
seem, in the latter half of his life, and all of them
adapted from the comedies of various Greek
dramatists, chiefly of the New Comedy.[1] Adaptations rather than translations they certainly were.
Apart from the many allusions in his comedies to
customs and conditions distinctly Roman, there is
evidence enough in Plautus's language and style

---

[1] The *Asinaria* was adapted from the 'Ὀναγός of Demophilus; the *Casina* from the Κληρούμενοι, the *Rudens* from an
unknown play, perhaps the Πήρα, of Diphilus; the *Stichus*,
in part, from the 'Ἀδελφοί ά of Menander. Menander's
Δὶς ἐξαπατῶν was probably the source of the *Bacchides*,
while the *Aulularia* and *Cistellaria* probably were adapted
from other plays (titles unknown) by Menander. The
Mercator and *Trinummus* are adaptations of Philemon's
'Ἔμπορος and Θησαυρός; the *Mostellaria* very possibly is
an adaptation of his Φάσμα, the *Amphitruo*, perhaps, an
adaptation of his Νὺξ μακρά.

that he was not a close translator.   Modern translators who have struggled vainly to reproduce
faithfully in their own tongues, even in prose, the
countless puns and quips, the incessant alliteration
and assonance in the Latin lines, would be the
last to admit that Plautus, writing so much, writing
in verse, and writing with such careless, jovial,
exuberant ease, was nothing but a translator in the
narrow sense of the term.

Very few of his extant comedies can be dated,
so far as the year of their production in Rome is
concerned, with any great degree of certainty.
The *Miles Gloriosus* appeared about 206, the *Cistellaria* about 202, *Stichus* in 200, *Pseudolus* in 191
B.C.; the *Truculentus*, like *Pseudolus*, was composed
when Plautus was an old man, not many years
before his death in 184 B.C.

Welcome as a full autobiography of Plautus
would be, in place of such scant and tasteless bio-
graphical morsels as we do have, only less welcome, perhaps, would be his own stage directions
for his plays, supposing him to have written stage
directions and to have written them with something
more than even modern fullness. We should learn
how he met the stage conventions and limitations
of his day; how successfully he could, by make-up
and mannerism, bring on the boards palpably
different persons in the Scapins and Bobadils and
Doll Tear-sheets that on the printed page often
seem so confusingly similar; and most important,
we should learn precisely what sort of dramatist
he was and wished to be.

If Plautus himself greatly cared, or expected
his restless, uncultivated, fun-seeking audience to

xii

care, about the construction of his plays, one must criticize him and rank him on a very different basis than if his main, and often his sole, object was to amuse the groundlings. If he often took himself and his art with hardly more seriousness than does the writer of the vaudeville skit or musical comedy of to-day, if he often wished primarily to gain the immediate laugh, then much of Langen's long list of the playwright's dramatic delinquencies is somewhat beside its intended point.

And in large measure this—to hold his audience by any means—does seem to have been his ambition : if the joke mars the part, down with the part ; if the ludicrous scene interrupts the development of the plot, down with the plot. We have plenty of verbal evidence that the dramatist frequently chose to let his characters become caricatures : we have some verbal evidence that their " stage business " was sometimes made laughably extravagant : in many cases it is sufficiently obvious that he expected his actors to indulge in grotesqueries, well or ill timed, no matter, provided they brought guffaws. It is probable, therefore, that in many other cases, where the tone and " stage business " are not as obvious, where an actor's high seriousness might elicit catcalls, and burlesque certainly would elicit chuckles, Plautus wished his players to avoid the catcalls.

This is by no means the universal rule. In the writer of the *Captivi*, for instance, we are dealing with a dramatist whose aims are different and higher. Though Lessing's encomium of the play is one to which not all of us can assent, and though even the *Captivi* shows some technical flaws, it is a work which must be rated according to the standards we apply to a *Minna von Barnhelm* rather than according to those applied to a *Pinafore* : here, certainly, we have comedy, not farce.

But whatever standards be applied to his plays their outstanding characters, their amusing situations, their vigour and comicality of dialogue remain. Euclio and Pyrgopolynices, the straits of the brothers Menaechmus and the postponement of Argyrippus's desires, the verbal encounter of Tranio and Grumio, of Trachalio and the fishermen —characters, situations, and dialogues such as these should survive because of their own excellence, not because of modern imitations and parallels such as Harpagon and Parolles, the misadventures of the brothers Antipholus and Juliet's difficulties with her nurse, the remarks of Petruchio to the tailor, of Touchstone to William.

Though his best drawn characters can and should stand by themselves, it is interesting to note how many favourite personages in the modern drama and in modern fiction Plautus at least prefigures. Long though the list is, it does not contain a large proportion of thoroughly respectable names. Plautus rarely introduces us to people, male or female, whom we should care to have long in the same house with us. A real lady seldom appears in these comedies, and—to approach a paradox— when she does she usually comes perilously close to being no lady : the same is usually true of the real gentleman. The generalization in the Epilogue of *The Captives* may well be made particular : "Plautus finds few plays such as this which make good men better." Yet there is little in his

plays which makes **men**—to say nothing of good
men—worse. A bluff Shakespearean coarseness
of thought and expression there often is, together
with a number of atrocious characters and scenes
and situations. But compared with the worst
of a Congreve or a Wycherley, compared with
the worst of our own contemporary plays and
musical comedies, the worst of Plautus, now because of its being too revolting, now because of its
being too laughable, is innocuous. His moral land
is one of black and white, mostly black, without
many of those really dangerous half-lights and
shadows in which too many of our present day
playwrights virtuously invite us to skulk and peer
and speculate.

Comparatively harmless though they are, the
translator has felt obliged to dilute certain phrases
and lines.

The text accompanying his version is that of
Leo, published by Weidmann, 1895–96. In the few
cases where he has departed from this text brief
critical notes are given: a few changes in punc-
tuation have been accepted without comment. In
view of the wish of the Editors of the Library
that the text pages be printed without unnecessary
defacements, it has seemed best to omit the lines
that Leo brackets as un-Plautine [1]: attention is
called to the omission in each case and the omitted
lines are given in the note: the numbering, of
course, is kept unchanged. Leo's daggers and

---

[1] It seemed best to make no exceptions to this rule:
even such a line as Bacchides 107 is therefore omitted
Cf. Lindsay, *Classical Quarterly,* 1913, pp. 1, 2; Havet,
Classical Quarterly, 1913, pp. 120, 121.

asterisks indicating corruption and lacunæ are omitted, again with brief notes in each case.

The translator gladly acknowledges his indebtedness to several of the English editors of the plays, notably to Lindsay, and to two or three English translators, for a number of phrases much more happily turned by them than by himself: the difficulty of rendering verse into prose—if one is to remain as close as may be to the spirit and letter of the verse, and at the same time not disregard entirely the contributions made by the metre to gaiety and gravity of tone—is sufficient to make him wish to mitigate his failure by whatever means. He is also much indebted to Professors Charles Knapp, K. C. M. Sills, and F. E. Woodruff for many valuable suggestions.

Brunswick, Me.,
September, 1913.

BIBLIOGRAPHY

Principal Editions :

Merula, Venice, 1472; the first edition.

Camerarius, Basel, 1552.

Lambinus, Paris, 1576; with a commentary.

Pareus, Frankfurt, 1619, 1623, and 1641.

Gronovius, Leyden, 1664–1684.

Bothe, Berlin, 1809–1811.

Ritschl, Bonn, 1848–1854; a most important edition; contains only nine plays.

Goetz, Loewe, and Schoell, Leipzig, 1871–1902; begun by Ritschl, as a revision and continuation of the previous edition.

Ussing, Copenhagen, 1875–1892; with a commentary.

Leo, Berlin, 1895–1896.

Lindsay, Oxford, 1904–1905.

Goetz and Schoell, Leipzig, 1892–1904.

English Translations :

Thornton, and others, London, second edition, 1769–1774; in blank verse.

Sugden, London, 1893; the first five plays, in the original metres.

General :

Ritschl, *Parerga*, Leipzig, 1845; *Neue plautinische Excurse*, Leipzig, 1869.

xvii

BIBLIOGRAPHY

Müller, *Plautinische Prosodie*, Berlin, 1869.

Reinhardstoettner (Karl von), *Spätere Bearbeitungen plautinischer Lustspiele*, Leipzig, 1886.

Langen, *Beiträge zur Kritik und Erklärung des Plautus*, Leipzig, 1880; *Plautinische Studien*, Berlin, 1886.

Sellar, *Roman Poets of the Republic*, Oxford, third edition, 1889, pp. 153–203.

Skutsch, *Forschungen zur lateinischen Grammatik und Metrik*, Leipzig, 1892.

Leo, *Plautinische Forschungen*, Berlin, 1895; second edition, 1912; *Die plautinischen Cantica und die hellenistische Lyrik*, Berlin, 1897.

Lindsay, *Syntax of Plautus*, Oxford, 1907.

Lodge, *Lexicon Plautinum*, Leipzig, 1901—.

PRINCIPAL MANUSCRIPTS

Ambrosianus palimpsestus (A), 4th century.
Palatinus Vaticanus (B), 10th century.
Palatinus Heidelbergensis (C), 11th century.
Vaticanus Ursinianus (D), 11th century.
Leidensis Vossianus (V), 12th century.
Ambrosianus (E), 12th century.
Londinensis (J), 12th century.

P = the supposed archetype of BCDVEJ.

SOME ANNOTATED EDITIONS OF
PLAYS IN THE FIRST VOLUME

Amphitruo, Palmer; London, Macmillan & Co., 1890.

Asinaria, Gray; Cambridge, University Press, 1894.

Aulularia, Wagner; London, George Bell & Sons, 1878.

Captivi, Brix; 6th edition, revised by Niemeyer; Leipzig, Teubner, 1910.

Captivi, Sonnenschein; London, W. Swan Sonnenschein & Allen, 1880.

Captivi, Lindsay; London, Methuen, 1900.

AMPHITRYON

ARGVMENTVM I[1]

In faciem versus Amphitruonis Iuppiter,
dum bellum gereret cum Telobois hostibus,
Alcmenam uxorem cepit usurariam.
Mercurius formam Sosiae servi gerit
absentis: his Alcmena decipitur dolis.
postquam rediere veri Amphitruo et Sosia,
uterque deluduntur in mirum modum.
hinc iurgium, tumultus uxori et viro,
donec cum tonitru voce missa ex aethere
adulterum se Iuppiter confessus est.   10

ARGVMENTVM II

Amore captus Alcumenas Iuppiter
Mutavit sese in formam eius coniugis,
Pro patria Amphitruo dum decernit cum hostibus.
Habitu Mercurius ei subservit Sosiae.
Is advenientis servum ac dominum frustra habet.
Turbas uxori ciet Amphitruo, atque invicem
Raptant pro moechis. Blepharo captus arbiter
Vter sit non quit Amphitruo decernere.
Omnem rem noscunt. geminos Alcumena eniti-
    tur.[2]

[1] None of the Arguments prefixed to the plays is by
Plautus. Their date is disputed, the acrostics having
been written during the first century B.C., perhaps, the
non-acrostics later.
[2] Corrupt (Leo): *Alcumena* MSS : *illa* Bothe.

ARGUMENT OF THE PLAY (I)

While Amphitryon was engaged in a war with his
foes, the Teloboians, Jupiter assumed his appearance and took the loan of his wife, Alcmena.
Mercury takes the form of an absent slave, Sosia,
and Alcmena is deceived by the two impostors.
After the real Amphitryon and Sosia return they
both are deluded in extraordinary fashion. This
leads to an altercation and quarrel between wife
and husband, until there comes from the heavens,
with a peal of thunder, the voice of Jupiter, who
owns that he has been the guilty lover.

ARGUMENT OF THE PLAY (II)

Jupiter, being seized with love for Alcmena,
changed his form to that of her husband, Amphitryon, while he was doing battle with his enemies
in defence of his country. Mercury, in the guise
of Sosia, seconds his father and dupes both servant
and master on their return. Amphitryon storms
at his wife: charges of adultery, too, are bandied
back and forth between him and Jupiter. Blepharo
is appointed arbiter, but is unable to decide which
is the real Amphitryon. They learn the whole
truth at last, and Alcmena gives birth to twin sons.

3

PERSONAE

MERCVRIVS DEUS
SOSIA SERVUS
IVPPITER DEUS
ALCVMENA MATRONA
AMPHITRVO DUX
BLEPHARO GUBERNATOR
BROMIA ANCILLA

DRAMATIS PERSONÆ

Mercury, *a god.*
Sosia, *slave of Amphitryon.*
Jupiter, *a god.*
Alcmena, *wife of Amphitryon.*
Amphitryon, *commander-in-chief of the Theban army.*
Blepharo, *a pilot.*
Bromia, *maid to Alcmena.*

PROLOGVS [1]

MERCVRIVS

DEVS

Ut vos in vostris voltis mercimoniis
emundis vendundisque me laetum lucris
adficere atque adiuvare in rebus omnibus
et ut res rationesque vostrorum omnium
bene me expedire voltis peregrique et domi
bonoque atque amplo auctare perpetuo lucro
quasque incepistis res quasque inceptabitis,
et uti bonis vos vostrosque omnis nuntiis
me adficere voltis, ea adferam, ea uti nuntiem
quae maxime in rem vostram communem sient—   10
nam vos quidem id iam scitis concessum et datum
mi esse ab dis aliis, nuntiis praesim et lucro —:
haec ut me voltis adprobare adnitier,[2]
ita huic facietis fabulae silentium
itaque aequi et iusti hic eritis omnes arbitri.
    Nunc cuius iussu venio et quam ob rem venerim
dicam simulque ipse eloquar nomen meum.
Iovis iussu venio, nomen Mercurio est mihi.
pater huc me misit ad vos oratum meus,   20
tam etsi, pro imperio vobis quod dictum foret,
scibat facturos, quippe qui intellexerat
vereri vos se et metuere, ita ut aequom est Iovem;
verum profecto hoc petere me precario
a vobis iussit, leniter, dictis bonis.

[1] The genuineness of the Prologues of these plays has
long been a moot question. The tendency of the more
recent investigators has been to hold that all were, at
least in part, written by Plautus himself.

[2] Leo brackets following v., 14 : *lucrum ut perenne vobis
semper suppetat.*

Scene :—Thebes.   A street before Amphitryon's house.

PROLOGUE

According as ye here assembled would have me prosper you and bring you luck in your buyings and in your sellings of goods, yea, and forward you in all things; and according as ye all would have me find your business affairs and speculations happy outcome in foreign lands and here at home, and crown your present and future undertakings with fine, fat profits for evermore; and according as ye would have me bring you and all yours glad news, reporting and announcing matters which most contribute to your common good (for ye doubtless are aware ere now that 'tis to me the other gods have yielded and granted plenipotence o'er messages and profits); according as ye would have me bless you in these things, then in such degree will ye (*suddenly dropping his pomposity*) keep still while we are acting this play and all be fair and square judges of the performance.

Now I will tell you who bade me come, and why I came, and likewise myself state my own name. Jupiter bade me come : my name is Mercury (*pauses, evidently hoping he has made an impression*). My father has sent me here to you to make a plea, yea, albeit he knew that whatever was told you in way of command you would do, inasmuch as he realized that you revere and dread him as men should Jupiter.   But the fact remains that he has bidden me make this request in suppliant wise, with gentle, kindly words. (*confidentially*) For you

7

etenim ille, cuius huc iussu venio, Iuppiter
non minus quam vostrum quivis formidat malum:
humana matre natus, humano patre,
mirari non est aequom, sibi si praetimet;
atque ego quoque etiam, qui Iovis sum filius,   30
contagione mei patris metuo malum.
propterea pace advenio et pacem ad vos affero.[1]:
iustam rem et facilem esse oratam a vobis volo,
nam iusta ab iustis iustus sum orator datus.
nam iniusta ab iustis impetrari non decet,
iusta autem ab iniustis petere insipientia est;
quippe illi iniqui ius ignorant neque tenent.
nunc iam huc animum omnes quae loquar advortite.
debetis velle quae velimus: meruimus
et ego et pater de vobis et re publica;   40
nam quid ego memorem,—ut alios in tragoediis
vidi, Neptunum Virtutem Victoriam
Martem Bellonam, commemorare quae bona
vobis fecissent,—quis bene factis meus pater,
deorum regnator[2] architectust[3] omnibus?
sed mos numquam illi fuit patri meo,[4]
ut exprobraret quod bonis faceret boni;
gratum arbitratur esse id a vobis sibi
meritoque vobis bona se facere quae facit.

Nunc quam rem oratum huc veni primum proloquar,   50
post argumentum huius eloquar tragoediae.
quid? contraxistis frontem, quia tragoediam
dixi futuram hanc? deus sum, commutavero.
eandem hanc, si voltis, faciam ex tragoedia

---

[1] Corrupt (Leo): *affero* MSS: *fero* Acidalius, followed
by Lindsay and others.   [2] Leo assumes lacuna here.
[3] *architectust* Pareus: *architectus* MSS. Lambinus
suggests that the actor who took the part of Jupiter may
have been a builder.   [Lindsay.
[4] Corrupt (Leo): *illi* MSS: *ille illi* Ussing, followed by

8

see, that Jupiter that " bade me come here " is just like any one of you in his horror of (*rubbing his shoulders reflectively*) trouble [1] : his mother being human, also his father, it should not seem strange if he does feel apprehensive regarding himself. Yes, and the same is true of me, the son of Jupiter : once my father has some trouble I am afraid I shall catch it, too. (*rather pompously again*) Wherefore I come in peace and peace do I bring to you. It is a just and trifling request I wish you to grant : for I am scnt as a just pleader pleading with the just for what is just. It would be unfitting, of course, for unjust favours to be obtained from the just, while looking for just treatment from the unjust is folly ; for unfair folk of that sort neither know nor keep justice. Now then, pay attention all of you to what I am about to say. Our wishes should be yours : we deserve it of you, my father and I, of you and of your state. Ah well, why should I—after the fashion of other gods, Neptune, Virtue, Victory, Mars, Bellona, whom I have seen in the tragedies recounting their goodness to you—rehearse the benefits that my father, ruler of the gods, hath builded up for all men? It never was a habit of that sire of mine to twit good people with the good he did them ; he considers you grateful to him for it and worthy of the good things he does for you.

Now first as to the favour I have come to ask, and then you shall hear the argument of our tragedy. What? Frowning because I said this was to be a tragedy? I am a god : I'll transform it. I'll convert this same play from tragedy to

---

[1] Actors might be whipped on occasion.

comoedia ut sit omnibus isdem vorsibus.
utrum sit an non voltis? sed ego stultior,
quasi nesciam vos velle, qui divos siem.
teneo quid animi vostri super hac re siet:
faciam ut commixta sit: sit tragicomoedia.
nam me perpetuo facere ut sit comoedia,   60
reges quo veniant et di, non par arbitror.
quid igitur? quoniam hic servos quoque partes
   habet,
faciam sit, proinde ut dixi, tragicomoedia.
nunc hoc me orare a vobis iussit Iuppiter,
ut conquaestores singula in subsellia
eant per totam caveam spectatoribus,
si cui favitores delegatos viderint,
ut is in cavea pignus capiantur togae;
sive qui ambissint palmam histrionibus
sive cuiquam artifici, si per scriptas litteras   70
sive qui ipse ambissit seu per internuntium,
sive adeo aediles perfidiose cui duint,
sirempse legem iussit esse Iuppiter,
quasi magistratum sibi alterive ambiverit.
virtute dixit vos victores vivere,
non ambitione neque perfidia: qui minus
eadem histrioni sit lex quae summo viro?
virtute ambire oportet, non favitoribus.
sat habet favitorum semper qui recte facit,
si illis fides est quibus est ea res in manu.   80
hoc quoque etiam mihi pater in mandatis dedit,
ut conquaestores fierent histrionibus:
qui sibi mandasset delegati ut plauderent
quive quo placeret alter fecisset minus,
10

comedy, if you like, and never change a line.
Do you wish me to do it, or not? But there! how
stupid of me! As if I didn't know that you do
wish it, when I'm a deity. I understand your
feelings in the matter perfectly. I shall mix things
up: let it be tragi-comedy. Of course it would
never do for me to make it comedy out and out,
with kings and gods on the boards. How about
it, then? Well, in view of the fact that there is a
slave part in it, I shall do just as I said and make
it tragi-comedy. Now here is the favour Jove
bade me ask of you: (*with great solemnity*) let inspectors go from seat to seat throughout the house,
and should they discover claqueurs planted for the
benefit of any party, let them take as security
from all such in the house—their togas. Or if
there be those who have solicited the palm for
actors, or for any artist—whether by letter, or by
personal solicitation, or through an intermediary—
or further, if the aediles do bestow the said palm
upon anyone unfairly, Jove doth decree that the
selfsame law obtain as should the said party solicit
guiltily, for himself or for another, public office.
'Tis worth has won your wars for you, saith he, not
solicitation or unfairness: why should not the same
law hold for player as for noblest patriot? Worth,
not hired support, should solicit victory. He who
plays his part aright ever has support enough, if it
so be that honour dwells in those whose concern it
is to judge his acts. This injunction, too, did Jove
lay upon me: that inspectors should be appointed
for the actors, to the end that whosoever has en-
joined claqueurs to clap himself, or whosoever has
endeavoured to compass the failure of another.

eius ornamenta et corium uti conciderent.
mirari nolim vos, quapropter Iuppiter
nunc histriones curet; ne miremini :
ipse hanc acturust Iuppiter comoediam.
quid? admirati estis? quasi vero novom
nunc proferatur, Iovem facere histrioniam; 90
etiam, histriones anno cum in proscaenio hic
Iovem invocarunt, venit, auxilio is fuit.[1]
hanc fabulam, inquam, hic Iuppiter hodie ipse
    aget,
et ego una cum illo. nunc vos animum advortite,
dum huius argumentum eloquar comoediae.

    Haec urbs est Thebae. in illisce habitat aedibus
Amphitruo, natus Argis ex Argo patre,
quicum Alcumena est nupta, Electri filia.
is nunc Amphitruo praefectust legionibus, 100
nam cum Telobois bellum est Thebano poplo.
is prius quam hinc abiit ipsemet in exercitum,
gravidam Alcumenam uxorem fecit suam.
nam ego vos novisse credo iam ut sit pater meus.
quam liber harum rerum multarum siet
quantusque amator sit quod complacitum est semel.
is amare occepit Alcumenam clam virum
usuramque eius corporis cepit sibi,
et gravidam fecit is eam compressu suo.
nunc de Alcumena ut rem teneatis rectius, 110
utrimque est gravida, et ex viro et ex summo Iove.
et meus pater nunc intus hic cum illa cubat,
et haec ob eam rem nox est facta longior,
dum cum illa quacum volt voluptatem capit;
sed ita adsimulavit se, quasi Amphitruo siet.

---

[1] Leo brackets following v., 93 : *praeterea certo prodit in tragoedia.*

may have his player's costume cut to shreds, also his hide. I would not have you wonder why Jove is now regardful of actors; do not so: he himself, Jove, will take part in this comedy. What? Surprised? As if it were actually a new departure, this, Jove's turning actor! Why, just last year when the actors on this very stage called upon Jupiter, he came,[1] and helped them out. This play, then, Jove himself will act in to-day, and I along with him. Now give me your attention while I unfold the argument of our comedy.

This city here is Thebes. In that house there (*pointing*) dwells Amphitryon, born in Argos, of an Argive father: and his wife is Alcmena, Electrus's daughter. At present this Amphitryon is at the head of the Theban army, the Thebans being at war with the Teloboians. Before he himself left to join his troops, his wife, Alcmena, was with child by him. (*apologetically*) Now I think you know already what my father is like—how free he is apt to be in a good many cases of this sort and what an impetuous lover he is, once his fancy is taken. Well, Alcmena caught his fancy, without her husband knowing it, and he enjoyed her and got her with child. So now Alcmena, that you may see it quite clearly, is with child by both of them, by her husband and by almighty Jove. And my father is there inside this very moment with her in his arms, and it is on this account that the present night has been prolonged while he enjoys the society of his heart's delight. All this in the guise of Amphitryon, you understand.

[1] An allusion to some play in which Jupiter appeared in time to save some situation.

Nunc ne hunc ornatum vos meum admiremini,
quod ego huc processi sic cum servili schema:
veterem atque antiquam rem novam ad vos pro-
    feram,
propterea ornatus in novom incessi modum.
nam meus pater intus nunc est eccum Iuppiter; 120
in Amphitruonis vertit sese imaginem
omnesque eum esse censent servi qui vident:
ita versipellem se facit quando lubet.
ego servi sumpsi Sosiae mi imaginem,
qui cum Amphitruone abiit hinc in exercitum,
ut praeservire amanti meo possem patri
atque ut ne, qui essem, familiares quaererent,
versari crebro hic cum viderent me domi;
nunc, cum esse credent servom et conservom suom,
haud quisquam quaeret qui siem aut quid venerim. 130
    Pater nunc intus suo animo morem gerit:
cubat complexus cuius cupiens maxime est;
quae illi ad legionem facta sunt memorat pater
meus Alcumenae: illa illum censet virum
suom esse, quae cum moecho est. ibi nunc meus
    pater
memorat, legiones hostium ut fugaverit,
quo pacto sit donis donatus plurimis.
ea dona, quae illic Amphitruoni sunt data,
abstulimus: facile meus pater quod volt facit.
nunc hodie Amphitruo veniet huc ab exercitu 140
et servos, cuius ego hanc fero imaginem.
nunc internosse ut nos possitis facilius,
ego has habebo usque in petaso pinnulas;
tum meo patri autem torulus inerit aureus
sub petaso: id signum Amphitruoni non erit.
ea signa nemo horum familiarium
videre poterit: verum vos videbitis.

AMPHITRYON

Now don't be surprised at this get-up of mine
and because I appear here in the character of a
slave as I do: I am going to submit to you a new
version of a worn and ancient tale, hence my
appearance in a new get-up. The point is, my
father Jupiter is now inside there, mark you. He
has turned himself into the very image of Amphitryon, and all the servants that see him believe
that's who he is. See how he can change his skin
when he likes! And as for me, I have assumed the
form of Amphitryon's slave Sosia, who went away
to the army with him, my idea being to subserve
my amorous sire and not have the domestics ask
who I am when they see me busy about the house
here continually. As it is, when they think I am
a servant and one of their own number, not a soul
will ask me who I am or what I've come for.

So now my father is inside indulging his heart's
desire as he lies there with his arms around the
lady-love he particularly dotes on. He is telling
Alcmena what happened during the campaign:
and she all the time thinking him her husband
when he's not. On he goes there with his stories
of putting the legions of the foe to flight and being
presented with prizes galore. The prizes Amphitryon did receive there we stole—things my father
fancies do come easy to him! Now Amphitryon
will return from the army to-day, and the slave I
am representing, too. To make it easier for you
to tell us apart I shall always wear this little plume
on my hat: yes, and as for my father he will have
a little gold tassel hanging from his: Amphitryon
will not have this mark. They are marks that
none of the household here will be able to see, but

sed Amphitruonis illic est servos Sosia:
a portu illic nunc cum lanterna advenit.
abigam iam ego illum advenientem ab aedibus.   150
adeste: erit operae pretium hic spectantibus
Iovem et Mercurium facere histrioniam.

you will. *(looking down street)* But there is Amphitryon's servant Sosia—just coming from the harbour with a lantern. I'll bustle him away from the house as soon as he gets here. Watch now! It will be worth your while to attend when Jove and Mercury take up the histrionic art. *(steps aside)*

TITUS MACCIUS PLAUTUS

ACTVS I

Sos.   Qui me alter est audacior homo aut qui confidentior,
         iuventutis mores qui sciam, qui hoc noctis solus
             ambulem?
         quid faciam nunc, si tres viri me in carcerem com-
             pegerint?
         inde cras quasi e promptaria cella depromar ad
             flagrum,
         nec causam liceat dicere mihi, neque in ero quic-
             quam auxili
         nec quisquam sit quin me malo omnes esse dignum
             deputent.
             ita quasi incudem me miserum homines octo
                 validi caedant: 159–16(
             ita peregre adveniens hospitio publicitus acci-
                 piar.   161–16?
                 haec eri immodestia
             coegit, me qui hoc noctis a portu ingratiis ex-
                 citavit.
             nonne idem hoc luci me mittere potuit?
                 opulento homini hoc servitus dura est,
                 hoc magis miser est divitis servos
             noctesque diesque assiduo satis superque est,
             quod facto aut dicto adeost opus, quietus ne sis.
             ipse dominus dives, operis et laboris expers,   17(
             quodcumque homini accidit libere, posse retur:

18

AMPHITRYON

ACT I

(Time, night.)

ENTER *Sosia*, LANTERN IN HAND.

Sos.   *(stopping and peering around timorously)* Who's a
bolder man, a more audacious man than I am—
know all about the young bloods and their capers,
I do, yet here I am strolling around all alone at
this time of night! *(seems to hear something and
jumps)* What if the police should lock me up in
jail? To-morrow I should be taken out of that
preserve closet and get served—to a rope's end;
and not a word would they let me say for myself,[1]
and not a bit of help could I get from master, and
there wouldn't be a soul but what would reckon I
deserved a hiding. Those eight strong wardens
would pound my poor carcass just as if I was an
anvil: that is how I should be entertained on coming
home from abroad—a public reception. *(disgustedly)*
It's master's impatience forced me into this, routing
me out from the harbour at this time of night,
against my will. Might have sent me on the same
errand by daylight, mightn't he? This is where it
comes hard slaving it for a nabob, this is where
a plutocrat's servant is worse off—night and day
there's work enough and more for him, no end,
always something to be done, yes, or said, so that
you can't rest. And your plutocrat of a master,
that never does a handsturn of work himself, takes
it for granted that any whim that comes into a

---

[1] Being a slave.

aequom esse putat, non reputat laboris quid
    sit [1]
ergo in servitute expetunt multa iniqua :
habendum et ferundum hoc onust cum labore.

Mer. Satius me queri illo modo servitutem :
        hodie qui fuerim liber,
    eum nunc potivit pater servitutis,
    hic qui verna natus est queritur.

Sos. Sum vero verna verbero : num numero mi in men-
        tem fuit,   180
    dis advenientem gratias pro meritis agere atque al-
        loqui ?
    ne illi edepol si merito meo referre studeant gratiam,
    aliquem hominem allegent qui mihi advenienti os
        occillet probe,
    quoniam bene quae in me fecerunt ingrata ea
        habui atque inrita.

Mer. Facit ille quod volgo haud solent, ut quid se sit
        dignum sciat.

Sos. Quod numquam opinatus fui neque alius quisquam
        civium
    sibi eventurum, id contigit, ut salvi poteremur domi.
    victores victis hostibus legiones reveniunt domum,
    duello exstincto maximo atque internecatis hostibus.
    quod multa Thebano poplo acerba obiecit funera,   190
    id vi et virtute militum victum atque expugnatum
        oppidum est
    imperio atque auspicio eri mei Amphitruonis max-
        ime.
    praeda atque agro adoriaque adfecit populares suos
    regique Thebano Creoni regnum stabilivit suom.

---

[1] Leo brackets following v., 173 : *nec aequom anne
iniquom imperet cogitabit.*

20

man's head can be gratified: yes, he counts that the fair thing, and never takes account of how much the work is. Ah, I tell you, there's a great deal of injustice this slavery lets you in for: you've got to take your load and carry it, and that is work.

Mer. (*aside*) It would be more in order for Mercury to do some of this grumbling about menial station— was free this very day, and now his father has made a slave of him. It's this fellow, a born drudge, that is grumbling.

Sos. (*frightened again*) I need a drubbing, I do, drudge that I am. I was not too quick, was I, to think of addressing the gods and giving 'em due thanks on my arrival? Oh Lord! if they took a notion to pay me back my dues, they'd commission some one to mash my face for me in fine shape on my arrival, now that I haven't appreciated the good turns they've done me and have let 'em go for nothing. (*makes sure he is safe*)

Mer. (*aside*) Rather uncommon that,—his knowing what he deserves to get.

Sos. What I never dreamed would happen nor anyone else on our side, either, has happened, and here we are safe and sound. (*magnificently*) Our legions come back victorious, our foes vanquished, a mighty contest concluded and our enemies massacred to a man. The town that has brought an untimely death to many a Theban citizen has been crushed and captured by the strength and valour of our soldiery, aye, and chiefly under the command and auspices of my own master, Amphitryon. He has furnished forth his countrymen with booty and land and fame, and fixed King Creon firm upon his Theban throne. (*subsiding*) As for me, he has sent

me a portu praemisit domum, ut haec nuntiem
    uxori suae,
ut gesserit rem publicam ductu imperio auspicio
    suo.
ea nunc meditabor quo modo illi dicam, cum illo
    advenero.
si dixero mendacium, solens meo more fecero.
nam cum pugnabant maxume, ego tum fugiebam
    maxume;
verum quasi adfuerim tamen simulabo atque audita
    eloquar.   200
sed quo modo et verbis quibus me deceat fabularier,
prius ipse mecum etiam volo hic meditari.   sic hoc
    proloquar.
    Principio ut illo advenimus, ubi primum terram
        tetigimus,
continuo Amphitruo delegit viros primorum prin-
    cipes;
eos legat, Telobois iubet sententiam ut dicant suam;
si sine vi et sine bello velint rapta et raptores
    tradere,
si quae asportassent redderent, se exercitum ex-
    templo domum
reducturum, abituros agro Argivos, pacem atque
    otium
dare illis; sin aliter sient animati neque dent quae
    petat,
sese igitur summa vi virisque eorum oppidum oppu-
    gnassere.   210
    Haec ubi Telobois ordine iterarunt quos praefe-
        cerat
Amphitruo, magnanimi viri freti virtute et viribus
superbe nimis ferociter legatos nostros increpant,
respondent bello se et suos tutari posse, proinde uti

me on ahead home from the harbour to tell his
wife the news: how the state was served under
the leadership, command, and auspices of—his very
own self. (*meditating*) Now let me think how I
am to tell her the tale when I get there. If I
do work in a lie or two, it won't be anything extraordinary for me. The fact is, it was just when
they were doing their hardest fighting that I was
doing my hardest running. Oh well, I'll pretend I
was there just the same, and recite what I heard
tell about it. But the neatest way to narrate my
story—and the words to use—I must practise a bit
by myself beforehand here. (*pauses*) Here's how
we'll begin. (*lays lantern down and addresses supposed
Alcmena importantly*)

First and foremost, when we reached there, as
soon as we had touched land, straightway Amphitryon picks out the most illustrous of his captains.
These he sends forth as legates and bids convey his
terms to the Teloboians, to wit: should they wish,
without contention and without strife, to deliver up
pillage and pillagers and restore whatsoever they
had carried off, he himself would lead his army home
forthwith and the Argives would leave their land
and grant them peace and quietude; but were they
otherwise disposed, and disinclined to yield what
he sought, he would thereupon with all the force
at his command make onslaught on their city.

When Amphitryon's ambassadors had duly made
this proclamation to the Teloboians, they, doughty
warriors, confiding in their courage and glorying
in their strength, made right rough and haughty
answer to our embassy, saying that they could
defend themselves and theirs by force of arms, and

propere irent, de suis finibus exercitus deducerent.
haec ubi legati pertulere, Amphitruo castris ilico
producit omnem exercitum. Teloboae contra ex
    oppido
legiones educunt suas nimis pulcris armis praeditas.
    postquam utrimque exitum est maxima copia,
    dispertiti viri, dispertiti ordines,   220
    nos nostras more nostro et modo instruximus
legiones, item hostes contra legiones suas instruont.
    deinde utrique imperatores in medium exeunt,
    extra turbam ordinum colloquontur simul.
    convenit, victi utri sint eo proelio,
    urbem agrum aras focos seque uti dederent.
    postquam id actum est, tubae contra utrimque
    occanunt,
    consonat terra, clamorem utrimque efferunt.
    imperator utrimque, hinc et illinc, Iovi
    vota suscipere, utrimque hortari exercitum.   230
    tum pro se quisque id quod quisque potest et
    valet
    edit, ferro ferit, tela frangunt, boat
caelum fremitu virum, ex spiritu atque anhelitu
nebula constat, cadunt volnerum vi viri.
    Denique, ut voluimus, nostra superat manus :
hostes crebri cadunt, nostri contra ingruont
vi [1] feroces.
sed [2] fugam in se tamen nemo convortitur
nec recedit loco quin statim rem gerat ;
animam omittunt prius quam loco demigrent :   240
quisque ut steterat iacet optinetque ordinem.
    hoc ubi Amphitruo erus conspicatust,
ilico equites iubet dextera inducere.

        [1] *vicimus vi* MSS : Leo brackets *vicimus*.
    [2] Corrupt (Leo). " *Convertitur pro convertit,*" Nonius 480.

24

that accordingly they should depart at once and
lead their troops out from the Teloboian borders.
On receiving this report from his legates, Amphitryon at once led forth his whole army from camp.
And from the city, too, the Teloboians led out their
legions in goodly panoply. After both sides had
marched out in full force, troops arrayed, and ranks
arrayed, we drew up our legions according to our
usual method and manner: our foemen likewise
draw up their legions facing ours. Then forward into
the centre of the field stride the leaders of both
hosts, and there out beyond the serried lines they
hold colloquy. This pact was made, that they who
were conquered in this battle should surrender city
and land, shrines, homes, and persons. This done,
the trumpets blared on either side; earth echoes;
on either side the battle cry is raised. The generals
on either side, both here and there, offer their
vows to Jove, and on either side cheer their warriors. Then each man lays about him with his every
ounce of strength and strikes home with his
blade: lances shiver: the welkin rings with the roar
of heroes: up from their gasping, panting breath
a cloud arises: men drop beneath the weight of
wounds.

At last, as we wished, our host prevails: the
foemen fall in heaps: on and on we press, fired by
our might. Yet for all that, none turns in flight
nor yields an inch, but stands his ground and
hews away. They lose their lives sooner than quit
their post. As each had stood, so he lies, and
keeps the line unbroken. When my lord Amphitryon noted this, he straightway ordered that the
cavalry on our right be led to the charge. Swift

25

equites parent citi: ab dextera maximo
    cum clamore involant impetu alacri,
foedant et proterunt hostium copias
      iure iniustas.

Mer. Numquam etiam quicquam adhuc verborum est
    prolocutus perperam:
namque ego fui illi in re praesenti et meus, cum
    pugnatum est, pater.

Sos. Perduelles penetrant se in fugam; ibi nostris ani-
    mus additust: 250
vortentibus Telobois telis complebantur corpora,
ipsusque Amphitruo regem Pterelam sua obtrun-
    cavit manu.
haec illic est pugnata pugna usque a mani ad ve-
    sperum—
hoc adeo hoc commemini magis, quia illo die
    inpransus fui—
sed proelium id tandem diremit nox interventu suo.
postridie in castra ex urbe ad nos veniunt flentes
    principes:
velatis manibus orant ignoscamus peccatum suom,
deduntque se, divina humanaque omnia, urbem et
    liberos
indicionem atque in arbitratum cuncti Thebano poplo.
post ob virtutem ero Amphitruoni patera donata
    aurea est, 260
qui Pterela potitare solitus est rex. haec sic dicam
    erae
nunc pergam eri imperium exequi et me domum
    capessere.

Mer. Attat, illic huc iturust. ibo ego illi obviam,
neque ego huc hominem hodie ad aedis has sinam
    umquam accedere;
quando imago est huius in me, certum est homi-
    nem eludere.

they obey, and with terrific yells swooping down from the right in mad career they mangle and trample underfoot the forces of our foes and right our wrongs. (*wipes his brow and meditates*)

er. (*aside*) Not a single, solitary word of fiction has he uttered yet: for I was there myself while the battle was actually going on, and my father too.

s. (*gathering himself together*) Their warriors take to flight; at this new courage animates our men. When the Teloboians turn their backs we stick them full of spears, and Amphitryon himself cut down King Pterelas with his own hand. This fight was fought out all through the day there from morn till eve. (*reflectively*) I remember this point more distinctly because that noon I went without my lunch. But darkness at last intervened and terminated the engagement. The following day their foremost men come tearfully from the city to our camp, their hands veiled in suppliant wise, and entreat us to pardon their transgression: and one and all they surrender their persons, their entire possessions sacred and profane, their city and their children to the Theban people to have and to hold as they deem fit. Then, for his valour, my lord Amphitryon was presented with a golden bowl from which King Pterelas was wont to drink. (*heaves deep sigh of relief*) This is how I will tell it to the mistress. Now I'll go finish up the job for master and take myself home. (*picks up lantern*)

er. (*aside*) Oho! about to come this way! I'll step up and meet him. The fellow shall never reach this house at present: I won't have it. Now that I am his double I fully intend to befool the fellow. And I say, considering I have taken on

27

et enim vero quoniam formam cepi huius in med
et statum,

decet et facta moresque huius habere me similes
item.

itaque me malum esse oportet, callidum, astutum
admodum

atque hunc, telo suo sibi, malitia a foribus pellere.

sed quid illuc est? caelum aspectat. observabo
quam rem agat.   270

Sos.   Certe edepol, si quicquamst aliud quod credam
aut certo sciam,

credo ego hac noctu Nocturnum obdormivisse ebrium.

nam neque se Septentriones quoquam in caelo
commovent,

neque se Luna quoquam mutat atque uti exorta est
semel,

nec Iugulae neque Vesperugo neque Vergiliae
occidunt.

ita statim stant signa, neque nox quoquam conce-
dit die.

Mer.   Perge, Nox, ut occepisti, gere patri morem meo:

optumo optume optumam operam das, datam pulchre locas.

Sos.   Neque ego hac nocte longiorem me vidisse censeo,

nisi item unam, verberatus quam pependi perpetem;   280

eam quoque edepol etiam multo haec vicit longi-
tudine.

credo edepol equidem dormire Solem, atque adpo-
tum probe;

mira sunt nisi invitavit sese in cena plusculum.

Mer.   Ain vero, verbero? deos esse tui similis putas?

ego pol te istis tuis pro dictis et male factis, furcifer,

accipiam; modo sis veni huc: invenies infortunium.

Sos.   Ubi sunt isti scortatores, qui soli inviti cubant?

28

his looks and dress, it is appropriate for me to ape
his ways and general conduct, too. I must be a sly
rapscallion, then, shifty as the deuce, yes, and
drive him away from the door with his own weapon,
roguery. (*looking at Sosia who is gaping at the stars*)
What's he at, though? Staring at the sky! I must
keep an eye on him.

Sos. My goodness, if there's anything I can believe or
know for sure, I surely do believe old Nocturnus
went to bed this night in liquor. Why, the Great
Bear hasn't moved a step anywhere in the sky,
and the moon's just as it was when it first rose,
and Orion's Belt, and the Evening Star, and the
Pleiades aren't setting, either. Yes, the constel-
lations are standing stock still, and no sign of day
anywhere.

Mer. (*aside*) Go on as you have begun, Night: oblige
my father: you're doing splendidly in a splendid
work for a splendid deity: you'll find it a fine
investment.

Sos. I don't think I ever did see a longer night—bar-
ring that one when I got whipped and was left
strung up till morning. And goodness me, in length
this one's way ahead of even that one. Gad, I
certainly do believe old Sol's asleep, asleep and
dead drunk. It's a wonder if he hasn't drunk his
own health a bit too much at dinner.

Mer. (*aside*) So, you scoundrel? Think the gods are
like yourself, eh? By heaven, I'll give you a
reception to match this talk and roguery of
yours, you gallows-bird. Just you be good enough
to step this way, and you shall meet with a
mishap.

Sos. Where are those young blades that hate a lonely

haec nox scita est exercendo scorto conducto male.

Mer. Meus pater nunc pro huius verbis recte et sapienter facit,

qui complexus cum Alcumena cubat amans animo
obsequens. 290

Sos. Ibo ut erus quod imperavit Alcumenae nuntiem.

sed quis hic est homo, quem ante aedis video hoc
noctis? non placet.

Mer. Nullust hoc metuculosus aeque.

Sos. Mi in mentem venit,

illic homo hoc de umero volt pallium detexere.

Mer. Timet homo: deludam ego illum.

Sos. Perii, dentes pruriunt;

certe advenientem hic me hospitio pugneo accep-
turus est.

credo misericors est: nunc propterea quod me
meus erus

fecit ut vigilarem, hic pugnis faciet hodie ut dormiam.

oppido interii. obsecro hercle, quantus et quam
validus est.

Mer. Clare advorsum fabulabor, ut hic auscultet quae
loquar; 300

igitur magis demum maiorem in sese concipiet
metum.

agite, pugni, iam diu est quom ventri victum non
datis:

iam pridem videtur factum, heri quod homines
quattuor

in soporem collocastis nudos.

Sos. Formido male,

ne ego hic nomen meum commutem et Quintus
fiam e Sosia;

quattuor nudos sopori se dedisse hic autumat;

metuo ne numerum augeam illum.

couch? Here is your lovely night for gallivanting
with an expensive lady.

er. (*aside*) According to this chap, my father's making
good, intelligent use of his time—loving to his
heart's content with Alcmena in his fond embrace.

s. Now for the message master told me to give mistress. (*aside as he moves toward house and sees
Mercury*) But who's that fellow in front of the
house at this time o' night? (*halts, frightened*) I
don't like it.

er. (*aside*) Of all the pusillanimous rogues!

s. (*aside*) It looks to me as if this fellow wants to take
my cloak off for me.

er. (*aside*) Our friend is scared: we'll have some sport
with him.

s. (*aside*) Oh Lord, my teeth do—itch! He's going
to give me a welcome on my arrival, he surely is,
—a fisty welcome! He's a kind-hearted soul, I do
believe. Seeing how master's kept me awake all
night, he's going to up with his fists now and put
me to sleep. Oh, I'm dead entirely! For God's
sake look at the size of him, and strong, heavens!

er. (*aside*) I'll speak out aloud, so that he can hear what
I say, and then I warrant he'll feel shakier still.
(*loudly, with melodramatic fierceness*) Fists, be up
and doing! 'Tis long since ye have made provision
for my paunch. It seems an age since yesterday
when ye stripped stark four men and laid them
away in slumber.

s. (*aside*) Oh, but I'm awfully scared my name will be
changed here and now, from Sosia to Sosia the
Fifth. Four men he's stripped already and sent to
slumberland, so he says: I'm afraid I'm going to
swell that list.

Mer.   Em, nunciam ergo: sic volo.

Sos.   Cingitur; certe expedit se.

Mer.   Non feret quin vapulet.

Sos.   Quis homo?

Mer.   Quisquis homo huc profecto venerit, pugnos edet.

Sos.   Apage, non placet me hoc noctis esse: cenavi
           modo: 310

     proin tu istam cenam largire, si sapis, esurientibus.

Mer.   Haud malum huic est pondus pugno.

Sos.   Perii, pugnos ponderat.

Mer.   Quid si ego illum tractim tangam, ut dormiat?

Sos.   Servaveris,
     nam contiuas has tris noctes pervigilavi.

Mer.   Pessumest,
     facimus nequiter, ferire malam male discit manus;
     alia forma esse oportet quem tu pugno legeris.

Sos.   Illic homo me interpolabit meumque os finget
           denuo.

Mer.   Exossatum os esse oportet quem probe percusseris.

Sos.   Mirum ni hic me quasi murenam exossare cogitat.
     ultro istunc qui exossat homines. perii, si me
           aspexerit.   320

Mer.   Olet homo quidam malo suo.

Sos.   Ei, numnam ego obolui?

AMPHITRYON

Mer. (*tightening his girdle*) There, now then! 'Tis well.

Sos. (*aside*) Loins girded! He is surely getting ready for business.

Mer. He shall not escape a trouncing.

Sos. (*aside, anxiously*) Who, who?

Mer. I tell ye, any man that comes this way shall eat fists.

Sos. (*aside*) No you don't! I don't care about eating at this time o' night. It wasn't long ago I dined. So if you've got any sense, you just bestow that dinner on the hungry.

Mer. (*examining his right fist*) There's some weight in that fist.

Sos. (*aside*) I'm finished! He's a-weighing his fists!

Mer. (*sparring*) What if I should stroke him softly into somnolence?

Sos. (*aside*) You'd save my life: I haven't slept a wink for three nights running.

Mer. (*swinging heavily*) Downright sinful, this! This is a shame! 'Tis wrong of my arm to learn really to jab a jaw! (*to arm as he feels biceps*) Merely graze a man with thy fist and his shape must needs be altered.

Sos. (*aside*) That bully's going to do me up and mould my face all over again for me.

Mer. The face that thou shalt smite in earnest is bound thereafter to be boneless.

Sos. (*aside*) Sure enough he's reckoning on boning me like a lamprey. I—I object to these man-boners. It's all up if he catches sight of me.

Mer. (*sniffing the air*) Ha! I smell somebody, and woe to him!

Sos. (*aside*) Oh, dear! It can't be he's got a whiff of me?

33

Mer.   Atque haud longe abesse oportet, verum longe hinc
         afuit.

Sos.   Illi homo superstitiosust.

Mer.   Gestiunt pugni mihi.

Sos.   Si in me exercituru's, quaeso in parietem ut
         primum domes.

Mer.   Vox mi ad aures advolavit.

Sos.   Ne ego homo infelix fui,
         qui non alas intervelli : volucrem vocem gestito.

Mer.   Illic homo a me sibi malam rem arcessit iumento suo.

Sos.   Non equidem ullum habeo iumentum.

Mer.   Onerandus est pugnis probe.

Sos.   Lassus sum hercle, navi ut vectus huc sum : etiam
         nunc nauseo ;

         vix incedo inanis, ne ire posse cum onere existimes.   330

Mer.   Certe enim hic nescio quis loquitur.

Sos.   Salvos sum, non me videt :
         nescioquem loqui autumat ; mihi certo nomen
         Sosiaest.

Mer.   Hinc enim mihi dextra vox auris, ut videtur,
         verberat.

Sos.   Metuo, vocis ne vicem hodie hic vapulem, quae
         hunc verberat.

Mer.   Optume eccum incedit ad me.

Sos.   Timeo, totus torpeo.
         non edepol nunc ubi terrarum sim scio, si quis roget,
         neque miser me commovere possum prae formidine.
         ilicet, mandata eri perierunt una et Sosia.
         verum certum est confidenter hominem contra con-
         loqui,

Mer.   Aye, and he must be near at hand, albeit he has been afar from here.

Sos.   (*aside*) The fellow's got second sight.

Mer.   My fists are rampant.

Sos.   (*in low tone*) If you intend to put 'em through their paces on me, for heaven's sake break 'em in first on the wall.

Mer.   A voice hath flown unto my ear.

Sos.   (*aside*) There you are! I swear I am an unlucky devil not to have clipped its wings, and me with such a bird-like voice.

Mer.   Yon wight doth summon me to wallop his beast's back for him.

Sos.   (*aside*) Never a beast do I own, not I.

Mer.   He needs a lusty load of buffets.

Sos.   (*in low tone*) Oh Lord! and me all done up with that sea trip home! I'm seasick even now. It's all I can do to stump along empty handed, so don't think I can travel with a load.

Mer.   Yea, of a truth some one is talking here.

Sos.   (*in lower tone*) Saved! He doesn't see me. It's Some one he says is talking : and my name is Sosia, I know that for a fact.

Mer.   Yes, a voice from the right here, as it seems, doth strike my ear.

Sos.   (*aside*) I'm afraid he'll soon pummel me instead of my voice for its striking him. (*steps forward timidly*)

Mer.   Oho! Splendid! He moves this way.

Sos.   (*aside*) I'm scared, I'm simply stiff! Good gracious, I don't know where in the world I am, not if anyone asked me. Oh dear, I can't move a step for fear! This ends me! Master's orders are done for, and Sosia, too. But I'm resolved —I'm going to speak right up to him boldly, so

	qui possim videri huic fortis, a me ut abstineat manum.	34(
Mer.	Quo ambulas, tu qui Volcanum in cornu conclusum geris?	
Sos.	Quid id exquiris tu, qui pugnis os exossas hominibus?	
Mer.	Servosne es an liber?	
Sos.	Utcumque animo conlibitum est meo.	
Mer.	Ain vero?	
Sos.	Aio enim vero.	
Mer.	Verbero.	
Sos.	Mentiris nunc.	
Mer.	At iam faciam ut verum dixas dicere.	
Sos.	Quid eo est opus?	
Mer.	Possum scire, quo profectus, cuius sis aut quid veneris?	
Sos.	Huc eo, eri iussu, eius sum servos. numquid nunc es certior?	
Mer.	Ego tibi istam hodie, sceleste, comprimam linguam.	
Sos.	Haud potes: bene pudiceque adservatur.	
Mer.	Pergin argutarier? quid apud hasce aedis negoti est tibi?	
Sos.	Immo quid tibi est?	350
Mer.	Rex Creo vigiles nocturnos singulos semper locat.	
Sos.	Bene facit: quia nos eramus peregre, tutatust domi; at nunc abi sane, advenisse familiares dicito.	
Mer.	Nescio quam tu familiaris sis: nisi actutum hinc abis, familiaris accipiere faxo haud familiariter.	
Sos.	Hic inquam habito ego atque horunc servos sum.	

36

that I can make him think I'm a dangerous character and let me be. (*tries to swagger*)

Mer. Whither dost stroll, thou who conveyest (*pointing
to lantern*) Vulcan pent within yon horn?

Sos. What dost want to know for, thou who bonest
folks' faces for 'em with yon fists?

Mer. Art slave or free?

Sos. Whichever I please.

Mer. So? In sooth?

Sos. Yes, so in sooth.

Mer. Thou whipped slave!

Sos. You lie: I'm none.

Mer. (*advancing*) But I shall soon make thee say 'tis true.

Sos. (*shrinking back*) Oh, what's the use of that?

Mer. (*sternly*) May I be informed where thou art bound,
who owns thee, or why thou camest? (*halts*)

Sos. (*encouraged*) I'm bound for here—master's orders
—and I'm his slave. Are you any wiser now?

Mer. I'll soon make thee hold thy tongue, miscreant!

Sos. No chance : she's chaperoned in nice modest fashion.

Mer. Still at thy quips, eh? What business hast thou
at this house?

Sos. Well, and what have you?

Mer. King Creon posts separate sentries about here
every night.

Sos. (*in superior manner*) Much obliged. Seeing we
were abroad, he's kept guard for us at home. But
now you can be off: say the family servants have
got back.

Mer. Thou a family servant, indeed! Unless thou dost
disappear instantly, I warrant ye I'll welcome servants of the family with strange familiarity.

Sos. Here's where I live, I tell you. This is my master's
house.

Mer.   At scin quo modo?
faciam ego hodie te superbum, nisi hinc abis.

Sos.   Quonam modo?

Mer. Auferere, non abibis, si ego fustem sumpsero.

Sos. Quin me esse huius familiai familiarem praedico.

Mer. Vide sis quam mox vapulare vis, nisi actutum hinc
abis.   360

Sos. Tun domo prohibere peregre me advenientem postulas?

Mer. Haecine tua domust?

Sos.   Ita inquam.

Mer.   Quis erus est igitur tibi?

Sos. Amphitruo, qui nunc praefectust Thebanis legionibus,
quicum nupta est Alcumena.

Mer.   Quid ais? quid nomen tibi est?

Sos. Sosiam vocant Thebani, Davo prognatum patre.

Mer. Ne tu istic hodie malo tuo compositis mendaciis
advenisti, audaciai columen, consutis dolis.

Sos. Immo equidem tunicis consutis huc advenio, non
dolis.

Mer. At mentiris etiam: certo pedibus, non tunicis venis.

Sos. Ita profecto.

Mer.   Nunc profecto vapula ob mendacium.   370

Sos. Non edepol volo profecto.

Mer.   At pol profecto ingratiis.
hoc quidem profecto certum est, non est arbitrarium.

Sos. Tuam fidem obsecro.

Mer.   Tun te audes Sosiam esse dicere,
qui ego sum?

Sos.   Perii.

38

Mer.	But knowest thou what? I'll soon be making an exalted man of thee, an' thou decampest not.
Sos.	Exalted! How is that?
Mer.	You shall be carried off on people's shoulders—no walking—once I take my club to you.
Sos.	I'm a member of the household here, I do avow.
Mer.	Kindly consider how soon you want a thrashing, unless you vanish instantly.
Sos.	So you want to forbid me the house when I'm getting back from foreign parts, you?
Mer.	Is this the house where you belong?
Sos.	That's what I say.
Mer.	Who is your master, then?
Sos.	Amphitryon, now in command of the Theban army, and his wife is Alcmena.
Mer.	How say you? Your name!
Sos.	Sosia the Thebans call me, Sosia, son of Davus.
Mer.	Ah! 'twas an evil hour for thee, when thou camest here, thou pinnacle of impudence, with thy premeditated lies and patched-up fabrications.
Sos.	You're wrong, I vow: I've come with my tunic patched up, not my fabrications.
Mer.	Ha, lying again! Thou dost clearly come with thy feet, not thy tunic.
Sos.	(*dryly*) Naturally.
Mer.	And naturally now get thrashed for fibbing. (*advances*)
Sos.	(*retreats*) Oh dear, I object, naturally.
Mer.	Oh well, naturally that is immaterial. My " naturally," at least, is a cold hard fact, no matter of opinion. (*beats him*)
Sos.	(*squirming*) Easy, easy, for heaven's sake!
Mer.	Durst say that thou art Sosia when I am he?
Sos.	Murder! murder!

Mer. Parum etiam, praeut futurum est, praedicas.
quoius nunc es?

Sos. Tuos, nam pugnis usu fecisti tuom.
pro fidem, Thebani cives.

Mer. Etiam clamas, carnifex?
loquere, quid venisti?

Sos. Ut esset quem tu pugnis caederes.

Mer. Cuius es?

Sos. Amphitruonis, inquam, Sosia.

Mer. Ergo istoc magis,
quia vaniloquo's, vapulabis: ego sum, non tu, Sosia.

Sos. Ita di faciant, ut tu potius sis atque ego te ut ver-
berem. 380

Mer. Etiam muttis?

Sos. Iam tacebo.

Mer. Quis tibi erust?

Sos. Quem tu voles.

Mer. Quid igitur? qui nunc vocare?

Sos. Nemo nisi quem iusseris.

Mer. Amphitruonis te esse aiebas Sosiam.

Sos. Peccaveram.
nam Amphitruonis [1] socium ne me esse volui dicere.

Mer. Sciebam equidem nullum esse nobis nisi me
servom Sosiam.
fugit te ratio.

Sos. Utinam istuc pugni fecissent tui.

Mer. Ego sum Sosia ille quem tu dudum esse aiebas mihi.

Sos. Obsecro ut per pacem liceat te alloqui, ut ne vapulem.

Mer. Immo indutiae parumper fiant, si quid vis loqui.

Sos. Non loquar nisi pace facta, quando pugnis plus vales. 390

Mer. Dic si quid vis, non nocebo.

[1] Corrupt (Leo): *neme esse* MSS: among the many
emendations is *sane* (Palmer).

Mer. (*continuing to beat him*) Murder? A mere nothing compared with what is coming. Whose are you now?

Sos. Yours! Your fists have got a title to me by limitation. Help, Thebans, help!

Mer. So? Bellowing, varlet? Speak up, why camest thou?

Sos. Just to give you some one to punch, sir.

Mer. Whose are you?

Sos. Amphitryon's Sosia, I tell you.

Mer. Well then, you shall be pummelled the more for talking nonsense. You Sosia! I am he myself.

Sos. (*in low tone*) I wish to God you were, instead of me, and I was thumping you.

Mer. Ha! Muttering, eh?

Sos. I won't, I won't, sir!

Mer. Who is your master?

Sos. Anyone you like, sir.

Mer. Indeed? And your name now?

Sos. Nothing but what you order, sir.

Mer. You were saying you were Amphitryon's Sosia.

Sos. All a mistake, sir; " Amphitryon's associate " I meant, sir, really I did.

Mer. Ah, I knew quite well there was no servant Sosia at our place except me. You made a slip.

Sos. Oh, how I wish your fists had!

Mer. I am that Sosia you claimed to be a while ago.

Sos. For heaven's sake, sir, let me have a word with you in peace without getting pummelled.

Mer. No peace—but I consent to a short armistice, if you have anything to say.

Sos. I won't say it, not unless peace is made : your fists are too much for me.

Mer. Out with what you want : I shall not hurt you!

41

TITUS MACCIUS PLAUTUS

Sos.   Tuae fide credo?
Mer.   Meae.
Sos.   Quid si falles?
Mer.   Tum Mercurius Sosiae iratus siet.
Sos.   Animum advorte. nunc licet mihi libere quidvis loqui.
     Amphitruonis ego sum servos Sosia.
Mer.   Etiam denuo?
Sos.   Pacem feci, foedus feci.   vera dico.
Mer.   Vapula.
Sos.   Ut libet quid tibi libet fac, quoniam pugnis plus vales;
     verum, utut es facturus, hoc quidem hercle haud
       reticebo tamen.
Mer.   Tu me vivos hodie numquam facies quin sim Sosia.
Sos.   Certe edepol tu me alienabis numquam quin noster
     siem;

     nec nobis praeter med alius quisquam est servos Sosia.[1]   400
Mer.   Hic homo sanus non est.
Sos.   Quod mihi praedicas vitium, id tibi est.
     quid, malum, non sum ego servos Amphitruonis Sosia?
     nonne hac noctu nostra navis huc ex portu Persico
     venit, quae me advexit? nonne me huc erus misit
       meus?
     nonne ego nunc sto ante aedes nostras? non mi est
       lanterna in manu?
     non loquor, non vigilo? nonne hic homo modo me
       pugnis contudit?
     fecit hercle, nam etiam misero nunc mihi malae
       dolent.
     quid igitur ego dubito, aut cur non intro eo in no-
       stram domum?
Mer.   Quid, domum vostram?
Sos.   Ita enim vero.

[1] Leo brackets following v., 401 : *qui cum Amphitruone
hinc una ieram in exercitum.*

42

s. Can I take your word for that?

er. You can.

s. What if you fool me?

er. (*solemnly*) Then may Sosia feel the wrath of Mercury!

s. Listen here, sir. Now I'm free to come out plain with anything. I am Amphitryon's Sosia, I am.

er. (*advancing*) What? Again?

s. (*vigorously*) I made peace—I struck a treaty! It's the truth.

er. Be thrashed to you!

s. Suit yourself, do what suits you, seeing your fists are too much for me. (*doggedly*) But just the same, no matter what you do, I won't keep that back, by gad, not that.

er. You shall never live to make me anyone but Sosia, never.

s. And by thunder, you shall never do me out of being our family's servant. No sir, and I'm the only servant Sosia we have.

er. The man is crazy.

s Crazy? You're putting your own complaint off on to me. (*half to himself*) See here, dash it, an't I Amphitryon's servant Sosia? Didn't our ship arrive this night from Port Persicus, and I on it? Didn't my own master send me here? An't I standing in front of our own house this minute? Haven't I got a lantern in my hand? An't I talking? An't I awake? Didn't this chap just give me a bruising? Lord, but he did! Why, my poor jaws ache even now. What am I hesitating for, then? Or why don't I go inside our house?

er. What? Your house?

s. Yes, just so.

43

Mer.   Quin quae dixisti modo   410
omnia ementitu's: equidem Sosia Amphitruonis
    sum.

nam noctu hac soluta est navis nostra e portu
    Persico,

et ubi Pterela rex regnavit oppidum expugnavimus,

et legiones Teloboarum vi pugnando cepimus,

et ipsus Amphitruo optruncavit regem Pterelam in
    proelio.

Sos. Egomet mihi non credo, cum illaec autumare illum
    audio ;

hic quidem certe quae illic sunt res gestae memorat
    memoriter.

sed quid ais ? quid Amphitruoni doni a Telobois
    datum est ?

Mer. Pterela rex qui potitare solitus est patera aurea.

Sos. Elocutus est.   ubi patera nunc est ?

Mer.   Est in cistula ;   420
Amphitruonis obsignata signo est.

Sos.   Signi dic quid est ?

Mer. Cum quadrigis Sol exoriens.   quid me captas, car-
    nufex ?

Sos. Argumentis vicit, aliud nomen quaerundum est mihi.

nescio unde haec hic spectavit.   iam ego hunc deci-
    piam probe ;

nam quod egomet solus feci, nec quisquam alius
    affuit,

in tabernaclo, id quidem hodie numquam poterit
    dicere.

si tu Sosia es, legiones cum pugnabant maxume,

quid in tabernaclo fecisti ? victus sum, si dixeris.

Mer. Cadus erat vini : inde implevi hirneam.

Sos.   Ingressust viam.

Mer. Eam ego, ut matre fuerat natum, vini eduxi meri.   430

44

AMPHITRYON

Mer.	You lie, I tell you: your every word has been a lie. I am Amphitryon's Sosia, beyond dispute. Why, this very night we unmoored and left Port Persicus; and we have seized the city where King Pterelas held sway; and we subdued the legions of the Teloboians by our sturdy onslaught; and Amphitryon himself slew King Pterelas on the field of battle.
Sos.	(*aside*) I can't believe my own ears when I hear that fellow going on so. My word, he certainly does reel our doings there all off pat. (*aloud*) But I say—what was Amphitryon presented with from the Teloboian spoils?
Mer.	A golden bowl that King Pterelas was wont to drink from.
Sos.	(*aside*) He's hit it! (*aloud*) Where is the bowl now?
Mer.	In a little chest, sealed with Amphitryon's signet.
Sos.	What's on the signet, tell me that?
Mer.	Sol rising in a four horse chariot. (*blustering*) Why this attempt to catch me, caitiff?
Sos.	(*aside*) This evidence settles me. I've got to find me a new name. I don't understand where he saw all this from. (*reflecting*) Ah, now I'll trick him in good style. Yes, something I did when I was all alone, and not another soul there, in the tent,—he'll never be able to tell me about that, anyway. (*aloud*) Well, if you're Sosia, what did you do in the tent when the soldiers were in the thick of the fight? Answer me that and I give in.
Mer.	There was a cask of wine: I drew off a jugful.
Sos.	(*aside*) He's on the right track.
Mer.	Then I drained it, wine pure as it came from its mother.

c

45

Sos. Factum est illud, ut ego illic vini hirneam ebiberim
  meri.

  mira sunt nisi latuit intus illic in illac hirnea.

Mer. Quid nunc? vincon argumentis, te non esse Sosiam?

Sos. Tu negas med esse?

Mer.   Quid ego ni negem, qui egomet siem?

Sos. Per Iovem iuro med esse neque me falsum dicere.

Mer. At ego per Mercurium iuro, tibi Iovem non credere;

  nam iniurato scio plus credet mihi quam iurato tibi.

Sos. Quis ego sum saltem, si non sum Sosia? te interrogo.

Mer. Ubi ego Sosia nolim esse, tu esto sane Sosia;

  nunc, quando ego sum, vapulabis, ni hinc abis, ig-
   nobilis.   440

Sos. Certe edepol, quom illum contemplo et formam
  cognosco meam,

  quem ad modum ego sum—saepe in speculum
   inspexi—nimis similest mei;

  itidem habet petasum ac vestitum: tam consimilest
   atque ego;

  sura, pes, statura, tonsus, oculi, nasum vel labra,

  malae, mentum, barba, collus: totus. quid verbis
   opust?

  si tergum cicatricosum, nihil hoc similist similius.

  sed quom cogito, equidem certo idem sum qui
   semper fui.

  novi erum, novi aedis nostras; sane sapio et sentio.

  non ego illi obtempero quod loquitur. pultabo
   foris.

Mer. Quo agis te?

Sos. (*aside*) That's a fact—I did drink off a jug of wine, neat. Most probably the fellow was hiding in that same jug!

Mer. Well, have I convinced you that you are not Sosia?

Sos. You deny it, do you?

Mer. Of course I deny it, being Sosia myself.

Sos. No, I am,—I swear it by Jupiter, and swear I'm not lying, too!

Mer. But I swear by Mercury that Jupiter disbelieves you. Why, man, he will take my bare word against your solemn oath, no doubt about it.

Sos. For mercy's sake who am I, if I'm not Sosia? I ask you that.

Mer. When I do not wish to be Sosia, be Sosia yourself, by all means. Now that I am he, you either pack, or take a thrashing, you unknown riff-raff.

Sos. (*aside, looking him over carefully*) Upon my soul, now I look him over, and consider my own looks, my own appearance—I've peeped in a mirror many a time—he is precious like me. Has on a travelling hat, yes, and clothes the same as mine. He's as like me as I am myself! Same leg —foot—height—haircut—eyes—nose—lips, even —jaw—chin—beard—neck—everything. Well— well, well, well! If he's got a backful of whip scars, you couldn't find a liker likeness anywhere. (*pause*) But—when I think it over—I'm positive I'm the same man I always was, of course I am. (*with growing conviction*) I know master, I know our house: I'm sane and sound, I've got my senses. I won't take any notice of what he says, not I. I'll knock at the door. (*moves toward Amphitryon's house*)

Mer. (*blocking him off*) Where now?

Sos. Domum.

Mer.   Quadrigas si nunc inscendas Iovis   450
atque hinc fugias, ita vix poteris effugere infortu-
nium.

Sos. Nonne erae meae nuntiare quod erus meus iussit
licet?

Mer. Tuae si quid vis nuntiare: hanc nostram adire non
sinam.
nam si me inritassis, hodie lumbifragium hinc auferes.

Sos. Abeo potius. di immortales, obsecro vostram fidem,
ubi ego perii? ubi immutatus sum? ubi ego formam
perdidi?
an egomet me illic reliqui, si forte oblitus fui?
nam hic quidem omnem imaginem meam, quae antehac fuerat, possidet.
vivo fit quod numquam quisquam mortuo faciet
mihi.
ibo ad portum atque haec uti sunt facta ero dicam
meo;   460
nisi etiam is quoque me ignorabit; quod ille faxit
Iuppiter,
ut ego hodie raso capite calvos capiam pilleum.

I. 2.

Mer. Bene prospere hoc hodie operis processit mihi:
amovi a foribus maximam molestiam,
patri ut liceret tuto illam amplexarier.
iam ille illuc ad erum cum Amphitruonem advenerit,
narrabit servom hinc sese a foribus Sosiam
amovisse; ille adeo illum mentiri sibi
credet, neque credet huc profectum, ut iusserat.
erroris ambo ego illos et dementiae   470
complebo atque omnem Amphitruonis familiam,

Sos.	Home.
Mer.	(*advancing*) And shouldst thou climb into Jupiter's four horse chariot and seek to flee, e'en so thou canst hardly fly misfortune.
Sos.	I can tell my own mistress what my own master ordered me to tell her, can't I?
Mer.	Thy own mistress, aye,—whatever likes thee: but never shalt thou approach ours here. Yea, provoke me, and thou draggest hence a shipwreck of a man. (*advancing*)
Sos.	(*retreating*) Don't, don't,—I'll be off! (*aside*) Ye immortal gods! For heaven's sake, where did I lose myself? Where was I transformed? Where did I drop my shape? I didn't leave myself behind at the harbour, did I, if I did happen to forget it? For, my word, this fellow has got hold of my complete image, mine that was! Here I am alive and folks carry my image—more than anyone will ever do when I'm dead. I'll go down to the harbour and tell my master all about these goings on—that is unless he doesn't know me, too,—and I hope to Jupiter he won't, so that I may shave my hair off this very day and stick my bald head in a freeman's cap.

Scene 2.   [EXIT *Sosia.*

Mer.	Well, my little affair has progressed finely, famously. I have sent a confounded nuisance to the right-about from the door and given my father a chance to embrace the lady there in safety. Now when our friend gets back there to his master, Amphitryon, he'll tell his tale how it was servant Sosia that packed him off. Yes, and then Amphitryon will think he is lying, and never came here as he ordered. I'll muddle up the pair of them, bedevil them completely, and Amphitryon's whole house-

adeo usque, satietatem dum capiet pater
illius quam amat. igitur demum omnes scient
quae facta. denique Alcumenam Iuppiter
rediget antiquam coniugi in concordiam.
nam Amphitruo actutum uxori turbas conciet
atque insimulabit eam probri; tum meus pater
eam seditionem illi in tranquillum conferet.
nunc de Alcumena dudum quod dixi minus,
hodie illa pariet filios geminos duos   480
alter decumo post mense nascetur puer
quam seminatust, alter mense septumo;
eorum Amphitruonis alter est, alter Iovis:
verum minori puero maior est pater,
minor maiori. iamne hoc scitis quid siet?
sed Alcumenae huius honoris gratia
pater curavit uno ut fetu fieret,
uno ut labore absolvat aerumnas duas.[1]
quamquam, ut iam dudum dixi, resciscet tamen   491
Amphitruo rem omnem. quid igitur? nemo id probro
profecto ducet Alcumenae; nam deum
non par videtur facere, delictum suom
suamque ut culpam expetere in mortalem ut sinat.
orationem comprimam: crepuit foris.
Amphitruo subditivos eccum exit foras
cum Alcumena uxore usuraria.

I. 3.
Iup.   Bene vale, Alcumena, cura rem communem, quod
          facis;
       atque inperce quaeso: menses iam tibi esse actos vides.   500
       mihi necesse est ire hinc; verum quod erit natum
          tollito.
Alc.   Quid istuc est, mi vir, negoti, quod tu tam subito
          domo abeas?

───────

[1] Leo brackets following v., 489–90 : *et ne in suspicione
ponatur stupri* | *et clandestina ut celetur consuetio.*

hold, too, and keep it up till my father has his fill of her whom he loves: then all shall know the truth, but not before. And finally Jupiter will renew the former harmony between Alcmena and her spouse. For you see, Amphitryon, will be raging at his wife shortly, and accusing her of playing him false: then my father will step in and quell the riot. Now about Alcmena—something I left unsaid a while ago—now she shall bring forth twin sons, one being a ten months' boy, the other a seven. One is Amphitryon's child, the other Jove's: the younger boy, however, has the greater father, and vice versa. You see how it is now, do you? But out of consideration for Alcmena here, my father has provided that there shall be only one parturition: he intends to make one labour suffice for two. But Amphitryon, though, as I told you some time since, will be informed of the whole affair. But what of that? Certainly no one will hold Alcmena guilty: no, no, it would seem highly unbecoming for a god to let a mortal take the consequences of his misdeeds and his indiscretions. (*listening*) Enough of this: there goes the door. Ah, the counterfeit Amphitryon comes out with his borrowed wife, Alcmena! (*steps aside*)

ENTER *Jupiter* AND *Alcmena*
FROM THE HOUSE.

Scene 3.

Jup. Good-bye and God bless you, my dear. Continue to look out for our common interests, and do be sure not to overdo: you are near your time now, you know. I am obliged to leave you—but don't expose the child.

Alc. (*plaintively*) Why, my husband, what is it takes you away so suddenly?

Iup.   Edepol haud quod tui me neque domi distaedeat;
         sed ubi summus imperator non adest ad exercitum,
         citius quod non facto est usus fit quam quod facto
         est opus.

Mer.   Nimis hic scitust sycophanta, qui quidem meus sit
         pater.
         observatote eum, quam blande mulieri palpabitur.

Alc.   Ecastor te experior quanti facias uxorem tuam.

Iup.   Satin habes, si feminarum nulla est quam aeque
         diligam?

Mer.   Edepol ne illa si istis rebus te sciat operam dare,   510
         ego faxim ted Amphitruonem esse malis, quam
         Iovem.

Alc.   Experiri istuc mavellem me quam mi memorarier.
         prius abis quam lectus ubi cubuisti concaluit locus.
         heri venisti media nocte, nunc abis.   hocin placet?

Mer.   Accedam atque hanc appellabo et subparasitabor
         patri.
         numquam edepol quemquam mortalem credo ego
         uxorem suam
         sic ecflictim amare, proinde ut hic te ecflictim
         deperit.

Iup.   Carnufex, non ego te novi? abin e conspectu meo?
         quid tibi hanc curatio est rem, verbero, aut
         muttitio?
         quoii ego iam hoc scipione—

Alc.   Ah noli.

Iup.   Muttito modo.   520

Mer.   Nequiter paene expedivit prima parasitatio.

p.   No weariness of you and home, I swear to that.
But when the commander-in-chief is not with his
army, things are much more liable to go wrong
than right.

er.   (*aside*) Ah, he's a sly old dodger—does me [1] credit,
my father does! Notice how suavely he'll smooth
her down.

lc.   (*pouting*) Oh yes, I'm learning how much you
think of your wife.

p.   (*fondly*) Isn't it enough that you're the dearest
woman in the world to me? (*embraces her*)

er.   (*aside*) Now, now, sir! Just let the lady up yonder (*pointing thumb heavenward*) learn of your per-
formances here, and I'll guarantee you'd rather
be Amphitryon than Jove.

lc.   Actions speak louder than words. Here you are
leaving me before your place on the couch had
time to get warm. You came last night at mid-
night, and now you are going. Does that seem
right?

er.   (*aside*) I'll go slip a word in and play henchman to
my father. (*to Alcmena, stepping up*) Lord, ma'am,
I don't believe there's a mortal man alive loves
his own wife (*glancing slyly at Jupiter*) so madly as
the mad way he dotes on you.

p.   (*angrily*) You rascal, don't I know you? Out of my
sight, will you! What business have you to interfere
with this matter, or to breathe a word about it,
you scamp? I'll take my cane this instant and—

lc.   (*seizing his arm*) Oh, please don't!

p.   You just breathe a word now!

er.   (*aside dryly*) The henchman's first try at henching
pretty nearly came to grief.

---

[1] Mercury was the patron god of roguery.

Iup. Verum quod tu dicis, mea uxor, non te mi irasci
decet.

clanculum abii a legione: operam hanc subrupui
tibi,

ex me primo ut prima scires, rem ut gessissem
publicam.

ea tibi omnia enarravi. nisi te amarem plurimum,
non facerem.

Mer. Facitne ut dixi? timidam palpo percutit.

Iup. Nunc, ne legio persentiscat, clam illuc redeundum
est mihi,

ne me uxorem praevertisse dicant prae re publica.

Alc. Lacrimantem ex abitu concinnas tu tuam uxorem.

Iup. Tace,
ne corrumpe oculos, redibo actutum.

Alc. Id actutum diu est. 530

Iup. Non ego te hic lubens relinquo neque abeo abs te.

Alc. Sentio,
nam qua nocte ad me venisti, eadem abis.

Iup. Cur me tenes?
tempus est: exire ex urbe prius quam lucescat
volo.

nunc tibi hanc pateram, quae dono mi illi ob
virtutem data est,

Pterela rex qui potitavit, quem ego mea occidi
manu,

Alcumena, tibi condono.

Alc. Facis ut alias res soles.
ecastor condignum donum, qualest qui donum dedit.

Mer. Immo sic: condignum donum, qualest cui dono
datumst.

Iup. Pergin autem? nonne ego possum, furcifer, te
perdere?

Alc. Noli amabo, Amphitruo, irasci Sosiae causa mea. 540

54

up. But as to what you say, precious,—you oughtn't to be cross with me. It was on the sly that I left my troops: this is a stolen treat, stolen for your sake, so that your first news of how I served my country might come first from me. And now I have told you the whole story. I wouldn't have done such a thing, if I hadn't loved you with all my heart.

Ter. (*aside*) Doing as I said, eh? Stroking her down, patting her back, poor thing.

up. Now I must slip back, so that my men may not get wind of this and say I put my wife ahead of the public welfare.

lc. (*tearfully*) And make your own wife cry at your leaving her!

up. (*affectionately*) Hush! Don't spoil your eyes: I shall be back soon.

lc. That " soon " is a long, long time.

up. It's not that I like to leave you here and go away.

lc. So I perceive—going away the same night you came to me! (*clings to him*)

up. Why do you hold me? It is time: I wish to get out of the city before daybreak. (*producing a golden bowl*) Here is the bowl they presented me for bravery on the field—the one King Pterelas used to drink from, whom I killed with my own hand—take it as a gift from me, Alcmena.

lc. (*taking bowl eagerly*) That *is* so like you! Oh, your gift just matches the giver!

Ter. Oh no, not the giver—that gift matches the getter.

up. (*savagely*) So? At it again? Is there no choking you off, you jailbird? No? (*advances with upraised cane*)

lc. (*holding him back*) Please, Amphitryon, don't be angry with Sosia on my account.

55

Iup.   Faciam ita ut vis.

Mer.   Ex amore hic admodum quam saevos est.

Iup.   Numquid vis?

Alc.   Ut quom absim me ames, me tuam te absente
         tamen.

Mer.   Eamus, Amphitruo.   lucescit hoc iam.

Iup.   Abi prae, Sosia,
         iam ego sequar.   numquid vis?

Alc.   Etiam: ut actutum advenias.

Iup.   Licet,
         prius tua opinione hic adero: bonum animum habe.
         nunc te, nox, quae me mansisti, mitto uti cedas die,
         ut mortalis inlucescat luce clara et candida.
         atque quanto, nox, fuisti longior hac proxuma,
         tanto brevior dies ut fiat faciam, ut aeque disparet.
         sed dies e nocte accedat.   ibo et Mercurium sequar.   550

ACTVS II

Amph.   Age i tu secundum.

Sos.   Sequor, subsequor te.

Amph.   Scelestissimum te arbitror.

Sos.   Nam quam ob rem?

up.	(*halting*) Anything you please.
Ter.	(*aside*) Love has made an out-and-out savage of him.
up.	(*kissing Alcmena and turning to go*) Nothing else, then?
lc.	This,—even though I am not near you, love me still, your own true wife, absent or not.
Ter.	Let's go, sir; it is getting light already.
up.	Go ahead, Sosia; I shall be with you in a moment. [EXIT *Mercury*. (*kisses Alcmena again and turns to go*) Nothing further?
lc.	Yes, yes—do come back soon.
up.	Indeed I will: I shall be here sooner than you think. Come, come, cheer up! (*embraces her and moves away*) [EXIT *Alcmena* INTO HOUSE, SADLY. Now, Night, who hast tarried for me, I dismiss thee: give place to Day, that he may shine upon mortals in radiance and splendour. And Night, since thou wert longer than the last, I shall make the day so much the shorter, that there may be fair adjustment. But let day issue forth from night. Now to follow after Mercury. [EXIT *Jupiter*.

ACT II

(*Half an hour has elapsed.*)

ENTER *Amphitryon* FOLLOWED BY *Sosia*.   SLAVES WITH
BAGGAGE IN REAR.

Amph.	(*to lagging Sosia*) Here you! After me, come!
Sos.	Coming, sir! Right at your heels.
Amph.	It's my opinion you are a damned rascal.
Sos.	(*hurt*) Oh sir, why?

57

Amph. Quia id quod neque est neque fuit neque futurum est
mihi praedicas.

Sos.   Eccere, iam tuatim
facis tu, ut tuis nulla apud te fides sit.

Amph. Quid est? quo modo? iam quidem hercle ego tibi
istam
scelestam, scelus, linguam abscidam.

Sos.   Tuos sum,
proinde ut commodumst et lubet quidque facias
tamen quin loquar haec uti facta sunt hic,
numquam ullo modo me potes deterrere.   560

Amph. Scelestissime, audes mihi praedicare id,
domi te esse nunc, qui hic ades?

Sos.   Vera dico.

Amph. Malum quod tibi di dabunt, atque ego hodie
dabo.

Sos.   Istuc tibist in manu, nam tuos sum.

Amph. Tun me, verbero, audes erum ludificari?
tune id dicere audes, quod nemo umquam homo
antehac
vidit nec potest fieri, tempore uno
homo idem duobus locis ut simul sit?

Sos. Profecto, ut loquor res ita est.

Amph.   Iuppiter te
perdat.

Sos.   Quid mali sum, ere, tua ex re promeritus?   570

Amph. Rogasne, improbe, etiam qui ludos facis me?

Sos. Merito maledicas mihi, si id ita factum est.[1]
verum haud mentior, resque uti facta dico.

Amph. Homo hic ebrius est, ut opinor.

Sos. Utinam ita essem.

Amph.   Optas quae facta.   575

Sos. Egone?

---

[1] Corrupt (Leo): *si non id ita* J.

AMPHITRYON

mph. (*angrily*) Because what you tell me is not so, never was so, never will be.

os. See there now! Just like you—you can never trust your servants.

mph. (*misunderstanding*) What? How is that? Well, by heaven now, I'll cut out that villainous tongue for you, you villain!

os. (*stubbornly*) I am yours, sir: so do anything that suits your convenience and taste. However, I shall tell everything just as it happened here, and you shall never frighten me out of that, never.

mph. You confounded rascal, do you dare tell me you are at home this very minute, when you are here with me?

os. It is a fact, sir.

mph. A fact you shall soon suffer for—the gods will see to that, and so will I.

os. That rests with you, sir: I am your man.

mph. You dare make fun of me, scoundrel, your master? You dare tell me a thing no one ever saw before, an impossible thing—the same man in two places at one time?

os. Really, sir, it is just as I say.

mph. Jove's curse on you!

os. What harm have I done you to be punished, sir?

mph. Harm? You reprobate! Still making a joke of me, are you?

os. You would have a right to call me names, if that was so. But I am not lying, sir: it happened just as I say.

mph. The man is drunk, I do believe.

os. (*heartily*) Wish I was!

mph. (*dryly*) Your wish is already gratified.

os. Is it?

59

Amph.　　　　　　Tu istic. ubi bibisti?
Sos.　Nusquam equidem bibi.
Amph.　　　　　　　　　　Quid hoc sit　　　576
　hominis?
Sos.　　　　　　Equidem decies dixi:
　domi ego sum, inquam, ecquid audis?　　　577
　et apud te adsum Sosia idem.
　satin hoc plane, satin diserte,　　　578
　ere, nunc videor
　tibi locutus esse?
Amph.　　　·　　　　Vah,　　　579
　apage te a me.
　　　　　　　　Quid est negoti?　　　580
Amph.　Pestis te tenet.
Sos.　　　　　　Nam quor istuc
　dicis? equidem valeo et salvos
　sum recte, Amphitruo.
Amph.　　　　　　　At te ego faciam　　　583
　hodie proinde ac meritus es,
　ut minus valeas et miser sis,　　　584a
　salvos domum si rediero: iam　　　584b
　sequere sis, erum qui ludificas　　　585a
　dictis delirantibus,　　　585b
　qui quoniam erus quod imperavit neglexisti persequi,
　nunc venis etiam ultro inrisum dominum: quae
　　neque fieri
　possunt neque fando umquam accepit quisquam
　　profers, carnifex;
　quoius ego hodie in tergum faxo ista expetant
　　mendacia.
Sos.　Amphitruo, miserrima istaec miseria est servo bono,　590
　apud erum qui vera loquitur, si id vi verum vincitur.
Amph.　Quo id, malum, pacto potest nam—mecum argu-
　　mentis puta—
　fieri, nunc uti tu et hic sis et domi? id dici volo.
　60

Amph. It is. Where did you get drink?

Sos. I did not, not I, nowhere.

Amph. (*despairingly*) What am I to make of the fellow?

Sos. I have told you how it is ten times over: I am at home, I say. Do you hear that? Yes, and I am here with you, the same Sosia. There sir, do you think that is putting it plainly enough, lucidly enough for you?

Amph. (*shoving him aside*) Bah! Get away with you.

Sos. What is the matter?

Amph. You have the plague.

Sos. Why, what do you say that for? Really, sir, I feel well, I am all right.

Amph. But I shall soon see you get your deserts: you will not feel so well, you will be wretched enough, once I get back home all right. Be so good as to follow me, you that make a butt of your master with your idiotic drivel. Seeing you neglected to carry out your master's orders, you now have the effrontery to come and laugh at him, to boot,—with your tales of what can never happen, what no man ever heard of, you rapscallion. By heaven, those lies of yours shall fall on your own back, I promise you!

Sos. (*plaintively*) It is hard, sir, horribly hard, on a good servant that tells his master plain facts to have his facts confuted by a flogging.

Amph. Curse it! How in the world is it possible—argue it out with me—for you to be here now, and at home, too? Tell me that, will you?

Sos. Sum profecto et hic et illic. hoc cuivis mirari licet,
neque tibi istuc mirum [1] magis videtur quam mihi.

Amph. Quo modo?

Sos. Nihilo, inquam, mirum magis tibi istuc quam mihi;
neque, ita me di ament, credebam primo mihimet
Sosiae,
donec Sosia illic egomet fecit sibi uti crederem.
ordine omne, uti quicque actum est, dum apud hostis sedimus,
edissertavit. tum formam una abstulit cum nomine.   600
neque lac lactis magis est simile quam ille ego
similest mei.
nam ut dudum ante lucem a portu me praemisisti
domum—

Amph. Quid igitur?

Sos. Prius multo ante aedis stabam quam illo adveneram.

Amph. Quas, malum, nugas? satin tu sanus es?

Sos.   Sic sum ut vides.

Amph. Huic homini nescio quid est mali mala obiectum
manu,
postquam a me abiit.

Sos.   Fateor, nam sum obtusus pugnis pessume.

Amph. Quis te verberavit?

Sos.   Egomet memet, qui nunc sum domi.

Amph. Cave quicquam, nisi quod rogabo te, mihi responderis.
omnium primum iste qui sit Sosia, hoc dici volo.

Sos. Tuos est servos.

Amph.   Mihi quidem uno te plus etiam est quam volo,   610
neque postquam sum natus habui nisi te servom
Sosiam.

Sos. At ego nunc, Amphitruo, dico: Sosiam servom tuom
praeter me alterum, inquam, adveniens faciam ut
offendas domi,

---

[1] Leo notes slight *lacuna* here: *mirum* MSS: *mirum
mirum* Spengel.

Sos.   I am here and I am there, I positively am. I don't care who wonders at it: it is no more wonderful to you than it is to me, sir.

Amph.   How is that?

Sos.   I say it is not a bit more wonderful to you than to me. So help me heaven, I didn't believe my own self, Sosia, at first, not till that other Sosia, myself, made me believe him. He reeled off every thing just as it happened while we were on the field there with the enemy; and besides, he had stolen my looks along with my name. One drop of milk is no more like another than that I is like me. Why, when you sent me ahead home from the harbour before dawn a while ago—

Amph.   What then?

Sos.   I was standing in front of the house long before I got there.

Amph.   What confounded rubbish! Are you actually in your senses?

Sos.   You can see for yourself I am.

Amph.   The fellow is bewitched somehow: the evil hand has been laid on him since he left me.

Sos.   Right you are! Evil? The way I got beaten to jelly was damned evil.

Amph.   Who was it beat you?

Sos.   I beat myself—the I that is at home now.

Amph.   Mind now, not a word but what I ask you. In the first place, I wish to be informed who that Sosia is.

Sos.   Your own slave.

Amph.   As a matter of fact, I have one too many in you already, and never in my life did I own a slave named Sosia except yourself.

Sos.   Well sir, you mark my words now: I warrant you you will come upon a second servant Sosia of yours besides me when you reach home, yes sir, one

Davo prognatum patre eodem quo ego sum, forma,
   aetate item
qua ego sum. quid opust verbis? geminus Sosia
   hic factust tibi.

Amph. Nimia memoras mira. sed vidistin uxorem meam?

Sos.   Quin intro ire in aedis numquam licitum est.

Amph.   Quis te prohibuit?

Sos.   Sosia ille, quem iam dudum dico, is qui me contudit.

Amph. Quis istic Sosia est?

Sos.   Ego, inquam. quotiens dicendum est tibi?

Amph. Sed quid ais? num obdormivisti dudum?

Sos.   Nusquam gentium. 620

Amph. Ibi forte istum si vidisses quendam in somnis So-
       siam—

Sos.   Non soleo ego somniculose eri imperia persequi.
vigilans vidi, vigilans nunc te video, vigilans fabulor,
vigilantem ille me iam dudum vigilans pugnis contudit.

Amph. Quis homo?

Sos.   Sosia, inquam, ego ille. quaeso, nonne intellegis?

Amph. Qui, malum, intellegere quisquam potis est? ita
     nugas blatis.

Sos.   Verum actutum nosces, quom illum nosces servom
     Sosiam.

Amph. Sequere hac igitur me, nam mi istuc primum
     exquisito est opus.[1]

II. 2.

Alc.   Satin parva res est voluptatum in vita atque in
     aetate agunda   633
praequam quod molestum est? ita cuique compar-
    atum est in aetate hominum;

---

[1] Leo brackets following v., 629–632 : *sed vide ex navi
efferantur quae imperavi iam omnia.*

Sos.   *Et memor sum et diligens, ut quae imperes compareant ;
non ego cum vino simitu ebibi imperium tuom.*

Amph. *Vtinam di faxint, infecta dicta re eveniant tua.*

whose father was Davus the same as mine, and
who is just like me and just my age, too. Enough
said, sir. Sosia has twinned here for you.

Amph. (*impressed*) Strange, very strange indeed! But
did you see my wife?

Sos. Why, sir, never a foot was I allowed to put in the
house.

Amph. Who hindered you?

Sos. That Sosia I have been telling of all along, the one
that smashed me up.

Amph. Who is that Sosia?

Sos. I am, I say. How many times do you need to be told?

Amph. (*reflecting*) But look here, you were not asleep a
while ago, were you?

Sos. Not a bit of it, sir.

Amph. Then perhaps, if you had seen that, well, that
Sosia of yours in your dreams—

Sos. I don't do my master's orders drowsily. Wide
awake I was, eyes open; I am wide awake with
'em open on you now; I am wide awake telling my
story; and I was wide awake when he hammered me
a while back, yes, and (*ruefully*) he was wide awake.

Amph. Who?

Sos. Sosia, I tell you, that me. Pray do not you understand?

Amph. How the devil can any man understand? Such
stuff and nonsense!

Sos. (*significantly*) Well, you will know what I mean very
soon, once you know that servant Sosia.

Amph. (*going toward house*) Come then, this way. This
matter needs my investigation first of all. (*stops to
examine house from distance and talks with Sosia*)

Scene 2.   ENTER *Alcmena* INTO DOORWAY.

Alc. Oh, are not the pleasures in life, in this daily round,
trifling compared with the pains! It is our common

ita divis est placitum, voluptatem ut maeror comes
consequatur :

quin incommodi plus malique ilico adsit, boni si
optigit quid.

nam ego id nunc experior domo atque ipsa de me
scio, cui voluptas

parumper datast, dum viri mei mihi potestas videndi
fuit

noctem unam modo ; atque is repente abiit a me
hinc ante lucem.

sola hic mihi nunc videor, quia ille hinc abest quem
ego amo praeter omnes.   640

plus aegri ex abitu viri, quam ex adventu voluptatis
cepi.

          sed hoc me beat

saltem, quom perduellis vicit et domum laudis
compos revenit :

          id solacio est.

      absit, dum modo laude parta

    domum recipiat se ; feram et perferam usque

abitum eius animo forti atque offirmato. id modo
si mercedis

    datur mi, ut meus victor vir belli clueat.

        satis mi esse ducam.

      virtus praemium est optimum ;

    virtus omnibus rebus anteit profecto :

libertas salus vita res et parentes, patria et prognati   650
          tutantur, servantur :

    virtus omnia in sese habet, omnia adsunt

        bona quem penest virtus

Amph. Edepol me uxori exoptatum credo adventurum
domum,

    quae me amat, quam contra amo, praesertim re
gesta bene,

human lot, it is heaven's will, for sorrow to come
following after joy: yes, yes, and to have a larger
share of trouble and distress the moment something nice has happened. Ah, I am learning this
now at first hand, learning it of my own experience—a few short hours of happiness, allowed to
see my husband for just one night; and then away
he goes all of a sudden before daylight! It does
seem so lonely here now, when the one I love best
is gone. I have felt more unhappy at his going
than happy at his coming. But there is thus much
to be thankful for, at least: he has been victorious
and come home a hero—that is one comfort. He
may leave me, if only he returns to me with a
glorious name: I will bear his going, yes, and keep
on bearing it to the end firmly and unflinchingly,
only let me have the reward of hearing my husband
hailed conqueror. That is enough for me! Courage
is the very best gift of all; courage stands before
everything, it does, it does! It is what main-
tains and preserves our liberty, safety, life, and our
homes and parents, our country and children.
Courage comprises all things: a man with courage
has every blessing.

Amph. By Jove, my wife will certainly be delighted to
have me home—loving each other as we do!
Especially now that we have been successful, and
the enemy, that every one thought invincible,
beaten, beaten at the first set-to under my auspices

	victis hostibus: quos nemo posse superari ratust,	
	eos auspicio meo atque ductu primo coetu vicimus.	
	certe enim med illi expectatum optato venturum scio.	
Sos.	Quid? me non rere expectatum amicae venturum meae?	
Alc.	Meus vir hic quidem est.	
Amph.	Sequere hac tu me.	
Alc.	Nam quid ille revortitur,	660
	qui dudum properare se aibat? an ille me temptat sciens	
	atque id se volt experiri, suom abitum ut desiderem?	
	ecastor med haud invita se domum recipit suam.	
Sos.	Amphitruo, redire ad navem meliust nos.	
Amph.	Qua gratia?	
Sos.	Quia domi daturus nemo est prandium advenientibus.	
Amph.	Qui tibi nunc istuc in mentemst?	
Sos.	Quia enim sero advenimus.	
Amph.	Qui?	
Sos.	Quia Alcumenam ante aedis stare saturam intellego.	
Amph.	Gravidam ego illanc hic reliqui, quom abeo.	
Sos.	Ei perii miser.	
Amph.	Quid tibi est?	
Sos.	Ad aquam praebendam commodum adveni domum,	
	decumo post mense, ut rationem te putare intellego.	670
Amph.	Bono animo es.	
Sos.	Scin quam bono animo sim? si situlam cepero,	
	numquam edepol tu mihi divini creduis post hunc diem,	
	ni ego illi puteo, si occepso, animam omnem intertraxero.	
Amph.	Sequere hac me modo; alium ego isti rei allegabo, ne time.	

68

and leadership. Ah yes, my arrival will surely be a very welcome event to her.

os. What? And don't you think mine is going to be welcome to my lady friend?

Alc. (*seeing them*) Why, here is my husband!

Amph. (*to Sosia*) Here you, this way! (*goes on toward house*)

Alc. (*aside*) What in the world is he back for so soon after saying he must hurry off! Is he trying me on purpose, does he want to test how much I miss him when he goes? Bless his heart, I have no objection to his coming home again!

os. (*seeing her*) We had better make for the ship once more, sir.

Amph. Why?

os. No one at home is going to give the new arrivals a breakfast, that is why.

Amph. And how does that thought happen to occur to you?

os. Because we've come too late.

Amph. How so?

os. (*pointing*) Well, there's mistress in front of the house, and she has a sort of well-fed look about her.

Amph. I had hopes when I went away, Sosia, of being made a father.

os. Heaven help me!

Amph. What is the matter?

os. (*disgustedly*) I have got home exactly in time to draw the water: it is the tenth month since, according as I follow your reckoning.

Amph. (*laughing*) Cheer up, cheer up!

os. Know how cheerful I am, do you, sir? Let me get hold of a bucket, and by gad, don't ever trust my sacred oath again, if I do not drain that well of its last breath, once I begin.

Amph. Come now, this way with me. (*moves toward house again*) I will appoint some one else to that office, never fear.

Alc.   Magis nunc me meum officium facere, si huic eam
         advorsum, arbitror.

Amph. Amphitruo uxorem salutat laetus speratam suam,
         quam omnium Thebis vir unam esse optimam diiu-
            dicat,

         quamque adeo cives Thebani vero rumiferant
            probam.

         valuistin usque? exspectatum advenio?

Sos.   Haud vidi magis.

         exspectatum eum salutat magis haud quicquam
         quam canem.   680

Amph. Et quom te [1] gravidam et quom te pulchre plenam
         aspicio, gaudeo.

Alc.   Obsecro ecastor, quid tu me derediculi gratia
         sic salutas atque appellas, quasi dudum non videris
         quasique nunc primum recipias te domum huc ex
            hostibus? [2]

Amph. Immo equidem te nisi nunc hodie nusquam vidi
         gentium.

Alc.   Cur negas?

Amph.   Quia vera didici dicere.

Alc.   Haud aequom facit
         qui quod didicit id dediscit. an periclitamini
         quid animi habeam? sed quid huc vos revortimini
         tam cito?

         an te auspicium commoratum est an tempestas
         continet   690

         qui non abiisti ad legiones, ita uti dudum dixeras?

Amph. Dudum? quam dudum istuc factum est?

Alc.   Temptas. iam dudum, modo.

Amph. Qui istuc potis est fieri, quaeso, ut dicis: iam du-
         dum, modo?

---

[1] Corrupt (Leo): *quom te gravidam* MSS : *quom gravidam* Pylades.

Alc.	(*aside*) I suppose it would be more duteous of me to go to meet him. (*advances slowly*)
Amph.	(*with playful courtliness*) Gladly does Amphitryon greet his darling wife, whom her husband judges to be the one best lady in all Thebes; yea, and justly do the citizens of Thebes bruit her virtue. (*earnestly*) Have you been well all this time? Are you glad to see me?
Sos.	(*aside*) Glad? None more so! Welcomes him about as warmly as she would a dog!
Amph.	Ah, it is splendid to see your condition, dear, and to see you getting on so finely.
Alc.	Good gracious! Why are you making fun of me with all these greetings and salutations, as if you had not seen me a little while ago and were just this moment back from the war?
Amph.	(*surprised*) Why, why, but I have not seen you—no, nowhere at all except this very instant.
Alc.	What makes you deny it?
Amph.	Because I have learned to tell the truth.
Alc.	It is not a good plan to learn a thing and then unlearn it. Or is this a test of my feelings? But why are you returning so quickly? Were you delayed by bad omens, or is it the weather detains you, that you have not gone away to the army, as you spoke of doing a little while ago?
Amph.	A little while ago? How little a while ago was that?
Alc.	Tease! Oh, quite a little while ago—just now.
Amph.	For heaven's sake, how can those statements agree —" quite a little while ago " and " just now "?

---

[2] Leo brackets following v., 685 : *atque me nunc proinde appellas quasi multo post videris?*

Alc.   Quid enim censes? te ut deludam contra lusorem
        meum,
        qui nunc primum te advenisse dicas, modo qui hinc
        abieris.

Amph. Haec quidem deliramenta loquitur.

Sos.   Paulisper mane,
        dum edormiscat unum somnum.

Amph.   Quaene vigilans somniat?

Alc.   Equidem ecastor vigilo, et vigilans id quod factum
        est fabulor.
        nam dudum ante lucem et istunc et te vidi.

Amph.   Quo in loco?

Alc.   Hic in aedibus ubi tu habitas.

Amph.   Numquam factum est.

Sos.   Non taces? 700
        quid si e portu navis huc nos dormientis detulit?

Amph. Etiam tu quoque adsentaris huic?

Sos.   Quid vis fieri?
        non tu scis? Bacchae bacchanti si velis advor-
        sarier,
        ex insana insaniorem facies, feriet saepius;
        si obsequare, una resolvas plaga.

Amph.   At pol qui certa res
        hanc est obiurgare, quae me hodie advenientem
        domum
        noluerit salutare.

Sos.   Inritabis crabrones.

Amph.   Tace.
        Alcumena, unum rogare te volo.

Alc.   Quid vis roga.

Amph. Num tibi aut stultitia accessit aut superat superbia?

Alc.   Qui istuc in mentemst tibi ex me, mi vir, percon-
        tarier?   710

Amph. Quia salutare advenientem me solebas antidhac,

    72

Alc.   Well, how do you suppose? I am merely trying to make game of you for a change, after your making game of me by saying this is your first appearance here, when you just now left us.

Amph. *(to Sosia)* Upon my soul, she is raving!

Sos.   Wait a while till she has slept out just one sleep.

Amph. What, awake and dreaming?

Alc.   *(indignantly)* To be sure I am awake, and awake as I relate what happened. Why, just a little while ago before dawn I saw that man and you, both.

Amph. Where was this?

Alc.   Here in your very own house, sir.

Amph. Impossible!

Sos.   Hush, sir, hush! What if the ship carried us here from the harbour in our sleep?

Amph. Ha! you are siding with her too, are you?

Sos.   *(wisely)* Well, what do you want? Don't you understand? You but cross a Bacchante when the Bacchic frenzy fills her, and you'll make the crazy thing crazier still and she'll hit you all the more: humour her, and she'll call it quits after one blow.

Amph. Humour her? By the Lord, it will be bad humour, that's sure,—arriving home to-day and she unwilling to give me a decent welcome!

Sos.   You'll be poking up a hornet's nest.

Amph. Silence! *(to Alcmena, sternly)* Alcmena, there is something I wish to ask you.

Alc.   Anything you please.

Amph. Are you obsessed by some foolish notion, or is this pride running away with you?

Alc.   What makes it enter your head to ask me such a question, my husband?

Amph. Because till to-day you used to welcome me on my

73

	appellare, itidem ut pudicae suos viros quae sunt solent.
	eo more expertem te factam adveniens offendi domi.
Alc.	Ecastor equidem te certo heri advenientem ilico, et salutavi et valuissesne usque exquisivi simul, mi vir, et manum prehendi et osculum tetuli tibi.
Sos.	Tun heri hunc salutavisti?
Alc.	Et te quoque etiam, Sosia.
Sos.	Amphitruo, speravi ego istam tibi parituram filium; verum non est puero gravida.
Amph.	Quid igitur?
Sos.	Insania.
Alc.	Equidem sana sum et deos quaeso, ut salva pariam filium.

720

	verum tu malum magnum habebis, si hic suom officium facit:
	ob istuc omen, ominator, capies quod te condecet.
Sos.	Enim vero praegnati oportet et malum et malum dari,
	ut quod obrodat sit, animo si male esse occeperit.
Amph.	Tu me heri hic vidisti?
Alc.	Ego, inquam, si vis decies dicere.
Amph.	In somnis fortasse?
Alc.	Immo vigilans vigilantem.
Amph.	Ei misero mihi.
Sos.	Quid tibi est?
Amph.	Delirat uxor.
Sos.	Atra bili percita est. nulla res tam delirantis homines concinnat cito.
Amph.	Ubi primum tibi sensisti, mulier, impliciscier?
Alc.	Equidem ecastor sana et salva sum.

74

	arrival and greet me as modest wives generally do their husbands. Yet here I come home to find you have dropped the habit.
lc.	Why mercy me, when you came home yesterday I certainly did welcome you the moment you appeared, and asked you in the same breath if you had been well all the time, and seized your hand and gave you a kiss.
os.	Welcomed him yesterday, did you?
lc.	Yes, and you, too, Sosia.
os.	Sir, I hoped she was going to bear you a son; but it's no child she's got.
mph.	What, then?
os.	A crazy streak.
lc.	(*angrily*) Indeed I have not, and I pray heaven I may safely bear a son. But you, sir, shall have an ample supply of aches and pains, if your master here does his duty! You shall be well rewarded for that omen, Sir Omener.
os.	Really now, ma'am, it's a lady in your condition ought to have aches and pains, yes, and an apple supply, too, so as to have something to chew on in case she gets to feeling seedy.
mph.	You saw me here yesterday?
lc.	Yes, I,—if you must be told ten times over.
mph.	In your sleep, perhaps?
lc.	No, no, awake,—and you were awake, too.
mph.	Oh, this is terrible, terrible!
os.	What ails you?
mph.	My wife is raving!
os.	Bilious attack, sir, black bile. There's nothing sets 'em raving so soon.
mph.	When did you first feel it coming on, woman?
lc.	Goodness me! I'm perfectly sane and sound.

75

Amph.   Quor igitur praedicas, 730
  te heri me vidisse, qui hac noctu in portum advecti
   sumus?
  ibi cenavi atque ibi quievi in navi noctem perpetem,
  neque meum pedem huc intuli etiam in aedis, ut
   cum exercitu
  hinc profectus sum ad Teloboas hostis eosque ut
   vicimus.

Alc. Immo mecum cenavisti et mecum cubuisti.

Amph.   Quid est?

Alc. Vera dico.

Amph. Non de hac quidem hercle re; de aliis nescio.

Alc. Primulo diluculo abiisti ad legiones.

Amph.   Quo modo?

Sos. Recte dicit, ut commeminit: somnium narrat tibi.
  sed, mulier, postquam experrecta es, te prodigiali
   Iovi
  aut mola salsa hodie aut ture comprecatam oportuit. 740

Alc. Vae capiti tuo.

Sos.   Tua istuc refert—si curaveris.

Alc. Iterum iam hic in me inclementer dicit, atque id
   sine malo.

Amph. Tace tu. tu dic: egone abs te abii hinc hodie cum
   diluculo?

Alc. Quis igitur nisi vos narravit mi, illi ut fuerit
   proelium?

Amph. An etiam id tu scis?

Alc.   Quippe qui ex te audivi, ut urbem maximam
  expugnavisses regemque Pterelam tute occideris.

Amph. Egone istuc dixi?

mph. Then why are you declaring you saw me yesterday,
when we reached port last night? I took
dinner there and spent the whole livelong night
there on board my ship, and I have not set foot in
this house from the time I and my troops started
on our campaign against the Teloboians and
conquered them.

lc. The idea! You had dinner with me and went to
bed with me.

mph. What?

lc. I tell you the truth, sir.

mph. Good God! Not in that, anyhow: about other
matters I can't say.

lc. And at the very break of day you went away to the
army.

mph. How's that?

os. Quite straight, sir, as far as her memory goes: she's
giving you her dream. But I say, ma'am, this
morning after you woke up you ought to have taken
some salted cakes, or incense, and prayed to Jove
—he has charge of prodigies.

lc. Oh confound you, sir!

os. (*innocently*) That would do you good, ma'am—if
you would see to it.

lc. There he is, rude to me again, and not suffering for it!

mph. (*to Sosia*) Keep still, you! (*to Alcmena*) And you—
I left you this morning at daybreak, did I?

lc. Why, who else but you two told me how the battle
there went?

mph. You don't mean to say you know about that?

lc. Naturally, since I heard from your own lips how
you took that great city and killed King Pterelas
yourself.

mph. I told you that, I?

D

Alc.   Tute istic, etiam adstante hoc Sosia.

Amph.   Audivistin tu me narrare haec hodie?

Sos.   Ubi ego audiverim?

Amph.   Hanc roga.

Sos.   Me quidem praesente numquam factum est, quod
sciam.

Alc.   Mirum quin te adversus dicat.

Amph.   Sosia, age me huc aspice.   750

Sos.   Specto.

Amph.   Vera volo loqui te, nolo adsentari mihi.
audivistin tu hodie me illi dicere ea quae illa autumat?

Sos.   Quaeso edepol, num tu quoque etiam insanis,
quom id me interrogas,
qui ipsus equidem nunc primum istanc tecum conspicio simul?

Amph.   Quid nunc, mulier? audin illum?

Alc.   Ego vero, ac falsum dicere.

Amph.   Neque tu illi neque mihi viro ipsi credis?

Alc.   Eo fit quia mihi
plurimum credo et scio istaec facta proinde ut
proloquor.

Amph.   Tun me heri advenisse dicis?

Alc.   Tun te abiisse hodie hinc negas?

Amph.   Nego enim vero, et me advenire nunc primum aio
ad te domum.

Alc.   Obsecro, etiamne hoc negabis, te auream pateram
mihi   760
dedisse dono hodie, qua te illi donatum esse
dixeras?

Amph.   Neque edepol dedi neque dixi; verum ita animatus fui
itaque nunc sum, ut ea te patera donem.   sed quis
istuc tibi
dixit?

78

Jc.   Yes, you yourself,—with Sosia here standing by, too.

mph.   (*to Sosia*) Have you ever heard me say a word of this?

os.   Heard you? Where?

mph.   (*sullenly*) Ask her.

os.   You never did so far as I know, leastways with me at hand.

lc.   (*ironically*) It is strange he declines to contradict his own master.

mph.   Sosia, here! Look me in the eye.

os.   (*obeying*) Very good, sir.

mph.   What I want from you is the truth, no obsequiousness. Did you ever hear me utter a syllable of what she says?

os.   Well, upon my word, I should like to ask if you are not crazy yourself, asking me a question like that—and I just this minute setting eyes on her for the first time along with you?

mph.   What now, madam? Do you hear him?

lc.   To be sure I do—telling lies.

mph.   You won't believe him, or me, your own husband, either?

lc.   That is only because I believe myself most of all, and I know everything occurred just as I tell you.

mph.   And you say that I arrived yesterday?

lc.   And you deny that you left to-day?

mph.   Deny it? Of course I do. And I say I'm just now coming home to you for the first time.

lc.   And will you deny this, too, pray,—that you gave me the golden bowl to-day that was presented to you there, as you said?

mph.   By heaven! I neither gave it nor said it. But I did intend to make you a gift of that bowl, and do still. Who told you of that, though?

Alc.   Ego equidem ex te audivi et ex tua accepi manu
pateram.

Amph.   Mane, mane, obsecro te. nimis demiror, Sosia,
qui illaec illic me donatum esse aurea patera
sciat,
nisi tu dudum hanc convenisti et narravisti haec
omnia.

Sos.   Neque edepol ego dixi neque istam vidi nisi
tecum simul.

Amph.   Quid hoc sit hominis?

Alc.   Vin proferri pateram?

Amph.   Proferri volo.

Alc.   Fiat. heus tu, Thessala, intus pateram proferto
foras,   770
qua hodie meus vir donavit me.

Amph.   Secede huc tu, Sosia,
enim vero illud praeter alia mira miror maxime,
si haec habet pateram illam.

Sos.   An etiam credis id, quae in hac cistellula
tuo signo obsignata fertur?

Amph.   Salvom signum est?

Sos.   Inspice.

Amph.   Recte, ita est ut obsignavi.

Sos.   Quaeso, quin tu istanc iubes
pro cerrita circumferri?

Amph.   Edepol qui facto est opus;
nam haec quidem edepol larvarum plenast.

Alc.   Quid verbis opust?
em tibi pateram, eccam.

Amph.   Cedo mi.

Alc.   Age aspice huc sis nunciam
tu qui quae facta infitiare; quem ego iam hic con-
vincam palam.
estne haec patera qua donatu's illi?

lc. Why, I heard about it from your own lips and received the bowl from your own hand.

mph. One moment, please, one moment! (*turning to Sosia*) It is very extraordinary, Sosia, how she knows I was presented with a golden bowl there, unless you met her a while ago yourself and told her the whole story.

os. By gad, sir, I never told her, no, nor saw her, except here with you.

mph. (*helplessly*) What sort of a creature have I got here?

lc. Would you like to have the bowl brought?

mph. Indeed I should.

lc. Very well. (*calling to maid within*) Ho, there! Thessala, bring out the bowl my husband gave me to-day.

mph. Sosia! Come over here. (*they withdraw somewhat*) Upon my soul, it will be the most astounding of all these astounding circumstances, if she has that.

os. Do you really believe that, sir, when I've got it in this little chest here, sealed with your own signet?

mph. Is the seal intact?

os. (*showing chest*) Look and see.

mph. (*doing so*) It is all right—just as I sealed it.

os. For heaven's sake, why don't you have her treated for lunacy?

mph. By Jove, so I should! Why, bless my soul, she's full of evil spirits!

ENTER *Thessala* WITH BOWL.

lc. Are you satisfied, sir? There! Your bowl, see!

mph. (*dumbfounded*) Give it here!

lc. Come now, be so good as to look at it, you that do a thing and then disown it. I shall refute you plainly, sir, here and now. Is this the bowl which they presented to you there, or not?

81

Amph.   Summe Iuppiter,   780
quid ego video? haec ea est profecto patera.   perii,
Sosia.

Sos. Aut pol haec praestigiatrix multo mulier maxima est
aut pateram hic inesse oportet.

Amph.   Agedum, exsolve cistulam.

Sos. Quid ego istam exsolvam? obsignatast recte, res
gesta est bene:
tu peperisti Amphitruonem, ego alium peperi
Sosiam;
nunc si patera pateram peperit, omnes congemina-
vimus.

Amph. Certum est aperire atque inspicere.

Sos.   Vide sis signi quid siet,
ne posterius in me culpam conferas.

Amph.   Aperi modo;
nam haec quidem nos delirantis facere dictis postulat.

Alc. Unde haec igitur est nisi abs te quae mihi dono
data est?   790

Amph. Opus mi est istuc exquisito.

Sos.   Iuppiter, pro Iuppiter.

Amph. Quid tibi est?

Sos.   Hic patera nulla in cistulast.

Amph.   Quid ego audio?

Sos. Id quod verumst.

Amph.   At cum cruciatu iam, nisi apparet, tuo

Alc. Haec quidem apparet.

Amph.   Quis igitur tibi dedit?

Alc.   Qui me rogat.

Sos. Me captas, quia tute ab navi clanculum huc alia via
praecucurristi, atque hinc pateram tute exemisti
atque eam
huic dedisti, post hanc rursum obsignasti clanculum.

82

mph.   (*taking it*) Jove almighty! What do I see? The selfsame bowl, it is, it is! This is frightful, Sosia!

os.   By gad, she's either the greatest enchantress alive, easily, or the bowl must be inside here. (*pointing to chest*)

mph.   Come, come, unfasten the chest!

os.   Unfasten it? Why? It's sealed all right, everything is shipshape. You have spawned another Amphitryon; I have spawned another Sosia; now if the bowl has spawned another bowl, we've all doubled.

mph.   I'm resolved: it must be opened and inspected.

os.   You please take a look at the seal, sir, so that you won't blame me later.

mph.   (*looking*) Yes, yes, open up! Why, the woman is bent on driving us mad with her talk.

lc.   Where did this come from, then, if not as a present from you?

mph.   (*curtly*) This matter needs my investigation.

os.   (*busy with chest*) By Jove! Oh, by Jove!

mph.   (*excited*) What is it?

os.   There's no bowl in the chest here at all!

mph.   What's that you say?

os.   It's the honest truth.

mph.   But your skin shall soon pay for it, if it's not forthcoming.

lc.   This one is forthcoming, at any rate.

mph.   (*roughly*) Who gave it you, then?

lc.   (*calmly*) My questioner.

os.   (*to Amphitryon*) Trying to catch me! The fact is you ran on ahead from the ship yourself by another road on the sly, and took the bowl out yourself, and gave it to her, and then sealed up the chest again on the sly.

Amph. Ei mihi, iam tu quoque huius adiuvas insaniam?
ain heri nos advenisse huc?

Alc. Aio, adveniensque ilico
me salutavisti, et ego te, et osculum tetuli tibi.   800

Sos. Iam illud non placet principium de osculo.

Amph. Perge exsequi.

Alc. Lavisti.

Amph. Quid postquam lavi?

Alc. Accubuisti.

Sos. Euge optime.
nunc exquire.

Amph. Ne interpella.   perge porro dicere.

Alc. Cena adposita est; cenavisti mecum, ego accubui
simul.

Amph. In eodem lecto?

Alc. In eodem.

Sos. Ei, non placet convivium.

Amph. Sine modo argumenta dicat. quid postquam cena-
vimus?

Alc. Te dormitare aibas; mensa ablata est, cubitum
hinc abiimus.

Amph. Ubi tu cubuisti?

Alc. In eodem lecto tecum una in cubiculo.

Amph. Perdidisti.

Sos. Quid tibi est?

Amph. Haec me modo ad mortem dedit.

Alc. Quid iam, amabo?

Amph. Ne me appella.

Sos. Quid tibi est?

Amph. Perii miser,   810
quia pudicitiae huius vitium me hinc absente est
additum.

Alc. Obsecro ecastor, cur istuc, mi vir, ex ted audio?

84

mph. Oh, ye gods! So now you are abetting her delusions, too! (*to Alcmena, with forced calmness*) We came here yesterday, you say?

lc. Yes, and the moment you arrived you greeted me, and I you, and I gave you a kiss.

os. Now I don't like that, that beginning with a kiss!

mph. Go on, go on!

lc. Then you bathed.

mph. And after bathing?

lc. You took your place on the dining couch.

os. Bravo, sir! Great work! Now get to the bottom of it.

mph. (*to Sosia*) No interruptions! (*to Alcmena*) Go on with your story.

lc. Dinner was served: we dined together: I took my place on the couch, too.

mph. The same couch?

lc. Surely.

os. Oho! This banqueting looks bad!

mph. (*to Sosia*) That will do. Let her state her case. (*to Alcmena*) What after we dined?

lc. You said you were sleepy: the table was removed: we went off to bed.

mph. Where did you sleep?

lc. Why, with you, in our room.

mph. Oh, my God!

os. What ails you?

mph. She has killed me, killed me!

lc. Why, my dear man, what do you mean?

mph. (*furiously*) Don't speak to me!

os. What ails you?

mph. Oh, God help me! She's been seduced while I was gone!

lc. Good heavens! For mercy's sake how can you say such a thing, my dear husband?

Amph. Vir ego tuos sim? ne me appella, falsa, falso nomine.

Sos. Haeret haec res, si quidem haec iam mulier facta est
ex viro.

Alc. Quid ego feci, qua istaec propter dicta dicantur
mihi?

Amph. Tute edictas facta tua, ex me quaeris quid deli-
queris.

Alc. Quid ego tibi deliqui, si, cui nupta sum, tecum
fui?

Amph. Tun mecum fueris? quid illac impudente audacius?
saltem, tute si pudoris egeas, sumas mutuom.

Alc. Istuc facinus, quod tu insimulas, nostro generi non
decet.   820
tu si me inpudicitiai captas, capere non potes.

Amph. Pro di immortales, cognoscin tu me saltem, Sosia?

Sos. Propemodum.

Amph.   Cenavin ego heri in navi in portu Persico?

Alc. Mihi quoque adsunt testes, qui illud quod ego
dicam adsentiant.

Sos. Nescio quid istuc negoti dicam, nisi si quispiam est
Amphitruo alius, qui forte ted hinc absenti tamen
tuam rem curet teque absente hic munus fungatur
tuom.
nam quod de illo subditivo Sosia mirum nimis,
certe de istoc Amphitruone iam alterum mirum est
magis.

Amph. Nescio quis praestigiator hanc frustratur mulierem.   830

Alc. Per supremi regis regnum iuro et matrem familias
Iunonem, quam me vereri et metuere est par
maxume,
ut mi extra unum te mortalis nemo corpus corpore
contigit, quo me impudicam faceret.

86

Amph.   Am I your husband? Oh, you false wretch. none of your false names for me!

Sos.   Here's a pretty mess, if he is turned into a woman and is not her husband!

Alc.   What have I done to be talked to like that?

Amph.   You have recounted your doings yourself—and you ask me what the harm is!

Alc.   Pray tell me what I have done in being with you, the man I married?

Amph.   You with me? Of all brazen shamelessness! You might at least borrow some sense of decency, if you have none of your own!

Alc.   Such behaviour as you accuse me of does not become members of my family, sir. Angle for me if you wish, you cannot catch me in such unspeakable conduct.

Amph.   Great God! You know me, anyhow, Sosia, don't you?

Sos.   Well, rather!

Amph.   Didn't I dine yesterday on shipboard at Port Persicus?

Alc.   Yes, and I too have witnesses to corroborate what I say.

Sos.   I can't puzzle it out, sir, unless there's some other Amphitryon to manage your business, no matter if you are away, and to do your job for you when you have gone. I tell you what, that sham Sosia was monstrous surprising, but this second Amphitryon is certainly more so.

Amph.   Some magician or other has bedevilled the woman!

Alc.   (*slowly and impressively*) I swear by the kingdom of the King on high and by Juno, the matron goddess I most should reverence and fear—so may she bless me as no mortal man, save you only, has taken me to him as a wife.

Amph.   Vera istaec velim.

Alc.   Vera dico, sed nequiquam, quoniam non vis credere.

Amph.   Mulier es, audacter iuras.

Alc.   Quae non deliquit, decet
audacem esse, confidenter pro se et proterve loqui.

Amph.   Satis audacter.

Alc.   Ut pudicam decet.

Amph.   Enim verbis proba's.[1]

Alc.   Non ego illam mihi dotem duco esse, quae dos
      dicitur,

sed pudicitiam et pudorem et sedatum cupidinem,   840
deum metum, parentum amorem et cognatum con-
      cordiam,

tibi morigera atque ut munifica sim bonis, prosim
      probis.

Sos.   Ne ista edepol, si haec vera loquitur, examussim
      est optima.

Amph.   Delenitus sum profecto ita, ut me qui sim nesciam.

Sos.   Amphitruo es profecto, cave sis ne tu te usu perduis:
ita nunc homines immutantur, postquam peregre
      advenimus.

Amph.   Mulier, istam rem inquisitam certum est non amit-
      tere.

Alc.   Edepol me libente facies.

Amph.   Quid ais? responde mihi,
quid si adduco tuom cognatum huc ab navi Nau-
      cratem,

qui mecum una vectust una navi, atque is si denegat   850
facta quae tu facta dicis, quid tibi aequom est fieri?
numquid causam dicis, quin te hoc multem matri-
      monio?

Alc.   Si deliqui, nulla causa est.

---

[1] *enim verbis probas* Lachmann: *probas* vel *proba's*
Lindsay: *in verbis probas* MSS.

mph. Ah, I wish it was the truth!

lc. It is the truth, but what of that, when you refuse to believe me!

mph. You're a woman: you swear boldly.

lc. A woman who has done nothing wrong ought to be bold, yes, and self-confident and forward in her own defence.

mph. Bold, with a vengeance!

lc. As innocence should be.

mph. Yes, you're immaculate as far as talk goes.

lc. (*quietly*) Personally I do not feel that my dowry is that which people call a dowry, but purity and honour and self-control, fear of God, love of parents, and affection for my family, and being a dutiful wife to you, sir, lavish of loving-kindness and helpful through honest service.

os. My word! She's a regular pattern of perfection, if she's telling the truth.

mph. Upon my soul, I have been so bewitched I don't know who I am!

os. You're Amphitryon right enough, sir: but just look out you don't lose your title to yourself by limitation, the way folks are getting changed about these days since we came back from abroad.

mph. (*to Alcmena, sternly*) This matter shall not escape investigation, madam, I am resolved on that.

lc. Dear me, sir, do investigate, and welcome!

mph. See here, answer me this—what if I bring your own relative, Naucrates, over from the ship? He made the voyage with me on the same vessel: now if he denies that I did as you say, what do you deserve? Have you any reason to give that I should not divorce you?

lc. None, if I have done wrong.

89

Amph.   Convenit. tu, Sosia,
       duc hos intro. ego huc ab navi mecum adducam
       Naucratem.

Sos.   Nunc quidem praeter nos nemo est. dic mihi ve-
       rum serio:
       ecquis alius Sosia intust, qui mei similis siet?

Alc.   Abin hinc a me dignus domino servos?

Sos.   Abeo, si iubes.

Alc.   Nimis ecastor facinus mirum est, qui illi conlibitum
       siet
       meo viro sic me insimulare falso facinus tam malum.
       quicquid est, iam ex Naucrate cognato id cognos-
       cam meo.   860

ACTVS III

Iup.   Ego sum ille Amphitruo, cui est servos Sosia,
       idem Mercurius qui fit, quando commodumst,
       in superiore qui habito cenaculo,
       qui interdum fio Iuppiter, quando lubet;
       huc autem quom extemplo adventum adporto, ilico
       Amphitruo fio et vestitum immuto meum.
       nunc huc honoris vostri venio gratia,
       ne hanc incohatam transigam comoediam;
       simul Alcumenae, quam vir insontem probri
       Amphitruo accusat, veni ut auxilium feram: 870
       90

AMPHITRYON

Amph. Agreed! (*turning to Sosia*) Sosia, take these fellows in. (*pointing to slaves with luggage*) I will bring Naucrates here from the ship. (*Sosia sends slaves inside*) [EXIT *Amphitryon.*

Sos. (*to Alcmena, confidentially*) Now then, ma'am, no one's here besides us. (*elaborately makes sure of it*) Do be serious and tell me the truth—is there another Sosia inside who's just like me?

Alc. (*indignantly*) Will you leave my sight, sir—you slave worthy of your master!

Sos. Sure, ma'am, if you say so. [EXIT INTO HOUSE.

Alc. Merciful heavens! It's simply unintelligible, how my husband could think fit to accuse me of such atrocious conduct without the slightest cause. Well, whatever it is, I shall soon know about it from Naucrates, one of my own family.

[EXIT INTO HOUSE.

ACT III

(*A couple of hours have elapsed.*)

ENTER *Jupiter.*

Jup. (*in jocular, self-satisfied tone*) I am that Amphitryon who has a servant Sosia, which same turns into Mercury on occasion, I being the Amphitryon who lodge in the upper attic (*pointing heavenward*) and become Jupiter at times, when the humour seizes me. As soon as I wend my way into these parts, however, on the spot I am Amphitryon and change my clothes. I now appear out of regard for you, so as not to terminate this inchoate comedy. At the same time I am here to help out Alcmena, poor innocent, denounced as disloyal by her lord, Amphitryon. For it would be sinful of me, if the

91

nam mea sit culpa, quod egomet contraxerim,
si id Alcumenae innocenti expetat.
nunc Amphitruonem memet, ut occepi semel,
esse adsimulabo, atque in horum familiam
frustrationem hodie iniciam maxumam ;
post igitur demum faciam res fiat palam
atque Alcumenae in tempore auxilium feram
faciamque ut uno fetu et quod gravida est viro
et me quod gravidast pariat sine doloribus.
Mercurium iussi me continuo consequi,   880
si quid vellem imperare.   nunc hanc adloquar.

III. 2.

Alc.   Durare nequeo in aedibus.   ita me probri,
stupri, dedecoris a viro argutam meo !
ea quae sunt facta infecta ut reddat clamitat,
quae neque sunt facta neque ego in me admisi
    arguit ;
atque id me susque deque esse habituram putat.
non edepol faciam. neque me perpetiar probri
falso insimulatam, quin ego illum aut deseram
aut satis faciat mi ille atque adiuret insuper,
nolle esse dicta quae in me insontem protulit.   890

Iup.   Faciundum est mi illud, fieri quod illaec postulat,
si me illam amantem ad sese studeam recipere,
quando ego quod feci, id factum Amphitruoni offuit
atque illi dudum meus amor negotium
insonti exhibuit, nunc autem insonti mihi
illius ira in hanc et male dicta expetent.

Alc.   Sed eccum video qui me miseram arguit
stupri, dedecoris.

Iup.   Te volo, uxor, conloqui.

92

storm I have brewed should descend on the head
of guileless Alcmena. I will pretend for the present to be Amphitryon myself, as I have already,
and thoroughly confound this family to-day. Then,
after that, I will eventually clear matters up, yes,
and aid Alcmena in due season, contriving that she
give birth at one time to both the children she
carries, her husband's and my own, without a pang.
Mercury has his orders to attend me closely, in
case I have commands to give. Now for a word
with the lady.

Scene 2.   ENTER *Alcmena* FROM HOUSE.

Alc.   I can't stand staying in the house! To be branded
so with shame, disloyalty, disgrace, by my own
husband! How he clamours to make facts no facts!
And what never happened, things I never, never
did, he accuses me of, and thinks I'll consider it
quite immaterial. Good gracious, but I won't! I
won't endure such an awful, unjustified accusation:
I will leave him, or he must apologize, one or the
other, yes, and swear he is sorry, too, for the things
he has said to an innocent woman.

Jup.   (*aside, dryly*) Hm! It's incumbent upon me to
meet her demands, if I wish the loving creature
to take me into her good graces again. Since my
doings offended Amphitryon, and this love affair of
mine lately occasioned his guiltless self some con-
sternation, it is turn about now, and my guiltless
self has to suffer for the scorn and contumely he
heaped on her.

Alc.   (*aside, seeing him*) Ah, there he is—the man that
charges his wretched wife with disloyalty and
shame!

Jup.   I wish to speak with you, my dear. (*circling her as*

93

quo te avortisti? [1]

Alc.   Ita ingenium mcumst:
inimicos semper osa sum optuerier.   900

Iup. Heia autem inimicos?

Alc.   Sic est, vera praedico;
nisi etiam hoc falso dici insimulaturus es.

Iup. Nimis iracunda es.

Alc.   Potin ut abstineas manum?
nam certo, si sis sanus aut sapias satis,
quam tu impudicam esse arbitrere et praedices,
cum ea tu sermonem nec ioco nec serio
tibi habeas, nisi sis stultior stultissimo.

Iup. Si dixi, nihilo magis es, neque ego esse arbitror,
et id huc revorti uti me purgarem tibi.
nam numquam quicquam meo animo fuit aegrius,   910
quam postquam audivi ted esse iratam mihi.
cur dixisti? inquies. ego expediam tibi.
non edepol quo te esse impudicam crederem;
verum periclitatus sum animum tuom,
quid faceres et quo pacto id ferre induceres.
equidem ioco illa dixeram dudum tibi,
ridiculi causa. vel hunc rogato Sosiam.

Alc. Quin huc adducis meum cognatum Naucratem,
testem quem dudum te adducturum dixeras,
te huc non venisse?

Iup.   Si quid dictum est per iocum,   920
non aequom est id te serio praevortier.

Alc. Ego illud scio quam doluerit cordi meo.

Iup. Per dexteram tuam te, Alcumena, oro obsecro.

---

[1] Leo notes lacuna here. *Ita ingenium* MSS: *Ita ingeni ingenium* Seyffert, followed by Lindsay.

Alc.   *she turns her back on him*) Turned away?   Where to?
Alc.   It is natural I should, sir: I always loathed looking at enemies.

Jup.   Oh, I say now!   Enemies?

Alc.   Yes, enemies: and that's the truth of it—unless you intend to term this a lie, too.

Jup.   (*trying to fondle her*) You're too irritable.

Alc.   (*pulling away*) Can't you keep your hands off? Why surely, sir, if you were sane or had a particle of sense about you, when you think your wife is immodest and tell her so yourself, you wouldn't hold any conversation with her at all in jest or earnest, unless you were the silliest of silly men.

Jup.   My saying so doesn't make you so any the more, And I don't think you so, either; and I've come back to set myself right with you.   For I never did feel sicker at heart about anything than after I heard you were provoked with me.   " Why did you say it? " you'll ask.   I'll clear up that point for you. Bless your heart, it wasn't because I believed you were immodest.   I was just testing your feelings to see what you'd do and how you'd take it. (*forcing a laugh*) Really it was all a joke, what I said just now, merely a bit of fun.   Why, you can ask Sosia here. (*pointing to house*)

Alc.   (*coldly*) Why do you not bring my relative Naucrates, as you just now said you would, to prove you had not been here?

Jup.   If something is said in joke, it's not fair to take it in earnest.

Alc.   I know one thing—that joke of yours cut me to the heart, sir.

Jup.   (*seizing her hand*) I beg and beseech you, Alcmena,

95

	da mihi hanc veniam, ignosce, irata ne sies.	
Alc.	Ego istaec feci verba virtute irrita;	
	nunc, quando factis me impudicis abstini,	
	ab impudicis dictis avorti volo.	
	valeas, tibi habeas res tuas, reddas meas.	
	iuben mi ire comites	
Iup.	Sanan es?	
Alc.	Si non iubes,	
	ibo egomet; comitem mihi Pudicitiam duxero.[1]	930
Iup.	Mane. arbitratu tuo ius iurandum dabo,	
	me meam pudicam esse uxorem arbitrarier.	
	id ego si fallo, tum te, summe Iuppiter,	
	quaeso, Amphitruoni ut semper iratus sies.	
Alc.	A, propitius sit potius.	
Iup.	Confido fore;	
	nam ius iurandum verum te advorsum dedi.	
	iam nunc irata non es?	
Alc.	Non sum.	
Iup.	Bene facis.	
	nam in hominum aetate multa eveniunt huius modi:	
	capiunt voluptates, capiunt rursum miserias;	
	irae interveniunt, redeunt rursum in gratiam.	940
	verum irae si quae forte eveniunt huius modi	
	inter eos, rursum si reventum in gratiam est,	
	bis tanto amici sunt inter se quam prius.	
Alc.	Primum cavisse oportuit ne diceres,	
	verum eadem si isdem purgas mi, patiunda sunt.	
Iup.	Iube vero vasa pura adornari mihi,	
	ut quae apud legionem vota vovi, si domum	
	rediissem salvos, ea ego exsolvam omnia.	
Alc.	Ego istuc curabo.	

---

[1] Corrupt (Leo): *duxero* MSS: *adsero* Leo.

by this right hand of yours, do forgive me for it: pardon me: don't be angry!

Alc. Your charges are refuted by my honest life; now, sir, having been guiltless of gross behaviour, I will not be subjected to gross language. Good-bye. Keep your own things and return me mine. Will you order my attendants to follow me? (*turns to go*)

Jup. Are you in your senses?

Alc. If you decline to do so, I will go with my woman's honour as my only escort. (*walks away*)

Jup. (*holding her*) Wait, wait! I'll swear to it—at your dictation—that I believe my wife is virtuous. If I deceive you in this, then, Jove almighty, I invoke thy curse upon Amphitryon for evermore.

Alc. (*hurriedly*) Oh no! His blessing, his blessing!

Jup. I trust to have it, for it is a reliable oath I have given you. (*drawing her close*) Now you're not angry, are you?

Alc. (*submitting*) No.

Jup. (*caressing her*) That's a good girl. Why, life is full of incidents of this sort. Human beings lay hold on pleasures and then again on pains. Quarrels come between them, and then they are reconciled again. But if any such quarrel as this does happen to arise between them, then when it blows over they are twice as fond of one another as they were before.

Alc. You should have been careful not to say such a thing in the first place: but if you apologize so nicely for hurting me so, I can't complain.

Jup. Well, well, then, have the sacrificial vessels prepared for me so that I can pay all the vows I vowed for a safe return home when I was in the field.

Alc. I will attend to that.

Iup.   Evocate huc Sosiam;

gubernatorem, qui in mea navi fuit   950
Blepharonem arcessat, qui nobiscum prandeat.
is adeo [1] inpransus ludificabitur,
cum ego Amphitruonem collo hinc obstricto traham.

Alc.   Mirum quid solus secum secreto ille agat.
atque aperiuntur aedis.   exit Sosia.

III. 3.

Sos.   Amphitruo, assum.   si quid opus est, impera, im-
        perium exequar.

Iup.   Sosia, optume advenis.

Sos.   Iam pax est inter vos duos?
nam quia vos tranquillos video, gaudeo et volup est
    mihi.
atque ita servom par videtur frugi sese instituere:
proinde eri ut sint, ipse item sit; voltum e voltu
    comparet: 960
tristis sit, si eri sint tristes; hilarus sit, si gaudeant.
sed age responde: iam vos rediistis in concordiam?

Iup.   Derides. qui scis haec dudum me dixisse per iocum.

Sos.   An id ioco dixisti?   equidem serio ac vero ratus.

Iup.   Habui expurigationem; facta pax est.

Sos.   Optume est.

Iup.   Ego rem divinam intus faciam, vota quae sunt.

Sos.   Censeo.

Iup.   Tu gubernatorem a navi huc evoca verbis meis
Blepharonem, qui re divina facta mecum prandeat.

Sos.   Iam hic ero, cum illic censebis esse me.

Iup.   Actutum huc redi.

---

[1] Leo notes lacuna here and suggests *is a Mercurio impransus.*

Jup.	(*to maids in doorway*) Call Sosia out. I want him to invite Blepharo, the pilot aboard my ship, to lunch with us (EXEUNT *maids*). (*aside*) As a matter of fact, friend Blepharo will be left unlunched and looking foolish when I turn Amphitryon out neck and crop.
Alc.	(*aside*) I wonder what he's talking about all to himself! Ah, there goes the door! Sosia's coming out.
Scene 3.	ENTER *Sosia*.
Sos.	Present, sir. If anything's needed, order away and I'll fulfil orders.
Jup.	Sosia, you are the very man I want.
Sos.	Is there peace between you two now, sir? I tell you what, it's a pleasure, it's a joy, to see you looking peaceful. Yes, and to my way of thinking, an honest servant ought to stick to this principle: be like what his betters are, model his expression on theirs, be in the dumps if they are in the dumps, and jolly if they are happy. But come, sir, answer me. Have you made friends again now, eh?
Jup.	(*reprovingly*) Mocker! What I said a while ago was all in fun, and you know it.
Sos.	In fun, was it? Upon my soul, I thought it was the solemn truth.
Jup.	I have explained: peace is made.
Sos.	That's grand, sir.
Jup.	I will make those offerings I vowed, inside.
Sos.	Very good, sir.
Jup.	As for you, convey my invitation to Pilot Blepharo to come over from the ship and lunch with me after the sacrifice is done.
Sos.	I'll be here by the time you think I'm there, sir.
Jup.	Yes, hurry back home. [EXIT *Sosia*.

Alc. Numquid vis, quin abeam iam intro, ut apparentur
    quibus opust?   970
Iup. I sane, et quantum potest parata fac sint omnia.
Alc. Quin venis quando vis intro? faxo haud quicquam
    sit morae.
Iup. Recte loquere et proinde diligentem ut uxorem
    decet.
    iam hisce ambo, et servos et era, frustra sunt duo,
    qui me Amphitruonem rentur esse: errant probe.
    nunc tu divine huc fac adsis Sosia—
    audis quae dico, tam etsi praesens non ades—
    fac Amphitruonem advenientem ab aedibus
    ut abigas; quovis pacto fac commentus sis.
    volo deludi illunc, dum cum hac usuraria   980
    uxore nunc mihi morigero.   haec curata sint
    fac sis, proinde adeo ut velle med intellegis,
    atque ut ministres mihi, mihi cum sacruficem.

III. 4.
Mer. Concedite atque abscedite omnes, de via decedite,
    nec quisquam tam audax fuat homo, qui obviam
    obsistat mihi.
    nam mihi quidem hercle qui minus liceat deo mini-
    tarier
    populo, ni decedat mihi, quam servolo in comoediis?
    ille navem salvam nuntiat aut irati adventum
    senis:
    ego sum Iovi dicto audiens, eius iussu nunc huc me
    adfero.
    quam ob rem mihi magis par est via decedere et
    concedere.   990
    pater vocat me, eum sequor, eius dicto imperio sum
    audiens;
    ut filium bonum patri esse oportet, itidem ego sum
    patri.

Alc.   Is there anything else, or shall I go in now and see to the things you'll need?

Jup.   Do, by all means, and get everything ready as quickly as you can.

Alc.   Come in as soon as you wish. I'll make sure there's nothing to delay you.

Jup.   (*tenderly*) That's the way for an attentive wife to talk. [EXIT *Alcmena*.

There we are! Both of 'em fooled, servant and mistress, took in thinking me Amphitryon. A sad mistake! Hark ye, Sosia the divine, appear! You hear what I say, even though absent in the flesh. Drive Amphitryon away from the house when he arrives—any device you please. He must be hood-winked while I proceed to divert myself with my wife on loan. Kindly see that this is managed precisely as you know I wish it to be, and do me service while I am sacrificing to myself.

[EXIT *Jupiter*.

Scene 4.   ENTER *Mercury* HURRIEDLY WITH BURLESQUE IMPORTANCE.

Mer.   (*to imaginary passers-by*) Get away, get out, get off the street, every one! Let no man be so bold as to block my path. (*to audience*) For damme, just tell me why a god like me hasn't as much right to hector people that hinder him as your paltry slave in the comedies? He brings word the ship is safe, or the choleric old man approaching: (*magnificently*) as for me, I hearken to the word of Jove and at his bidding do I now hie me hither. Wherefore 'tis still more seemly to get out, to get off the street for me. My father calls me; I come, obedient to his hest and will. (*confidingly*) I am a good son to my father, as a son should be. I back him

amanti subparasitor, hortor, adsto, admoneo, gaudeo.
si quid patri volup est, voluptas ea mihi multo
    maxumast.
amat: sapit; recte facit, animo quando obsequitur suo,
quod omnis homines facere oportet, dum id modo
    fiat bono.
nunc Amphitruonem volt deludi meus pater : faxo
    probe
iam hic deludetur, spectatores, vobis inspectantibus.
capiam coronam mi ni caput, adsimulabo me esse
    ebrium ;
atque illuc sursum escendero : inde optume aspel-
    lam virum   1000
de supero, cum huc accesserit ; faciam ut sit madi-
    dus sobrius.
deinde illi actutum sufferet suos servos poenas Sosia :
eum fecisse ille hodie arguet quae ego fecero hic.
quid mea ?
meo me aequomst morigerum patri, eius studio
    servire addecet.
sed eccum Amphitruonem, advenit ; iam ille hic
    deludetur probe,
siquidem vos voltis auscultando operam dare.
ibo intro, ornatum capiam qui potis decet ;
dein susum ascendam in tectum, ut illum hinc
    prohibeam.

ACTVS IV

Amph. Naucratem quem convenire volui, in navi non erat,
neque domi neque in urbe invenio quemquam qui
    illum viderit.   1010
nam omnis plateas perreptavi, gymnasia et myropolia;
apud emporium atque in macello, in palaestra atque
    in foro,
in medicinis, in tonstrinis, apud omnis aedis sacras

up in his gallantries, encourage him, stand by him, advise him, rejoice with him. If anything gratifies my father, it gratifies me infinitely more. He's in love: he's wise; he does well to indulge his inclinations. It is what every one ought to do, that is within due bounds. At present my father wishes Amphitryon to be fooled: fooled he shall be finely, I promise you, here and now, spectators, and under your inspection. I'm going to put a garland on my head and make believe I'm drunk, yes, and I'll climb out on the roof yonder (*pointing to Amphitryon's house*) and repel our returning hero in glorious style from up above there. I'll see that he's both soaked and sober. Then that servant Sosia of his shall promptly smart for it, Sosia being accused of doing what I do here. But what of that? I must humour my own father: it is only dutiful to meet his desires. (*looking down street*) But there's Amphitryon coming! Here and now he'll be finely fooled—if you'll only take the trouble to attend. I'll go inside and make up as a person flown with wine; then I'll up on the roof to keep him off. 　　　　　[EXIT INTO HOUSE.

ACT IV

ENTER *Amphitryon* WEARILY.

Amph. Naucrates, whom I wanted to get hold of wasn't on the ship, and not a soul can I find at his house or in the city who has seen him. Why, I've hobbled through every street, gymnasium, and perfumery shop: down in the bazaar and the market, at the athletic field and the forum, too, at the doctor's, the barber's, the holy temples from

sum defessus quaeritando: nusquam invenio Naucratem.

nunc domum ibo atque ex uxore hanc rem pergam
exquirere,

quis fuerit quem propter corpus suom stupri com-
pleverit.

nam me, quam illam quaestionem inquisitam hodie
amittere,

mortuom satiust. sed aedis occluserunt. eugepae,
pariter hoc fit atque ut alia facta sunt. feriam
foris.

aperite hoc. heus, ecquis hic est? ecquis hoc aperit
ostium?   1020

IV. 2.

Mer.   Quis ad fores est?

Amph.   Ego sum.

Mer.   Quid ego sum?

Amph.   Ita loquor.

Mer.   Tibi Iuppiter
dique omnes irati certo sunt, qui sic frangas fores.

Amph.   Quo modo?

Mer.   Eo modo, ut profecto vivas aetatem miser.

Amph.   Sosia.

Mer.   Ita, sum Sosia, nisi me esse oblitum existimas.
quid nunc vis?

Amph.   Sceleste, at etiam quid velim, id tu me rogas?

Mer.   Ita, rogo. paene effregisti, fatue, foribus cardines.
an foris censebas nobis publicitus praeberier?
quid me aspectas, stolide? quid nunc vis tibi? aut
quid tu es homo?

Amph.   Verbero, etiam quis ego sim me rogitas, ulmorum
Acheruns?
quem pol ego hodie ob istaec dicta faciam ferven-
tem flagris.   1030

first to last,—I'm tired to death looking for him, and not a sign of Naucrates anywhere. Now I'm going home and ask my wife some more questions about this, and (*savagely*) find out who it is she has prostituted herself for. Ah, I'd sooner die than let the day pass without having this matter settled. (*trying door*) Well! they've locked up the house! Nice doings! Quite in accord with the rest of it. I'll knock. (*does so*) Open up here! Hey! is anyone in? Open—somebody! (*knocks more lustily*)

Scene 2.   *Mercury,* MUCH DISHEVELLED, APPEARS ON ROOF.

Mer. (*thickly*) Who's at the door?

Amph. I am.

Mer. I am, eh?

Amph. (*sharply*) So I say.

Mer. Jupiter and . . . all the . . . gods . . . are surely . . . angry at you . . . demolishing our door so.

Amph. What do you mean?

Mer. Here's . . . what I mean: you're certainly going to have a bad, bad time of it.

Amph. (*sternly*) Sosia!

Mer. Just so! That's me . . . unless you think I've forgotten. Now what do . . . you want?

Amph. Rascal! Do you actually dare ask me that—what I want?

Mer. Of course I do. You've almost hammered the doors off their hinges, you . . . stupid. Didn't suppose we were supplied with doors at public expense, did you? What are you staring at me for, you . . . booby? What are you after now? Who are you?

Amph. You scoundrel! Still asking me who I am, you death-on-rods, you? By gad, I'll warm you up with a whip to-day for this insolence!

Mer. Prodigum te fuisse oportet olim in adulescentia.

Amph. Quidum?

Mer.   Quia senecta aetate a me mendicas malum.

Amph. Cum cruciatu tuo istaec hodie, verna, verba funditas.

Mer. Sacrufico ego tibi.

Amph.   Qui?

Mer.   Quia enim te macto infortunio.

Amph. At ego te cruce et cruciatu mactabo, mastigia.   I

Mer. Erus Amphitruost occupatus.   II

Mer.   abiendi nunc tibi etiam occasiost.   III (XV LG)

Mer. Optimo iure infringatur aula cineris in caput.   IV (III)

106

AMPHITRYON

Mer. You must have been a waster . . . in your . . . younger days.

Imph. How so?

Mer. Well . . . here you are in your declining years begging . . . me for trouble.

Imph. You shall soon suffer for this flow of language, you drudge.

Mer. I'm sacrificing to ye, I am.

Imph. How?

Mer. (*slyly poising a pail of water*) Why, because I'm making you an offering of a . . . calamity.

[*At this point there is a gap in the MSS. Only a few lines have been preserved. Leo outlines the lost part as follows: After Mercury has had sufficient amusement with Amphitryon, the disturbance calls Alcmena from within. She has a dispute with her husband—Jupiter had left her earlier so that he might offer sacrifice—and shuts him out of the house. Perhaps Amphitryon went away to summon friends to aid him: at any rate, Sosia appears with Blepharo and gets a bad welcome from his master, despite Blepharo's patronage, and then escapes. Jupiter comes out of the house. Husband and lover abuse each other vigorously and a scuffle ensues. Blepharo is appealed to by Amphitryon, only to be made ridiculous by Jupiter.*]

Imph. But I'll make you an offering of torture and torment, you whipping post.

Mer. The master, Amphitryon, is busy.

I

Mer. — — now you still have a chance to leave.

II

Mer. It would serve you right to have a pot of ashes broken on your head.

Mer. Ne tu postules matulam unam tibi aquae infundi
in caput v (IV)

Mer. Larvatu's. edepol hominem miserum. medicum
quaerita. VI (VII)

Alc. Exiuravisti te mihi dixe per iocum. VII (XI)

Alc. Quaeso advenienti morbo medicari iube: VIII (XII)
tu certe aut larvatus aut cerritus es.

Alc. Nisi hoc ita factum est, proinde ut factum esse
autumo, IX (XIII)
non causam dico quin vero insimules probri

Amph. Cuius? quae me absente corpus volgavit suom. x (XVI)

Amph. Quid minitabas te facturum, si istas pepulissem
fores? XI (V)

Amph. Ibi scrobes ecfodito tu plus sexagenos in die. XII (VI)

Amph. Noli pessimo precari. XIII (XVII)

Bleph. animam comprime XIV (XVIII)

Iup. Manifestum hunc optorto collo teneo furem
flagiti. XV (IX)

Amph. Immo ego hunc, Thebani cives, qui domi uxorem
meam XVI (X)
impudicitia impedivit, teneo, thensaurum stupri.

Amph. Nilne te pudet, sceleste, populi in conspectum in-
gredi? XVII (VIII)

Amph. clandestino XVIII (XIX)

Amph. Qui nequeas nostrorum uter sit Amphitruo de-
sive Iup. cernere. XIX (XIV)

IV. 3.

Bleph. Vos inter vos partite; ego abeo, mihi negotium est;

Ier. You would certainly ask to have one jar of water
emptied on your head.

Ier. Bewitched! Dear, dear! poor man! Look for a
doctor.

Alc. You swore solemnly that you said it to me in
fun.

Alc. For mercy's sake have this disease treated at the
outset; you surely are bewitched or crazed.

Alc. If this did not take place just as I state, you have
every right to accuse me of unchastity.

Amph. Whose? A woman that prostituted herself in my
absence!

Amph. What were you threatening to do, if I pounded on
that door?

Amph. There dig more than sixty ditches a day.

Amph. Don't intercede for an utter rascal.

Bleph. — save your breath.

up. I have him by the scruff of the neck, an outrageous
thief caught in the act.

Amph. No, no, Theban citizens, I have him, the monster
of lust who has brought disgrace on my wife at home.

Amph. Aren't you at all ashamed, you villain, to come out
into public sight?

Amph. — clandestinely.

Amph. You who are unable to decide which of us is Am
r Jup. phitryon.

Scene 3.

Bleph. (*disgustedly*) You must untangle your own selves:
I'm going: I have an engagement. (*aside*) Never

neque ego umquam usquam tanta mira me vidisse
censeo.

Amph. Blepharo, quaeso ut advocatus mi adsis neve abeas.

Bleph. Vale.

quid opust me advocato, qui utri sim advocatus
nescio?

Iup. Intro ego hinc eo.   Alcumena parturit.

Amph. Perii miser.

quid ego faciam, quem advocati iam atque amici
deserunt? 1040

numquam edepol me inultus istic ludificabit, quisquis est;

nam iam ad regem recta me ducam resque ut facta
est eloquar.[1]

ego pol illum ulciscar hodie Thessalum veneficum,

qui pervorse perturbavit familiae mentem meae.

sed ubi illest? intro edepol abiit, credo ad uxorem
meam.

qui me Thebis alter vivit miserior? quid nunc agam?

quem omnes mortales ignorant et ludificant ut lubet.

certumst, intro rumpam in aedis: ubi quemque
hominem aspexero,

si ancillam seu servom sive uxorem sive adulterum

seu patrem sive avom videbo, obtruncabo in aedibus. 1050

neque me Iuppiter neque di omnes id prohibebunt,
si volent,

quin sic faciam ut constitui.   pergam in aedis nunciam.

---

[1] Corrupt (Leo): *nam iam* MSS: *iam* Gruter.

did I see such marvels anywhere. I do believe.
(*turns to go*)

Amph. Blepharo! Stand by me, for mercy's sake, and be
my assistant: don't go!

Bleph. Good-bye. What's the use of my being an assistant when I don't know which to be it to?

[EXIT *Blepharo.*

Jup. (*aside*) I'm going inside myself: Alcmena's delivery
is at hand.

[EXIT *Jupiter* INTO HOUSE, UNSEEN BY *Amphitryon.*

Amph. (*wildly*) Heavens! oh, Heavens! What shall I
do now when assistants and friends desert me? By
the Lord, that villain shall never make game of me
and escape, whoever he is! I'll go straight to the
king this moment and tell him all as it happened.
I swear I'll have my revenge this day on that Thes-
salian sorcerer who has turned the wits of my
household topsy-turvy. (*looking around*) Where is
he, though? Good God! He's gone inside—to
my wife, no doubt! Oh, of all miserable men
in Thebes! What shall I do now? Disowned and
humbugged by every mortal soul to suit their
humour! (*pause*) My mind's made up—I'll burst
into the house, and every human creature there
I set my eyes on, maid or man, wife or paramour,
father or grandfather, I'll cut them down in my
halls! And rot the will of Jupiter and all the
gods shall stop my doing as I've determined! I'll
in this minute! (*he rushes toward door : a peal of
thunder : he falls to ground motionless*)

ACTVS V

Brom. Spes atque opes vitae meae iacent sepultae in
pectore,
neque ullast confidentia iam in corde, quin ami-
serim;
ita mihi videntur omnia, mare terra caelum, consequi,
iam ut opprimar, ut enicer. me miseram, quid
agam nescio.
ita tanta mira in aedibus sunt facta. vae miserae mihi,
animo malest, aquam velim. corrupta sum atque
absumpta sum.
caput dolet, neque audio, nec oculis prospicio satis,
nec me miserior femina est neque ulla videatur
magis.   1060
ita erae meae hodie contigit. nam ubi parturit,
deos sibi invocat,
strepitus, crepitus, sonitus, tonitrus: ut subito,
ut propere, ut valide tonuit!
ubi quisque institerat, concidit crepitu. ibi nescio quis maxuma
voce exclamat: " Alcumena, adest auxilium,
ne time:
et tibi et tuis propitius caeli cultor advenit.
exsurgite " inquit " qui terrore meo occidistis prae
metu."
ut iacui, exsurgo. ardere censui aedis, ita tum
confulgebant.
ibi me inclamat Alcumena; iam ea res me horrore
adficit,
erilis praevertit metus: accurro, ut sciscam quid
velit.
atque illam geminos filios pueros peperisse conspicor; 1070
neque nostrum quisquam sensimus, quom peperit,

112

AMPHITRYON

ACT V

(Half an hour has elapsed.)

ENTER *Bromia* FROM HOUSE, IN A PANIC.

Brom. Oh, my hopes and chances of getting out of this alive are dead and buried inside of me! There's not a thing left to keep my courage up now! The way everything—sea, land, sky—does seem set on crushing me, killing me off this instant! Oh dear, oh dear! What to do I don't know. Such amazing things as did happen in there! Oh, poor me! I feel faint. Oh, for some water! I'm a wreck, I'm all done up. My head's splitting, and I can't hear or see right, either. There isn't a wretcheder woman on earth, or one that could seem so, either. The experience mistress did have this day! As soon as her time comes she calls on the gods to help her, and there's a grumbling and rumbling and smashing and crashing—what a crash, so sudden and quick and heavy it was! Every one fell flat where he stood at the peal. And then some one or other called out in a mighty voice: "Alcmena, help is at hand: be not afraid. To thee and thine the sovereign of the skies comes in kindliness. Rise," he said, "ye who have fallen in terror, from dread of me." Having dropped, I got on my feet: I thought the house was afire, the way it was all lit up then. Just then Alcmena calls for me to come. I was trembling already at what happened, but fear of mistress prevailed, and up I run to find out what she wants. And there I see she has given birth to twins, boys, and not a soul of us noticed when it

113

       neque providimus.

       sed quid hoc? quis hic est senex, qui ante aedis
         nostras sic iacet?

                     numnam hunc percussit Iuppiter?

   credo edepol, nam, pro Iuppiter, sepultust quasi sit
      mortuos.

   ibo et cognoscam, quisquis est. Amphitruo hic
      quidem est erus meus.

   Amphitruo.

Amph.   Perii.

Brom.   Surge.

Amph.   Interii.

Brom.   Cedo manum.

Amph.   Quis me tenet?

Brom. Tua Bromia ancilla.

Amph.   Totus timeo, ita me increpuit Iuppiter.

   nec secus est, quasi si ab Acherunte veniam. sed
      quid tu foras

   egressa es?

Brom.   Eadem nos formido timidas terrore impulit

   in aedibus, tu ubi habitas. nimia mira vidi. vae mihi, 1080

   Amphitruo, ita mihi animus etiam nunc abest.

Amph.   Agedum expedi:

   scin me tuom esse erum Amphitruonem?

Brom.   Scio.

Amph.   Vide etiam nunc.

Brom.   Scio.

Amph. Haec sola sanam mentem gestat meorum familiarium.

Brom. Immo omnes sani sunt profecto.

Amph.   At me uxor insanum facit

   suis foedis factis.

Brom.   At ego faciam, tu idem ut aliter praedices,

   Amphitruo, piam et pudicam esse tuam uxorem ut
      scias.

happened, or is ready for it! (*sees prostrate Amphitryon*) But what's this? Who's this old man lying like this in front of our house? Why, can it be he's struck by lightning? Why, mercy me, I do believe so! For, good gracious, he's as completely disposed of as if he was a corpse! I'll go find out, whoever it is. (*approaches*) It's Amphitryon! **It's** my master! (*calling*) Amphitryon!

mph. (*feebly*) Heaven help me!

rom. Get up, sir.

mph. I'm dead!

rom. Give me your hand, sir. (*takes it*)

mph. Who has hold of me?

rom. Your servant maid, sir, Bromia.

mph. I'm paralysed with fear! Oh, Jove, what a bolt! I feel as if I were getting back—from the next world. (*he gets up*) But what made you come out?

rom. We poor women were struck with the same terror in this house of yours, sir. I've seen the most amazing things! Oh deary me, master, I'm just clean dazed even now!

mph. Come, come, quick, tell me—do you know me for your master, Amphitryon?

rom. Surely, sir.

mph. Here, look, look again!

rom. (*obeying*) Surely, sir.

mph. (*half aside*) She's the only one of my household that has any sanity about her.

rom. Oh no, sir, they're all sane, of course they are.

mph. Well, my wife had driven me insane with her infamous actions!

rom. (*warmly*) Well, I'll make you change that tune, sir, your very own self, and make you realize that **your** wife is a pious, honest woman, sir. I'll soon

	de ea re signa atque argumenta paucis verbis eloquar.
	omnium primum: Alcumena geminos peperit filios.
Amph.	Ain tu, geminos?
Brom.	Geminos.
Amph.	Di me servant.
Brom.	Sine me dicere, ut scias tibi tuaeque uxori deos esse omnis propitios. 1090
Amph.	Loquere.
Brom.	Postquam parturire hodie uxor occepit tua, ubi utero exorti dolores, ut solent puerperae invocat deos immortales, ut sibi auxilium ferant, manibus puris, capite operto. ibi continuo contonat sonitu maxumo; aedes primo ruere rebamur tuas. aedes totae confulgebant tuae, quasi essent aureae.
Amph.	Quaeso absolvito hinc me extemplo, quando satis deluseris. quid fit deinde?
Brom.	Dum haec aguntur, interea uxorem tuam neque gementem neque plorantem nostrum quisquam audivimus; ita profecto sine dolore peperit.
Amph.	Iam istuc gaudeo, 1100 utut erga me merita est.
Brom.	Mitte ista atque haec quae dicam accipe. postquam peperit, pueros lavere iussit nos. occepimus. sed puer ille quem ego lavi, ut magnust et multum valet! neque eum quisquam colligare quivit incunabulis.
Amph.	Nimia mira memoras; si istaec vera sunt, divinitus non metuo quin meae uxori latae suppetiae sient.
Brom.	Magis iam faxo mira dices. postquam in cunas conditust,

give you signs and proofs of that. First of all, she has given birth to twin sons.

mph. What's that—twins?

rom. Twins.

mph. The gods are with me!

rom. Let me go on, so that you may know all the gods mean well by you and your wife, sir.

mph. Yes, yes.

rom. After she began to feel near her time to-day and her pains were setting in, she called on the immortal gods to help her—as women do, sir, in labour—with clean washed hands and covered head. She had no sooner begun than there was a frightful thunder clap. At first we thought your house was tumbling down: your whole house was shining, sir, just as if it was gold.

mph. For heaven's sake hurry up and don't keep me on tenterhooks! I have had enough of your trifling! What happened next?

rom. While this was going on, not one of us heard your wife groan or whimper a bit, sir, the whole time: that's how she bore those boys, sir—never a pang, that's plain.

mph. (*heartily*) Well now, I'm glad of that, no matter what her behaviour to me has been.

rom. Do let that be, sir, and listen. After they were born she told us to bathe them. We began. But that boy I bathed! How big and strong he was! Not a soul of us could wrap him in his swaddling clothes.

mph. A most astounding story! If it be true, there's no doubt that my wife received divine aid.

rom. You'll call this more astounding still, sir, I warrant you. After he was tucked in his cradle, two enor-

        devolant angues iubati deorsum in impluvium duo
        maximi : continuo extollunt ambo capita.

Amph.   Ei mihi.

Brom.   Ne pave.   sed angues occulis omnis cirumvisere.   1110
        postquam pueros conspicati, pergunt ad cunas
          citi.
        ego cunas recessim rursum vorsum trahere et du-
          cere,
        metuens pueris, mihi formidans ; tantoque angues
          acrius
        persequi.   postquam conspexit angues ille alter
          puer,
        citus e cunis exilit, facit recta in anguis impetum :
        alterum altera prehendit eos manu perniciter.

Amph.   Mira memoras, nimis formidolosum facinus prae-
          dicas ;
        nam mihi horror membra misero percipit dictis tuis.
        quid fit deinde ?   porro loquere.

Brom.   Puer ambo angues enicat.
        dum haec aguntur, voce clara exclamat uxorem
          tuam—   1120

Amph.   Quis homo ?

Brom.   Summus imperator divom atque hominum
          Iuppiter.
        is se dixit cum Alcumena clam consuetum cubitibus,
        eumque filium suom esse qui illos angues vicerit ;
        alterum tuom esse dixit puerum.

Amph.   Pol me haud paenitet,
        si licet boni dimidium mihi dividere cum Iove.
        abi domum, iube vasa pura actutum adornari mihi,
        ut Iovis supremi multis hostiis pacem expetam.
        ego Teresiam coniectorem advocabo et consulam
        quid faciundum censeat ; simul hanc rem ut facta
          est eloquar.

mous crested serpents came slipping down into the
fountain basin: the next second both of them
were lifting up their heads.

nph. Heavens and earth!

om. Don't be scared. Well, the serpents glared around
at all of us. As soon as they spied the boys they
made for the cradles like a flash. I backed away,
fearful for the boys and frightened for myself,
pulling and hauling the cradles along after me
with the serpents a-chasing us all the angrier. The
minute that boy I was telling of sets eyes on the
serpents he's up and out of that cradle in a trice,
rushing straight for 'em and grabbing 'em one in
each hand quick as a wink.

nph. Astounding! Astounding! A perfectly horrify-
ing tale! Mercy on us! why, your very words
palsy me! What then? Go on, go on!

om. The boy chokes both serpents to death. While this
is going on, in a clear voice he calls out the name
of your wife—

nph. Who does?

om. The almighty ruler of gods and men, Jupiter. He
said that he himself had secretly shared Alcmena's
bed and that that was his son who had crushed the
serpents: the other one, he said, was your own child.

nph. Well, well, well! I make no complaint at being
permitted to have Jove as partner in my blessings.
In with you, girl! Have sacrificial vessels made
ready for me instantly so that I may seek the
favour of omnipotent Jove with ample offerings.

[EXIT *Bromia.*

I'll summon Tiresias the prophet and consult with
him as to what he thinks should be done, and at
the same time tell him all that's happened. (*thun-*

sed quid hoc? quam valide tonuit. di, obsecro
vostram fidem. 1130

V. 2.

Iup. Bono animo es, adsum auxilio, Amphitruo, tibi et
tuis:
nihil est quod timeas. hariolos, haruspices
mitte omnes; quae futura et quae facta eloquar,
multo adeo melius quam illi, quom sum Iuppiter.
primum omnium Alcumenae usuram corporis
cepi, et concubitu gravidam feci filio.
tu gravidam item fecisti, cum in exercitum
profectu's: uno partu duos peperit simul.
eorum alter, nostro qui est susceptus semine,
suis factis te immortali adficiet gloria. 1140
tu cum Alcumena uxore antiquam in gratiam
redi: haud promeruit quam ob tem vitio vorteres;
mea vi subactast facere. ego in caelum migro.

V. 3.

Amph. Faciam ita ut iubes et te oro, promissa ut serves tua.
ibo ad uxorem intro, missum facio Teresiam senem.

nunc, spectatores, Iovis summi causa clare plaudite.

der) But what's this? That awful thunder peal! Heaven preserve us!

Scene 2.   *Jupiter* APPEARS ABOVE.

Jup. Be of good cheer. I am here with aid, Amphitryon, for thee and thine. Thou hast naught to fear. Seers, soothsayers—have none of them. I will make known to thee future and past alike, and better far than they, moreover, for I am Jupiter. First of all, then, I took thy Alcmena to myself and by me she was made a mother. By thee too was she with child when thou didst go forth to war: at one birth she bore them both. The one begotten of my seed shall win thee undying glory by his works. Live again in fond concord as of old with thy wife Alcmena: she has done naught to merit thy reproach: my power was on her. I now depart to heaven.   [EXIT *Jupiter.*

Scene 3.

mph. (*reverently*) Thy will shall be done: and keep thy word with me, I beg thee. (*after a pause*) I'll in and see my wife! No more of old Tiresias!

(*to the audience*)

Now, spectators, for the sake of Jove almighty, give us some loud applause.   [EXIT.

ASINARIA

OR

THE COMEDY OF ASSES

ARGVMENTVM

Amanti argento filio auxiliarier
Sub imperio vivens volt senex uxorio.
Itaque ob asinos relatum pretium Saureae
Numerari iussit servolo Leonidae.
Ad amicam id fertur. cedit noctem filius.
Rivalis amens ob praereptam mulierem,
Is rem omnem uxori per parasitum nuntiat.
Accurrit uxor ac virum e lustris rapit.

PERSONAE

LIBANVS SERVVS
DEMAENETVS SENEX
ARGYRIPPVS ADVLESCENS
CLEARETA LENA
LEONIDA SERVVS
MERCATOR
PHILAENIVM MERETRIX
DIABOLVS ADVLESCENS
PARASITVS
ARTEMONA MATRONA

ARGUMENT OF THE PLAY

An old gentleman, whose wife is the head of the household, desires to give his son financial support in a love affair. He therefore had some money, brought to Saurea in payment for some asses, counted out to a certain rascally servant of his own, Leonida. This money goes to the young fellow's mistress, and he concedes his father an evening with her. A rival of his, beside himself at being deprived of the girl, sends word, by a parasite, to the old gentleman's wife, of the whole matter. In rushes the wife and drags her husband from the house of vice.

DRAMATIS PERSONAE

LIBANUS, *slave of Demaenetus.*
DEMAENETUS, *an old gentleman of Athens.*
ARGYRIPPUS, *his son.*
CLEARETA, *a procuress.*
LEONIDA, *slave of Demaenetus.*
A TRADER.
PHILAENIUM, *a courtesan, daughter of Cleareta.*
DIABOLUS, *a young gentleman of Athens.*
A PARASITE.
ARTEMONA, *wife of Demaenetus.*

PROLOGVS

Hoc agite sultis, spectatores, nunciam,
quae quidem mihi atque vobis res vertat bene
gregique huic et dominis atque conductoribus.
face nunciam tu, praeco, omnem auritum poplum.
age nunc reside, cave modo ne gratiis.
nunc quid processerim huc et quid mihi voluerim
dicam: ut sciretis nomen huius fabulae;
nam quod ad argumentum attinet, sane brevest.
nunc quod me dixi velle vobis dicere,
dicam: huic nomen Graece Onagost fabulae;   10
Demophilus scripsit, Maccus vortit barbare;
Asinariam volt esse, si per vos licet.
inest lepos ludusque in hac comoedia,
ridicula res est.   date benigne operam mihi,
ut vos, ut alias, pariter nunc Mars adiuvet.

Scene :—Athens. A street running in front of the houses of Demaenetus and Cleareta : between the houses is a narrow lane.

PROLOGUE

Kindly give us your entire attention now, spectators: I heartily hope it will result in benefit to me, also to you, and to this company and its managers, and to those that hire them. (*turning to a herald*) Herald, provide all this crowd with ears at once. (*the herald proclaims silence*) Enough enough! Sit down—and be sure you put that in your bill! (*to audience*) Now I shall say why I have come out before you here and what I wished : I have come to acquaint you with the name of this play. For as far as the plot is concerned, that is quite simple. Now I shall say what I said I wished to say: the Greek name of this play is ONAGOS: Demophilus wrote it: Maccus translated it into a foreign tongue. He wishes to call it THE COMEDY OF ASSES, by your leave. It is a clever comedy, full of drollery and laughable situations. Do oblige me by being attentive, that now too, as in other days, Mars may be with you.

TITUS MACCIUS PLAUTUS

ACTVS I

Lib. Sicut tuom vis unicum gnatum tuae
superesse vitae sospitem et superstitem,
ita ted obtestor per senectutem tuam
perque illam, quam tu metuis, uxorem tuam,
si quid med erga hodie falsum dixeris,   20
ut tibi superstes uxor aetatem siet
atque illa viva vivos ut pestem oppetas.

Dem. Per Dium Fidium quaeris: iurato mihi
video necesse esse eloqui quidquid roges.[1]
proinde actutum istuc quid sit quod scire expetis
eloquere: ut ipse scibo, te faciam ut scias.

Lib. Dic obsecro hercle serio quod te rogem,
cave mihi mendaci quicquam.

Dem.   Quin tu ergo rogas?   30

Lib. Num me illuc ducis, ubi lapis lapidem terit?

Dem. Quid istuc est? aut ubi istuc est terrarum loci?[2]

Lib. Apud fustitudinas, ferricrepinas insulas,
ubi vivos homines mortui incursant boves.

Dem. Modo pol percepi, Libane, quid istuc sit loci:
ubi fit polenta, te fortasse dicere.

Lib.   Ah,

---

[1] Leo brackets following v., 25–26: *ita me obstinate ad-*
gressu's, ut non audeam
   profecto, percontanti quin promam omnia.
[2] Leo brackets following v., 33: *ubi flent nequam ho-*
mines, qui polentam pinsitant.

128

THE COMEDY OF ASSES

ACT I

<small>ENTER</small> *Demaenetus*, <small>FROM HIS HOUSE, BRINGING</small>

Libanus.

Lib. (*very solemnly*) As you hope to have your only son
survive hale and hearty, sir, when you're gone
yourself, I implore you, sir, by your hoary hairs
and by the one you dread, your wife, sir—if you
tell me any lie to-day, may she outlast you by
years and years, yes, sir, and you die a living death
with her alive.

Dem. (*laughing*) You beg me by the very God of Truth.
Once under oath, I see I must tell you whatever
you ask. Come then, quick! Let me hear what
you wish to know, and so far as I know myself, I
shall let you know.

Lib. For God's sake, sir, do please answer my question
seriously! No lying to me, sir, mind that!

Dem. Then why not ask your question?

Lib. (*anxiously*) You won't take me where stone rubs
stone, sir?

Dem. What do you mean? Where in the world is that?

Lib. There at the Clubbangian-Chainclangian Islands,
sir, where dead oxen attack living men.

Dem. (*reflecting, then with a chuckle*) Bless my soul! At
last I get your meaning, Libanus—the barley mill [1]:
I daresay that's the place you mention.

Lib. (*in grotesque terror*) Oh Lord, no! I'm not men-

---

[1] Where he might be beaten with ox-hide whips.

129

	neque hercle ego istuc dico nec dictum volo,	
	teque obsecro hercle, ut quae locutu's despuas.	
Dem.	Fiat, geratur mos tibi.	
Lib.	Age, age usque excrea.	40
Dem.	Etiamne?	
Lib.	Age quaeso hercle usque ex penitis faucibus.	
	etiam amplius.	
Dem.	Nam quo usque?	
Lib.	Usque ad mortem volo.	
Dem.	Cave sis malam rem.	
Lib.	Uxoris dico, non tuam.	
Dem.	Dono te ob istuc dictum, ut expers sis metu.	
Lib.	Di tibi dent quaecumque optes.	
Dem.	Redde operam mihi.	
	cur hoc ego ex te quaeram? aut cur miniter tibi	
	propterea quod me non scientem feceris?	
	aut cur postremo filio suscenseam,	
	patres ut faciunt ceteri?	
Lib.	Quid istuc novi est?	50
	demiror quid sit et quo evadat sum in metu.	
Dem.	Equidem scio iam, filius quod amet meus	
	istanc meretricem e proxumo Philaenium.	
	estne hoc ut dico, Libane?	
Lib.	Rectam instas viam.	
	ea res est. sed eum morbus invasit gravis.	
Dem.	Quid morbi est?	
Lib.	Quia non suppetunt dictis data.	
Dem.	Tune es adiutor nunc amanti filio?	
Lib.	Sum vero, et alter noster est Leonida.	
Dem.	Bene hercle facitis et a me initis gratiam.	

130

tioning that, and I don't want it mentioned, either, and for the love of heaven, sir, do spit away that word!

Dem. (*spitting*) All right. Anything to humour you.

Lib. Go on, sir, go on! Hawk it way up!

Dem. (*spitting again*) Will that do?

Lib. Go on, sir, for God's sake, way from the bottom of your gullet! (*Demaenetus spits violently*) Farther down still, sir!

Dem. Eh? How far?

Lib. (*half aside*) To the door of death, I hope.

Dem. (*angrily*) Kindly look out, my man, look out!

Lib. (*hastily*) Your wife's, sir, I mean, not yours.

Dem. (*laughing*) Never fear—for that remark I grant you immunity.

Lib. And heaven grant you all your prayers, sir.

Dem. Now listen to me for a change. Why should I ask you about this? Or threaten you because you haven't informed me? Or for that matter, why should I fly into a rage at my son, as other fathers do?

Lib. (*aside*) Hm! What's this surprise? Wonder what it means! Where it will end is what scares me.

Dem. As a matter of fact, I know already that my son has an affair with that wench, Philaenium, next door. Isn't that so, Libanus?

Lib. You're on the right track, sir. That's how it is. But he has suffered a severe shock.

Dem. Shock? What?

Lib. Well, his presents are falling short of his promises.

Dem. Are you aiding my son in this amour?

Lib. Indeed I am, sir, and so is my mate, your servant Leonida.

Dem. Well, well, my lad, thanks! You are both earning

131

	verum meam uxorem, Libane, nescis qualis sit?	60
Lib.	Tu primus sentis, nos tamen in pretio sumus.	
Dem.	Fateor eam esse importunam atque incommodam.	
Lib.	Posterius istuc dicis quam credo tibi.	
Dem.	Omnes parentes, Libane, liberis suis	

qui mi auscultabunt, facient obsequellam [1]
quippe qui mage amico utantur gnato et benevolo.
atque ego me id facere studeo, volo amari a meis;
volo me patris mei similem, qui causa mea
nauclerico ipse ornatu per fallaciam
quam amabam abduxit ab lenone mulierem;   70
neque puduit eum id aetatis sycophantias
struere et beneficiis me emere gnatum suom sibi.
eos me decretumst persequi mores patris.
nam me hodie oravit Argyrippus filius,
uti sibi amanti facerem argenti copiam;
et id ego percupio obsequi gnato meo.[2]
quamquam illum mater arte contenteque habet,
patres ut consueverunt: ego mitto omnia haec.
praesertim quom is me dignum quoi concrederet   80
habuit, me habere honorem eius ingenio decet;
quom me adiit, ut pudentem gnatum aequomst
     patrem,
cupio esse amicae quod det argentum suae.

Lib.	Cupis id quod cupere te nequiquam intellego.
	dotalem servom Sauream uxor tua
	adduxit, cui plus in manu sit quam tibi.
Dem.	Argentum accepi, dote imperium vendidi.

[1] Corrupt (Leo): *obsequellam* MSS: *obsequellam eam* Acidalius.
[2] Leo brackets following v., 77: *volo amori obsecutum illius, volo amet me patrem.*

132

my gratitude. But (*looking cautiously around*) my
wife, Libanus, don't you know her temperament?

Lib. (*with certainty*) You feel it first, sir, but we get
plenty of it.

Dem. (*awkwardly*) I confess that she is . . . high-handed
and . . . hard to get along with.

Lib. I believe that before you speak a word, sir.

Dem. (*with an air of profound moral conviction*) Libanus, all
parents who take my advice will be a bit indulgent
to their children, seeing it makes a son more friendly
and affectionate. Yes, and I am anxious to be so
myself. I wish to be loved by my own flesh and
blood; I wish to model myself on my own father
who dressed up as a shipmaster for my sake and
swindled a slave-dealer out of a girl I was in love
with. He felt no shame at going in for hocus-
pocus at his time of life, and buying his son's
affection, mine, by his kindnesses. These methods
of my father's I have resolved to follow out
myself. Well now, this very day my boy Argyrippus begged me to supply him with some money,
saying he was in love: and I heartily desire to
oblige the dear lad. No matter if his mother does
keep a firm, tight rein on him and play the ordinary father's part, none of that for me. And seeing
he has regarded me as worthy of his confidence, I
have special reason to respect his inclinations.
Now that he has applied to me, as a respectful son
should to his father, I am desirous that he should
have some money for his mistress.

Lib. You're desirous of something you'll desire in vain,
sir, I reckon. Your wife's brought along Saurea, that
dower slave of hers, to have more power than you.

Dem. (*bitterly*) Sold myself! Gave up my authority for a

	nunc verba in pauca conferam quid te velim.	
	viginti iam usust filio argenti minis:	
	face id ut paratum iam sit.	90

Lib.   Unde gentium?

Dem.   Me defraudato.

Lib.   Maxumas nugas agis:
nudo detrahere vestimenta me iubes.
defraudem te ego? age sis, tu sine pennis vola.
tene ego defraudem, cui ipsi nihil est in manu,
nisi quid tu porro uxorem defraudaveris?

Dem.   Qua me, qua uxorem, qua tu servom Sauream
potes, circumduce, aufer; promitto tibi
non offuturum, si id hodie effeceris.

Lib.   Iubeas una opera me piscari in aere,
venari autem rete iaculo in medio mari.[1]   100

Dem.   Tibi optionem sumito Leonidam,
fabricare quidvis, quidvis comminiscere:
perficito, argentum hodie ut habeat filius,
amicae quod det.

Lib.   Quid ais tu, Demaenete?

Dem.   Quid vis?

Lib.   Si forte in insidias devenero,
tun redimes me, si me hostes interceperint?

Dem.   Redimam.

Lib.   Tum tu igitur aliud cura quid lubet.
ego eo ad forum, nisi quid vis.

Dem.   Ei, bene ambula.
atque audin etiam?

---

[1] Corrupt (Leo): *venari autem rete iaculo* MSS: *reti, iaculo venari autem* Vahlen.

dowry! (*pause*) Now, in a word, here is what I
want of you. My son needs eighty pounds [1] at
once: will you see it is procured at once.

ib. Where in the world from?

em. Cheat me out of it.

ib. What awful nonsense you do talk! You're telling
me to strip the clothes off a naked man. I cheat
you out of it? Come, sir, will you kindly fly without
wings! I cheat you out of it, when you don't own
a thing, unless you've played the same game and
cheated your wife out of something?

em. Well, me, or my wife, or servant Saurea—do your
best, swindle us, rook us; I promise you your interests won't suffer, if you accomplish this to-day.

ib. You might as well order me to go a-fishing in the
air, yes, and to take my casting-net and do some
deep sea—hunting.

em. Have Leonida for your adjutant: manufacture
something, devise something—anything: see you
get the money to-day for my son to give his girl.

ib. Look here.

em. Well?

ib. Suppose I happen to fall into an ambuscade, ransom
me, will you, if I'm intercepted by the enemy?

em. I will.

ib. (*after a pause, airily*) Well then, in that case you
may dismiss the matter from your mind. I'm off to
the forum, unless you want me further.

em. Go ahead! A pleasant stroll to you! (*Libanus
walks away*) And I say,—listening still, are you?

---

[1] It has seemed advisable to use the terms of the English
coinage system throughout this version: the value of the
money metals, however, has shrunk very considerably since
Plautus's day.

Lib.   Ecce.

Dem.   Si quid te volam,
ubi eris?

Lib.   Ubicumque libitum erit animo meo.   110
profecto nemo est quem iam dehinc metuam mihi
ne quid nocere possit, cum tu mihi tua
oratione omnem animum ostendisti tuom.
quin te quoque ipsum facio haud magni, si hoc patro.
pergam quo occepi atque ibi consilia exordiar.

Dem.   Audin tu? apud Archibulum ego ero argentarium.

Lib.   Nempe in foro?

Dem.   Ibi, si quid opus fuerit.

Lib.   Meminero.

Dem.   Non esse servos peior hoc quisquam potest
nec magis versutus nec quo ab caveas aegrius.
eidem homini, si quid recte curatum velis,   120
mandes: moriri sese misere mavolet,
quam non perfectum reddat quod promiserit.
nam ego illud argentum tam paratum filio
scio esse quam me hunc scipionem contui.
sed quid ego cesso ire ad forum, quo inceperam?
[1] atque ibi manebo apud argentarium.

I. 2.

Argyr.   Sicine hoc fit? foras aedibus me eici?
promerenti optume hocin preti redditur?
bene merenti mala es, male merenti bona es;
at malo cum tuo, nam iam ex hoc loco   130
ibo ego ad tres viros vostraque ibi nomina
faxo erunt, capitis te perdam ego et filiam,

---

[1] Leo notes lacuna here: *atqui ibi* MSS: *ibo atque ibi*
Camerarius.

Lib. (*pertly, without turning*) Behold me!

Dem. If I want you for anything, where will you be?

Lib. Precisely where it pleases my fancy. (*half aside*) I tell you what, from now on I won't be scared of a man alive, for fear he can do me any harm, after your showing me all the secrets of your soul. Why, you won't count for much with me your own self, either, if I carry this through. (*setting off again*) I'll go along to where I was bound and lay my plans there.

Dem. Look here! I shall be at banker Archibulus's.

Lib. In the forum, you mean?

Dem. Yes, there,—if anything's needed.

Lib. (*nonchalantly*) I'll keep it in mind.

[EXIT *Libanus* TO FORUM.

Dem. A more rascally servant than this of mine can't be found, or a wilier one, or one harder to guard against. But he's just your man to commit a matter to, if you want it well managed: he'd prefer to expire in pain and torment rather than fail to fulfil his promise to the letter. Why, I'm just as confident that that money is in store for my son as that I've got my eyes on this cane here. But I must be off to the forum, where I was going. Yes, and I'll wait there at the banker's. [EXIT *Demaenetus.*

Scene 2. ENTER *Argyrippus* PRECIPITATELY FROM HOUSE OF *Cleareta.*

Argyr. (*violently to those within*) So that's the way, is it? Thrown out of doors, am I? This is my reward for all the good turns I've done you, eh? Evil for good and good for evil is your system. But it will be evil for you! I'll go direct from here to the police and leave your names with 'em. I'll humble you and your daughter! You decoys, you de-

137

perlecebrae, permities, adulescentum exitium.
nam mare haud est mare, vos mare acerrumum;
nam in mari repperi, his elavi bonis.
ingrata atque inrita esse omnia intellego
quae dedi et quod bene feci, at posthac tibi
 male quod potero facere faciam, meritoque id
  faciam tuo.
 ego pol te redigam eodem unde orta es, ad
  egestatis terminos,
 ego edepol te faciam ut quae sis nunc et quae
  fueris scias.   140
 quae prius quam istam adii atque amans ego animum meum isti dedi,
 sordido vitam oblectabas pane in pannis inopia,
 atque ea si erant, magnas habebas omnibus dis
  gratias;
 eadem nunc, cum est melius, me, cuius opera est,
  ignoras mala.
 reddam ego te ex fera fame mansuetem, me
  specta modo.
 nam isti quid succenseam ipsi? nihil est, nihil
  quicquam meret;
 tuo facit iussu, tuo imperio paret: mater tu,
  eadem era es.
 te ego ulciscar, te ego ut digna es perdam
  atque ut de me meres.
 at scelesta viden ut ne id quidem, me dignum
  esse existumat
 quem adeat, quem conloquatur quoique irato
  supplicet?   150
 atque eccam inlecebra exit tandem; opinor hic
  ante ostium
 meo modo loquar quae volam, quoniam intus non
  licitum est mihi.

stroyers, you wreckers of young fellows! Why, the
sea's no sea: you are—the wildest sea of all! Why
at sea I made my money, here I am cleaned out of
it. All I've given you and all I've done for you gets
no thanks, goes for nothing, I find: but after this
all I can do against you I'll do, and do it with good
reason. By the Lord, I'll put you down where
you came from, the depths of destitution, I will.
By heaven, I'll make you appreciate what you
are now and what you were. You, who before
I courted that girl of yours and offered her my
loving heart, used to regale yourself on coarse bread
in rags and poverty: yes, and gave hearty thanks
to Heaven, if you got your bread and rags. Yet
here you are, now that you are better off, snubbing
me that made you so, curse you! I'll tame you
down, you wild beast, by the famine treatment:
trust me for that. As for that girl of yours,
why should I be angry with her? She's done
nothing, she's not at all to blame. It is your dic-
tates she follows, your orders she obeys: you're
mother and mistress both. You're the one I'll
have revenge on; you're the one I'll ruin as you
deserve, as your behaviour to me merits. (*pauses
and glares at house*) But d'ye see how the wretch
doesn't even think it worth while to come to me,
talk with me, go on her knees to me, when I'm in
a rage? (*Cleareta's door opens*) Ah, there she is
coming out at last, the decoy! I wager I'll have
my full say in my own fashion out in front of the
door here, seeing I couldn't do it inside.

I. 3.

Cle.   Unum quodque istorum verbum nummis Philippis
        aureis
       non potest auferre hinc a me si quis emptor venerit;
       nec recte quae tu in nos dicis, aurum atque argen-
        tum merumst:
       fixus hic apud nos est animus tuos clavo Cupidinis.
       remigio veloque quantum poteris festina et fuge:
       quam magis te in altum capessis, tam aestus te in
        portum refert.

Argyr. Ego pol istum portitorem privabo portorio;
       ego te dehinc ut merita es de me et mea re tractare
        exsequar,   160
       quom tu med ut meritus sum non tractas atque
        eicis domo.

Cle.   Magis istuc percipimus lingua dici, quam factis fore.

Argyr. Solus solitudine ego ted atque ab egestate abstuli;
       solus si ductem, referre gratiam numquam potes.

Cle.   Solus ductato, si semper solus quae poscam dabis;
       semper tibi promissum habeto hac lege, dum
        superes datis.

Argyr. Qui modus dandi? nam numquam tu quidem ex-
        pleri potes;
       modo quom accepisti, haud multo post aliquid
        quod poscas paras.

Cle.   Quid modist ductando, amando? numquamne ex-
        pleri potes?
       modo remisisti, continuo iam ut remittam ad te
        rogas: 170

Argyr. Dedi equidem quod mecum egisti.

Cle.   Et tibi ego misi mulierem:
       par pari datum hostimentumst, opera pro pecunia.

Scene 3.   ENTER *Cleareta* FROM HOUSE.

Cle.   (*calmly and pleasantly*) Not a single one of those words do I part with for golden sovereigns, not if some purchaser comes along: uncomplimentary remarks about us from you are good coin of the realm. Your heart is fastened to us here with one of Cupid's spikes through it. Out with oar and up with sail, speed your fastest and scud away: the more you put out to sea, the more the tide brings you back to harbour.

Argyr. (*grimly*) By the Lord, I'll hold back that harbour master's harbour dues; from this time forth you'll get the treatment you merit of me and my exchequer, for this unmerited treatment of me, this turning me out of the house.

Cle.   (*lightly*) Such things are easier said than done, I observe.

Argyr. I, and I alone, am the man that rescued you from loneliness and destitution; even if I should take the girl for myself alone, you'd still be in my debt.

Cle.   Take her for yourself alone, if you alone will always give me what I demand. You can always be sure of her—on condition your presents are the biggest.

Argyr. And what end to the presents? Why, you can never be sated. Now you get something, and a minute later you're devising some new demand.

Cle.   And what end to the taking her, to the lovey-doveying? Can you never be sated? Now you have sent her back to me, and the next instant you're crying for me to send her back to you.

Argyr. Well, I paid you what we agreed on.

Cle.   And I let you have the girl: my policy has been fair give and take—services rendered for cash

F'   141

Argyr. Male agis mecum.

Cle.   Quid me accusas, si facio officium meum?

nam neque fictum usquamst neque pictum neque scriptum in poematis

ubi lena bene agat cum quiquam amante, quae frugi esse volt.

Argyr. Mihi quidem te parcere aequomst tandem, ut tibi durem diu.

Cle. Non tu scis? quae amanti parcet, eadem sibi parcet parum.

quasi piscis, itidemst amator lenae: nequam est, nisi recens;

is habet sucum, is suavitatem, eum quo vis pacto condias

vel patinarium vel assum, verses quo pacto lubet: 180

is dare volt, is se aliquid posci, nam ibi de pleno promitur;

neque ille scit quid det, quid damni faciat: illi rei studet,

volt placere sese amicae, volt mihi, volt pedisequae,

volt famulis, volt etiam ancillis; et quoque catulo meo

subblanditur novos amator, se ut quom videat gaudeat.

vera dico: ad suom quemque hominem quaestum esse aequomst callidum.

Argyr. Perdidici istaec esse vera damno cum magno meo.

Cle. Si ecastor nunc habeas quod des, alia verba praehibeas;

nunc quia nihil habes, maledictis te eam ductare postulas.

A-gyr. Non meum est.

Cle. Nec meum quidem edepol, ad te ut mittam gratiis.   190

verum aetatis atque honoris gratia hoc fiet tui,

quia nobis lucro fuisti potius quam decori tibi:

142

Argyr. You're using me shamefully.

Cle. Why find fault with me for doing my plain duty? Why, nowhere in stone, paint, or poem is a lady in my line portrayed as using any lover well—if she wants to get on.

Argyr. (*appealingly*) You really ought to use me sparingly, though, so that I may last you a long time.

Cle. (*coolly*) You miss the point? The lady that spares her lover spares herself too little. Lovers are the same as fish to us—no good unless they're fresh. Your fresh ones are juicy and sweet; you can season them to taste in a stew, bake them, and turn them every way. Your fresh one wants to give you things, wants to be asked for something: in his case it all comes from a full cupboard, you see; and he has no idea what he's giving, what it costs him. This is his only thought: he wants to please, please his girl, please me, please the waiting-woman, please the men servants, please the maid servants, too: yes, the new lover makes up to my little dog, even, so that he may be glad to see him. This is the plain truth: every one ought to keep a sharp eye for the main chance.

Argyr. I have thoroughly learned the truth of that, and a pretty penny it's cost me.

Cle. Tut, tut! If you had anything left to give us, your language would be different; now that you have nothing, you expect to get her by abuse.

Argyr. That's not my way.

Cle. Nor mine, sir, to let you have her gratis—mercy, no! But, considering your youth and our high regard for you, this shall be done, seeing you have been more of an income to us than a credit to yourself: just hand me over (*casually*) four

       si mihi dantur duo talenta argenti numerata in
           manum,
       hanc tibi noctem honoris causa gratiis dono dabo.

Argyr. Quid si non est?

Cle.   Tibi non esse credam, illa alio ibit tamen.

Argyr. Ubi illaec quae dedi ante?

Cle.   Abusa. nam si ea durarent mihi,
       mulier mitteretur ad te, numquam quicquam
           poscerem.
       diem aquam solem lunam noctem, haec argento
           non emo :
       ceterum quae volumus uti Graeca mercamur fide.
       quom a pistore panem petimus, vinum ex oenopolio,   200
       si aes habent, dant mercem : eadem nos discipulina
           utimur.
       semper oculatae manus sunt nostrae, credunt quod
           vident.
       vetus est : " nihili coactiost "—scis cuius. non dico
           amplius.

Argyr. Aliam nunc mi orationem despoliato praedicas,
       longe aliam, inquam, praebes nunc atque olim,
           quom dabam,
       aliam atque olim, quom inliciebas me ad te blande
           ac benedice.
       tum mi aedes quoque arridebant, cum ad te venie-
           bam, tuae ;
       me unice unum ex omnibus te atque illam amare
           aibas mihi ;
       ubi quid dederam, quasi columbae pulli in ore
           ambae meo
       usque eratis, meo de studio studia erant vostra omnia,   210
       usque adhaerebatis : quod ego iusseram, quod
           volueram
       faciebatis, quod nolebam ac votueram, de industria

hundred pounds in cash and you shall have this
evening with her, in token of said high regard, as
a free gift from me.

Argyr. What if I haven't it?

Cle. (*smiling, but firm*) I'll give you credit—that you
haven't it: the girl shall go to some one else,
however.

Argyr. Where is what I gave you before?

Cle. Spent. Why, if it had lasted, you should have
your lady, and not a thing would I be asking for.
Daylight, water, sunlight, moonlight, darkness—
for these things I have to pay no money: everything else we wish to use we purchase on Greek
credit. When we go to the baker for bread, to
the vintner for wine, their rule is commodities
for cash: we use the same system ourselves.
Our hands have eyes always: seeing is believ-
ing with them. As the old proverb has it:
"There's no getting"—you know what. I say
no more.

Argyr. It's a different sort of eloquence you use on me
now I've been fleeced, very different, I say, from
that former sort when I was giving you things,
different from that former sort when you were
luring me on with your smooth, suave talk. Then
your very house used to be wreathed in smiles,
when I turned up. You used to say I was the one
and only love in all the world for you and her. After
I'd given you anything the both of you used to
keep hanging on my lips like a pair of young doves.
Whatever I fancied, you fancied, and nothing else.
You used to keep clinging to me. I ordered a
thing, wished a thing,—you used to do it: I dis-
liked a thing, forbade a thing,—you used to take

145

fugiebatis, neque conari id facere audebatis prius.
nunc neque quid velim neque nolim facitis magni,
    pessumae.

Cle. Non tu scis? hic noster quaestus aucupi simillimust.
auceps quando concinnavit aream, offundit cibum;
aves adsuescunt: necesse est facere sumptum qui
    quaerit lucrum;
saepe edunt: semel si sunt captae, rem solvont
    aucupi.
itidem hic apud nos: aedes nobis area est, auceps
    sum ego,   219, 220
esca est meretrix, lectus inlex est, amatores aves;
bene salutando consuescunt, compellando blanditer,
osculando, oratione vinnula, venustula.
si papillam pertractavit, haud est ab re aucupis;
savium si sumpsit, sumere eum licet sine retibus.
haecine te esse oblitum, in ludo qui fuisti tam diu?

Argyr. Tua ista culpa est, quae discipulum semidoctum
    abs te amoves.

Cle. Remeato audacter, mercedem si eris nactus; nunc
    abi.

Argyr. Mane, mane, audi. dic, quid me aequom censes
    pro illa tibi dare,
annum hunc ne cum quiquam alio sit?

Cle.   Tene? viginti minas;   230
atque ea lege: si alius ad me prius attulerit, tu vale.

Argyr. At ego est etiam prius quam abis quod volo loqui.

Cle.   Dic quod lubet.

Argyr. Non omnino iam perii, est relicuom quo peream
    magis.

pains to avoid doing it: you didn't dare attempt to do it then. Now you don't care tuppence what I like, or don't like, you vile wretches!

le. (*still cheerfully superior*) You miss the point? This profession of ours is a great deal like bird-catching. The fowler, when he has his fowling-floor prepared, spreads food around; the birds become familiarized: you must spend money, if you wish to make money. They often get a meal: but once they get caught they recoup the fowler. It is quite the same with us here: our house is the floor, I am the fowler, the girl the bait, the couch the decoy, the lovers the birds. They become familiar through pleasant greetings, pretty speeches, kisses, cooey, captivating little whispers. If he cuddles her close in his arms, well, no harm to the fowler. If he takes a naughty kind of kiss, he can be taken himself, and no net needed. You to forget all this, and so long in the school, too?

rgyr. It's your fault, if I have: you expelled your pupil when he was half taught.

le. Trot along back to us boldly, if you find the tuition fee: for the present run away. (*turns to go in*)

rgyr. Wait, wait, listen! Tell me, what do you think I ought to give you to have her all to myself this next year?

le. (*laughingly*) What? You? (*after a pause*) Eighty pounds: yes, and on this condition—if some one else brings me the money before you do, good-bye to you. (*again turning to go*)

rgyr. But there's something more I want to say before you go.

le. Say on, anything.

rgyr. I'm not entirely ruined yet: there is a balance left for further ruin. I can give you what you ask.

      habeo unde istuc tibi quod poscis dem ; sed in leges
        meas
      dabo, uti scire possis, perpetuom annum hunc mihi
        uti serviat
      nec quemquam interea alium admittat prorsus
        quam me ad se virum.

Cle.   Quin, si tu voles, domi servi qui sunt castrabo viros.
      postremo ut voles nos esse, syngraphum facito
        adferas ;
      ut voles, ut tibi lubebit, nobis legem imponito :
      modo tecum una argentum adferto, facile patiar
        cetera.   240
      portitorum simillumae sunt ianuae lenoniae :
      si adfers, tum patent, si non est quod des, aedes
        non patent.

Argyr. Interii, si non invenio ego illas viginti minas,
      et profecto, nisi illud perdo argentum, pereundum
        est mihi.
      nunc pergam ad forum atque experiar opibus, omni
        copia,
      supplicabo, exobsecrabo ut quemque amicum
        videro,
      dignos indignos adire atque experiri certumst
        mihi,[1]
      nam si mutuas non potero, certumst sumam faenore.

ACTVS II

Lib.   Hercle vero, Libane, nunc te meliust expergiscier
      atque argento comparando fingere fallaciam.   250
      iam diu est factum quom discesti ab ero atque abiisti
        ad forum,[2]

---

[1] Corrupt (Leo) : *experiri* MSS : *experi* Skutsch.
[2] Leo brackets following v., 252 : *igitur inveniundo argento ut fingeres fallaciam.*

But I'll give it to you on my own terms, and here
they are—she's to be at my disposal this whole
next year through, and all that time not a single
man but me is to come near her.

le.   (*cheerfully ironical*) Why, if you choose, I'll change
all the men servants in the house to maids. In
short, bring along a contract stating how you wish
us to behave. All you desire, all you like,—impose
your own terms on us: only bring along the money,
too; the rest is easy for me. Our doors are much
like those of a custom house: pay your fee, and
they are open: if you can't, they are—(*going into
house and closing the door in his face with a provoking
laugh*) not open.

rgyr.   (*drearily*) It's all over with me, if I don't get hold
of that eighty pounds: yes, one thing is sure, that
money goes to pot, or else my life must. (*a pause,
then with animation*) I'll off to the forum this
moment and try to raise it by every means in my
power: I'll entreat, ex-supplicate every friend I
see. Good and bad—I'll up and try them all,
I'm resolved on that: and if I can't get it as a
friendly loan, I'm resolved to borrow it at usury.

[EXIT *Argyrippus.*

ACT II

(*A couple of hours have elapsed.*)

ENTER *Libanus* WITH WORRIED AIR.

ib.   By gad, Libanus, you'd certainly better rouse
yourself now and contrive some trick for collecting
that cash. It's a long time since you left your
master and hied yourself to the forum, to loaf

149

ibi tu ad hoc diei tempus dormitasti in otio.

quin tu abs te socordiam omnem reice et segnitiem
amove

atque ad ingenium vetus versutum te recipis tuom.

serva erum, cave tu idem faxis alii quod servi
solent,

qui ad eri fraudationem callidum ingenium gerunt.

unde sumam? quem intervortam? quo hanc celo-
cem conferam?

impetritum, inauguratumst : quovis admittunt aves,

picus et cornix ab laeva, corvos parra ab dextera   260

consuadent; certum herclest vostram consequi
sententiam.

sed quid hoc, quod picus ulmum tundit? non
temerariumst.

certe hercle ego quantum ex augurio eius pici
intellego,

aut mihi in mundo sunt virgae aut atriensi Saureae.

sed quid illuc quod exanimatus currit huc Leonida?

metuo quom illic obscaevavit meae falsae fallaciae.

II. 2.

Leon.   Ubi ego nunc Libanum requiram aut familiarem
filium,

ut ego illos lubentiores faciam quam Lubentiast?

maximam praedam et triumphum eis adfero adventu meo.

quando mecum pariter potant, pariter scortari
solent,   270

hanc quidem, quam nactus, praedam pariter cum
illis partiam.

Lib.   Illic homo aedis compilavit, more si fecit suo.

150

and snooze away there till this time of day. Come
on, shake off all this dull sloth, away with slug-
gishness, yes, and get back that old gift of guile of
yours! Save your master: mind you don't do the
same as other servants that use their wily wits to
gull him. (*pause*) Where shall I get it? Who shall
I swindle? Where shall I steer this cutter? (*looking upwards, then jubilantly*) I've got my auspices,
my auguries: the birds let me steer it where I
please! Woodpecker and crow on the left, raven
and barn owl on the right. "Go ahead," they
say! By Jove, I'll follow your advice, I certainly
will. (*looking upward again*) What's this, though,—
the woodpecker tapping an elm? [1] That's not for
nothing! Lord! So far as I understand the omen
of this woodpecker, that certainly means there are
rods in pickle for me, or for steward Saurea.
(*looking down street*) But what's wrong—Leonida
running up here all out of breath? I'm afraid now
that the bird there has predicted trouble for my
artful arts.

Scene 2. ENTER *Leonida* IN GREAT EXCITEMENT, WITHOUT
SEEING *Libanus*.

Leon. Where shall I look for Libanus now, or young
master, so that I can make them more delighted
than Delight herself? Oh, the mighty prize
and triumph my coming confers on 'em! Seeing
they guzzle along with me, and chase the girls
along with me, I'll certainly go shares in this
prize I've got along with them.

Lib. (*aside*) The fellow's been robbing a house if he's

---

[1] The elm corresponded to our birch in being used for
corporal punishment.

         vae illi, qui tam indiligenter observavit ianuam.

Leon.   Actatem velim servire, Libanum ut conveniam
         modo.

Lib.   Mea quidem hercle opera liber numquam fies ocius.

Leon.   Etiam de tergo ducentas plagas praegnatis dabo.

Lib.   Largitur peculium, omnem in tergo thensaurum
         gerit.

Leon.   Nam si huic sese occasioni tempus supterduxerit,
         numquam edepol quadrigis albis indipiscet postea;
         erum in obsidione linquet, inimicum animos auxerit.   280
         sed si mecum occasionem opprimere hanc, quae
            obvenit, studet,
         maximas opimitates, gaudio exfertissimas
         suis eris ille una mecum pariet, gnatoque et patri,
         adeo ut aetatem ambo ambobus nobis sint obnoxii,
         nostro devincti beneficio.

Lib.   Vinctos nescio quos ait;
         non placet: metuo, in commune ne quam fraudem
            frausus sit.

Leon.   Perii ego oppido, nisi Libanum invenio iam, ubiubi
         est gentium.

Lib.   Illic homo socium ad malam rem quaerit quem
         adiungat sibi.
         non placet: pro monstro extemplo est, quando qui
         sudat tremit.

Leon.   Sed quid ego hic properans concesso pedibus,
         lingua largior?   290
         quin ego hanc iubeo tacere, quae loquens lacerat
         diem?

acted naturally. Lord help the poor devil that minded the door so carelessly!

on. I'd be willing to slave it all my life, only let me meet Libanus.

b. (*aside*) By Jove, you'll never be free a minute sooner for any help you get from me.

on. I'll even give two hundred swollen welts from off my back to see him.

b. (*aside*) He's generous with what he has: carries all his coffers on his back.

on. For if this chance is let slide, he'll never catch it again, by Jove, not with a chariot and four, white [1] horses. He'll be leaving his master under siege and increasing the courage of his enemies. But if he's ready to take part with me and pounce on this opportunity that's turned up, he'll be my partner in hatching the biggest, joy-stuffedest jubilee that ever was for his masters, son and father both, yes, and put the pair of 'em under obligations to the pair of us for life, too, chained tight by our services.

b. (*aside*) Chained, he says: some one or other chained! I don't like it. I'm afraid he's been trumping up some trumpery that'll involve the both of us.

on. (*quivering with excitement*) I'm absolutely done for, if I don't find Libanus at once, wherever he is.

b. That chap's after a mate to yoke with in a race for a thrashing. I don't like it! it means something bad soon, when a man in a sweat shivers.

on. But why am I holding in my feet and letting out my tongue, and I in such a hurry? Why don't I tell it to shut up, with its wagging the day to shreds?

---

[1] White horses were supposed to be the fastest.

Lib.   Edepol hominem infelicem, qui patronam con-
primat.

nam si quid sceleste fecit, lingua pro illo perierat.

Leon.   Adproperabo, ne post tempus praedae praesidium
parem.

Lib.   Quae illaec praeda est? ibo advorsum atque ele-
ctabo, quidquid est.

iubeo te salvere voce summa, quo ad vires va-
lent.

Leon.   Gymnasium flagri, salveto.

Lib.   Quid agis, custos carceris?

Leon.   O catenarum colone.

Lib.   O virgarum lascivia.

Leon.   Quot pondo ted esse censes nudum?

Lib.   Non edepol scio.

Leon.   Scibam ego te nescire, at pol ego, qui ted expendi,
scio:

nudus vinctus centum pondo es, quando pendes
per pedes.

Lib.   Quo argumento istuc?

Leon.   Ego dicam, quo argumento et quo modo.

ad pedes quando adligatumst aequom centumpon-
dium,

ubi manus manicae complexae sunt atque adductae
ad trabem,

nec dependes nec propendes—quin malus nequam-
que sis.

Lib.   Vae tibi.

Leon.   Hoc testamento Servitus legat tibi.

Lib.   Verbivelitationem fieri compendi volo.

quid istud est negoti?

Leon.   Certum est credere.

Lib.   Audacter licet.

Leon.   Sis amanti subvenire familiari filio,

300

ib.   (*aside*) Good Lord! Poor devil—choking off his patroness! Why, once he's been up to some rascality, it's that same tongue perjures herself for him.

eon.   I'll cut along, so as not to procure protection for the prize when it's too late. (*moves away*)

ib.   What's that prize? I'll up and worm it out of him, whatever it is. (*aloud*) Good day to you—(*raising his voice, Leonida having paid no attention*) as loud a one as my lungs allow!

eon.   Ah there, (*turning and stopping*) you whip developer!

ib.   How goes it, gaol guard?

eon.   Oh you fetter farmer.

ib.   Oh you rod tickler!

eon.   How much do you think you weigh, stripped?

ib.   Lord! I don't know.

eon.   I knew you didn't know: but by the Lord, I know for I've weighed you. Stripped and tied you weigh a hundred pounds—when you're hanging by your heels.

ib.   What's your proof of that?

eon.   I'll tell you my proof and my method. When a fair hundredweight is fastened to your feet, with the handcuffs hugging your hands lashed to a beam, you're not a bit under or over the weight of—a good-for-nothing rascal.

ib.   You be damned!

eon.   Precisely what you are down for yourself in Slavery's will.

ib.   Let's cut short this war of words. What's that business of yours?

eon.   I've determined to trust you.

ib.   You can—boldly.

eon.   If you've got a mind to help the young master in his love affair, there's such an unexpected supply

tantum adest boni inproviso, verum commixtum
   malo: 310
omnes de nobis carnificum concelebrabuntur dies.
Libane, nunc audacia usust nobis inventa et dolis.
tantum facinus modo inveni ego, ut nos dicamur
   duo
omnium dignissumi esse, quo cruciatus confluant.

Lib. Ergo mirabar quod dudum scapulae gestibant
      mihi,
hariolari quae occeperunt, sibi esse in mundo
   malum.
quidquid est, eloquere.

Leon.   Magna est praeda cum magno malo.
Lib. Si quidem omnes coniurati cruciamenta conferant,
habeo opinor familiare tergum, ne quaeram
   foris.

Leon. Si istam firmitudinem animi optines, salvi sumus. 320
Lib. Quin si tergo res solvenda est, rapere cupio pu-
      blicum:
pernegabo atque obdurabo, periurabo denique.

Leon. Em ista virtus est, quando usust qui malum fert
      fortiter;
fortiter malum qui patitur, idem post potitur
   bonum.

Lib. Quin rem actutum edisseris? cupio malum nan-
      ciscier.

Leon. Placide ergo unum quidquid rogita, ut adquiescam.
   non vides
me ex cursura anhelitum etiam ducere?

Lib.   Age, age, mansero
tuo arbitratu, vel adeo usque dum peris.

Leon.   Ubinam est erus?
Lib. Maior apud forumst, minor hic est intus.
Leon.   Iam satis est mihi.

of good luck come to hand—mixed with bad,
though—that the public torturers will have a regular festival at our expense every day. Libanus,
now we need grit and guile. I've just now come
upon such a deed for us to do, that we two will be
called the worthiest men alive—to be where the
torture's thickest.

.ib. (*dryly*) Aha! I was wondering what made my
shoulders tingle a while ago: they began prog-
nosticating trouble was in pickle for 'em. Whatever it is, out with it!

.eon. It's a big prize and a big risk.

.ib. No matter if they all combine to pile the torments
on, I fancy I've got a back of my own, without
having to look for one outside.

.eon. That's the spirit, hold to it and we're safe.

.ib. Pooh! if it's my back that is to pay the score, I'm
ripe for sacking the Treasury: then I'll say up and
down I didn't, stick to it I didn't, yes, yes, take
my solemn oath I didn't.

.eon. There! That's courage—to take hard knocks like
a man when occasion calls. The chap that endures
hard knocks like a man enjoys a soft time later on.

.ib. Why don't you hurry up and unfold your tale? I
long for some hard knocks.

.eon. Easy then with each question, so that I can get a
rest. Don't you see I'm still puffing after that run
of mine?

.ib. All right, all right, I'll wait till you're ready, yes,
ready to expire, for that matter.

.eon. (*after a pause*) Where the deuce is master?

.ib. Old one's at the forum, young one's inside here.
(*pointing to Cleareta's house*)

.eon. That'll do! I'm satisfied.

157

Lib. Tum igitur tu dives es factus?

Leon.   Mitte ridicularia.   330

Lib. Mitto.[1] istuc quod adfers aures exspectant meae.

Leon. Animum adverte, ut aeque mecum haec scias.

Lib.   Taceo.

Leon.   Beas.

meminstin asinos Arcadicos mercatori Pellaeo

nostrum vendere atriensem?

Lib.   Memini.   quid tum postea?

Leon. Em ergo is argentum huc remisit, quod daretur
    Saureae

pro asinis.   adulescens venit modo, qui id argentum
    attulit.

Lib. Ubi is homost?

Leon.   Iam devorandum censes, si conspexeris?

Lib. Ita enim vero. sed tamen, tu nempe eos asinos
    praedicas

vetulos, claudos, quibus subtritae ad femina iam
    erant ungulae?   340

Leon. Ipsos, qui tibi subvectabant rure huc virgas ulmeas.

Lib. Teneo, atque idem te hinc vexerunt vinctum rus.

Leon.   Memor es probe.

verum in tonstrina ut sedebam, me infit percon-
    tarier,

ecquem filium Stratonis noverim Demaenetum.

dico me novisse extemplo et me eius servom praedico

esse, et aedis demonstravi nostras.

Lib.   Quid tum postea?

Leon. Ait se ob asinos ferre argentum atriensi Saureae,

viginti minas, sed eum sese non nosse hominem qui
    siet,

ipsum vero se novisse callide Demaenetum.

quoniam ille elocutus haec sic—

[1] Leo notes lacuna here : *istuc* MSS : *istuc, istuc* Palmer.

Lib.   Satisfied? So you're a millionaire already, are you?

Leon.   Don't try to be funny.

Lib.   I won't. (*grandly*) My ears await your tidings.

Leon.   Listen here, and you'll know about things as well as I do.

Lib.   I'm dumb.

Leon.   (*ironically*) Oh, bliss! Do you remember those Arcadian asses our steward sold to the merchant from Pella?

Lib.   I do. Well, what next?

Leon.   Now then! He's sent the money for 'em, to be paid to Saurea. A young chap's just arrived with it.

Lib.   (*with a start*) Where is he?

Leon.   Think he ought to be swallowed down the minute you spy him, eh?

Lib.   Aye, that I do! But let me see, of course you mean those poor old lame asses with their hoofs worn away up to their hocks?

Leon.   Precisely! the ones that used to come down from the farm with loads of elm rods for you.

Lib.   I have you: yes, the same ones that carried you off to the farm in fetters.

Leon.   Remarkable memory, yours! However, when I was in the barber's chair he speaks up and asks me if I know a Demaenetus, the son of Strato. I say yes at once, and declare that I'm his servant, and I told him where our house was.

Lib.   Well, what next?

Leon.   He says he's bringing money for the asses to steward Saurea, eighty pounds; but that he doesn't know the man at all: says he knows Demaenetus himself well, though. After he had given me an account of things this way——

TITUS MACCIUS PLAUTUS

Lib. Quid tum?

Leon. Ausculta ergo, scies. 350
extemplo facio facetum me atque magnificum virum,
dico med esse atriensem. sic hoc respondit mihi:
"ego pol Sauream non novi neque qua facie sit scio.
te non aequomst suscensere. si erum vis Demaenetum,
quem ego novi, adduce: argentum non morabor
 quin feras."
ego me dixi erum adducturum et me domi praesto
 fore;
ille in balineas iturust, inde huc veniet postea.
quid nunc consili captandum censes? dic.

Lib. Em istuc ago,
quo modo argento intervortam et adventorem et
 Sauream.
iam hoc opus est exasciato [1]; nam si ille argentum
 prius 360
hospes huc affert, continuo nos ambo exclusi sumus.
nam me hodie senex seduxit solum sorsum ab aedibus,
mihi tibique interminatust nos futuros ulmeos,
ni hodie Argyrippo essent viginti argenti minae;
iussit vel nos atriensem vel nos uxorem suam
defraudare, dixit sese operam promiscam dare.
nunc tu abi ad forum ad erum et narra haec ut nos
 acturi sumus:
te ex Leonida futurum esse atriensem Sauream,
dum argentum afferat mercator pro asinis.

Leon. Faciam ut iubes.

Lib. Ego illum interea hic oblectabo, prius si forte advenerit. 370

Leon. Quid ais?

---

[1] Corrupt (Leo): *exasciato* Acidalius: *exasceatum* MSS.

THE COMEDY OF ASSES

Lib.   What next?

Leon.   Well, listen and you'll find out. Instantly I pose as a fine, superior sort of creature and tell him I am the steward. Here's the way he answered me: " Well, well," says he, " I am not acquainted with Saurea personally and I don't know what he looks like. You have no reason to take offence. Bring along your master Demaenetus whom I do know, if you please: I'll let you have the money without delay." I told him I would bring my master and be at home waiting for him. He's going to the baths: then he'll be here later. What do you propose now for a plan of campaign? Tell me.

Lib.   (*thinking*) That's the point! Just what I'm casting about for—some way to relieve newcomer and Saurea of the cash. We must have our scheme roughed out at once; for let that stranger fetch his money before we're ready and the next minute we're both shut out of it. You see, the old man took me aside out of the house to-day all by myself: swore he'd made the pair of us perfectly elmy, if eighty pounds was not forthcoming for Argyrippus this very day. He gave us orders to do the steward out of it, or else his wife: said he'd stand by us whichever it was. Now you be off to the forum to master and tell him what our game will be: that you are going to change from Leonida to steward Saurea when the trader brings the money for the asses.

Leon.   I'll do as you say. (*moves off*)

Lib.   I'll entertain him here myself meanwhile, if he happens to come before you do.

Leon.   (*halting*) I say.

Lib.	Quid vis?
Leon.	Pugno malam si tibi percussero,
	mox cum Sauream imitabor, caveto ne suscenseas.
Lib.	Hercle vero tu cavebis ne me attingas, si sapis,
	ne hodie malo cum auspicio nomen commutaveris.
Leon.	Quaeso, aequo animo patitor.
Lib.	Patitor tu item, cum ego te referiam.
Leon.	Dico ut usust fieri.
Lib.	Dico hercle ego quoque ut facturus sum.
Leon.	Ne nega.
Lib.	Quin promitto, inquam, hostire contra ut merueris.
Leon.	Ego abeo, tu iam, scio, patiere. sed quis hic est?
	is est,
	ille est ipsus. iam ego recurro huc. tu hunc
	interea hic tene.
	volo seni narrare.
Lib.	Quin tuom officium facis ergo ac fugis? 380
II. 3.	
Merc.	Ut demonstratae sunt mihi, hasce aedis esse
	oportet,
	Demaenetus ubi dicitur habitare. i, puere, pulta
	atque atriensem Sauream, si est intus, evocato huc.
Lib.	Quis nostras sic frangit fores? ohe, inquam, si
	quid audis.
Merc.	Nemo etiam tetigit. sanun es?
Lib.	At censebam attigisse

162

Lib. What do you want?

Leon. (*gravely*) In case I punch your jaw for you later on when I'm imitating Saurea, take care you don't get angry.

Lib. By gad, you'd just better take care yourself not to touch me, if you know what's what, or you'll find you've picked an unlucky day for changing your name.

Leon. Come, come, put up with it patiently.

Lib. Yes, and you put up with it when I hit you back.

Leon. I'm telling how it's got to be done.

Lib. And by the Lord, I'm telling how I'm going to do it.

Leon. Don't refuse.

Lib. Oh, I agree, I agree—to pay you back all you earn.

Leon. (*turning to go*) I'm off: you'll put up with it now, I know you will. (*looking down street*) Hullo! Who's this! It's he, the very man! I'll hurry back here soon! You keep him here while I'm gone. I must tell the old man. (*stops to look again*)

Lib. (*sneeringly*) Why don't you play your part then, and—run away?   [EXIT *Leonida.*

Scene 3.   ENTER *Trader*, WITH SERVANT.

Trader (*looking at house of Demaenetus*) According to directions, this must be the house where they say Demaenetus lives. (*to servant*) Go knock, my lad, and if steward Saurea is in there, call him out. (*servant goes toward house*)

Lib. (*stepping forward*) Who's that battering our door so? Whoa there, I say—if you're not deaf!

Trader No one has touched it yet. Are you in your senses?

Lib. Well, I was thinking you had touched it, seeing you were making this way. I don't want you to

  propterea, huc quia habebas iter. nolo ego fores
   conservas
  meas a te verberarier. sane ego sum amicus
   nostris.

Merc. Pol haud periclum est, cardines ne foribus effrin-
   gantur,
  si istoc exemplo omnibus qui quaerunt respondebis.

Lib. Ita haec morata est ianua : extemplo ianitorem 390
  clamat, procul si quem videt ire ad se calcitronem.
  sed quid venis ? quid quaeritas ?

Merc.   Demaenetum volebam.

Lib. Si sit domi, dicam tibi.

Merc.   Quid eius atriensis ?

Lib. Nihilo mage intus est.

Merc.   Ubi est ?

Lib.   Ad tonsorem ire dixit.

Merc. Conveni. sed post non redit ?

Lib.   Non edepol. quid volebas ?

Merc. Argenti viginti minas, si adesset, accepisset.

Lib. Qui pro istuc ?

Merc.   Asinos vendidit Pellaeo mercatori
  mercatu.

Lib.   Scio. tu id nunc refers ? iam hic credo eum
   adfuturum.

Merc. Qua facie voster Saurea est ? si is est, iam scire
   potero.

Lib. Macilentis malis, rufulus aliquantum, ventriosus,
  truculentis oculis, commoda statura, tristi fronte. 400

Merc. Non potuit pictor rectius describere eius formam.

Lib. Atque hercle ipsum adeo contuor, quassanti capite
   incedit.
  quisque obviam huic occesserit irato, vapulabit.

Merc. Siquidem hercle Aeacidinis minis animisque exple-
   tus incedit,

rader beat that door—it's a fellow servant of mine. I tell you what, I love my fellow servants.

rader Gad! No danger of the door being battered off its hinges, if you answer all callers in that style.

ib. Here's the way this door has been trained: once it sights some bully in the distance coming towards it, it bawls for the porter directly. But what's your business? What are you after?

rader I wished to see Demaenetus.

ib. If he was at home, I'd tell you.

rader What about his steward?

ib. No, he's not in, either.

rader Where is he?

ib. Said he was going to the barber's.

rader I met him. But he has not been back since?

ib. Lord, no! What did you want?

rader He would have got eighty pounds, if he was here.

ib. What for?

rader He sold some asses at the market to a trader from Pella.

ib. I know. Bringing the cash now, are you? He'll be here soon, I, fancy.

rader What does your Saurea look like? (*aside*) Now I can find out if that fellow is my man.

ib. (*reflectively*) Lantern-jawed—reddish hair—pot-bellied—savage eyes—average height—and a scowl.

rader (*aside*) No painter could give me a more living likeness of that fellow.

ib. (*looking down street*) Yes, and what's more, he's in sight himself, by gad,—swaggering along and shaking his head! Anyone that crosses his path when he's angry gets thrashed.

rader Good Lord! No matter if he swaggers along as

si med iratus tetigerit, iratus vapulabit.

II. 4.

Leon. Quid hoc sit negoti, neminem meum dictum magni
   facere?
   Libanum in tonstrinam ut iusseram venire, is nullus
   venit.
   ne ille edepol tergo et cruribus consuluit haud
   decore.

Merc. Nimis imperiosust.

Lib. Vae mihi.

Leon. Hodie salvere iussi   410
   Libanum libertum? iam manu emissu's?

Lib. Obsecro te.

Leon. Ne tu hercle cum magno malo mihi obviam occes-
   sisti.
   cur non venisti, ut iusseram, in tonstrinam?

Lib. Hic me moratust.

Leon. Siquidem hercle nunc summum Iovem te dicas
   detinuisse
   atque is precator adsiet, malam rem effugies numquam.
   tu, verbero, imperium meum contempsisti?

Lib. Perii, hospes.

Merc. Quaeso hercle noli, Saurea, mea causa hunc verberare.

Leon. Utinam nunc stimulus in manu mihi sit.

Merc. Quiesce quaeso.

Leon. Qui latera conteram tua, quae occalluere plagis.
   abscede ac sine me hunc perdere, qui semper me
   ira incendit,   420
   cui numquam unam rem me licet semel praecipere
   furi,

full of fire and fury as Achilles—if your angry
man lays a hand on me, it's your angry man gets
thrashed.

Scene 4. ENTER *Leonida,* APPARENTLY IN A RAGE.

Leon. What does this mean? Does no one mind what I
say? I told Libanus to come to the barber's shop,
and he never came at all. By the Lord, he hasn't
given due thought to the welfare of his hide and
shanks, that's a fact!

Trader (*aside*) A precious domineering chap!

Lib. (*affecting terror*) Oh, I'm in for it!

Leon. (*to Libanus ironically*) Ah, greetings to Libanus the
freedman, is it, to-day? Have you been manu-
mitted now? (*advancing*)

Lib. (*cowering*) Please, please, sir!

Leon. By heaven, I'll certainly give you good reason to
regret crossing my path. Why didn't you come
to the barber's, as I ordered?

Lib. (*pointing to trader*) This gentleman delayed me.

Leon. (*without looking at trader*) Damme! You can go on
and say Jove Almighty detained you, yes, and he
can come here and plead your case, but you shall
never escape a flogging. You scorned my
authority, you whipping post?

Lib. (*running behind trader*) Oh kind stranger, I'm a
dead man!

Trader By Jove, Saurea! Now, now, don't flog him, for
my sake!

Leon. (*paying no attention*) Oh, if I could only get hold
of an ox goad now!

Trader Now, now, calm down.

Leon. So as to stave in those ribs of yours that have grown
callous to blows! (*to trader*) Out of my way, and
let me murder the rascal that always sets me afire

167

quin centiens eadem imperem atque ogganniam,
    itaque iam hercle
clamore ac stomacho non queo labori suppeditare.
iussin, sceleste, ab ianua hoc stercus hinc auferri?
iussin columnis deici operas araneorum?
iussin in splendorem dari bullas has foribus nostris?
nihil est: tamquam si claudus sim, cum fustist am-
    bulandum.
quia triduom hoc unum modo foro operam adsiduam
    dedo,
dum reperiam qui quaeritet argentum in faenus,
    hic vos
dormitis interea domi, atque erus in hara, haud
    aedibus habitat.   430
em ergo hoc tibi.

Lib.   Hospes, te obsecro, defende.
Merc.   Saurea, oro,
mea causa ut mittas.
Leon.   Eho, ecquis pro vectura olivi
rem solvit?
Lib.   Solvit.
Leon.   Cui datumst?
Lib.   Sticho vicario ipsi
tuo.
Leon.   Vah, delenire apparas, scio mihi vicarium esse,
neque eo esse servom in aedibus eri qui sit pluris
    quam illest.
sed vina quae heri vendidi vinario Exaerambo,
iam pro eis satis fecit Sticho?
Lib.   Fecisse satis opinor,
nam vidi huc ipsum adducere trapezitam Exaer-
    ambum.
Leon.   Sic dedero.   prius quae credidi vix anno post
    exegi;

with rage, that never lets one order from me suffice for one job, the criminal, but keeps me commanding and growling the same thing a hundred times over. Good Lord, it's come to the point where I can't stand the work, what with yelling and storming at him! Didn't I tell you to carry off this dung from the doorway, you villain? Didn't I tell you to clean the spiders' webs off the columns? Didn't I tell you to rub these door knobs till they shone? It's no good: anyone would think I was lame, the way I have to travel around after you with a cane. Because I've been constantly busy at the forum just for the last three days, trying to find some one to place a loan with, here you've been drowsing all the time at home, and your master living in a pig-pen, not a house. There now, take that! (*strikes him*)

b.   Kind stranger! For heaven's sake protect me!

ader Come, Saurea, do let him off for my sake.

on.   (*to Libanus*) Hey, you! Did anyone pay for the shipping of that oil?

b.   Yes, sir.

on.   Who to?

b.   To Stichus himself, sir, your own deputy.

on.   Hm-m! trying to smooth me down! To be sure I have a deputy, and there's not a slave in the master's house that is a more valuable man than that deputy, either. But how about the wine I sold to Exaerambus the vintner yesterday—has he settled with Stichus for it yet?

b.   I reckon he has, sir: for I saw Exaerambus bringing the banker here himself.

on.   That's the style for me! Last time I trusted him I barely got the money out of him a year after-

169

	nunc satagit: adducit domum etiam ultro et scribit nummos.
	Dromo mercedem rettulit? 440
Lib.	Dimidio minus opinor.
Leon.	Quid relicuom?
Lib.	Aibat reddere quom extemplo redditum esset; nam retineri, ut quod sit sibi operis locatum efficeret.
Leon.	Scyphos quos utendos dedi Philodamo, rettulitne?
Lib.	Non etiam.
Leon.	Hem non? si velis, da,[1] commoda homini amico.
Merc.	Perii hercle, iam hic me abegerit suo odio.
Lib.	Heus iam satis tu. audin quae loquitur?
Leon.	Audio et quiesco.
Merc.	Tandem, opinor, conticuit. nunc adeam optimum est, prius quam incipit tinnire.
	quam mox mi operam das?
Leon.	Ehem, optume. quam dudum tu advenisti? non hercle te provideram—quaeso ne vitio vortas— 450 ita iracundia obstitit oculis.
Merc.	Non mirum factum est. sed si domi est, Demaenetum volebam.
Leon.	Negat esse intus. verum istuc argentum tamen mihi si vis denumerare,
	repromittam istoc nomine solutam rem futuram.

---

[1] Leo notes lacuna here: *da* MSS: *dare* Fleckeisen.

    wards. Now he pays his bills: even brings his
banker over to the house besides, and writes his
cheque. Has Dromo brought home his wages?

b.   Only half, I think.

eon.   And the rest?

b.   He said he'd give it to you as soon as it was given
to him; claimed it was kept back so that he'd
finish up a job that was placed with him.

eon.   Those cups that I lent Philodamus—has he returned 'em?

b.   Not yet.

eon.   Hey? No? (*sourly*) Give things away, if you like,
—give 'em to a friend on loan.

rader (*half aside, wearily*) Oh, the devil! The fellow will
be driving me off before long with his confounded
talk.

b.   (*aside to Leonida*) Hi, you! That's enough now!
D'ye hear what he says?

eon.   (*aside to Libanus*) I hear; I'll calm down.

rader (*aside*) Silent at last, I do believe. Best approach
him now before he begins to rattle on again.
(*aloud to Leonida*) How soon can you give me your
attention?

eon.   (*looking at him and affecting surprise*) Aha! Splendid! How long have you been here? Well, well,
I hadn't noticed you before! I trust you won't
feel offended. I was so angry that it affected my
eyesight.

rader   Nothing strange in that. But I wished to see
Demaenetus, if he is at home.

eon.   He (*indicating Libanus*) says he's not in. But as to
that money, though,—count it out to me, if you
like, and then I'll engage that your account with
us is settled.

171

Merc.   Sic potius, ut Demaeneto tibi ero praesente reddam.

Lib.   Erus istunc novit atque erum hic.

Merc.   Ero huic praesente reddam.

Lib.   Da modo meo periculo, rem salvam ego exhibebo;
        nam si sciat noster senex fidem non esse huic ha-
            bitam,
        suscenseat, quoi omnium rerum ipsus semper credit.

Leon.   Non magni pendo. ne duit, si non volt. sic sine
        astet.   460

Lib.   Da, inquam. vah, formido miser, ne hic me tibi
        arbitretur
        suasisse, sibi ne crederes. da, quaeso, ac ne for-
        mida :
        salvom hercle erit.

Merc.   Credam fore, dum quidem ipse in manu habebo.
        peregrinus ego sum, Sauream non novi.

Lib.   At nosce sane.

Merc.   Sit, non sit, non edepol scio. si is est, eum esse
        oportet.
        ego certe me incerto scio hoc daturum nemini ho-
        mini.

Leon.   Hercle istum di omnes perduint. verbo cave
        supplicassis.
        ferox est viginti minas meas tractare sese.
        nemo accipit aufer te domum, abscede hinc, mo-
        lestus ne sis.

Merc.   Nimis iracunde. non decet superbum esse homi-
        nem servom.   470

Leon.   Malo hercle iam magno tuo, ni isti nec recte dicis.

Lib.   Impure, nihili. non vides irasci?

rader I should prefer to make the payment in the presence of your master Demaenetus.

ib. (*protestingly*) Oh, master knows him and he knows master.

rader (*firmly*) I shall pay him in his master's presence.

ib. Oh now, give it to him, at my risk: I'll make it all right. Why, if our old man knew Saurea here was doubted, he'd be furious: he always trusts him with everything himself.

eon. (*very superior*) It's of no importance. He can keep it, if he wants. Let him stand by with it there.

ib. (*aside to trader*) I say, do give it to him. Oh dear, this is awful! I'm afraid he'll think I persuaded you not to trust him. Give it to him, for mercy's sake, and don't be afraid. Good Lord, it'll be all right!

rader I trust it will be, so long as I keep hold of it myself, anyway. I am a stranger here: I don't know Saurea.

ib. (*pointing to Leonida*) Well, just make his acquaintance, then.

rader Whether he is the man or not, I don't know by, gad. If he is, he is, of course. I certainly do know that when I am uncertain I give this (*showing a wallet*) to nobody on earth.

eon. Be damned to the fellow! (*to Libanus*) Not a word of entreaty, you! He's puffed up at having the handling of my eighty pounds. (*to trader*) No one will take it! Home with you! Away with you! Don't bother me!

rader (*scoffingly*) Quite in a pet! The idea of a mere slave being arrogant!

eon. (*to Libanus*) By heaven, you'll soon pay dear for it, if you don't abuse him!

ib. (*loudly to trader*) You dirty thing, you, you good

G

Leon.   Perge porro.

Lib. Flagitium hominis. da, obsecro, argentum huic, ne
male loquatur.

Merc. Malum hercle vobis quaeritis.

Leon.   Crura hercle diffringentur,
ni istum impudicum percies.

Lib.   Perii hercle. age impudice,
sceleste, non audes mihi scelesto subvenire?

Leon. Pergin precari pessimo?

Merc.   Quae res? tun libero homini
male servos loquere?

Leon.   Vapula.

Merc.   Id quidem tibi hercle fiet,
ut vapules, Demaenetum simul ac conspexero hodie.[1]   479

Leon. Quid, verbero? ain tu, furcifer? erum nos fugitare censes?   484-485
ei nunciam ad erum, quo vocas, iam dudum quo
volebas.

Merc. Nunc demum? tamen numquam hinc feres argenti
nummum, nisi me
dare iusserit Demaenetus.

Leon.   Ita facito, age ambula ergo.
tu contumeliam alteri facias, tibi non dicatur?
tam ego homo sum quam tu.

Merc.   Scilicet. ita res est

Leon.   Sequere hac ergo.   490

[1] Leo brackets following vv., 480-483 :
in ius voco te.
Leon.   *Non eo.*
Merc.   *Non is? memento.*
Leon.   *Memini.*
Merc. *Dabitur pol supplicium mihi de tergo vostro.*
Leon   *Vae te.*
tibi quidem supplicium, carnufex, de nobis detur?
Merc.   *Atque etiam*
pro dictis vostris maledicis poenae pendentur mi hodie.

174

for nothing! (*in lower tone*) Don't you see he's angry?

Leon. (*to Libanus*) Go on, get at him!

Lib. (*loudly*) You scandal of a man! (*in lower tone*) Do give him the money, for heaven's sake, so that he won't call you bad names.

Trader Gad! It's a bad time you two are looking for.

Leon. (*to Libanus*) By the Lord, your legs shall be broken to splinters, if you don't give that shameless rascal a blowing up.

Lib. (*to trader in low tone*) Oh Lord! I'm in for it! (*loudly*) Come, you shameless rascal, you wretch, won't you help me, poor wretch that I am?

Leon. (*to Libanus*) Continuing to coax that criminal, are you?

Trader (*getting indignant*) How is this? You dare to abuse a free man, you, you slave?

Leon. You be thrashed!

Trader Be thrashed? Precisely what will be done to you, by gad, the moment I set eyes on Demaenetus to-day!

Leon. What, you whipping post? So, you gallows-bird? D'ye think we skulk from our master? On with you straight to the master you summon us to, the master you've wanted to see this long time past. (*goes toward forum*)

Trader At last, eh? But never a penny do you get from me, unless I am instructed to give it to you by Demaenetus.

Leon. All right, all right! Come, step along, then! Do you want to insult another man and not get it back? I'm as much of a man as you are!

Trader No doubt. Quite so.

Leon. Come along this way, then. (*stops*) If I may say so

175

      praefiscini hoc nunc dixerim : nemo etiam me
        accusavit

      merito meo, neque me alter est Athenis hodie quis-
        quam,

      cui credi recte aeque putent.

Merc.   Fortassis. sed tamen me

      numquam hodie induces, ut tibi credam hoc argen-
        tum ignoto.

      lupus est homo homini, non homo, quom qualis sit
        non novit.

Leon.   Iam nunc secunda mihi facis. scibam huic te
        capitulo hodie.

      facturum satis pro iniuria; quamquam ego sum
        sordidatus,

      frugi tamen sum, nec potest peculium enumerari.

Merc.   Fortasse.

Leon.   Etiam [1] Periphanes Rhodo mercator dives

      absente ero solus mihi talentum argenti soli   500

      adnumeravit et mihi credidit, nequest deceptus in
        eo.

Merc.   Fortasse.

Leon.   Atque etiam tu quoque ipse, si esses percontatus
      me ex aliis, scio pol crederes nunc quod fers.

Merc.   Haud negassim.

ACTVS III

Cle.   Nequeon ego ted interdictis facere mansuetem
      meis ?

        [1] *etiam nunc dico* MSS : Lindsay excises *nunc dico.*

without presumption, let me tell you this now: no
one has ever yet accused me justly, and there's
not a single other man in all Athens that people
think worthy of such confidence as me, either.

Trader I dare say. But notwithstanding, never will you
induce me to-day to trust this money to you, a
stranger. (*somewhat apologetically*) "Man is no
man, but a wolf, to a stranger."

Leon. (*encouraged*) Now there, that's decent of you! I
knew you'd soon be making amends to a good fellow for doing him an injustice. No matter if I do
look shabby, I'm an honest man just the same,
and as for the cash I've laid by—it can't be
counted.

Trader (*sceptically*) I dare say.

Leon. Even Periphanes, the rich trader from Rhodes,
counted out two hundred pounds to me when
master was away and we were all by ourselves,—
he trusted me, and he wasn't deceived in doing
so, either.

Trader I dare say.

Leon. Yes, and even you yourself, too, if you had only
inquired from others about me, I know you would
trust me with what you've got there, good Lord,
yes!

Trader (*icily*) I should be sorry to deny it. (*motions
Leonida to lead the way to Demaenetus*)
[EXEUNT THE THREE TO THE FORUM, *Leonida* IREFUL.

ACT III

(Half an hour has elapsed.)

ENTER *Cleareta* AND *Philaenium* FROM THEIR HOUSE.

Cle. Have I no power to make you submit when I pro-

	an ita tu es animata, ut qui matris expers imperio sies ?
Phil.	Ubi piem Pietatem, si istoc more moratam tibi postulem placere, mater, mihi quo pacto prae cipis ? [1]
Cle.	Hocine est pietatem colere, matris imperium minuere ?
Phil.	Neque quae recte faciunt culpo neque quae delinquont amo.
Cle.	Satis dicacula es amatrix.
Phil.	Mater, is quaestus mihi est : lingua poscit, corpus quaerit ; animus orat, res monet.
Cle.	Ego te volui castigare, tu mi accusatrix ades.
Phil.	Neque edepol te accuso neque id me facere fas existimo. verum ego meas queror fortunas, cum illo quem amo prohibeor.
Cle.	Ecqua pars orationis de die dabitur mihi ?
Phil.	Et meam partem loquendi et tuam trado tibi ; ad loquendum atque ad tacendum tute habeas porticulum. quin pol si reposivi remum, sola ego in casteria ubi quiesco, omnis familiae causa consistit tibi.
Cle.	Quid ais tu, quam ego unam vidi mulierem audacissimam ? quotiens te votui Argyrippum filium Demaeneti compellare aut contrectare, conloqui aut contui ? quid dedit ? quid ad nos iussit deportari ? an tu tibi verba blanda esse aurum rere, dicta docta pro datis ?

510

520

---

[1] Leo brackets following v., 508 :

Cle.   *An decorum est adversari meis te praeceptis ?*

Phil.   *Quid est ?*

hibit a thing? Can it be that you feel inclined to
rid yourself of your mother's authority?

il. How should I be showing myself duteous to
Filial Duty, mother, if I tried to please you by
practising such practices and doing as you pre-
scribe?

?. Is this regarding filial duty, to lessen a mother's
authority?

il. I don't find fault with mothers that do right, and
I don't like ones that do wrong.

?. A glib enough little hussy!

il. (*lightly*) All in my profession, mother: tongue
asks, body teases; fancy prompts, circumstances
suggest.

e. I intended to scold you, and here you are turning
on me!

il. Oh, no! I'm not turning on you: I don't think
that would be right. But I do think it's a cruel
fate to be kept away from the man I love.

?. Am I to get some share of the speechmaking
before nightfall?

il. I give you my share and your own, too: you can be
boatswain yourself and give the signal for talking
and keeping still. But goodness me, if I once lay
down the oar, I, and stay by myself resting in the
rowers' room, the progress of this whole household
stops short, you see.

e. Look here! Of all the impudent young misses I
have ever seen! How many times have I forbidden
you to have communication or contact or chitchat
with Demaenetus's son, Argyrippus, or to cast
your eyes on him? What has he given us? What
has he had sent us? Do you think pretty speeches
are gold pieces, witty words presents? You

179

ultro amas, ultro expetessis, ultro ad te accersi
    iubes.

illos qui dant, eos derides; qui deludunt, deperis.

an te id exspectare oportet, si quis promittat tibi

te facturum divitem, si moriatur mater sua?

ecastor [1] nobis periclum magnum et familiae por-
    tenditur,   530

dum eius exspectamus mortem, ne nos moriamur
    fame.

nunc adeo nisi mi huc argenti adfert viginti minas,

ne ille ecastor hinc trudetur largus lacrumarum
    foras.

hic dies summust quo est [2] apud me inopiae excu-
    satio.

Phil. Patiar, si cibo carere me iubes, mater mea.

Cle. Non voto ted amare qui dant quoia amentur
    gratia.

Phil. Quid si hic animus occupatust, mater, quid faciam?
    mone.

Cle.   Em,
    meum caput contemples, si quidem ex re consultas
    tua.

Phil. Etiam opilio qui pascit, mater, alienas ovis,   539, 540
    aliquam habet peculiarem, qui spem soletur suam.
    sine me amare unum Argyrippum animi causa,
    quem volo.

Cle. Intro abi, nam te quidem edepol nihil est impu-
    dentius.

Phil. Audientem dicto, mater, produxisti filiam.

III. 2.

Lib. Perfidiae laudes gratiasque habemus merito ma
    gnas,

---

[1] Corrupt (Leo): *nobis* excised by Bothe.
[2] *quo est* Leo : not in MSS.

make love to him yourself, run after him yourself, have him called yourself. Men that give you things you treat with contempt; those that trifle with you you dote on. Have you any business waiting for it to happen, if a man does promise to make you rich, if his mother dies? Mercy me, while we wait for her to die, up looms a big risk of ourselves and our household dying of starvation! Now let me tell you this: unless he brings me eighty pounds, I swear to goodness that fellow shall be bundled out of the house, liberal as he is —of tears! This is the last day I accept pleas of poverty.

hil.   Tell me to do without food, mother dear, and I'll endure that.

le.   I have nothing to say against your loving men who give you something to be loved for.

hil.   What if my heart isn't free, mother? What then? Advise me.

le.   Look! Consider these grey hairs of mine, if you really have any regard for your own good.

hil.   Even the shepherd that pastures other peoples' sheep has some ewe lamb of his very own, mother, one that he builds happy hopes on. Do let me love Argyrippus alone, the man I want, just for love's sake.

le.   Inside with you! Why, mercy on us, a more shameless minx than you really can't exist.

hil.   (*tearfully*) You've trained . . . your . . . daughter . . . to . . . be obedient . . . mother.

[EXIT *Philaenium* INTO HOUSE, FOLLOWED BY *Cleareta.*

ene 2.   ENTER FROM FORUM *Libanus* AND *Leonida*, LATTER CARRYING A WALLET.

ib.   (*chanting ecstatically*) All praise and thanks be to

quom nostris sycophantiis, dolis astutiisque,[1]
advorsum stetimus lamminas,[2] crucesque compedes-
   que,
nervos, catenas, carceres, numellas, pedicas, boias 549, 550
inductoresque [3] acerrumos gnarosque nostri tergi.[4]
eae nunc legiones, copiae exercitusque eorum
vi pugnando periuriis nostris fugae potiti.
id virtute huius collegae [5] meaque comitate
factumst. qui me vir fortior ad sufferundas plagas?

Leon.   Edepol virtutes qui tuas non possis conclaudare
sic ut ego possim, quae domi duellique male fecisti.
ne illa edepol pro merito tuo memorari multa pos-
    sunt: 560
ubi fidentem fraudaveris, ubi ero infidelis fueris,
ubi verbis conceptis sciens libenter periuraris,
ubi parietes perfoderis, in furto ubi sis prehensus,
ubi saepe causam dixeris pendens adversus octo
artutos, audacis viros, valentis virgatores.

Lib.   Fateor profecto ut praedicas, Leonida, esse vera;
verum edepol ne etiam tua quoque malefacta
   iterari multa
et vero possunt; ubi sciens fideli infidus fueris,
ubi prensus in furto sies manifesto et verberatus,[6] 569
ubi eris damno, molestiae et dedecori saepe fueris,

---

[1] Leo brackets following v., 547 : *scapularam confidentia,
virtute ulmorum freti.*

[2] *advorsum stetimus* Ussing : *qui advorsum stimulos,*
MSS.

[3] *Inductoresque* Acidalius and others : *indoctoresque*
MSS.

[4] Leo brackets following v., 552—*qui saepe ante in
nostras scapulas cicatrices indiderunt*—and assumes lacuna
following.

holy Perfidy as she deserves, since by our swindles, shams, and wiles we have defied hot irons and crosses and gyves, and thongs, chains, cells, shackles, fetters, collars, and painters—painters keen as can be and intimate with our backs! All these regiments, battalions, and armies of theirs have been put to flight, after fierce fighting, by our fabrications. 'Tis the valour of my colleague hath done it, with my own kind assistance. Who's a stouter-hearted hero than I am at taking thwacks?

on. (*sneeringly*) Good Lord! Your deeds of valour—you couldn't celebrate them the way I could your villainies at home and in the field. Gad! you certainly can be acredited with a lengthy list of things along that line. Item, cheated a confiding friend; item, faithless to master; item, committed perjury consciously, cheerfully, in set form of words; item, dug your way into houses through the walls; item, caught at thieving; item, strung up repeatedly and plead your case before eight bold, brawny beef-eaters with a gift for club swinging.

b. I am quite ready to admit that is a just statement of the case, Leonida; but, Lord! the list of even your own villainies, too, can certainly be made lengthy enough, without injustice. Item, consciously treacherous to a trusting friend; item, caught stealing redhanded and whipped; item, repeatedly brought loss, trouble, and disgrace on

---

[5] Corrupt (Leo): *collegae* MSS: *collegae mei* Leo.
[6] Leo brackets following v., 570: *ubi periuraris, ubi sacro manus sis admolitus.*

ubi creditum quod sit tibi datum esse pernegaris,[1]
ubi saepe ad languorem tua duritia dederis octo
validos lictores, ulmeis adfectos lentis virgis.
num male relata est gratia, ut collegam collaudavi?

Leon. Ut meque teque maxime atque ingenio nostro
decuit.

Lib. Iam omitte ista atque hoc quod rogo responde.

Leon.   Rogita quod vis.

Lib. Argenti viginti minas habesne?

Leon.   Hariolare.

edepol senem Demaenetum lepidum fuisse nobis: 580
ut adsimulabat Sauream med esse quam facete!
nimis aegre risum contini, ubi hospitem inclamavit,
quod se absente mihi fidem habere noluisset.
ut memoriter me Sauream vocabat atriensem

Lib. Mane dum

Leon.   Quid est?

Lib.   Philaenium estne haec quae intus exit
atque Argyrippus una?

Leon.   Opprime os, is est.   subauscultemus.

Lib. Lacrumantem lacinia tenet lacrumans. quidnam
esse dicam?

taciti auscultemus.

Leon.   Attatae, modo hercle in mentem venit,
nimis vellem habere perticam.

Lib.   Quoi rei?

Leon.   Qui verberarem
asinos, si forte occeperint clamare hinc ex crumina. 590

---

[1] Leo brackets following v., 573: *ubi amicae quam amico tuo fueris magis fidelis.*

your masters; item, had money left in your keeping
and swore and swore it wasn't; item, repeatedly
exhausted by your toughness eight strong lictors
equipped with pliant elm rods. (*pause*) Have I
celebrated my colleague highly enough to pay
him back—eh, what?

eon. (*thoughtfully*) Yes, pretty much what you and I
and our characters deserved.

ib. Drop your nonsense now and answer me this
question.

con. Ask your question.

ib. (*triumphantly*) The eighty pounds, have you got it?

eon. You're a prophet! By gad, old Demaenetus did
do the handsome thing by us. The way he pretended I was Saurea—clever, my word! I did
have a deuce of a time holding in when he
hauled our guest over the coals for not being
willing to trust me in his absence. The way
he remembered to keep calling me steward
Saurea!

ib. (*looking toward Cleareta's house*) Wait, though!

eon. What's up?

ib. Isn't this Philaenium coming out here, yes, and
Argyrippus along with her?

eon. (*in low tone*) Shut your mouth—so it is. Let's do
some eaves-dropping. (*they retire*)

ib. Both crying and she holding on to the lappet of his
cloak! What on earth is the matter! Let's keep
still and listen.

eon. Oh-h! Jove! It has just occurred to me: how I
do wish I had a pole!

ib. What for?

eon. To whop those asses, if they happen to start
braying in the wallet here.

185

III. 3.

Argyr. Cur me retentas?

Phil.   Quia tui amans abeuntis egeo.

Argyr. Vale.

Phil.   Aliquanto amplius valerem, si hic maneres.

Argyr. Salve.

Phil.   Salvere me iubes, quoi tu abiens offers morbum?

Argyr. Mater supremam mihi tua dixit, domum ire iussit.

Phil. Acerbum funus filiae faciet, si te carendum est,

Lib. Homo hercle hinc exclusust foras.

Leon.   Ita res est.

Argyr.   Mitte quaeso.

Phil. Quo nunc abis? quin tu hic manes?

Argyr.   Nox, si voles, manebo.

Lib. Audin hunc opera ut largus est nocturna? nunc
     enim esse

negotiosum interdius videlicet Solonem,

leges ut conscribat, quibus se populus teneat. ger-
     rae!

qui sese parere apparent huius legibus, profecto

numquam bonae frugi sient, dies noctesque potent.

Leon. Ne iste hercle ab ista non pedem discedat, si
     licessit,

qui nunc festinat atque ab hac minatur sese abire.

Lib. Sermoni iam finem face tuo, huius sermonem ac-
     cipiam.

600

Scene 3. ENTER *Argyrippus* AND *Philaenium* FROM THE
DOORWAY OF *Cleareta's* HOUSE WHERE THEY HAVE
BEEN STANDING.

Argyr. (*sadly*) Why hold me back?

Phil. (*tearfully*) Because it's dreadful having you leave
me when I love you so.

Argyr. (*trying half-heartedly to release himself*) Farewell!

Phil. (*still clinging to him*) I should fare much better if
you'd stay with me.

Argyr. And God bless you!

Phil. You ask God to bless me when you curse me
yourself by going?

Argyr. Your mother said this was to be my last hour: she
has ordered me home.

Phil. She'll make her daughter die in misery, if I must
be deprived of you.

Lib. (*aside to Leonida*) By gad! He's been shut out of
the house here.

Leon. So he has.

Argyr. (*dismally*) Come, come, let go! (*pulls away from
her and turns to go*)

Phil. Where are you off to now? Why don't you stay here?

Argyr. I will at night, if you want.

Lib. Hear the chap—how free he is with his attentions
by night? For now in the daytime he's a hard-
working Solon, drawing up laws to bind the people
—oh, yes he is! Rot! Folks that set themselves
to obey his laws won't ever be good for anything,
that's sure,—except drinking day and night.

Leon. Good Lord! The fellow wouldn't move a step
from her, if he had his way, not he, for all this rush
of his and threats to leave her.

Lib. Come, make an end of your talk: I want to take
in some of his.

Argyr. Vale.

Phil.   Quo properas?

Argyr.   Bene vale, apud Orcum te videbo.

nam equidem me iam quantum potest a vita ab-
    iudicabo.

Phil. Cur tu, obsecro, immerito meo me morti dedere
    optas?

Argyr. Ego te? quam si intellegam deficere vita, iam
    ipse

vitam meam tibi largiar et de mea ad tuam addam.   610

Phil. Cur ergo minitaris mihi, te vitam esse amissurum?

nam quid me facturam putas, si istuc quod dicis
    faxis?

mihi certum est facere in me omnia eadem quae tu
    in te faxis.

Argyr. Oh melle dulci dulcior tu es.

Phil.   Certe enim tu vita es mi.

complectere.

Argyr.   Facio lubens.

Phil.   Utinam sic efferamur.

Leon. O Libane, uti miser est homo qui amat.

Lib.   Immo hercle vero,

qui pendet multo est miserior.

Leon.   Scio qui periclum feci.

circum sistamus, alter hinc, hinc alter appellemus.

ere, salve. sed num fumus est haec mulier quam
    amplexare?

Argyr. Quidum?

Leon.   Quia oculi sunt tibi lacrumantes, eo rogavi.   620

Argyr.	(*tragically*) Farewell! (*starts away*)
Phil.	Where are you hurrying to?
Argyr.	Farewell! Be happy. I shall see you in the world to come! For upon my soul, this world and I shall now be divorced as soon as possible!
Phil.	(*running up and clinging to him*) Oh, for heaven's sake, why, why do you wish to condemn me to death yourself, innocent as I am?
Argyr.	I you? If I saw your life was ebbing, I'd freely give you my own at once and add my years to yours.
Phil.	Then why do you theaten me with throwing away your life? For what do you think I will do, if you do what you say? My mind's made up: I'll do to myself just precisely what you do to yourself.
Argyr.	Oh, you're sweeter than sweet honey!
Phil.	And you're my very life, I know that. Do put your arms around me!
Argyr.	(*doing so*) Yes, yes, gladly!
Phil.	Oh, if we could only be carried to the grave like this!
Leon.	I say, Libanus, what a poor devil a chap in love is!
Lib.	By Jove, no! A chap hung up by his heels is a much poorer devil, believe me.
Leon.	I know that: I've tried it. (*a pause*) Let's surround him, and give him a salute, one from here (*pointing*) and the other from here. (*they station themselves : then, giving the signal to Libanus to chime in, loudly to Argyrippus*) Good day, sir! (*the lovers give a start*) But—this lady you're hugging isn't smoke, is she?
Argyr.	Smoke? Why so?
Leon.	Well, your eyes are watering; that's why I asked.

Argyr. Patronus qui vobis fuit futurus, perdidistis.
Leon. Equidem hercle nullum perdidi, ideo quia numquam
   ullum habui.
Lib. Philaenium, salve.
Phil.   Dabunt di quae velitis vobis.
Lib. Noctem tuam et vini cadum velim, si optata fiant.
Argyr. Verbum cave faxis, verbero.
Lib.   Tibi equidem, non mihi opto.
Argyr. Tum tu igitur loquere quod lubet.
Lib.   Hunc hercle verberare.
Leon. Quisnam istuc adcredat tibi, cinaede calamistrate?
   tun verberes, qui pro cibo habeas te verberari?
Argyr. Ut vostrae fortunae meis praecedunt, Libane,
   longe,
   qui hodie numquam ad vesperum vivam.
Lib.   Quapropter, quaeso? 630
Argyr. Quia ego hanc amo et haec me amat, huic quod
   dem nusquam quicquam est,
   hinc med amantem ex aedibus eiecit huius mater.
   argenti viginti minae me ad mortem appulerunt,
   quas hodie adulescens Diabolus ipsi daturus dixit,
   ut hanc ne quoquam mitteret nisi ad se hunc annum totum.
   videtin viginti minae quid pollent quidve possunt?
   ille qui illas perdit salvos est, ego qui non perdo
   pereo.
Lib. Iam dedit argentum?
Argyr.   Non dedit.
Lib.   Bono animo es, ne formida.

Argyr. (*tragically*) You have lost a man who would have freed you and been your patron, my lads.

Leon. Lord! I haven't lost any such, no, indeed, seeing I never had any such.

Lib. Good day to you, Philaenium.

Phil. God grant all your wishes, to both of you.

Lib. I'd wish an evening with you and a cask of wine, if wishing was having.

Argyr. Hold your tongue, you rascal!

Lib. Oh, wish 'em for you, I mean, sir, not for myself.

Argyr. Then in that case, say what you like.

Lib. Like? I'd like to give this chap (*pointing to Leonida*) a thrashing, by gad!

Leon. (*ironically*) Well, well, who'd believe it of you, you frizzle-headed girl hunter? You thrash me, you, you that live on thrashings?

Argyr. (*tragical again*) Ah, Libanus, how far preferable your lot is to mine—I who will never never live till evening!

Lib. How's that, for mercy's sake?

Argyr. Because I love her (*indicating Philaenium*) and she loves me; and (*bitterly*) never a penny can I find anywhere to give her; and her mother has thrown me out of the house here, me, her daughter's lover. I'm driven to my death by eighty pounds, eighty pounds young Diabolus promised to pay her to-day for letting no one else but him have my girl the whole of this next year. Do you see the power, the possibilities in eighty pounds? The man that loses them is saved: I don't lose them and I'm lost myself.

Lib. Has he paid 'em over already?

Argyr. No.

Lib. Cheer up: never you fear.

Leon. Secede huc, Libane, te volo.
Lib.   Si quid vis.
Argyr.   Obsecro vos,
    eadem istac opera suaviust complexos fabulari.   640
Lib. Non omnia eadem aeque omnibus, ere, suavia esse
    scito :
    vobis est suave amantibus complexos fabulari,
    ego complexum huius nil moror, meum autem hic
        aspernatur.
    proinde istud facias ipse quod faciamus nobis
        suades.
Argyr. Ego vero, et quidem edepol lubens. interea, si
    videtur,
    concedite istuc.
Leon.   Vin erum deludi ?
Lib.   Dignust sane.
Leon. Vin faciam ut te Philaenium praesente hoc am-
    plexetur ?
Lib. Cupio hercle.
Leon.   Sequere hac.
Argyr.   Ecquid est salutis ? satis locuti.
Leon. Auscultate atque operam date et mea dicta devor-
    ate.
    primum omnium servos tuos nos esse non negamus ;   650
    sed tibi si viginti minae argenti proferentur,
    quo nos vocabis nomine ?
Argyr.   Libertos.
Leon.   Non patronos ?
Argyr. Id potius.
Leon.   Viginti minae hic insunt in crumina,
    has ego, si vis, tibi dabo.

192

Leon.	Libanus! Come over here: I want you.
Lib.	(*obeying*) Anything to please. (*they withdraw and talk, heads close together*)
Argyr.	(*calling*) For heaven's sake, you two! You'd find it pleasanter to hug each other, while you do your chatting!
Lib.	Tastes differ about what's pleasant, sir, let me tell you that. A fond pair like you find it pleasant to hug each other while you do your chatting; but, personally, I don't care for this fellow's hugs, and as for mine, he scorns 'em. So you go on and practise yourself what you preach to us.
Argyr.	Indeed I will, by Jove, yes, and gladly. Meanwhile you two go on and step aside there, if you see fit. (*embraces Philaenium*)
Leon.	D'ye want to have some fun with master?
Lib.	That I do, serves him right.
Leon.	D'ye want me to make Philaenium give you a squeeze right before his face?
Lib.	(*enthusiastically*) Gad, I long for one!
Leon.	Come along. (*leads the way back to Argyrippus and* (*Philaenium*)
Argyr.	Any good news? You have talked enough.
Leon.	(*importantly*) Listen here, you two; pay attention and devour my remarks. (*to Argyrippus*) First of all, we are your slaves, we don't deny that; but if eighty pounds is produced for you, what will you call us?
Argyr.	(*eagerly*) Freedmen!
Leon.	Not patrons, eh?
Argyr.	Yes, yes, patrons!
Leon.	There's eighty pounds in this wallet here: I'll give it to you if you like.

Argyr.   Di te servassint semper,
      custos erilis, decus popli, thensaurus copiarum.
      salus interioris[1] corporis amorisque imperator.
      hic pone, hic istam colloca cruminam in collo plane.

Leon.   Nolo ego te, qui erus sis, mihi onus istuc sustinere.

Argyr. Quin tu labore liberas te atque istam imponis in
      me?

Leon.   Ego baiulabo, tu, ut dacet dominum, ante me ito
      inanis.   660

Argyr. Quid nunc?

Leon.   Quid est?

Argyr.   Quin tradis huc cruminam pressatum
      umerum?

Leon.   Hanc, cui daturu's hanc, iube petere atque orare
      mecum.
      nam istuc proclive est, quo iubes me plane collocare.

Phil.   Da, meus ocellus. mea rosa, mi anime, mea
      voluptas,
      Leonidā, argentum mihi, ne nos diiunge amantis.

Leon.   Dic me igitur tuom passerculum, gallinam. co-
      turnicem,
      agnellum haedillum me tuom dic esse vel vitellum,
      prehende auriculis, compara labella cum labellis.

Argyr. Ten osculetur, verbero?

Leon.   Quam vero indignum visum est?
      at qui pol hodie non feres, ni genua confricantur.   670

Argyr. Quidvis egestas imperat : fricentur. dan quod oro?

        [1] Corrupt (Leo): *interioric* MSS : *interior* Bothe.

194

rgyr. Heaven prosper you for evermore, you guardian of your master, you glory of the populace, you storehouse of supplies, saviour of the inner man, and generalissimo of love! Put it here, hang that wallet here around my neck in plain sight.

eon. Let my master hear such a load? No sir, not I.

rgyr. Why not take things easy yourself and let me stand the strain?

eon. I'll act as porter myself; as for you, you walk on ahead as a master should, empty handed.

rgyr. (*eagerly*) Well now?

eon. (*drawling*) Well what?

rgyr. Why don't you hand the wallet over and let it crush my shoulder?

eon. She's the one, (*pointing to Philaenium*) the one you'll give it to, tell her to ask me for it, tease me for it. You see that plain site you told me to put it on is a (*with a sly glance at Philaenium*) slope.

hil. Oh, Leonida, you apple of my eye, my rosebud, my heart's delight, my darling, do give me the money! Don't separate us lovers.

eon. (*with burlesque fondness*) Well then, call me your little sparrow, hen, quail, call me your little lamb-kin, kidlet, or calfyboy, if you prefer: take hold of me by the earlaps and match my little lips to your little lips.

rgyr. She kiss you, you scoundrel?

eon. Yes, it does seem a shame, doesn't it? However, you don't get the cash this day, by gad, unless you rub my knees.

rgyr. " Need knows no shame." Rubbed they shall be. (*gets down on ground, with poor grace, and clasps Leonida's knees*) Won't you grant my prayer? (*gets up*)

Phil.   Age, mi Leonida, obsecro, fer amanti ero salutem,
        redime istoc beneficio te ab hoc, et tibi eme hunc
          isto argento.

Leon.   Nimis bella es atque amabilis, et si hoc meum
          esset, hodie
        numquam me orares quin darem: illum te orare
          meliust,
        illic hanc mihi servandam dedit. ei sane bella belle.
        cape hoc sis, Libane.

Argyr.   Furcifer, etiam me delusisti?

Leon.   Numquam hercle facerem, genua ni tam nequiter
          fricares.
        age sis tu in partem nunciam hunc delude atque
          amplexare hanc.

Lib.   Taceas, me spectes.

Argyr.   Quin ad hunc, Philaenium, adgredimur,   680
        virum quidem pol optimum et non similem furis
          huius?

Lib.   Inambulandum est: nunc mihi vicissim supplica-
          bunt.

Argyr.   Quaeso hercle, Libane, sis erum tuis factis sospi-
          tari,
        da mihi istas viginti minas. vides me amantem
          egere.

Lib.   Videbitur. factum volo. redito huc conticinno.
        nunc istanc tantisper iube petere atque orare
          mecum.

Phil.   Amandone exorarier vis ted an osculando?

196

Phil.   Come, dear Leonida, please, please save your master that loves me so! Buy your freedom from him by this kindness, buy his favour for yourself with this money! (*embraces him*)

Leon.   (*leering at her*) Ah, you're pretty, perfectly adorable: and if this belonged to me, I'd never let you tease me twice for it, never. But he's the one for you to tease: (*pointing to Libanus*) he gave it to me to keep for him. At him now, my pretty, prettily. Libanus, catch hold of this, will you! (*tosses him the wallet*)

Argyr.   What, you villain! Have you been making a fool of me?

Leon.   Bless you, sir, I wouldn't, only you made such a bad job of rubbing my knees. (*aside to Libanus*) Come on now, will you; you take your turn at fooling him and cuddling her.

Lib.   (*aside to Leonida*) Shut up: you watch me!

Argyr.   (*aside to Philaenium*) Why not make up to him, Philaenium? He's a very decent sort, Libanus is, gad yes, nothing like this thief. (*indicating Leonida*)

Lib.   (*aside as they approach*) Now for some strutting around: here's where I come in for being supplicated. (*parades magnificently back and forth*)

Argyr.   Hang it all, Libanus, for mercy's sake be a good fellow and save your master's life! Give me that eighty pounds. You see I'm in love and need the money.

Lib.   We'll see about it. Happy if I can oblige. Come back early in the evening. Meanwhile now just tell the lady there to ask me for it and tease me for it.

Phil.   Tease it from you by loving you, or by kissing you, which?

Lib.   Enim vero utrumque.

Phil.   Ergo, obsecro, et tu utrumque nostrum serva.

Argyr. O Libane, mi patrone, mi trade istuc. magis
decorumst

libertum potius quam patronum onus in via por-
tare.   690

Phil. Mi Libane, ocellus aureus, donum decusque amoris,

amabo, faciam quod voles, da istuc argentum nobis.

Lib.   Dic igitur med aniticulam, columbam vel catellum,

hirundinem, monerulam, passerculum putillum,

fac proserpentem bestiam me, duplicem ut habeam
linguam,

circumda torquem bracchiis, meum collum circum-
plecte.

Argyr. Ten complectatur, carnufex?

Lib.   Quam vero indignus videor?

ne istuc nequiquam dixeris tam indignum dictum
in me,

vehes pol hodie me, si quidem hoc argentum ferre
speres.

Argyr. Ten ego veham?

Lib.   Tun hoc feras argentum aliter a me?   700

Argyr. Perii hercle. si verum quidem et decorum erum
vehere servom,

inscende.

Lib.   Sic isti solent superbi subdomari.

asta igitur, ut consuetus es puer olim. scin ut dicam?

em sic. abi, laudo, nec te equo magis est equos
ullus sapiens.

Argyr. Inscende actutum.

198

b. Oh well, try both of 'em.

il. (*fondling him*) And both of us, then,—do rescue us, please, please!

gyr. O Libanus, my dear patron, do hand it over to me! A freedman is the proper person to carry a load on the street, not his patron.

il. My own Libanus, my little golden treasure boy, love's gift and glory, oh, I'll adore you, do anything for you, only give us that money!

b. Then call me your little ducky, dovey, doggieboy, your swallow, your little jackdaw, your little tootsie wootsie sparrowkin: (*opening his mouth*) make a reptile of me and let me have a double tongue in my mouth; throw a chain of arms around me; clasp me close around my neck.

gyr. Put her arms around you, you gallows-bird!

b. An awful shame, isn't it, really now? Not to have you saying such shameful things of me free of charge, you'll carry me on your back to-day, by gad, that is, if you count on getting this cash.

gyr. I carry you on my back—I?

b. See any other way of getting this cash, do you— you?

gyr. O damnation! Well, if it is right and proper for a master to carry a servant on his back—get up.

b. Here's how those toplofty ones are tamified. Now then, stand by—the way you used to do years ago as a boy. Know how I mean? (*Argyrippus sidles up and bends over*) There! That's it! Good for you! Capital! There isn't a more knowing bit of horse-flesh than you anywhere.

gyr. Get up, and be quick about it!

Lib.   Ego fecero. hem quid istuc est? ut tu incedis?
    demam hercle iam de hordeo, tolutim ni badizas.

Argyr. Amabo, Libane, iam sat est.

Lib.   Numquam hercle hodie exorabis.
    nam iam calcari quadrupedo agitabo advorsum cli-
        vom,
    postidea ad pistores dabo, ut ibi cruciere currens.
    asta ut descendam nunciam in proclivi, quamquam
        nequam es.   710

Argyr. Quid nunc, amabo? quoniam, ut est libitum, nos
    delusistis,
    datisne argentum?

Lib.   Si quidem mihi statuam et aram statuis
    atque ut deo mi hic immolas bovem: nam ego tibi
        Salus sum.

Leon. Etiam tu, ere, istunc amoves abs te atque[1] ipse me
        adgredere
    atque illa, sibi quae hic iusserat, mihi statuis suppli-
        casque?

Argyr. Quem te autem divom nominem?

Leon.   Fortunam, atque Obsequentem.

Argyr. Iam istoc es melior.

Lib.   An quid est homini Salute melius?

Argyr. Licet laudem Fortunam, tamen ut ne Salutem
    culpem.

Phil. Ecastor ambae sunt bonae.

Argyr.   Sciam ubi boni quid dederint.

Leon. Opta id quod ut contingat tibi vis.

Argyr.   Quid si optaro?

Leon.   Eveniet.   720

---

[1] Corrupt (Leo): *atque ad me adgredire* Langen.

ib.	(*springing on his shoulders*) So I will. (*Argyrippus moves off slowly*) Hullo! What's the matter? How you do jog along! By gad, I'll dock your barley directly, if you don't stir yourself and gallop. (*Argyrippus gallops*)
rgyr.	There's a good fellow, Libanus,—that's enough now!
ib.	Not on your life—you don't beg off this day. Why, now I'm going to dig the spurs in and trot you up a hill: afterwards I'll hand you over to the millers to do some running for 'em at the end of a rawhide. Stand still! so that I can dismount on the slope now, even though you are a good-for-nothing beast. (*gets off*)
rgyr.	How about it now? There's a good fellow! Seeing you two have had your fill of sport with me, going to give us the money, are you?
ib.	Oh well, if you put me up an altar and statue, yes, and offer me up an ox here the same as a god: for I'm your goddess Salvation, I am.
eon.	Come, sir, get rid of that chap, won't you, and apply to me in person, yes, and let me have those statues and supplications he ordered for himself.
rgyr.	Ah, and by what name does your godship pass?
eon.	Fortune, yes sir, Indulgent Fortune.
rgyr.	Now there's where you are better.
ib.	Eh? what's better for a man than Salvation?
rgyr.	I can praise Fortune and still not disparage Salvation.
hil.	Mercy me, they're both good.
rgyr.	I'll know so when I get something good out of them.
eon.	Wish for something you want to happen to you.
rgyr.	What if I do?
eon.	It'll come true.

Argyr. Opto annum hunc perpetuom mihi huius operas.

Leon.   Impetrasti.

Argyr. Ain vero?

Leon.   Certe inquam.

Lib.   Ad me adi vicissim atque experire.

exopta id quod vis maxime tibi evenire: fiet.

Argyr. Quid ego aliud exoptem amplius nisi illud cuius
        inopiast,

viginti argenti commodas minas, huius quas dem
matri.

Lib. Dabuntur, animo sis bono face, exoptata optingent.

Argyr. Ut consuevere, homines Salus frustratur et Fortuna.

Leon. Ego caput huic argento fui hodie reperiundo.

Lib. Ego pes fui.

Argyr.   Quin nec caput nec pes sermoni apparet.

nec quid dicatis scire nec me cur ludatis possum.   73•

Lib. Satis iam delusum censeo. nunc rem ut est elo-
        quamur.

animum, Argyrippe, advorte sis. pater nos ferre
hoc iussit

argentum ad ted.

Argyr. ·   Ut temperi opportuneque attulistis.

Lib. Hic inerunt viginti minae bonae, mala opera partae;

has tibi nos pactis legibus dare iussit.

Argyr.   Quid id est, quaeso?

Lib. Noctem huius et cenam sibi ut dares.

202

Argyr. My wish is to have this lady's attentions this whole next year through.

Leon. You've got it.

Argyr. Really? really?

Leon. Sure thing I tell you.

Lib. It's my turn—come over here and give me a trial. Long for something you most want to come true: it will.

Argyr. What could I long for more than something I haven't got a trace of—a round eighty pounds to give this girl's mother?

Lib. Forthcoming. Keep your courage up: your longing will be gratified.

Argyr. (*incredulous*) Salvation is at her old tricks, fooling people, and Fortune too.

Leon. In lighting on this cash to-day—I'm the one that's been the head of it!

Lib. I'm the one that's been the foot of it!

Argyr. And upon my soul, your discourse is a puzzle from head to foot. I can't understand your talk, or why you're making game of me.

Lib. (*aside to Leonida*) I move he's been fooled with long enough. Come on, let's out with it. (*to Argyrippus*) Your kind attention, Argyrippus! Your father told us to bring this money to you. (*holding up wallet*)

Argyr. Oh, you've brought it just in time, just at the right moment!

Lib. You'll find in here eighty good sovereigns ill-gotten: he said to give 'em to you according to terms agreed upon.

Argyr. Terms? What terms, for mercy's sake?

Lib. That you're to give him an evening with this lady, and a dinner.

Argyr.   Iube advenire quaeso:
meritissimo eius quae volet faciemus, qui hosce
    amores
nostros dispulsos compulit.

Leon.   Patierin, Argyrippe,
patrem hanc amplexari tuom?

Argyr.   Haec faciet facile ut patiar.
Leonida, curre obsecro, patrem huc orato ut veniat.   740

Leon.   Iam dudum est intus.

Argyr.   Hac quidem non venit.

Leon.   Angiporto
illac per hortum circum iit clam, ne quis se videret
huc ire familiarium: ne uxor resciscat metuit.
de argento si mater tua sciat ut sit factum—

Argyr.   Heia,
bene dicite.

Lib.   Ite intro cito.

Argyr.   Valete.

Leon.   Et vos amate.

ACTVS IV

Diab.   Agedum istum ostende quem conscripsti syngra-
        phum
        inter me et amicam et lenam.   leges pellege.
        nam tu poeta es prorsus ad eam rem unicus.

Par.   Horrescet faxo lena, leges cum audiet.

Diab.   Age quaeso mi hercle translege.

204

rgyr. Tell him to come along, yes, yes! We'll do what he wants, and quite right we should, after the way he's gathered our scattered love to the fold. (*takes wallet from Libanus*)

eon. Going to put up with your father's hugging her, are you, Argyrippus?

rgyr. (*waving wallet*) This will easily enable me to put up with it. Leonida, for heaven's sake run and beg my father to come here.

eon. (*pointing to Cleareta's house*) He was in there long ago.

rgyr. He certainly didn't come this way.

eon. Sneaked in by the alley there through the garden, so that none of the servants would see him enter: he's afraid of his wife finding out. If your mother was to learn about the money, how it was—

rgyr. Hold on there! No ominous remarks!

ib. In with you, quick!

rgyr. Good-bye, you two.

eon. And spoon away, you two.

[EXEUNT *Argyrippus* AND *Philaenium* INTO *Cleareta's* HOUSE, *Libanus* AND *Leonida* INTO HOUSE OF *Demaenetus*.

ACT IV

ENTER *Diabolus* AND *Parasite*.

iab. Come on, show me that contract you drew up between me and my mistress and the Madame. Read over the terms. Ah, you're the one and only artist at this business.

ar. (*producing a document*) I warrant you Madame will shudder when she hears the terms.

iab. Come come, man, for the Lord's sake let's have 'em!

H

Par.	Audin?	
Diab.	Audio.	750
Par.	" Diabolus Glauci filius Clearetae	

       lenae dedit dono argenti viginti minas,
       Philaenium ut secum esset noctes et dies
       hunc annum totum."

Diab.   Neque cum quiquam alio quidem.

Par.   Addone?

Diab.   Adde, et scribas vide plane et probe.

Par.   " Alienum hominem intro mittat neminem.
       quod illa aut amicum aut patronum nominet,
       aut quod illa amicae [1] amatorem praedicet,
       fores occlusae omnibus sint nisi tibi.
       in foribus scribat occupatam esse se.   760
       aut quod illa dicat peregre allatam epistulam,
       ne epistula quidem ulla sit in aedibus
       nec cerata adeo tabula; et si qua inutilis
       pictura sit, eam vendat: ni in quadriduo
       abalienarit, quo abs te argentum acceperit,
       tuos arbitratus sit, comburas, si velis,
       ne illi sit cera ubi facere possit litteras.
       vocet convivam neminem illa, tu voces;
       ad eorum ne quem oculos adiciat suos.
       si quem alium aspexit, caeca continuo siet.   770
       tecum una potet, aeque pocla potitet:
       abs ted accipiat, tibi propinet, tu bibas,
       ne illa minus aut plus quam tu sapiat."

---

[1] Leo notes slight lacuna here : *amicae suae* Gulielmius.

ar.   Are you listening?

iab.   Yes.

ar.   (*reading*) " Diabolus, son of Glaucus, has given to
          Cleareta, Madame, a present of eighty pounds to
          the end that Philaenium throughout the coming
          year may spend her nights and days with him."

iab.   Yes, and not with anyone else, either.

ar.   Shall I add that?

iab.   Add that, and see you put it down in a good firm
          hand.

ar.   (*after doing so*) " She is to admit no male outsider
          into her house.   In case she call him a mere friend
          or guardian, or in case she allege him to be the
          lover of a friend of hers, her doors must be closed
          to all but you.   She must post a notice on the
          doors stating that she is engaged.   Or in case
          she say that a letter from foreign parts has been
          delivered to her, there must be no letter at
          all in the house, nor so much as a waxen tablet;
          and if there be any undesirable picture about,
          let her sell it : unless she shall have removed it
          within four days after receipt of your money, it
          shall be at your disposal : you may burn it up, if
          you deem fit, that she may have no wax whereon
          to write.   She must invite no guest to the house :
          you shall invite them ; and she must have eyes
          for none of them.   If her glance has fallen on an-
          other man, she must become blind forthwith.   She
          must drink with you only, and drink with you glass
          for glass : let her receive the glass from your
          hands, drink to your health, and then do you take
          it and drink, so that she may have no—(*unobtru-
          sively dropping the aspirate*) whit more than you, nor
          less."

207

Diab.   Satis placet.

Par.   " Suspiciones omnes ab se segreget.

        neque illaec ulli pede pedem homini premat,

        cum surgat, neque cum in lectum inscendat pro-
           ximum,

        neque cum descendat inde, det cuiquam manum:

        spectandum ne cui anulum det neque roget.

        talos ne cuiquam homini admoveat nisi tibi.

        cum iaciat, ' te ' ne dicat : nomen nominet.   780

        deam invocet sibi quam libebit propitiam,

        deum nullum ; si magis religiosa fuerit,

        tibi dicat : tu pro illa ores ut sit propitius.

        neque illa ulli homini nutet, nictet, annuat.

        post, si lucerna exstincta sit, ne quid sui

        membri commoveat quicquam in tenebris."

Diab.   Optumest.

        ita scilicet facturam.   verum in cubiculo—

        deme istuc—equidem illam moveri gestio.

        nolo illam habere causam et votitam dicere.

Par.   Scio, captiones metuis.

Diab.   Verum.

Par.   Ergo ut iubes   790

        tollam.

Diab.   Quid ni?

Par.   Audi relicua.

Diab.   Loquere, audio.

Par.   " Neque ullum verbum faciat perplexabile,

        neque ulla lingua sciat loqui nisi Attica.

        forte si tussire occepsit. ne sic tussiat,

THE COMEDY OF ASSES

iab. (*not noticing*) Quite satisfactory.

ar. " She must keep herself above every suspicion. She must not touch feet with any man when she arises from table: and when she steps upon the adjoining couch, or steps down therefrom, she must take no one's hand. She must give no one her ring to look at, nor ask to look at his. To no man save yourself must she pass the dice. On making a throw she must not say, ' Thee [1] I invoke! ' She is to name your name. Let her call upon any goddess she pleases for favour, but upon no god; if she have religious scruples in regard to this, let her tell you, and do you make the prayer for his favour in her stead. To no man shall she nod, wink, or signify compliance. Further, if the lamp go out, she is not to move a single limb in the darkness."

iab. Excellent! To be sure she mustn't. (*pause*) But in our own room—cut that clause out—why, I'm keen as can be for her to be lively there! I don't want her to have an excuse and say the contract forbids.

ar. I see, you fear some catch.

iab. Exactly.

ar. Well then, I shall strike that out, as you order.

iab. Of course you will.

ar. Listen to the rest.

iab. Go on: I am listening.

ar. " She must use no phrase of double meaning, and must know how to speak no language but the Attic. If she should happen to cough, she is not to cough so, (*illustrating*) in such a way as to extend

---

[1] Naming one's sweetheart, on making a throw, was a common custom.

ut cuiquam linguam in tussiendo proserat.
quod illa autem simulet, quasi gravedo profluat,
hoc ne sic faciat: tu labellum abstergeas
potius quam cuiquam savium faciat palam.
nec mater lena ad vinum accedat interim,
nec ulli verbo male dicat. si dixerit, 800
haec multa ei esto, vino viginti dies
ut careat."

Diab.   Pulchre scripsti. scitum syngraphum.
Par.   "Tum si coronas, serta, unguenta iusserit
ancillam ferre Veneri aut Cupidini,
tuos servos servet, Venerine eas det an viro.
si forte pure velle habere dixerit,
tot noctes reddat spurcas quot pure habuerit."
haec sunt non nugae, non enim mortualia.

Diab. Placent profecto leges. sequere intro.
Par.   Sequor.

IV. 2.

Diab. Sequere hac. egone haec patiar aut taceam? emori 810
me malim, quam haec non eius uxori indicem.
ain tu? apud amicam munus adulescentuli
fungare, uxori excuses te et dicas senem?
praeripias scortum amanti atque argentum obicias
lenae? suppiles clam domi uxorem tuam?
suspendam potius me, quam tu haec tacita auferas.
iam quidem hercle ad illam hinc ibo, quam tu pro-
    pediem,

her tongue toward anyone. Moreover, in case she
pretends to have a running cold, she must not do
this : (*purses his lips*) you are to wipe her little lip
yourself rather than let her pucker up her mouth
for anyone so obviously. Nor shall the Madame,
her mother, drop in while you are having your
wine, or say a single abusive word to anyone. If
such a word be said by her, the penalty shall be
this—no wine for her for twenty days."

ab. Splendid document ! Capital contract !

r. " Then if she bid her maid carry chaplets, wreaths,
perfumes to Venus or to Cupid, your servant shall
observe whether she gives them to Venus, or to a
man. Should she happen to express a wish for
religious seclusion, she must give you as many
hours of love as she has of loneliness." These be no
trifles ; these be no dirges for dead folk, I tell you.

ab. The terms are highly satisfactory. Follow me in.

r. Very well.

[EXEUNT INTO *Cleareta's* HOUSE : SOUND OF WRANGLING
WITHIN : RE-ENTER *Diabolus* AND *Parasite* FROM HOUSE.

ene 2.

ab. (*incensed*) Come along ! I put up with this ? I hold
my tongue ? I'd rather perish from the earth than
not let it out to his wife ! (*shouting to Demaenetus
within*) You will, will you ? You will play the gay
young spark with a mistress and excuse yourself to
your wife on the plea of old age, eh ? You will snatch
a girl from her lover and toss your money to the
Madame, eh ? You will filch things from your lady
at home on the sly, eh ? I'd sooner hang myself
than let you carry it off so and nothing said. By
the Lord, I'll go to her this very minute, I will,
the woman you're bound to bring to pauperism

	nisi quidem illa ante occupassit te, effliges scio,	
	luxuriae sumptus suppeditare ut possies.	
Par.	Ego sic faciundum censeo: me honestiust,	820
	quam te palam hanc rem facere, ne illa existimet	
	amoris causa percitum id fecisse te	
	magis quam sua causa.	
Diab.	At pol qui dixti rectius.	
	tu ergo fac ut illi turbas lites concias;	
	cum suo sibi gnato unam ad amicam de die	
	potare, illam expilare narra.	
Par.	Ne mone.	
	ego istud curabo.	
Diab.	At ego te opperiar domi.[1]	

ACTVS V

Dem.	Numquidnam tibi molestumst, gnate mi, si haec	
	nunc mecum accubat?	830
Argyr.	Pietas, pater, oculis dolorem prohibet. quamquam	
	ego istanc amo,	
	possum equidem inducere animum, ne aegre patiar	
	quia tecum accubat.	
Dem.	Decet verecundum esse adulescentem, Argyrippe.	
Argyr.	Edepol, pater,	
	merito tuo facere possum.	

[1] Leo brackets following v., 828, 829:

Argyr.	*Age, decumbamus sis, pater.*
Dem.	*Ut iusseris,*
	mi gnate, ita fiet.
Argyr.	*Pueri, mensam adponite.*
Argyr.	Come, father, let's take our places, please.
Dem.	Just as you say, my dear boy.
Argyr.	(*to slaves*) Bring the table, my lads.

shortly,—if she doesn't forestall you, that is,—just
so that you may be kept in funds for your orgies!

r. (*calmly, judiciously*) In my opinion, this is the way
we should handle the case: it would look better
for me to appear in the matter than you; she
might think you were hard hit and did it more out
of jealousy than out of regard for her.

ab. Right you are, gad yes, that is better! Then raise
hell for him yourself; stir up a row; notify her
that he's having a daylight carouse with his own
son, one girl between 'em there at her house, and
she herself being rooked for it!

r. No advice needed! I shall take care of that.

ab. Well, I'll wait for you at home. [EXIT.

ACT V

THE DOOR OF *Cleareta's* HOUSE IS OPEN, SHOWING
Argyrippus, Demaenetus, AND *Philaenium* BANQUET-
ING, *Philaenium* BEING ON A COUCH BESIDE *Demaenetus*
AND TRYING NOT TO SEEM BORED BY HIS GALLANTRIES.

m. You don't mind it, do you, my boy,—her being on
the couch here with me? (*merrily chucks Philaenium
under the chin*)

gyr. (*dolefully*) My duty as a son takes the sting out of
the sight, father. Even though I do love her, of
course I can persuade myself not to be disturbed
at her being with you.

m. A young fellow should be modest, Argyrippus.

gyr. Ah yes, father, I can behave as you deserve.

Dem.   Age ergo, hoc agitemus convivium
vino et [1] sermoni suavi.   nolo ego metui, amari ma-
    volo,
mi gnate, me abs te.

Argyr.   Pol ego utrumque facio, ut aequom est filium.

Dem.   Credam istuc, si esse te hilarum videro.

Argyr.   An tu me tristem putas?

Dem.   Putem ego, quem videam aeque esse maestum ut
    quasi dies si dicta sit?

Argyr. Ne dixis istuc.

Dem.   Ne sic fueris: ilico ego non dixero.   839. 840

Argyr. Em aspecta: rideo.

Dem.   Utinam male qui mihi volunt sic rideant.

Argyr. Scio equidem quam ob rem me, pater, tu tristem
    credas nunc tibi:
quia istaec est tecum.   atque ego quidem hercle ut
    verum tibi dicam, pater,
ea res me male habet; at non eo, quia tibi non
    cupiam quae velis;
verum istam amo.   aliam tecum esse equidem facile
    possum perpeti.

Dem.   At ego hanc volo.

Argyr.   Ergo sunt quae exoptas: mihi quae ego exoptem
    volo.

Dem.   Unum hunc diem perpetere, quoniam tibi potesta-
    tem dedi,
cum hac annum ut esses, atque amanti argenti
    feci copiam.

Argyr. Em istoc me facto tibi devinxti.

Dem.   Quin te ergo hilarum das mihi?   849, 850

---

[1] *et* Pius: *ut* MSS.

m. (*jovially*) Come on then, let's have a lively banquet—wine and sweet converse, my dears! None of your filial awe for me: your love is what I want, my lad.

gyr. (*still more dolefully*) Ah yes, father, I give you both, as a son should.

m. I'll believe that, once I see you looking jolly.

gyr. (*with a deep sigh*) You don't think I'm ... melancholy ... do you?

m. Think so? When you look as sepulchral as if you were docketed for trial!

gyr. Don't say that.

m. Don't be that, and I'll stop saying it soon enough.

gyr. (*making a dismal effort to look happy*) Here now! See! I'm smiling.

m. (*dryly*) I wish my enemies were blessed with a smile like that.

gyr. Of course I know why you think my bearing toward you now is melancholy, father,—because she's with you. And good heavens, father, to tell you the truth, I—it does make me miserable; not because I'm not eager to have your wishes gratified; but I love that girl. If it was some other one, I shouldn't mind at all, really I shouldn't.

m. I want this one, though.

gyr. Well then, you've got your desire: I wish I could have the same luck!

m. Oh, you'll take it calmly this one day, now that I've given you the chance to be with her for a year, and furnished forth my young gallant with funds.

gyr. Just the point! You have me bound hard and fast by that.

m. Come then, surrender and be jolly, won't you?

V. 2.

Art. Ain tu meum virum hic potare, obsecro, cum filio
et ad amicam detulisse argenti viginti minas
meoque filio sciente id facere flagitium patrem?

Par. Neque divini neque mi humani posthac quicquam
accreduas,
Artemona, si huius rei me esse mendacem inveneris.

Art. At scelesta ego praeter alios meum virum[1] frugi
rata,
siccum, frugi, continentem, amantem uxoris maxume.

Par. At nunc dehinc scito illum ante omnes minimi
mortalem preti,
madidum, nihili, incontinentem atque osorem
uxoris suae.

Art. Pol ni istaec vera essent, numquam faceret ea quae
nunc facit.   860

Par. Ego quoque hercle illum antehac hominem semper
sum frugi ratus,
verum hoc facto sese ostendit, qui quidem cum filio
potet una atque una amicam ductet, decrepitus
senex.

Art. Hoc ecastor est quod ille it ad cenam cottidie.
ait sese ire ad Archidemum, Chaeream, Chaere-
stratum,
Cliniam, Chremem, Cratinum, Diniam, Demosthe-
nem:
is apud scortum corruptelae est liberis, lustris studet.

Par. Quin tu illum iubes ancillas rapere sublimen domum?

Art. Tace modo.   ne ego illum ecastor miserum habebo.

Par.   Ego istuc scio,
ita fore illi dum quidem cum illo nupta eris.

[1] Corrupt (Leo): *fui* Pylades: *fueram* Leo.

216

THE COMEDY OF ASSES

Scene 2. ENTER *Artemona* AND *Parasite* FROM HOUSE OF
Demaenetus.

Art. (*tempestuously*) What's that, for heaven's sake,—my
husband carousing here with his son, and brought
eighty pounds to a mistress, and my son conniving
at such an outrage on the part of his father, his
father?

Par. Never trust me in another thing divine or human,
madam, if you find I have misinformed you in this.

Art. But oh dear me! I thought my husband was the
very paragon of men, a sober man, a worthy, moral
man that loved his wife devotedly.

Par. But from now on you must realize that he is the
very scum of the earth, a toping man, a worthless,
immoral man that hates the wife of his bosom.

Art. Mercy yes! unless all that was true, he would never
be acting as he does now.

Par. I always thought he was a worthy man myself before to-day, upon my soul I did: but now he shows
himself in his true colours—carousing with his own
son and sharing his mistress with him, the old
ruin!

Art. Good gracious! This explains his going out to
dinner every day! He with his tales of going to
dine with Archidemus, Chaerea, Chaerestratus,
Clinia, Chremes, Cratinus, Dinias, Demosthenes—
and all the time corrupting his children at a harlot's,
haunting houses of ill fame!

Par. Why not tell your maids to pick him up and take
him off home?

Art. You just keep still. Oh, but I'll make life miserable for him, I swear I will!

Par. I have no doubt about that, just as long as he is
your husband.

217

Art.   Ego censeo.   870
      eum [1] etiam hominem in senatu dare operam aut
        clientibus,
      ibi labore delassatum noctem totam stertere:
      ille opere foris faciendo lassus noctu ad me advenit;
      fundum alienum arat, incultum familiarem deserit.
      is etiam corruptus porro suom corrumpit filium.

Par.   Sequere hac me modo, iam faxo ipsum hominem
        manifesto opprimas.

Art.   Nihil ecastor est quod facere mavelim.

Par.   Mane dum.

Art.   Quid est?

Par.   Possis, si forte accubantem tuom virum conspexeris
      cum corona amplexum amicam, si videas, cogno-
        scere?

Art.   Possum ecastor.

Par.   Em tibi hominem.

Art.   Perii.

Par.   Paulisper mane.   880
      aucupemus ex insidiis clanculum quam rem gerant.

Argyr. Quid modi, pater, amplexando facies?

Dem.   Fateor, gnate mi—

Argyr. Quid fatere?

Dem.   Me ex amore huius corruptum oppido.

Par.   Audin quid ait?

Art.   Audio.

Dem.   Egon ut non domo uxori meae
      subripiam in deliciis pallam quam habet, atque ad
        te deferam?
      non edepol conduci possum vita uxoris annua.

---

[1] Corrupt (Leo): *hominem (aut)* Camerarius.

rt.   (*too irate to notice unflattering accent*) Yes, indeed! He busy in the Senate or helping his clients! He wearied out by his labours there, there, that he spends the whole night snoring! It is business away from home that makes him turn up at night all weary—the business of ploughing other people's fields and leaving his own uncultivated. Corrupt himself, he actually goes on and corrupts his own son.

ar.   Just follow me this way : I'll soon make you drop on our gentleman in the very act.

rt.   Ah—h—h! There's nothing I'd like better!

ar.   Hm! wait! (*goes quietly to Cleareta's door, peeps in and comes back*)

rt.   What's the matter?

ar.   If you happened to spy your husband stretched out on a banquet couch with a garland on and a girl in his arms—if you saw him, could you recognize him?

rt.   Indeed I can!

ar.   (*taking her cautiously to the door*) Behold your man!

rt.   (*peeping*) Dreadful, dreadful!

ar.   (*drawing her aside*) Wait a bit! Let's lie in ambush and spy what's going on without being seen.

rgyr.   (*resentfully*) Father! When is that hug going to end?

em.   (*somewhat embarrassed*) I admit, my dear boy,—

rgyr.   Admit what?

em.   That this lady is altogether too much for my sense of decorum.

ar.   (*to Artemona*) Do you hear what he says?

rt.   I hear!

em.   (*to Philaenium*) Not steal my wife's pet mantle from home and bring it to you? By heaven, I couldn't be hired not to—not if she should die within the year.

Par.   Censen tu illum hodie primum ire adsuetum esse
       in ganeum?

Art.   Ille ecastor suppilabat me, quod ancillas meas
       suspicabar atque insontis miseras cruciabam.

Argyr.   Pater,
       iube dari vinum; iam dudum factum est cum
       primum bibi.   890

Dem.   Da, puere, ab summo. age, tu interibi ab infimo
       da savium.

Art.   Perii misera, ut osculatur carnufex, capuli decus.

Dem.   Edepol animam suaviorem aliquanto quam uxoris
       meae.

Phil.   Dic amabo, an fetet anima uxoris tuae?

Dem.   Nauteam
       bibere malim, si necessum sit, quam illam oscu-
       larier.

Art.   Ain tandem? edepol ne tu istuc cum malo magno
       tuo
       dixisti in me. sine, revenias modo domum, faxo
       ut scias
       quid pericli sit dotatae uxori vitium dicere.

Phil.   Miser ecastor es.

Art.   Ecastor dignus est.

Argyr.   Quid ais, pater?
       ecquid matrem amas?

Dem.   Egone illam? nunc amo, quia non adest.   900

Argyr.   Quid cum adest?

Dem.   Periisse cupio.

Par.   Amat homo hic te, ut praedicat.

Art.   Ne illa ecastor faenerato funditat: nam si domum
       redierit hodie, osculando ego ulciscar potissimum.

Par.   (*to Artemona*) Do you think to-day is the first time that gentleman has used such resorts?

Art.   Mercy on us! So he was the thief all those times I suspected my maids, yes, and tortured the poor innocent things.

Argyr.   Tell them to set the wine going, father; it seems an age since I had my first drink.

Dem.   (*to servant*) Boy, send round the wine from the head of the table. (*to Philaenium*) Come, my dear, meanwhile you send round a naughty, naughty kiss from the foot. (*Philaenium obeys*)

Art.   Oh-h-h! Good heavens! The way he kisses, the villain, fit only to grace a coffin!

Dem.   My word! Rather sweeter breath than my wife's!

Phil.   Do tell me, there's a dear—your wife's breath isn't bad, is it?

Dem.   I'd rather drink bilge water, if it came to that, than kiss her.

Art.   (*aside*) So? You would, would you? Good gracious, sir, that fling at me will cost you dear. Very well! just you come back home, sir! I'll show you the danger of vilifying a wife with money.

Phil.   Goodness me, you poor thing!

Art.   (*aside*) Goodness me, he deserves to be!

Argyr.   Look here, father. Do you love my mother?

Dem.   Love her? I? I love her now for not being near.

Argyr.   And when she is near?

Dem.   I yearn for a death in the family.

Par.   (*to Artemona*) This gentleman is fond of you, it seems.

Art.   (*aside*) Oh-h-h! won't he pay interest on that flow of words! Just let him come back home to-day, and that will be my favourite method of · revenge—kissing him.

Argyr. Iace, pater, talos, ut porro nos iaciamus.
Dem.   Maxime.
te, Philaenium, mihi atque uxoris mortem. hoc
    Venerium est.
pueri, plaudite et mi ob iactum cantharo mulsum
    date.
Art. Non queo durare.
Par.   Si non didicisti fulloniam,
non mirandum est.[1] in oculos invadi optumum est.
Art. Ego pol vivam et tu istaec hodie cum tuo magno
    malo invocavisti.
Par.   Ecquis currit pollictorem accersere?   910
Argyr. Mater, salve.
Art.   Sat salutis.
Par.   Mortuost Demaenetus.
tempus est subducere hinc me; pulchre hoc gliscit
    proelium.
ibo ad Diabolum, mandata dicam facta ut voluerit,
atque interea ut decumbamus suadebo, hi dum
    litigant.
poste demum huc cras adducam ad lenam, ut vi-
    ginti minas
ei det, in partem hac amanti ut liceat ei potirier.
Argyrippus exorari spero poterit, ut sinat
sese alternas cum illo noctes hac frui. nam ni im-
    petro,
regem perdidi: ex amore tantum est homini in-
    cendium.

[1] *non mirandumst,* (*Artemona.* Art.).   *In* Havet.

222

THE COMEDY OF ASSES

Argyr. (*pushing some dice toward Demaenetus*) Your throw, father: come, so that I can take my turn.

Dem. By all means. (*as he throws*) Here's to you for me, Philaenium, and my wife for the tomb! (*looking at throw*) Ha! The Venus![1] (*to servants*) A cheer, lads, and some mead from the tankard for that throw!

Art. (*aside to Parasite*) This is intolerable!

Par. (*aside to Artemona*) No wonder, if you never learned the fuller's[2] trade. Your best plan is to make a dash for his eyes.

Art. (*bursting into house*) My heavens, sir, I will live, and you shall pay dear for that petition of yours just now! (*tableau*)

Par. (*gleefully*) Run, some one, and fetch the undertaker!

Argyr. (*innocently*) How do you do, mother?

Art. Enough of your how d'ye do-ing!

Par. (*aside*) Demaenetus is dead. Time for me to retire from the scene; the battle waxes finely. I'll off to Diabolus and tell him his mandates are executed to the letter, yes, and suggest our taking dinner meantime, while they fight it out. Then to-morrow when it's over I'll bring him back to the Madame so that he may give her the eighty pounds and get her permission for his fond self to go shares in the girl here. I do hope Argyrippus can be induced to let him have her half the time. For if I don't get so much out of him, I have lost a patron— all one blaze of love, as the fellow is.

[EXIT *Parasite.*

---

[1] The highest throw.
[2] Fullers being accustomed to unpleasant smells.

Art. Quid tibi hunc receptio ad te est meum virum?

Phil.   Pol me quidem 920
miseram odio enicavit.

Art.   Surge, amator, i domum.

Dem. Nullus sum.

Art.   Immo es, ne nega, omnium unus pol nequissimus.
at etiam cubat cuculus. surge, amator, i domum.

Dem. Vae mihi.

Art.   Vera hariolare. surge, amator, i domum.

Dem. Abscede ergo paululum istuc.

Art.   Surge, amator, i domum.

Dem. Iam obsecro, uxor.

Art.   Nunc uxorem me esse meministi tuam?
modo, cum dicta in me ingerebas, odium, non
uxor eram.

Dem. Totus perii.

Art.   Quid tandem? anima fetetne uxoris tuae?

Dem. Murram olet.

Art.   Iam subrupuisti pallam, quam scorto dares?

Phil. Ecastor qui subrupturum pallam promisit tibi. 930

Dem. Non taces?

Argyr.   Ego dissuadebam, mater.

Art.   Bellum filium.
istoscine patrem aequom est mores liberis largirier?
nilne te pudet?

Art. (*to Philaenium*) What do you mean by receiving this man at your house—my husband?

Phil. Dear, dear! Why, I'm fairly bored to death by him, for my part.

Art. (*standing over Demaenetus*) Get up, my gallant; home with you!

Dem. (*half aside, afraid to move*) I'm a dead man!

Art. Good gracious, no! You're the vilest man living, and you needn't deny it. But he's roosting there still, the cuckoo! Get up, my gallant; home with you!

Dem. (*half aside*) Oh, I'm in for it!

Art. You are a true prophet. Get up, my gallant; home with you!

Dem. Well then, do stand a bit farther off.

Art. Get up, my gallant; home with you!

Dem. For heaven's sake now, my dear!

Art. Now you recollect that I am your dear, do you? A moment ago, when you were saying things about me, I was your abomination, not your dear.

Dem. (*half aside*) It's all up with me, absolutely!

Art. You really meant it, did you? Your dear's breath smells, does it?

Dem. (*hastily*) Smells of myrrh, myrrh!

Art. (*ironically*) Have you stolen the mantle yet to give this creature?

Phil. He promised he would steal it from you, indeed he did!

Dem. (*aside to Philaenium*) Shut up, won't you?

Argyr. I tried to dissuade him, mother.

Art. A pretty son! (*to Demaenetus*) Is this the way for a father to edify his children? Is there nothing you're ashamed of? (*helps him off the couch by the ear*)

225

Dem.   Pol, si aliud nil sit, tui me, uxor, pudet.

Art.   Cano capite te cuculum uxor ex lustris rapit.

Dem.   Non licet manere—cena coquitur—dum cenem
  modo?

Art.   Ecastor cenabis hodie, ut dignus es, magnum malum.

Dem.   Male cubandum est: iudicatum me uxor abducit
  domum.

Argyr. Dicebam, pater, tibi, ne matri consuleres male.

Phil.   De palla memento, amabo.

Dem.   Iuben hanc hinc abscedere?

Art.   I domum.

Phil.   Da savium etiam prius quam abis.

Dem.   I in crucem.   940

Phil.   Immo intro potius. sequere hac me, mi anime.

Argyr.   Ego vero sequor.

Dem. Oh Lord! You make me ashamed, my dear, if nothing else would.

Art. (*guiding him toward the door*) It's your dear that is dragging you from this den of vice, your hoary-headed cuckoo!

Dem. Mayn't I stay—dinner's being cooked—just till I've dined?

Art. Good heavens, sir! You shall dine as you deserve to-day—on dire distress.

Dem. (*aside*) It's a poorish night I'm in for: here I am sentenced, and my wife leading me off—home. (*Argyrippus and Philaenium follow them to door*)

Argyr. I kept telling you, father, not to play any tricks on mother.

Phil. Remember about the mantle, there's a dear!

Dem. (*to wife*) Tell her to get out of here, won't you?

Art. (*jerking him along*) Home with you!

Phil. Do give me another naughty, naughty kiss before we part.

Dem. Go to hell!

Phil. Oh no, inside, instead. (*to Argyrippus, as she goes back inside*) Come along with me, darling.

Argyr. Indeed I will.   [EXEUNT OMNES.

GREX

Hic senex si quid clam uxorem suo animo fecit
    volup,
neque novum neque mirum fecit nec secus quam
    alii solent;
nec quisquam est tam ingenio duro nec tam firmo
    pectore,
quin ubi quicque occasionis sit sibi faciat bene.
nunc si voltis deprecari huic seni ne vapulet,
remur impetrari posse, plausum si clarum datis.

EPILOGUE

(Spoken by the Company)

If this old gentleman has indulged his inclinations
a bit without informing his wife, he has done nothing new or strange, or different from what other
men ordinarily do. No one has such an iron
nature, such an unyielding heart, as not to do
himself a good turn whenever he has any chance.
So now in case you wish to beg the old fellow
off from a beating, we opine that you can succeed,
if you—give us some loud applause.

AULULARIA

OR

THE POT OF GOLD

ARGVMENTVM I

Senex avarus vix sibi credens Euclio
domi suae defossam multis cum opibus
aulam invenit, rursumque penitus conditam
exanguis amens servat.   eius filiam
Lyconides vitiarat.   interea senex
Megadorus a sorore suasus ducere
uxorem avari gnatam deposcit sibi.
durus senex vix promittit, atque aulae timens
domo sublatam variis abstrudit locis.
insidias servos facit huius Lyconidis
qui virginem vitiarat; atque ipse obsecrat   10
avonculum Megadorum sibimet cedere
uxorem amanti.   per dolum mox Euclio
cum perdidisset aulam, insperato invenit
laetusque natam conlocat Lyconidi.

ARGVMENTVM II

Aulam repertam auri plenam Euclio
Vi summa servat, miseris adfectus modis.
Lyconides istius vitiat filiam.
Volt hanc Megadorus indotatam ducere,
Lubensque ut faciat dat coquos cum obsonio.
Auro formidat Euclio, abstrudit foris.
Re omni inspecta compressoris servolus
Id surpit.   illic Euclioni rem refert.
Ab eo donatur auro, uxore et filio.

ARGUMENT OF THE PLAY (I)

A miserly old man named Euclio, a man who would hardly trust his very self, on finding a pot full of treasure buried within his house, hides it away again deep in the ground, and, beside himself with terror, keeps watch over it. His daughter had been wronged by Lyconides. Meanwhile an old gentleman, one Megadorus, is persuaded by his sister to marry, and asks the miser for his daughter's hand. The dour old fellow at length consents, and, fearing for his pot, takes it from the house and hides it in one place after another. The servant of this Lyconides, the man who had wronged the girl, plots against the miser; and Lyconides himself entreats his uncle, Megadorus, to give up the girl, and let him, the man that loves her, marry her. After a time Euclio, who had been tricked out of his pot, recovers it unexpectedly and joyfully bestows his daughter upon Lyconides.

ARGUMENT OF THE PLAY (II)

Euclio, on finding a pot full of gold, is dreadfully worried, and watches over it with the greatest vigilance. Lyconides wrongs his daughter. This girl, undowered though she is, Megadorus wishes to marry, and he cheerfully supplies cooks and provisions for the wedding feast. Anxious about his gold, Euclio hides it outside the house. Everything he does having been witnessed, a rascally servant of the girls' assailant steals it. His master informs Euclio of it, and receives from him gold, wife, and son.

233

PERSONAE.

LAR FAMILIARIS PROLOGVS
EVCLIO SENEX
STAPHYLA ANVS
EVNOMIA MATRONA
MEGADORVS SENEX
PYTHODICVS SERVVS

CONGRIO
ANTHRAX } COCI
STROBILVS SERVVS
LYCONIDES ADVLESCENS
PHAEDRIA PVELLA
TIBICINAE

DRAMATIS PERSONAE

THE HOUSEHOLD GOD OF EUCLIO, *the Prologue.*

EUCLIO, *an old gentleman of Athens.*

STAPHYLA, *his old slave.*

EUNOMIA, *a lady of Athens.*

MEGADORUS, *an old gentleman of Athens, Eunomia's brother.*

PYTHODICUS, *his slave.*

CONGRIO ⎱ *cooks.*
ANTHRAX ⎰

STROBILUS, *slave of Lyconides.*

LYCONIDES, *a young gentleman of Athens, Eunomia's son.*

PHAEDRIA, *Euclio's daughter.*

MUSIC GIRLS.

PROLOGVS

Lar Familiaris.

Ne quis miretur qui sim, paucis eloquar.
ego Lar sum familiaris ex hac familia
unde exeuntem me aspexistis.   hanc domum
iam multos annos est cum possideo et colo
patri avoque iam huius qui nunc hic habet.
sed mi avos huius obsecrans concredidit
thensaurum auri clam omnis : in medio foco
defodit, venerans me ut id servarem sibi.
is quoniam moritur—ita avido ingenio fuit—
numquam indicare id filio voluit suo,   10
inopemque optavit potius eum relinquere,
quam eum thensaurum commonstraret filio ;
agri reliquit ei non magnum modum,
quo cum labore magno et misere viveret.

Ubi is obiit mortem qui mihi id aurum credidit,
coepi observare, ecqui maiorem filius
mihi honorem haberet quam eius habuisset pater.
atque ille vero minus minusque impendio
curare minusque me impertire honoribus.
item a me contra factum est, nam item obiit diem.   20
is ex se hunc reliquit qui hic nunc habitat filium
pariter moratum ut pater avosque huius fuit.
huic filia una est.   ea mihi cottidie
aut ture aut vino aut aliqui semper supplicat,
dat mihi coronas.   eius honoris gratia
feci, thensaurum ut hic reperiret Euclio,
quo illam facilius nuptum, si vellet, daret

236

Scene :—Athens.   A street on which are the houses of Euclio and Megadorus, a narrow lane between them ; in front, an altar.

PROLOGUE

SPOKEN BY EUCLIO'S HOUSEHOLD GOD.

That no one may wonder who I am, I shall inform you briefly. I am the Household God of that family from whose house you saw me come. For many years now I have possessed this dwelling, and preserved it for the sire and grandsire of its present occupant. Now this man's grandsire as a suppliant entrusted to me, in utter secrecy, a hoard of gold : he buried it in the centre of the hearth, entreating me to guard it for him.   When he died he could not bear—so covetous was he— to reveal its existence to his own son, and he chose to leave him penniless rather than apprise him of this treasure. Some land, a little only, he did leave him, whereon to toil and moil for a miserable livelihood.

After the death of him who had committed the gold to my keeping, I began to observe whether the son would hold me in greater honour than his father had.   As a matter of fact, his neglect grew and grew apace, and he showed me less honour. I did the same by him : so he also died.   He left a son who occupies this house at present, a man of the same mould as his sire and grandsire.   He has one daughter. She prays to me constantly, with daily gifts of incense, or wine, or something : she gives me garlands.   Out of regard for her I caused Euclio to discover the treasure here in order that he might the more easily find her a husband,

1

nam eam compressit de summo adulescens loco.
is scit adulescens quae sit quam compresserit,
illa illum nescit, neque compressam autem pater.　　30
　　Eam ego hodie faciam ut hic senex de proxumo
sibi uxorem poscat.　id ea faciam gratia,
quo ille eam facilius ducat qui compresserat.
et hic qui poscet eam sibi uxorem senex,
is adulescentis illius est avonculus,
qui illam stupravit noctu, Cereris vigiliis.
sed hic senex iam clamat intus ut solet.
anum foras extrudit, ne sit conscia.
credo aurum inspicere volt, ne subreptum siet.

if he wished. For she has been ravished by a young gentleman of very high rank. He knows who it is that he has wronged; who he is she does not know, and as for her father, he is ignorant of the whole affair.

I shall make the old gentleman who lives next door here (*pointing*) ask for her hand to-day. My reason for so doing is that the man who wronged her may marry her the more easily. And the old gentleman who is to ask for her hand is the uncle of the young gentleman who violated her by night at the festival of Ceres. (*an uproar in Euclio's house*) But there is old Euclio clamouring within as usual, and turning his ancient servant out of doors lest she learn his secret. I suppose he wishes to look at his gold and see that it is not stolen.   [EXIT.

ACTVS I

Eucl.	Exi, inquam. age exi. exeundum hercle tibi hinc
	est foras, 40
	circumspectatrix cum oculis emissiciis.
Staph.	Nam cur me miseram verberas?
Eucl.	Ut misera sis
	atque ut te dignam mala malam aetatem exigas.
Staph.	Nam qua me nunc causa extrusisti ex aedibus?
Eucl.	Tibi ego rationem reddam, stimulorum seges?
	illuc regredere ab ostio. illuc sis vide,
	ut incedit. at scin quo modo tibi res se habet?
	si hercle hodie fustem cepero aut stimulum in
	manum,
	testudineum istum tibi ego grandibo gradum.
Staph.	Utinam me divi adaxint ad suspendium 50
	potius quidem quam hoc pacto apud te serviam.
Eucl.	At ut scelesta sola secum murmurat.
	oculos hercle ego istos, improba, ecfodiam tibi,
	ne me observare possis quid rerum geram.
	abscede etiam nunc—etiam nunc—etiam—ohe,
	istic astato. si hercle tu ex istoc loco
	digitum transvorsum aut unguem latum excesseris
	aut si respexis, donicum ego te iussero,

THE POT OF GOLD

ACT I

Eucl. (*within*) Out with you, I say! Come now, out with you! By the Lord, you've got to get out of here, you snook-around, you, with your prying and spying. ENTER *Staphyla* FROM *Euclio's* HOUSE, FOLLOWED BY *Euclio* WHO IS PUSHING AND BEATING HER.

Staph. (*groaning*) Oh, what makes you go a-hitting a poor wretch like me, sir?

Eucl. (*savagely*) To make sure you are a poor wretch, so as to give a bad lot the bad time she deserves.

Staph. Why, what did you push me out of the house for now?

Eucl. I give my reasons to you, you,—you patch of beats, you? Over there with you, (*pointing*) away from the door! (*Staphyla hobbles to place indicated*) Just look at her, will you,—how she creeps along! See here, do you know what'll happen to you? Now by heaven, only let me lay my hand on a club or a stick and I'll accelerate that tortoise crawl for you!

Staph. (*aside*) Oh, I wish Heaven would make me hang myself, I do! Better that than slaving it for you at this rate, I'm sure.

Eucl. (*aside*) Hear the old criminal mumbling away to herself, though! (*aloud*) Ah! those eyes of yours, you old sinner! By heaven, I'll dig 'em out for you, I will, so that you can't keep watching me whatever I do. Get farther off still! still farther! still— Whoa! Stand there! You budge a finger's breadth a nail's breadth, from that spot; you so much as turn your head till I say the word, and by the

241

     continuo hercle ego te dedam discipulam cruci.
     scelestiorem me hac anu certo scio   60
     vidisse numquam, nimisque ego hanc metuo male,
     ne mi ex insidiis verba imprudenti duit
     neu persentiscat aurum ubi est absconditum,
     quae in occipitio quoque habet oculos pessima.
     nunc ibo ut visam sitne ita aurum ut condidi,
     quod me sollicitat plurimis miserum modis.

Staph.   Noenum mecastor quid ego ero dicam meo
     malae rei evenisse quamve insaniam,
     queo comminisci; ita me miseram ad hunc modum
     decies die uno saepe extrudit aedibus.   70
     nescio pol quae illunc hominem intemperiae tenent:
     pervigilat noctes totas, tum autem interdius
     quasi claudus sutor domi sedet totos dies.
     neque iam quo pacto celem erilis filiae
     probrum, propinqua partitudo cui appetit,
     queo comminisci; neque quicquam meliust mihi,
     ut opinor, quam ex me ut unam faciam litteram
     longam, meum laqueo collum quando obstrinxero.

I. 2.
Eucl.   Nunc defaecato demum animo egredior domo,
     postquam perspexi salva esse intus omnia.   80
     redi nunciam intro atque intus serva.

Staph.   Quippini?
     ego intus servem? an ne quis aedes auferat?
     nam hic apud nos nihil est aliud quaesti furibus,
     ita inaniis sunt oppletae atque araneis.

Almighty, the next minute I'll send you to the gallows for a lesson, so I will. (*aside*) A worse reprobate than this old crone I never did see, no, never. Oh, but how horribly scared I am she'll come some sly dodge on me when I'm not expecting it, and smell out the place where the gold is hidden. She has eyes in the very back of her head, the hellcat. Now I'll just go see if the gold is where I hid it. Dear, dear, it worries the life out of me!

[EXIT *Euclio* INTO HOUSE.

ph. Mercy me! What's come over master, what crazy streak he's got, I can't imagine,—driving a poor woman out of the house this way ten times a day, often. Goodness gracious, what whim-whams the man's got into his head I don't see. Never shuts his eyes all night: yes, and then in the daytime he's sitting around the house the whole livelong day, for all the world like a lame cobbler. How I'm going to hide the young mistress's disgrace now is beyond me, and she with her time so near. There's nothing better for me to do, as I see, than tie a rope round my neck and dangle myself out into one long capital I.

ene 2.

RE-ENTER *Euclio* FROM HOUSE.

cl. (*aside*) At last I can feel easy about leaving the house, now I have made certain everything is all right inside. (*to Staphylu*) Go back in there this instant, you, and keep watch inside.

ph. (*tartly*) I suppose so! So I'm to keep watch inside, am I? You aren't afraid anyone'll walk away with the house, are you? I vow we've got nothing else there for thieves to take—all full of emptiness as it is, and cobwebs.

Eucl.　Mirum quin tua me causa faciat Iuppiter
　　　Philippum regem aut Dareum, trivenefica.
　　　araneas mihi ego illas servari volo.
　　　pauper sum; fateor, patior; quod di dant fero.
　　　abi intro, occlude ianuam.　iam ego hic ero.
　　　cave quemquam alienum in aedis intro miseris.　　　90
　　　quod quispiam ignem quaerat, extingui volo,
　　　ne causae quid sit quod te quisquam quaeritet.
　　　nam si ignis vivet, ut extinguere extempulo.
　　　tum aquam aufugisse dicito, si quis petet.
　　　cultrum, securim, pistillum, mortarium,
　　　quae utenda vasa semper vicini rogant,
　　　fures venisse atque abstulisse dicito.
　　　profecto in aedis meas me absente neminem
　　　volo intro mitti.　atque etiam hoc praedico tibi,
　　　si Bona Fortuna veniat, ne intro miseris.　　　100

Staph.　Pol ea ipsa credo ne intro mittatur cavet,
　　　nam ad aedis nostras numquam adit, quamquam
　　　　　prope est.

Eucl.　Tace atque abi intro.

Staph.　　　　　　　　Taceo atque abeo.

Eucl.　　　　　　　　　　　　　　Occlude sis
　　　fores ambobus pessulis.　iam ego hic ero.
　　　discrucior animi, quia ab domo abeundum est mihi.
　　　nimis hercle invitus abeo.　sed quid agam scio.
　　　nam noster nostrae qui est magister curiae
　　　dividere argenti dixit nummos in viros;
　　　id si relinquo ac non peto, omnes ilico
　　　me suspicentur, credo, habere aurum domi.　　　110

ucl. It is surprising Providence wouldn't make a King Philip or Darius of me for your benefit, you viper, you! (*threateningly*) I want those cobwebs watched! I'm poor, poor; I admit it, I put up with it; I take what the gods give me. In with you, bolt the door. I shall be back soon. No outsider is to be let in, mind you. And in case anyone should be looking for a light, see you put the fire out so that no one will have any reason to come to you for it. Mark my words, if that fire stays alive, I'll extinguish you instantly. And then water—if anyone asks for water, tell him it's all run out. As for a knife, or an axe, or a pestle, or a mortar,—things the neighbours are all the time wanting to borrow —tell 'em burglars got in and stole the whole lot. I won't have a living soul let into my house while I'm gone—there! Yes, and what's more, listen here, if Dame Fortune herself comes along. don't you let her in.

taph. Goodness me, she won't get in: she'll see to that herself, I fancy. Why, she never comes to our house at all, no matter how near she is.

ucl. Keep still and go inside. (*advances on her*)

taph. (*hurrying out of reach*) I'm still, sir, I'm going!

ucl. Mind you lock the door, both bolts. I'll soon be back.

[EXIT *Staphyla* INTO HOUSE.

It's agony having to leave the house, downright agony. Oh my God, how I do hate to go! But I have my reasons. The director of our ward gave notice he was going to make us a present of two shillings a man; and the minute I let it pass without putting in my claim, they'd all be suspecting I had gold at home, I'm sure they would. No, it

245

nam non est veri simile, hominem pauperem
pauxillum parvi facere quin nummum petat.
nam nunc cum celo sedulo omnis, ne sciant,
omnes videntur scire et me benignius
omnes salutant quam salutabant prius;
adeunt, consistunt, copulantur dexteras,
rogitant me ut valeam, quid agam, quid rerum ge-
    ram.
nunc quo profectus sum ibo; postidea domum
me rursum quantum potero tantum recipiam.

ACTVS II

Eun.   Velim te arbitrari med haec verba, frater,   120
meai fidei tuaique rei
causa facere, ut aequom est germanam sororem.
quamquam haud falsa sum nos odiosas haberi;
nam multum loquaces merito omnes habemur,
nec mutam profecto repertam ullam esse
aut hodie dicunt mulierem aut ullo in saeclo.
verum hoc, frater, unum tamen cogitato,
tibi proximam me mihique esse item te;
ita aequom est quod in rem esse utrique arbitremur
et mihi te et tibi me consulere et monere;   130
neque occultum id haberi neque per metum mus-
    sari,
quin participem pariter ego te et tu me ut facias.
eo nunc ego secreto ted huc foras seduxi,
ut tuam rem ego tecum hic loquerer familiarem.

246

doesn't look natural for a poor man to think so little of even a tiny bit of money as not to go ask for his two shillings. Why, even now, hard as I try to keep every one from finding out, it seems as if every one knew: it seems as if every one has a heartier way of saying good day than they used to. Up they come, and stop, and shake hands, and keep asking me how I'm feeling, and how I'm getting on, and what I'm doing. Well, I must get along to where I'm bound; and then I'll come back home just as fast as I possibly can.

[EXIT *Euclio.*

ACT II

ENTER *Eunomia* AND *Megadorus* FROM LATTER'S HOUSE.

un. Brother, I do hope you'll believe I say this out of my loyalty to you and for your welfare, as a true sister should. Of course I'm well enough aware you men think us women are a bother; yes, awful chatterboxes—that's the name we all have, and (*ruefully*) it fits. And then that common saying: "Never now, nor through the ages, never any woman dumb." But just the same, do remember this one thing, brother,—that I am closer to you and you to me than anyone else in the whole world. So both of us ought to advise and counsel each other as to what we feel is to either's advantage, not keep such things back or be afraid to speak out openly; we ought to confide in one another fully, you and I. This is why I've taken you aside out here now—so that we can have a quiet talk on a matter that concerns you intimately.

247

Mega. Da mi, optuma femina, manum.

Eun. Ubi ea est? quis ea est nam optuma?

Mega. Tu.

Eun.   Tune ais?

Mega.   Si negas, nego.

Eun. Decet te equidem vera proloqui;
nam optuma nulla potest eligi:
alia alia peior, frater, est.

Mega.   Idem ego arbitror,   140
ned tibi advorsari certum est de istac re umquam,
     soror.

Eun. Da mihi operam amabo.

Mega.   Tuast, utere atque impera, si quid vis.

Eun. Id quod in rem tuam optumum esse arbitror, ted
     id monitum advento.

Mega. Soror, more tuo facis.

Eun.   Factum volo.

Mega. Quid est id, soror?

Eun.   Quod tibi sempiternum
salutare sit: liberis procreandis—
ita di faxint—volo te uxorem
domum ducere.

Mega.   Ei occidi.

Eun.   Quid ita?   150

Mega. Quia mihi misero cerebrum excutiunt
tua dicta, soror: lapides loqueris.

Eun. Heia, hoc face quod te iubet soror.

Mega.   Si lubeat, faciam.

Eun. In rem hoc tuam est.

Mega. (*warmly*) Let's have your hand, you best of women!

un. (*pretending to look about*) Where is she? Who on earth is that best of women?

Mega. Yourself.

un. You say that—you?

Mega. (*banteringly*) Oh well, if you deny it—

un. Really now, you ought to be truthful. There's no such thing, you know, as picking out the best woman: it's only a question of comparative badness, brother.

Mega. My own opinion precisely: I'll never differ with you there, sister, you may count on that.

un. Now do give me your attention, there's a dear.

Mega. It is all your own: use me, command me—anything you wish.

un. I'm going to advise you to do something that I think will be the very best thing in the world for you.

Mega. Quite like you, sister.

un. I certainly hope so.

Mega. And what is this something, my dear?

un. Something that will make for your everlasting welfare. You should have children—God grant you may!—and I want you to marry.

Mega. Oh-h-h, murder!

un. How so?

Mega. Well, you're knocking my poor brains out with such a proposition, my dear girl: you're talking cobble-stones.

un. Now, now, do what your sister tells you.

Mega. I would, if it appealed to me.

un. It would be a good thing for you.

249

Mega.   Ut quidem emoriar prius quam ducam.
sed his legibus si quam dare vis ducam:
quae cras veniat, perendie foras feratur;
his legibus dare vis? cedo: nuptias adorna.

Eun.   Cum maxima possum tibi, frater, dare dote;
sed est grandior natu: media est mulieris aetas.
eam si iubes, frater, tibi me poscere, poscam.   160

Mega.   Num non vis me interrogare te?

Eun.   Immo, si quid vis, roga.

Mega.   Post mediam aetatem qui media ducit uxorem domum,
si eam senex anum praegnatem fortuito fecerit,
quid dubitas, quin sit paratum nomen puero Postumus?
nunc ego istum, soror, laborem demam et deminuam tibi.
ego virtute deum et maiorum nostrum dives sum satis.
istas magnas factiones, animos, dotes dapsiles,
clamores, imperia, eburata vehicla, pallas, purpuram,
nil moror quae in servitutem sumptibus redigunt viros.

Eun.   Dic mihi, quaeso, quis ea est quam vis ducere uxorem?

Mega.   Eloquar.   170
nostin hunc senem Euclionem ex proximo pauperculum?

Eun.   Novi, hominem haud malum mecastor.

Mega.   Eius cupio filiam
virginem mihi desponderi. verba ne facias. soror.
scio quid dictura es: hanc esse pauperem. haec pauper placet.

250

Mega.   Yes—to die before marrying. (*pause*) **All right,
I'll marry anyone you please, on this condition,
though**: her wedding to-morrow, and her wake
the day after. Still wish it, on this condition?
Produce her! Arrange for the festivities!

Eun.   I can get you one with ever so big a dowry, dear.
To be sure, she's not a young girl—middle-aged, as
a matter of fact. I'll see about it for you, brother,
if you want.

Mega.   You don't mind my asking you a question, I dare say?

Eun.   Why, of course not; anything you like.

Mega.   Now supposing a man pretty well on in life marries a lady of maturity and this aged female should
happen to show intentions of making the old fellow a father—can you doubt but that the name in
store for that youngster is Postumus? [1] See here,
sister, I'll relieve you of all this and save you
trouble. I'm rich enough, thanks be to heaven and
our forbears. And I have no fancy at all for those
ladies of high station and hauteur and fat dowries,
with their shouting and their ordering and their
ivory trimmed carriages and their purple and fine
linen that cost a husband his liberty.

Eun.   For mercy's sake tell me who you do want to
marry, then!

Mega.   I'm going to. You know the old gentleman—
rather hard up, poor fellow,—that lives next door,
Euclio?

Eun.   Yes indeed. Why, he seems quite nice.

Mega.   It's his daughter—there's the engagement I'm
eager for. Now don't make a fuss, sister. I know
what you're about to say—that she's poor. But
this particular poor girl suits me.

---

[1] The last born, or born after the father's death.

25

Eun. Di bene vortant.

Mega.   Idem ego spero.

Eun.   Quid me? num quid vis?

Mega.   Vale.

Eun. Et tu, frater.

Mega.   Ego conveniam Euclionem, si domi est.
            sed eccum video. nescio unde sese homo recipit
            domum.

II. 2.

Eucl. Praesagibat mi animus frustra me ire, quom exi-
            bam domo;
         itaque abibam invitus; nam neque quisquam curia-
            lium
         venit neque magister quem dividere argentum
            oportuit.   180
         nunc domum properare propero, nam egomet sum
            hic, animus domi est.

Mega. Salvos atque fortunatus, Euclio, semper sies.

Eucl. Di te ament, Megadore.

Mega.   Quid tu? recten atque ut vis vales?

Eucl. Non temerarium est, ubi dives blande appellat
            pauperem.
         iam illic homo aurum scit me habere, eo me salutat
            blandius.

Mega. Ain tu te valere?

Eucl.   Pol ego haud perbene a pecunia.

Mega. Pol si est animus aequos tibi, sat habes qui bene
            vitam colas.

Eucl. Anus hercle huic indicium fecit de auro, perspicue
            palam est,
         cui ego iam linguam praecidam atque oculos effo-
            diam domi.

Eun. God's blessing on your choice, dear!

Mega. I trust so.

Eun. (*about to leave*) Well, there's nothing I can do?

Mega. Yes—take good care of yourself.

Eun. You too, brother.   [EXIT *Eunomia.*

Mega. Now for an interview with Euclio, if he's at home. (*looking down street*) Hullo, though! here he is! Just getting back from somewhere or other.

Scene 2.   ENTER *Euclio.*

Eucl. (*without seeing Megadorus*) I knew it! Something told me I was going on a fool's errand when I left the house; that's why I hated to go. Why, there wasn't a single man of our ward there, or the director either, who ought to have distributed the money. Now I'll hurry up and hurry home: I'm here in the body, but that's where my mind is.

Mega. (*advancing with outstretched hand*) Good day to you, Euclio, yes, and the best of everything to you always!

Eucl. (*taking hand gingerly*) God bless you, Megadorus.

Mega. How goes it? All right, are you? Feeling as well as you could wish?

Eucl. (*aside*) There's something behind it when a rich man puts on that smooth air with a poor one. Now that fellow knows I've got gold: that's why he's so uncommon smooth with his salutations.

Mega. You say you are well?

Eucl. Heavens, no: I feel low, very low—in funds.

Mega. (*cheerily*) Well, well, man, if you have a contented mind, you've got enough to enjoy life with.

Eucl. (*aside, frightened*) Oh, good Lord! The old woman has let on to him about the gold! It's discovered, clear as can be! I'll cut her tongue out, I'll tear her eyes out, the minute I get at her in the house!

253

Mega. Quid tu solus tecum loquere?

Eucl.   Meam pauperiem conqueror.   190
     virginem habeo grandem, dote cassam atque inlo-
        cabilem,
     neque eam queo locare cuiquam.

Mega.   Tace, bonum habe animum, Euclio.
     dabitur, adiuvabere a me. dic, si quid opust,
        impera.

Eucl. Nunc petit, cum pollicetur; inhiat aurum ut
        devoret.
     altera manu fert lapidem, panem ostentat altera.
     nemini credo qui large blandust dives pauperi:
     ubi manum inicit benigne, ibi onerat aliqua zamia.
     ego istos novi polypos, qui ubi quidquid tetigerunt
        tenent.

Mega. Da mi operam parumper. paucis, Euclio, est quod
        te volo
     de communi re appellare mea et tua.

Eucl.   Ei misero mihi,   200
     aurum mi intus harpagatum est. nunc hic eam
        rem volt, scio,
     mecum adire ad pactionem. verum intervisam
        domum.

Mega. Quo abis?

Eucl.   Iam ad te revortar: nunc est quod visam domum.

Mega. Credo edepol, ubi mentionem ego fecero de filia,
     mi ut despondeat, sese a me derideri rebitur;
     neque illo quisquam est alter hodie ex paupertate
        parcior.

Eucl. Di me servant, salva res est. salvom est si quid
        non perit.
     nimis male timui. prius quam intro redii, exani-
        matus fui.
     redeo ad te, Megadore, si quid me vis.

Mega. What is that you're saying to yourself?

Eucl. (*startled*) Just . . . how awful it is to be poor. And I with a grown-up girl, without a penny of dowry, that I can't get off my hands or find a husband for.

Mega. (*clapping him on the back*) There, there, Euclio! Cheer up. She shall be married: I'll help you out. Come now, call on me, if you need anything.

Eucl. (*aside*) When he agrees to give he wants to grab! Mouth wide open to gobble down my gold! Holds up a bit of bread in one hand and has a stone in the other! I don't trust one of these rich fellows when he's so monstrous civil to a poor man. They give you a cordial handshake, and squeeze something out of you at the same time. I know all about those octopuses that touch a thing and then—stick.

Mega. I should be glad to have a moment of your time, Euclio. I want to have a brief talk with you on a matter that concerns us both.

Eucl. (*aside*) Oh, God save us! My gold's been hooked, and now he wants to make a deal with me! I see it all! But I'll go in and look. (*hurries toward house*)

Mega. Where are you off to?

Eucl. Just a moment! . . . I'll be back . . . the fact is . . . I must see to something at home. [EXIT INTO HOUSE.

Mega. By Jove! I suppose he'll think I'm making fun of him when I speak about his giving me his daughter; poverty never made a fellow closer-fisted.

RE-ENTER Euclio

Eucl. (*aside*) Thank the Lord, I'm saved! It's safe—that is, if it's all there. Ah, but that was a dreadful moment! I nearly expired before I got in the house. (*to Megadorus*) Here I am, Megadorus, if you want anything of me.

255

Mega.   Habeo gratiam.
quaeso, quod te percontabor, ne id te pigeat pro-
    loqui.   210
Eucl. Dum quidem ne quid perconteris quod non lubeat
    proloqui.
Mega. Dic mihi, quali me arbitrare genere prognatum?
Eucl.   Bono.
Mega. Quid fide?
Eucl.   Bona.
Mega.   Quid factis?
Eucl.   Neque malis neque improbis.
Mega. Aetatem meam scis?
Eucl.   Scio esse grandem, item ut pecuniam.
Mega. Certe edepol equidem te civem sine mala omni
    malitia
semper sum arbitratus et nunc arbitror.
Eucl.   Aurum huic olet.
quid nunc me vis?
Mega.   Quoniam tu me et ego te qualis sis scio,
quae res recte vortat mihique tibique tuaeque
    filiae,
filiam tuam mi uxorem posco. promitte hoc
    fore.
Eucl. Heia, Megadore, haud decorum facinus tuis factis
    facis,   220
ut inopem atque innoxium abs te atque abs tuis me
    inrideas.
nam de te neque re neque verbis merui ut faceres
    quod facis.
Mega. Neque edepol ego te derisum venio neque derideo,
    neque dignum arbitror.
Eucl.   Cur igitur poscis meam gnatam tibi?
Mega. Ut propter me tibi sit melius mihique propter te et
    tuos.

THE POT OF GOLD

Mega. Thanks. Now I trust you won't mind answering
the questions I'm going to ask.

Eucl. (*cautiously*) No-no—that is, if you don't ask any I
don't like to answer.

Mega. Frankly now, what do you think of my family connections?

Eucl. (*grudgingly*) Good.

Mega. And my sense of honour?

Eucl. Good.

Mega. And my general conduct?

Eucl. Not bad, not disreputable.

Mega. You know my age?

Eucl. Getting on, getting on, I know that—(*aside*) finan-
cially, too.

Mega. Now Euclio, I've always considered you a citizen
of the true, trusty type, by Jove, I certainly have,
and I do still.

Eucl. (*aside*) He's got a whiff of my gold. (*aloud*) Well,
what do you want?

Mega. Now that we appreciate each other, I'm going to
ask you—and may it turn out happily for you and
your girl and me—to give me your daughter in
marriage. Promise you will.

Eucl. (*whining*) Now, now, Megadorus! This is unlike
you, unworthy of you, making fun of a poor man
like me that never harmed you or yours. Why, I
never said or did a thing to you to deserve being
treated so.

Mega. Good Lord, man! I didn't come here to make fun
of you, and I'm not making fun of you: I couldn't
think of such a thing.

Eucl. Then why are you asking for my daughter?

Mega. Why? So that we may all of us make life pleasanter
for one another.

Eucl. Venit hoc mihi, Megadore, in mentem, ted esse
    hominem divitem,
factiosum, me autem esse hominem pauperum pau-
    perrimum;
nunc si filiam locassim meam tibi, in mentem venit
te bovem esse et me esse asellum: ubi tecum con-
    iunctus siem,
ubi onus nequeam ferre pariter, iaceam ego asinus
    in luto,   230
tu me bos magis haud respicias, gnatus quasi num-
    quam siem.
et te utar iniquiore et meus me ordo inrideat,
neutrubi habeam stabile stabulum, si quid divorti
    fuat:
asini me mordicibus scindant, boves incursent cor-
    nibus.
hoc magnum est periclum, ab asinis ad boves tran-
    scendere.
Mega. Quam ad probos propinquitate proxime te adiunxeris,
tam optumum est. tu condicionem hanc accipe,
    ausculta mihi,
atque eam desponde mi.
Eucl.   At nihil est dotis quod dem.
Mega.   Ne duas.
dum modo morata recte veniat, dotata est satis.
Eucl. Eo dico, ne me thensauros repperisse censeas.   240
Mega. Novi, ne doceas. desponde.
Eucl.   Fiat. sed pro Iuppiter,
num ego disperii?
Mega.   Quid tibi est?
Eucl.   Quid crepuit quasi ferrum modo?
Mega. Hic apud me hortum confodere iussi. sed ubi hic
    est homo?
abiit neque me certiorem fecit. fastidit mei,

258

ucl. Now here's the way it strikes me, Megadorus,—you're a rich man, a man of position: but as for me, I'm poor, awfully poor, dreadfully poor. Now if I was to marry off my daughter to you, it strikes me you'd be the ox and I'd be the donkey. When I was hitched up with you and couldn't pull my share of the load, down I'd drop, I, the donkey, in the mud; and you, the ox, wouldn't pay any more attention to me than if I'd never been born at all. You would be too much for me: and my own kind would haw-haw at me: and if there should be a falling out, neither party would let me have stable quarters: the donkeys would chew me up and the oxen would run me through. It is a very hazardous business for donkeys to climb into the ox set.

Mega. But honourable human beings—the more closely connected you are with them, the better. Come, come, accept my offer: listen to what I say and promise her to me.

ucl. But not one penny of dowry can I give.

Mega. Don't. Only let me have a girl that's good, and she has dowry enough.

ucl. (*forcing a laugh*) I mention this just so that you mayn't think I've found some treasure.

Mega. Yes, yes, I understand. Promise.

ucl. So be it. (*aside, starting at noise*) Oh, my God! Can it be I'm ruined, ruined?

Mega. What's the matter?

ucl. That noise? What was it—a sort of clinking sound?   [EXIT INTO HOUSE HURRIEDLY.

Mega. (*not noticing his departure*) I told them to do some digging in my garden here. (*looking around*) But where is the man? Gone away and left me—without a word! Scorns me, now he sees I de-

259

       quia videt me suam amicitiam velle : more homi-
          num facit ;
       nam si opulentus it petitum pauperioris gratiam,
       pauper metuit congrediri, per metum male rem
          gerit.
       idem, quando occasio illaec periit, post sero cupit.

Eucl. Si hercle ego te non elinguandam dedero usque ab
       radicibus,   250
       impero auctorque ego sum, ut tu me cuivis ca-
          strandum loces.

Mega. Video hercle ego te me arbitrari, Euclio, hominem
          idoneum,
       quem senecta aetate ludos facias, haud merito meo.

Eucl. Neque edepol, Megadore, facio, neque, si cupiam,
          copia est.

Mega. Quid nunc ? etiam mihi despondes filiam ?

Eucl.   Illis legibus,
       cum illa dote quam tibi dixi.

Mega.   Sponden ergo ?

Eucl.   Spondeo.

Mega. Di bene vertant.

Eucl.   Ita di faxint.   illud facito ut memineris,
       convenisse ut ne quid dotis mea ad te afferret filia.

Mega. Memini.

Eucl.   At scio quo vos soleatis pacto perplexarier :
       pactum non pactum est, non pactum pactum est,
          quod vobis lubet.   260

Mega. Nulla controversia mihi tecum erit.   sed nuptias
       num quae causa est quin faciamus hodie ?

sire his friendship! Quite the usual thing, that. Yes, let a wealthy man try to get the regard of a poorer one, and the poor one is afraid to meet him half-way: his timidity makes him injure his own interests. Then when it's too late and the opportunity is gone he longs to have it again.

RE-ENTER *Euclio.*

Eucl. (*to Staphyla within*) By heaven, if I don't have your tongue torn out by the very roots, I give you orders, give you full authority, to hand me over to anyone you please to be skinned alive. (*approaches Megadorus*)

Mega. Upon my word, Euclio! So you think I am the proper sort of man to make a fool of, at my time of life, and without the slightest reason.

Eucl. Bless my soul! I'm not making a fool of you, Megadorus: I couldn't if I would.

Mega. (*doubtfully*) Well now, do you mean I am to have your daughter?

Eucl. On the understanding she goes with the dowry I mentioned.

Mega. You consent, then?

Eucl. I consent.

Mega. And may God prosper us!

Eucl. Yes, yes,—and mind you remember our agreement about the dowry: she doesn't bring you a single penny.

Mega. I remember.

Eucl. But I know the way you folks have of juggling things: now it's on and now it's off, now it's off and now it's on, just as you like.

Mega. You shall have no occasion to quarrel with me. But about the marriage—there's no reason for not having it to-day, is there?

Eucl.   Immo edepol optuma.

Mega. Ibo igitur, parabo.   numquid me vis?

Eucl.   Istuc.   ei et vale.

Mega. Heus, Pythodice, sequere propere me ad macellum
strenue.

Eucl. Illic hinc abiit.   di immortales, obsecro, aurum
quid valet.[1]

id inhiat, ea affinitatem hanc obstinavit gratia.

Ubi tu es, quae deblateravisti iam vicinis omnibus,

meae me filiae daturum dotem?   heus, Staphyla,
te voco.

II. 3. ecquid audis?   vascula intus pure propera atque
elue: 270

filiam despondi ego: hodie huic nuptum Mega-
doro dabo.

Staph. Di bene vortant.   verum ecastor non potest, subi-
tum est nimis.

Eucl. Tace atque abi.   curata fac sint cum a foro redeam
domum;

atque aedis occlude;   iam ego hic adero.

Staph.   Quid ego nunc agam?

nunc nobis prope adest exitium, mi atque erili
filiae,

nunc probrum atque partitudo prope adest ut fiat
palam;

quod celatum atque occultatum est usque adhuc,
nunc non potest.

ibo intro, ut erus quae imperavit facta, cum veniat,
sient.

nam ecastor malum maerore metuo ne mixtum
bibam.

---

[1] Leo brackets following v., 266 :   *credo ego illum iam
inaudivisse mi esse thensaurum domi.*

ucl. Dear, dear, no! The very thing, the very thing!

Mega. I'll go and make arrangements, then. (*turning to leave*) Anything else I can do?

ucl. Only that. Go along. Good-bye.

Mega. (*calling at the door of his house*) Hey, Pythodicus! quick! [ENTER *Pythodicus*] Down to the market with me—come, look alive! [EXEUNT.

ucl. (*looking after them*) He's gone! Ah, ye immortal gods, doesn't money count! That is what he's gaping after. That is why he's so set on being my son-in-law. (*goes to the door and calls*) Where are you, you blabber, telling the whole neighbourhood I'm going to give my daughter a dowry! Hi-i! Staphyla! It's you I'm calling. Can't you hear!

Scene 3.

[ENTER *Staphyla*] Hurry up with the dishes inside there and give them a good scouring. I have betrothed my daughter: she marries Megadorus here to-day.

Staph. God bless them! (*hastily*) Goodness, though! It can't be done. This is too sudden.

ucl. Silence! Off with you! Have things ready by the time I get back from the forum. And lock the door, mind; I shall be here soon. [EXIT *Euclio*.

Staph. What shall I do now? Now we're all but ruined, the young mistress and me: now it's all but public property about her being disgraced and brought to bed. We can't conceal it, we can't keep it dark any longer now. But I must go in and do what master ordered me before he gets back. Oh deary me! I'm afraid I've got to take a drink of trouble and tribulation mixed.

[EXIT *Staphyla* INTO HOUSE.

II. 4.

Pyth. Postquam obsonavit erus et conduxit coquos 280
    tibicinasque hasce apud forum, edixit mihi
    ut dispertirem obsonium hic bifariam.

Anthr. Me quidem hercle, dicam tibi palam, non divides.
    si quo tu totum me ire vis, operam dabo.

Cong. Bellum et pudicum vero prostibulum popli.
    post si quis vellet, te haud non velles dividi.

Pyth. Atque ego istuc, Anthrax, alio vorsum dixeram,
    non istuc quo tu insimulas. sed erus nuptias
    meus hodie faciet.

Anthr.   Cuius ducit filiam?

Pyth. Vicini huius Euclionis senis e proximo. 290
    ei adeo obsoni hinc iussit dimidium dari,
    cocum alterum itidemque alteram tibicinam.

Anthr. Nempe huc dimidium dicis, dimidium domum?

Pyth. Nempe sicut dicis.

Anthr.   Quid? hic non poterat de suo
    senex obsonari filiai nuptiis?

Pyth. Vah.

Anthr.   Quid negotist?

Pyth.   Quid negoti sit rogas?
    pumex non aeque est aridus atque hic est senex.
    264

Scene 4.   (*An hour has elapsed.*)

ENTER *Pythodicus* BRINGING COOKS, *Anthrax* AND *Congrio*, MUSIC GIRLS, *Phrygia* AND *Eleusium*, AND ATTENDANTS, WITH PROVISIONS FROM THE MARKET AND TWO LAMBS.

Pyth. (*importantly*) After master did the marketing and hired the cooks and these music girls at the forum, he told me to take and divide all he'd got into two parts.

Anthr. By Jupiter, you shan't make two parts of me, let me tell you that plainly! If you'd like to have the whole of me anywhere, why, I'll accommodate you.

Cong. (*to Anthrax*) You pretty boy, yes, you nice little everybody's darling, you! Why, if anyone wanted to make two parts of a real man out of you, you oughtn't to be cut up about it.

Pyth. Now, now, Anthrax, I mean that otherwise from what you make out. Look here, my master's marrying to-day.

Anthr. Who's the lady?

Pyth. Daughter of old Euclio that lives next door here. Yes sir, and what's more, he's to have half this stuff here, and one cook and one music girl, too, so master said.

Anthr. You mean to say half goes to him and half to you folks?

Pyth. Just what I do mean.

Anthr. I say, couldn't the old boy pay for the catering for his daughter's wedding his own self?

Pyth. (*scornfully*) Pooh!

Anthr. What's the matter?

Pyth. The matter, eh? You couldn't squeeze as much out of that old chap as you could out of a pumice stone.

Anthr. Ain tandem?

Pyth.   Ita esse ut dixi. tute existuma:
quin divom atque hominum clamat continuo fidem,[1]
suam rem periisse seque eradicarier,   300
de suo tigillo fumus si qua exit foras.
quin cum it dormitum, follem obstringit ob gulam.

Anthr. **Cur?**

Pyth.   ′ Ne quid animae forte amittat dormiens.

Anthr. Etiamne obturat inferiorem gutturem,
ne quid animai forte amittat dormiens?

Pyth. Haec mihi te ut tibi med aequom est, credo, credere.

Anthr. Immo equidem credo.

Pyth.   At scin etiam quomodo?
aquam hercle plorat, cum lavat, profundere.

Anthr. Censen talentum magnum exorari pote
ab istoc sene ut det, qui fiamus liberi?   310

Pyth. Famem hercle utendam si roges, numquam dabit.
quin ipsi pridem tonsor unguis dempserat:
collegit, omnia abstulit praesegmina.

Anthr. Edepol mortalem parce parcum praedicas.

Pyth. Censen vero adeo esse parcum et miserum vivere?
pulmentum pridem ei eripuit milvos:
homo ad praetorem plorabundus devenit;
infit ibi postulare plorans, eiulans,
ut sibi liceret milvom vadarier.

---

[1] 299, 300 inverted, Gulielmius. Leo, following Havet,
assumes lacuna after 298.

Anthr. (*incredulously*) Oh, really now!

Pyth. That's a fact. Judge for yourself. Why, I tell you he begins bawling for heaven and earth to witness that he's bankrupt, gone to everlasting smash, the moment a puff of smoke from his beggarly fire manages to get out of his house. Why, when he goes to bed he strings a bag over his jaws.

Anthr. What for?

Pyth. So as not to chance losing any breath when he's asleep.

Anthr. Oh yes! And he puts a stopper on his lower windpipe, doesn't he, so as not to chance losing any breath while he's asleep?

Pyth. (*ingenuously*) You should believe me, I believe, just as I should believe you.

Anthr. (*hurriedly*) Oh, no, no! I do believe, of course!

Pyth. But listen to this, will you? Upon my word, after he takes a bath it just breaks him all up to throw away the water.

Anthr. D'ye think the old buck could be induced to make us a present of a couple of hundred pounds to buy ourselves off with?

Pyth. Lord! He wouldn't make you a loan of his hunger, no sir, not if you begged him for it. Why, the other day when a barber cut his nails for him he collected all the clippings and took 'em home.

Anthr. My goodness, he's quite a tight one, from what you say.

Pyth. Honest now, would you believe a man could be so tight and live so wretched? Once a kite flew off with a bit of food of his: down goes the fellow to the magistrate's, blubbering all the way, and there he begins, howling and yowling, demanding to have the kite bound over for trial. Oh, I could tell

267

sescenta sunt quae memorem, si sit otium.   320
sed uter vestrorum est celerior?   memora mihi.

Anthr. Ego, et multo melior.

Pyth.   Cocum ego, non furem rogo.

Anthr. Cocum ergo dico.

Pyth.   Quid tu ais?

Cong.   Sic sum ut vides.

Anthr. Cocus ille nundinalest, in nonum diem
solet ire coctum.

Cong.   Tun, trium litterarum homo
me vituperas?   fur.

Anthr.   Etiam fur, trifurcifer.

II. 5.

Pyth. Tace nunciam tu, atque agnum hinc uter est pin-
        guior
cape atque abi intro ad nos.

Anthr.   Licet.

Pyth.   Tu, Congrio,
quem illic reliquit agnum, eum sume atque abi
[1] intro illuc, et vos illum sequimini.
vos ceteri ite huc ad nos.

Cong.   Hercle iniuria   330
dispertivisti: pinguiorem agnum isti habent.

Pyth. At nunc tibi dabitur pinguior tibicina.
i sane cum illo, Phrugia.   tu autem, Eleusium,
huc intro abi ad nos.

Cong.   O Pythodice subdole,
hucine detrusti me ad senem parcissimum?
ubi si quid poscam, usque ad ravim poscam prius
quam quicquam detur.

                [1] Leo notes lacuna here : *etiam tu* Leo.

268

       hundreds of stories about him if I had time. (*to both cooks*) But which of you is the quicker? Tell me that.

nthr. I am, and a whole lot better, too.

yth. At cooking I mean, not thieving.

nthr. Well, I mean cooking.

yth. (*to Congrio*) And how about you?

ong. (*with a meaning glance at Anthrax*) I'm what I look.

nthr. He's nothing but a market-day cook, that chap: he only gets a job once a week.

ong. You running me down, you? You five letter man, you! You T-H-I-E-F!

nthr. Five letter man yourself! Yes, and five times —penned!

cene 5.

yth. (*to Anthrax*) Come, come, shut up, you: and this fattest lamb here, (*pointing*) take it and go over to our house.

nthr. (*grinning triumphantly at Congrio*) Aye, aye, sir.

       [EXIT *Anthrax* INTO HOUSE OF *Megadorus* LEADING LAMB.

yth. Congrio, you take this one he's left (*pointing*) and go into that house there, (*pointing to Euclio's*) and as for you, (*indicating some of the attendants*) you follow him. The rest of you come over to our house.

ong. Hang it! That's no way to divide: they've got the fattest lamb.

yth. Oh well, I'll give you the fattest music girl. (*turning to girls*) That means you, Phrygia: you go with him. As for you, Eleusium, you step over to our place. [EXEUNT *Eleusium* AND OTHERS INTO HOUSE OF *Megadorus*.

ong. Oh, you're a wily one, Pythodicus! Shoving me off on this old screw, eh? If I ask for anything there, I can ask myself hoarse before I get a thing.

K

TITUS MACCIUS PLAUTUS

Pyth.   Stultus et sine gratia es.
[1] tibi recte facere, quando quod facias perit.

Cong. Qui vero?

Pyth.   Rogitas? iam principio in aedibus
turba istic nulla tibi erit: siquid uti voles,   340
domo abs te adferto, ne operam perdas poscere.
hic autem apud nos magna turba ac familia est
supellex, aurum, vestis, vasa argentea:
ibi si perierit quippiam—quod te scio
facile abstinere posse, si nihil obviam est—
dicant: coqui abstulerunt, comprehendite,
vincite, verberate, in puteo condite.
horum tibi istic nihil eveniet: quippe qui
ubi quid subripias nihil est. sequere hac me.

Cong.   Sequor.

II. 6.

Pyth. Heus, Staphyla, prodi atque ostium aperi.

Staph.   Qui vocat? 350

Pyth. Pythodicus.

Staph.   Quid vis?

Pyth.   Hos ut accipias coquos
tibicinamque obsoniumque in nuptias.
Megadorus iussit Euclioni haec mittere.

Staph. Cererin, Pythodice, has sunt facturi nuptias?

Pyth. Qui?

---

[1] Corrupt (Leo): *stultu's et sine gratiast ibi* Gulielmius.

Pyth. An ungrateful blockhead is what you are. The idea of doing you a favour, when it's only thrown away!

Cong. Eh? How so?

Pyth. How so? Well, in the first place there won't be an uproarious gang in that house to get in your way: if you need anything, just you fetch it from home so as not to waste time asking for it. Here at our establishment, though, we do have a great big uproarious gang of servants, and knick-knackery and jewellery and clothes and silver plate lying about. Now if anything was missing, —of course it's easy for you to keep your hands off, provided there's nothing in reach,—they'd say: " The cooks got away with it! Collar 'em! Tie 'em up! Thrash 'em! Throw 'em in the dungeon!" Now over there (*pointing to Euclio's*) nothing like this will happen to you—as there's nothing at all about for you to filch. (*going toward Euclio's house*) Come along.

Cong. (*sulkily*) Coming. (*he and the rest follow*)

Scene 6.

Pyth. (*knocking at door*) Hey! Staphyla! Come here and open the door.

Staph. (*within*) Who is it?

Pyth. Pythodicus.

Staph. (*sticking her head out*) What do you want?

Pyth. Take these cooks and the music girl and the supplies for the wedding festival. Megadorus told us to take 'em over to Euclio's.

Staph. (*examining the provisions disappointedly*) Whose festival are they going to celebrate, Pythodicus? Ceres'?

Pyth. Why hers?

271

Staph.	Quia temeti nihil allatum intellego.
Pyth.	At iam afferetur, si a foro ipsus redierit.
Staph.	Ligna hic apud nos nulla sunt.
Cong.	Sunt asseres?
Staph.	Sunt pol.
Cong.	Sunt igitur ligna, ne quaeras foris.
Staph.	Quid, impurate? quamquam Volcano studes,

cenaene causa aut tuae mercedis gratia   360
nos nostras aedis postulas comburere?

Cong.	Haud postulo.
Pyth.	Duc istos intro.
Staph.	Sequimini.

II. 7.

Pyth.   Curate.   ego intervisam quid faciant coqui;
quos pol ut ego hodie servem, cura maxuma est.
nisi unum hoc faciam, ut in puteo cenam coquant:
inde coctam sursum subducemus corbulis.
si autem deorsum comedent, si quid coxerint,
superi incenati sunt et cenati inferi.
sed verba hic facio, quasi negoti nil siet,
rapacidarum ubi tantum sit in aedibus.   370

II. 8.
Eucl.   Volui animum tandem confirmare hodie meum,
ut bene me haberem filiai nuptiis.

Staph. Well, no tipple's [1] been brought, as I notice.

Pyth. But there'll be some all right when the old gent gets back from the forum.

Staph. We haven't got any firewood in the house.

Cong. Any rafters in it?

Staph. Mercy, yes.

Cong. There's firewood in it, then: never mind going for any.

Staph. Hey? You godless thing! even though you are a devotee of Vulcan, do you want us to burn our house down, all for your dinner or your pay? (*advances on him*)

Cong. (*shrinking back*) I don't, I don't!

Pyth. Take 'em inside.

Staph. (*brusquely*) This way with you.

[EXEUNT *Congrio* AND OTHERS INTO *Euclio's* HOUSE.

Scene 7.

Pyth. (*as they leave*) Look out for things. (*starting for Megadorus's house*) I'll go see what the cooks are at. By gad, it's the devil's own job keeping an eye on those chaps. The only way is to make 'em cook dinner in the dungeon and then haul it up in baskets when it's done. Even so, though, if they're down there gobbling up all they cook, it's a case of starve in heaven and stuff in hell. But here I am gabbling away just as if there wasn't anything to do, and the house all full of those young Grabbits. [EXIT *Pythodicus.*

Scene 8. ENTER *Euclio* FROM FORUM CARRYING A SMALL PACKAGE AND A FEW FORLORN FLOWERS.

Eucl. Now I did want to be hearty to-day, and do the handsome thing for daughter's wedding, yes

---

[1] The use of wine was forbidden at the festival called the *Cereris nuptiae.*

venio ad macellum, rogito pisces: indicant
caros; agninam caram, caram bubulam,
vitulinam, cetum, porcinam: cara omnia.
atque eo fuerunt cariora, aes non erat.
abeo iratus illinc, quoniam nihil est qui emam.
ita illis impuris omnibus adii manum.
deinde egomet mecum cogitare intervias
occepi: festo die si quid prodegeris,   380
profesto egere liceat, nisi peperceris.
postquam, hanc rationem ventri cordique edidi,
accessit animus ad meam sententiam,
quam minimo sumptu filiam ut nuptum darem.
nunc tusculum emi hoc et coronas floreas:
haec imponentur in foco nostro Lari,
ut fortunatas faciat gnatae nuptias.
sed quid ego apertas aedis nostras conspicor?
et strepitust intus. numnam ego compilor miser?

Cong. Aulam maiorem, si pote, ex vicinia   390
   pete: haec est parva, capere non quit.

Eucl.   Ei mihi,
perii hercle. aurum rapitur, aula quaeritur.[1]
Apollo, quaeso, subveni mi atque adiuva,
confige sagittis fures thensaurarios,
si cui in re tali iam subvenisti antidhac.
sed cesso prius quam prorsus perii currere?

II. 9.
Anthr. Dromo, desquama piscis. tu, Machaerio,
   congrum, murenam exdorsua quantum potest.

---

[1] Leo brackets following v., 393: *nimirum occidor, nisi
ego intro huc propere propero currere.*

I did. Off I go to the market—ask for fish!
Very dear! And lamb dear . . . and beef dear
. . . and veal and tunny and pork . . . everything
dear, everything! Yes, and all the dearer for my
not having any money! It just made me furious,
and seeing I couldn't buy anything, I up and left.
That's how I circumvented 'em, the whole dirty
pack of 'em. Then I began to reason things out
with myself as I walked along. " Holiday feasting
makes everyday fasting," says I to myself, " unless
you economize." After I'd put the case this way
to my stomach and heart, my mind supported my
motion to cut down daughter's wedding expenses
just as much as possible. Now I've bought a little
frankincense here and some wreaths of flowers:
we'll put 'em on the hearth in honour of our
Household God, so that he may bless daughter's
marriage. (*looking toward house*) Eh! What's my
door open for? A clattering inside, too! Oh,
mercy on us! It can't be burglars, can it?

ong. (*within, to an attendant*) See if you can't get a bigger
pot from one of the neighbours: this here's a little
one: it won't hold it all.

ucl. Oh, my God! my God! I'm ruined! They're
taking my gold! They're after my pot! Oh, oh,
Apollo, help me, save me! Shoot your arrows
through them, the treasure thieves, if you've ever
helped a man in such a pinch before! But I
must rush in before they ruin me entirely!

[EXIT *Euclio.*

cene 9.   ENTER *Anthrax* FROM HOUSE OF *Megadorus.*

nthr. (*to servants inside*) Dromo, scale the fish. As for
you, Machaerio, you bone the conger and lamprey
as fast as you know how. I'm going over next

275

ego hinc artoptam ex proximo utendam peto   400
a Congrione.   tu istum gallum, si sapis,
glabriorem reddes mihi quam volsus ludiust.
sed quid hoc clamoris oritur hinc ex proximo?
coqui hercle, credo, faciunt officium suom.
fugiam intro, ne quid turbae hic itidem fuat.

ACTVS III

Cong. Attatae! cives,[1] populares, incolae, accolae, advenae
    omnes,
date viam qua fugere liceat, facite totae plateae
    pateant.
neque ego umquam nisi hodie ad Bacchas veni in
    Bacchanal coquinatum,
ita me miserum et meos discipulos fustibus male
    contuderunt.
totus doleo atque oppido perii, ita me iste habuit
    senex gymnasium;   410
    attat, perii hercle ego miser,
aperit bacchanal, adest,   411a
sequitur.   scio quam rem geram: hoc
ipsus magister me docuit.   412a
neque ligna ego usquam gentium praeberi vidi pul-
    chrius,
itaque omnis exegit foras, me atque hos, onustos
    fustibus.

III. 2.
Eucl. Redi.   quo fugis nunc?   tene, tene.
Cong.   Quid, stolide, clamas?

---

[1] *Attatae* Lindsay : *optati* MSS : *cives* V² : *vires* B, *vives*
D V¹.

door to ask Congrio for the loan of a bread-pan.
And you there! if you know what's good for you,
you won't hand me back that rooster till it's
plucked cleaner than a ballet dancer. (*sound of
scuffle in Euclio's house*) Hullo, though! What's
the row in the house next door? Hm! the cooks
settling down to business, I reckon! I'll hustle
back, or we'll be having a rumpus at our place, too.

[EXIT

ACT III

ENTER *Congrio* AND HIS ASSOCIATES TUMBLING OUT OF
Euclio's HOUSE, SLAMMING DOOR BEHIND THEM.

ong. (*in burlesque panic*) Hi—i—i! Citizens, natives,
inhabitants, neighbours, foreigners, every one—
give me room to run! Open up! Clear the street!
(*stopping at some distance from the house*) This is the
first time I ever came to cook for Bacchantes at a
Bacchante den. Oh dear, what an awful clubbing
I and my disciples did get! I'm one big ache!
I'm dead and gone! The way that old codger
took me for a gymnasium! (*Euclio's door opens and
he appears, cudgel in hand*) Oh—ow—ow! Good
Lord be merciful! I'm done for! He's opening
the den: he's at the door: he's after me! I know
what I'll do: (*retires*) he's taught me my lesson,
my master has. I never in all my life saw a place
where they were freer-handed with their wood:
(*rubbing his shoulders*) why, when he drove the lot
of us out he let us have big sticks of it, all we could
stagger under.

ene 2.

ucl. (*going into street*) Come back. Where are you running to now? Stop him, stop him!

ong. What are you yelling for, stupid?

277

Eucl. Quia ad tris viros iam ego deferam nomen tuom.

Cong. Quam ob rem?

Eucl. Quia cultrum habes.

Cong. Cocum decet.

Eucl. Quid comminatu's
mihi?

Cong. Istud male factum arbitror, quia non latus fodi.

Eucl. Homo nullust te scelestior qui vivat hodie
neque quoi ego de industria amplius male plus
libens faxim. 420

Cong. Pol etsi taceas, palam id quidem est: res ipsa
testist;
ita fustibus sum mollior magis quam ullus cinaedus.
sed quid tibi nos tactiost, mendice homo?

Eucl. Quae res?
etiam rogitas? an quia minus quam aequom erat
feci?

Cong. Sine, at hercle cum magno malo tuo, si hoc caput
sentit.

Eucl. Pol ego haud scio quid post fuat: tuom nunc caput
sentit.
sed in aedibus quid tibi meis nam erat negoti
me absente, nisi ego iusseram? volo scire.

Cong. Tace ergo.
quia venimus coctum ad nuptias.

Eucl. Quid tu, malum, curas,
utrum crudum an coctum ego edim, nisi tu mi es
tutor? 430

Cong. Volo scire, sinas an non sinas nos coquere hic
cenam?

Eucl. Volo scire ego item, meae domi mean salva futura?

278

cl. Because I am going to report your name to the police this instant.

ng. Why?

cl. Well, you carry a knife.

ng. And so a cook should.

cl. And how about your threatening me?

ng. It's a pity I didn't jab it through you, I'm thinking.

cl. There isn't a more abandoned villain than you on the face of the earth, or one I'd be gladder to go out of my way to punish more, either.

ng. Good Lord! That's evident enough, even if you didn't say so: the facts speak for themselves. I've been clubbed till I'm looser than any fancy dancer. Now what did you mean by laying hands on me, you beggar?

cl. What's that? You dare ask me? Didn't I do my duty by you—is that it? *(lifts cudgel)*

ng. *(backing away)* All right: but by gad, you'll pay heavy for it, or I'm a numskull.

cl. Hm! I don't know anything about the future of your skull, but *(chuckling and tapping his cudgel)* it must be numb now. *(savagely)* See here, what the devil were you doing in my house without my orders while I was gone? That's what I want to know.

ng. Well then, shut up. We came to cook for the wedding, that's all.

cl. And how does it concern you, curse you, whether I eat my food cooked or take it raw—unless you are my guardian?

ng. Are you going to let us cook dinner here or not? That's what I want to know.

cl. Yes, and I want to know whether my things at home will be safe?

Cong. Utinam mea mihi modo auferam, quae adtuli, salva:
me haud paenitet, tua ne expetam.

Eucl. Scio, ne doce, novi.

Cong. Quid est qua prohibes nunc gratia nos coquere hic
cenam?

quid fecimus, quid diximus tibi secus quam velles?

Eucl. Etiam rogitas, sceleste homo, qui angulos in
omnis

mearum aedium et conclavium mihi pervium facitis?

ibi ubi tibi erat negotium, ad focum si adesses,

non fissile auferres caput: merito id tibi factum
est. 440

adeo ut tu meam sententiam iam noscere possis

si ad ianuam huc accesseris, nisi iussero, propius,

ego te faciam miserrimus mortalis uti sis.

scis iam meam sententiam.

Cong. Quo abis? redi rursum.

ita me bene amet Laverna, uti te iam, nisi reddi

mihi vasa iubes, pipulo te hic differam ante aedis.

quid ego nunc agam? ne ego edepol veni huc auspicio malo.

nummo sum conductus: plus iam medico merce
dest opus.

III. 3.

Eucl. Hoc quidem hercle, quoquo ibo, mecum erit, mecum
feram,

neque isti id in tantis periclis umquam committam
ut siet. 45

280

ong.   All I hope is I can get safe away with my own
things that I brought there. That'll do for me:
don't worry about my hankering for anything you
own.

ucl.   (*incredulous*) I know. You needn't go on. I
quite understand.

ong.   Why won't you let us cook dinner here now?
What have we done? What have we said that
you didn't like?

ucl.   A pretty question, you villainous rascal, with your
making a public highway of every nook and cranny
in my whole house! If you had stayed by the
oven where your business lay, you wouldn't be
carrying that cloven pate: it serves you right.
(*with forced composure*) Now further, just to
acquaint you with my sentiments in the matter,—
you come any nearer this door without my permission, and I will make you the most forlorn
creature in God's world. Now you know my
sentiments.   [EXIT INTO HOUSE.

ong.   (*calling after him*) Where are you off to? Come
back! So help me holy Mother of Thieves, but
I'll soon make it warm for you, the way I'll rip up
your reputation in front of the house here, if you
don't have my dishes brought back! (*as Euclio
closes the door*) Now what? Oh, hell! It certainly
was an unlucky day when I came here! Two
shillings for the job, and now it'll take more than
that to pay the doctor's bill.

ene 3.

RE-ENTER *Euclio* FROM HOUSE WITH OBJECT UNDER
HIS CLOAK.

ucl.   (*aside*) By heaven, wherever I go this goes (*peering
under cloak*) too: I won't leave it there to run

281

ite sane nunciam omnes, et coqui et tibicinae,
etiam intro duce, si vis, vel gregem venalium,
coquite, facite, festinate nunciam, quantum libet.

Cong. Temperi, postquam implevisti fusti fissorum caput.

Eucl. Intro abite, opera huc conducta est vostra, non
    oratio.

Cong. Heus, senex, pro vapulando hercle ego abs te mer-
    cedem petam.

coctum ego, non vapulatum, dudum conductus fui.

Eucl. Lege agito mecum. molestus ne sis. i et cenam
    coque,

aut abi in malum cruciatum ab aedibus.

Cong.   Abi tu modo.
III. 4.

Eucl. Illic hinc abiit. di immortales, facinus audax
    incipit   460

qui cum opulento pauper homine coepit rem ha-
    bere aut negotium.[1]

veluti Megadorus temptat me omnibus miserum
    modis,

qui simulavit mei honoris mittere huc causa coquos:

is ea causa misit, hoc qui surriperent misero mihi.

condigne etiam meus med intus gallus gallinacius,

qui erat anu peculiaris, perdidit paenissume.

ubi erat haec defossa, occepit ibi scalpurrire ungulis

circum circa. quid opust verbis? ita mihi pectus
    peracuit:

[1] Corrupt (Leo): Goetz deletes *coepit.*

such risks, never. (*to Congrio and others*) Very well, come now, in with you, cooks, music girls, every one! (*to Congrio*) Go on, take your under-strappers inside if you like, the whole hireling herd of 'em. Cook away, work away, scurry around to your hearts' content now.

Cong. A nice time for it, after you've clubbed my head till it's all cracks!

Eucl. In with you. You were engaged to get up a dinner here, not a declamation.

Cong. I say, old boy, I'll come to you with my bill for that basting, by the Lord I will. I was hired a while ago to be cook, not to be thumped.

Eucl. Well, go to law about it. Don't bother me. Away with you: get dinner, or else get to the devil out of here.

Cong. You just get to—(*mildly, as he pushes in past him*) one side, then.

[EXEUNT *Congrio* AND HIS ASSOCIATES INTO HOUSE.

Scene 4.

Eucl. (*looking after them*) He's disappeared. My Lord, my Lord! It's an awful chance a poor man takes when he begins to have dealings or business with a wealthy man. Here's Megadorus now, trying to catch me—oh, dear, dear!—in all sorts of ways. Sending cooks over here and pretending it's because of regard for me! Sent 'em to steal this (*looking under cloak*) from a poor old man— that's what his sending 'em was because of! And then of course that dunghill cock of mine in there, that used to belong to the old woman, had to come within an inch of ruining me, begin-ning to scratch and claw around where this (*looking under cloak*) was buried. Enough said.

283

capio fustem, obtrunco gallum, furem manufesta-
　rium.
credo edepol ego illi mercedem gallo pollicitos
　coquos, 470
si id palam fecisset. exemi ex manu [1] manubrium.[2]
sed Megadorus meus affinis eccum incedit a foro.
iam hunc non ausim praeterire, quin consistam et
　conloquar.

III. 5.

Mega.　Narravi amicis multis consilium meum
de condicione hac. Euclionis filiam
laudant. sapienter factum et consilio bono.
nam meo quidem animo si idem faciant ceteri
opulentiores, pauperiorum filias
ut indotatas ducant uxores domum, 480
et multo fiat civitas concordior,
et invidia nos minore utamur quam utimur,
et illae malam rem metuant quam metuont magis,
et nos minore sumptu simus quam sumus.
in maximam illuc populi partem est optimum;
in pauciores avidos altercatio est,
quorum animis avidis atque insatietatibus
neque lex neque sutor capere est qui possit modum.
namque hoc qui dicat " quo illae nubent divites
dotatae, si istud ius pauperibus ponitur? " 490
quo lubeant, nubant, dum dos ne fiat comes.
hoc si ita fiat, mores meliores sibi
parent, pro dote quos ferant, quam nunc ferunt,

---

[1] Corrupt (Leo): *manupretium* Leo for *manubrium.*
[2] Leo brackets following v., 472: *quid opust verbis ?
acta est pugna in gallo gallinacio.*

284

It just got me so worked up I took a club and annihilated that cock, the thief, the redhanded thief! By heaven, I do believe the cooks offered that cock a reward to show them where this (*looking under cloak*) was. I took the handle (*looking under cloak*) out of their hands! (*looking down street*) Ah, but there is son-in-law Megadorus swaggering back from the forum. I suppose it would hardly do for me to pass him without stopping for a word or two, now.

Scene 5.   ENTER *Megadorus.*

Mega. (*not seeing Euclio*) Well, I've told a number of friends of my intentions regarding this match. They were full of praise for Euclio's daughter. Say it's the sensible thing to do, a fine idea. Yes, for my part I'm convinced that if the rest of our well-to-do citizens would follow my example and marry poor men's daughters and let the dowries go, there would be a great deal more unity in our city, and people would be less bitter against us men of means than they are, and our wives would stand in greater awe of marital authority than they do, and the cost of living would be lower for us than it is. It's just the thing for the vast majority of the people; the fight comes with a handful of greedy fellows so stingy and grasping that neither law nor cobbler can take their measure. And now supposing some one should ask: "Who are the rich girls with dowries going to marry, if you make this rule for the poor ones?" Why, anyone they please, let 'em marry, provided their dowry doesn't go along with 'em. In that case, instead of bringing their husbands money, they'd bring them better behaved wives than they do at present.

ego faxim muli, pretio qui superant equos,
sint viliores Gallicis cantheriis.

Eucl. Ita me di amabunt ut ego hunc ausculto lubens.
nimis lepide fecit verba ad parsimoniam.

Mega. Nulla igitur dicat " equidem dotem ad te adtuli
maiorem multo quam tibi erat pecunia;
enim mihi quidem aequomst purpuram atque
    aurum dari,   500
ancillas, mulos, muliones, pedisequos,
salutigerulos pueros, vehicla qui vehar."

Eucl. Ut matronarum hic facta pernovit probe.
moribus praefectum mulierum hunc factum velim.

Mega. Nunc quoquo venias plus plaustrorum in aedibus
videas quam ruri, quando ad villam veneris.
sed hoc etiam pulchrum est praequam ubi sumptus
    petunt.
stat fullo, phyrgio, aurifex, lanarius;
caupones patagiarii, indusiarii,
flammarii, violarii, carinarii;   510
stant manulearii, stant [1] murobatharii,
propolae linteones, calceolarii;
sedentarii sutores diabathrarii,
solearii astant, astant molocinarii; [2]
strophiarii astant, astant semul sonarii.
iam hosce absolutos censeas: cedunt, petunt
treceni, cum stant thylacistae in atriis
textores limbularii, arcularii.

---

[1] Corrupt (Leo): *myrobaptarii* Leo.
[2] Leo brackets following v., 515: *petunt fullones, sarcinatores petunt.*

	Those mules of theirs that cost more than horses do now—they'd be cheaper than Gallic geldings by the time I got through.
Eucl.	(*aside*) God bless my soul, how I do love to hear him talk! Those thoughts of his about econo- mizing—beautiful, beautiful!
Mega.	Then you wouldn't hear them saying: " Well, sir, you never had anything like the money I brought you, and you know it. Fine clothes and jewellery, indeed! And maids and mules and coachmen and footmen and pages and private carriages—well, if I haven't a right to them! "
Eucl.	(*aside*) Ah, he knows 'em, knows 'em through and through, these society dames! Oh, if he could only be appointed supervisor of public morals— the women's!
Mega.	Wherever you go nowadays you see more wagons in front of a city mansion than you can find around a farmyard. That's a perfectly glorious sight, though, compared with the time when the trades- men come for their money. The cleanser, the ladies' tailor, the jeweller, the woollen worker— they're all hanging round. And there are the dealers in flounces and underclothes and bridal veils, in violet dyes and yellow dyes, or muffs, or balsam scented foot-gear; and then the lingerie people drop in on you, along with shoemakers and squatting cobblers and slipper and sandal merchants and dealers in mallow dyes; and the belt makers flock around, and the girdle makers along with 'em. And now you may think you've got them all paid off. Then up come weavers and lace men and cabinet-makers—hundreds of 'em—who plant themselves like jailers in your halls and want you

       ducuntur, datur aes.   iam absolutos censeas,   520
       cum incedunt infectores corcotarii,
       aut aliqua mala crux semper est, quae aliquid petat.

Eucl.   Compellarem ego illum, ni metuam ne desinat
       memorare mores mulierum : nunc sic sinam.

Mega. Ubi nugivendis res soluta est omnibus,
       ibi ad postremum cedit miles, aes petit.
       itur, putatur ratio cum argentario ;
       miles inpransus astat, aes censet dari.
       ubi disputata est ratio cum argentario,
       etiam ipsus ultro debet argentario :   530
       spes prorogatur militi in alium diem.
       haec sunt atque aliae multae in magnis dotibus
       incommoditates sumptusque intolerabiles.
       nam quae indotata est, ea in potestate est viri ;
       dotatae mactant et malo et damno viros.
       sed eccum adfinem ante aedes.   quid agis, Euclio ?

Eucl.   Nimium lubenter edi sermonem tuom.

III. 6.

Mega. An audivisti ?

Eucl.   Usque a principio omnia.

Mega. Tamen meo quidem animo aliquanto facias rectius,
       si nitidior sis filiai nuptiis.   540

to settle up. You bring 'em in and square accounts. "All paid off now, anyway," you may be thinking, when in march the fellows who do the saffron dyeing—some damned pest or other, anyhow, eternally after something.

Eucl.   (*aside*) I'd hail him, only I'm afraid he'd stop talking about how the women go on. No, no, I'll let him be.

Mega.   When you've got all these fellows of fluff and ruffles satisfied, along comes a military man, bringing up the rear, and wants to collect the army tax. You go and have a reckoning with your banker, your military gentleman standing by and missing his lunch in the expectation of getting some cash. After you and the banker have done figuring, you find you owe him money too, and the military man has his hopes postponed till another day. These are some of the nuisances and intolerable expenses that big dowries let you in for, and there are plenty more. Now a wife that doesn't bring you a penny—a husband has some control over her: it's the dowered ones that pester the life out of their husbands with the way they cut up and squander. (*seeing Euclio*) But there's my new relative in front of the house! How are you, Euclio?

Scene 6.

Eucl.   Gratified, highly gratified with your discourse—I devoured it.

Mega.   Eh? you heard?

Eucl.   Every word of it.

Mega.   (*looking him over*) But I say, though, I do think it would be a little more in keeping, if you were to spruce up a bit for your daughter's wedding.

Eucl. Pro re nitorem et gloriam pro copia
qui habent, meminerunt sese unde oriundi sient.
neque pol, Megadore, mihi neque quoiquam pau-
    peri
opinione melius res structa est domi.

Mega. Immo est quod satis est, et di faciant ut siet
plus plusque et istuc sospitent quod nunc habes.

Eucl. Illud mihi verbum non placet " quod nunc habes."
tam hoc scit me habere quam egomet.   anus fecit
    palam.

Mega. Quid tu te solus e senatu sevocas?

Eucl. Pol ego ut te accusem merito meditabar.

Mega.   Quid est? 550

Eucl. Quid sit me rogitas?   qui mihi omnis angulos
furum implevisti in aedibus misero mihi,
qui mi intro misti in aedis quingentos coquos,
cum senis manibus, genere Geryonaceo ;
quos si Argus servet qui oculeus totus fuit,
quem quondam Ioni Iuno custodem addidit,
is numquam servet. praeterea tibicinam,
quae mi interbibere sola, si vino scatat,
Corinthiensem fontem Pirenam potest.
tum obsonium autem—

Mega.   Pol vel legioni sat est. 560
etiam agnum misi.

Eucl.   Quo quidem agno sat scio
magis curiosam [1] nusquam esse ullam beluam.

Mega. Volo ego ex te scire qui sit agnus curio.

---

[1] *curiosam* MSS : *curionem* Gulielmius, followed by Leo
and others.

290

Eucl.   (*whining*) Folks with the wherewithal and means to let 'em spruce up and look smart remember who they are. My goodness, Megadorus! I haven't got a fortune piled up at home (*peers slyly under cloak*) any more than people think, and no other poor man has, either.

Mega.   (*genially*) Ah well, you've got enough, and heaven make it more and more, and bless you in what you have now.

Eucl.   (*turning away with a start*) " What you have now! " I don't like that phrase! He knows I have this money just as well as I do! The old hag's been blabbing!

Mega.   (*pleasantly*) Why that secret session over there?

Eucl.   (*taken aback*) I was—damme sir,—I was framing the complaint against you that you deserve.

Mega.   What for?

Eucl.   What for, eh? When you've filled every corner of my house with thieves, confound it! When you've sent cooks into my house by the hundred and every one of 'em a Geryonian [1] with six hands apiece! Why, Argus, who had eyes all over him and was set to guarding Io once by Juno, couldn't ever keep watch on those fellows, not if he tried. And that music girl besides! She could take the fountain of Pirene at Corinth and drink it dry. all by herself, she could,—if it ran wine. Then as for the provisions——

Mega.   Bless my soul! Why, there's enough for a regiment. I sent you a lamb, too.

Eucl.   Yes, and a more shearable beast than that same lamb doesn't exist, I know that.

Mega.   I wish you would tell me how the lamb is shearable.

---

[1] Geryon was a giant with three heads and bodies.

Eucl.	Quia ossa ac pellis totust, ita cura macet.
	quin exta inspicere in sole ei vivo licet:
	ita is pellucet quasi lanterna Punica.
Mega.	Caedundum conduxi ego illum.
Eucl.	Tum tu idem optumumst
	loces efferendum; nam iam, credo, mortuost.
Mega.	Potare ego hodie, Euclio, tecum volo.
Eucl.	Non potem ego quidem hercle.
Mega.	At ego iussero 570
	cadum unum vini veteris a me adferrier.
Eucl.	Nolo hercle, nam mihi bibere decretum est aquam.
Mega.	Ego te hodie reddam madidum, si vivo, probe,
	tibi cui decretum est bibere aquam.
Eucl.	Scio quam rem agat:
	ut me deponat vino, eam adfectat viam,
	post hoc quod habeo ut commutet coloniam.
	ego id cavebo, nam alicubi abstrudam foris.
	ego faxo et operam et vinum perdiderit simul.
Mega.	Ego, nisi quid me vis, eo lavatum, ut sacruficem.
Eucl.	Edepol, ne tu, aula, multos inimicos habes 580
	atque istuc aurum quod tibi concreditum est.

THE POT OF GOLD

Eucl. Because it's mere skin and bones, wasted away till it's perfectly—*(tittering)* sheer. Why, why, you put that lamb in the sun and you can watch its inwards work: it's as transparent as a Punic [1] lantern.

Mega. *(protestingly)* I got that lamb in myself to be slaughtered.

Eucl. *(dryly)* Then you'd best put it out yourself to be buried, for I do believe it's dead already.

Mega. *(laughing and clapping him on the shoulder)* Euclio, we must have a little carouse to-day, you and I.

Eucl. *(frightened)* None for me, sir, none for me! Carouse! Oh my Lord!

Mega. But see here, I'll just have a cask of good old wine brought over from my cellars.

Eucl. No, no! I don't care for any! The fact is, I am resolved to drink nothing but water.

Mega. *(digging him in the ribs)* I'll get you properly soaked to-day, on my life I will, you with your " resolved to drink nothing but water."

Eucl. *(aside)* I see his game! Trying to fuddle me with his wine, that's it, and then give this *(looking under cloak)* a new domicile! *(pauses)* I'll take measures against that : yes, I'll secrete it somewhere outside the house. I'll make him throw away his time and wine together.

Mega. *(turning to go)* Well, unless I can do something for you, I'll go take a bath and get ready to offer sacrifice.   [EXIT INTO HOUSE.

Eucl. *(paternally to object under cloak)* God bless us both, pot, you do have enemies, ah yes, many enemies, you and the gold entrusted to you! As matters

---

[1] Perhaps of glass, of which the Phœnicians were reputedly the inventors.

nunc hoc mihi factu est optumum, ut ted au-
    feram,
aula, in Fidei fanum : ibi abstrudam probe.
Fides, novisti me et ego te : cave sis tibi,
ne in me mutassis nomen, si hoc concreduo.
ibo ad te fretus tua, Fides, fiducia.

ACTVS IV

Strob.   Hoc est servi facinus frugi, facere quod ego perse-
       quor,
    ne morae molestiaeque imperium erile habeat sibi.
    nam qui ero ex sententia servire servos postulat,
    in erum matura, in se sera condecet capessere.   590
    sin dormitet, ita dormitet, servom sese ut cogitet.[1]
    erile [2] imperium ediscat, ut quod frons velit oculi
       sciant ;
    quod iubeat citis quadrigis citius properet per-
       sequi.   600
    qui ea curabit, abstinebit censione bubula,
    nec sua opera rediget umquam in splendorem com-
       pedes.

   [1] Leo brackets following v., 592–598 :
nam qui amanti ero servitutem servit, quasi ego servio,
si erum videt superare amorem, hoc servi est officium
   reor,
retinere ad salutem, non enim quo incumbat eo impellere.
quasi pueri qui nare discunt scirpea induitur ratis,
qui laborent minus, facilius ut nent et moveant manus,
eodem modo servom ratem esse amanti ero aequom censeo,
ut eum toleret, ne pessum abeat tamquam—
   [2] Corrupt (Leo) : *eri ille* Wagner.

stand, pot, the best thing I can do for you is to carry you off to the shrine of Faith: I'll hide you away there, just as cosy! You know me, Faith, and I know you: don't change your name, mind, if I trust this to you. Yes, I'll go to you, Faith, relying on your faithfulness.   [EXIT *Euclio*.

ACT IV

ENTER *Strobilus*.

rob. (*self-complacently*) This is the way for a good servant to act, the way I do: no thinking master's orders are a botheration and nuisance. I tell you what, if a servant wants to give satisfaction, he'd just better make it a case of master first and man second.[1] Even if he should fall asleep, he ought to do it with an eye on the fact that he's a servant. He's got to know his master's inclinations like a book, so that he can read his wishes in his face. And as for orders, he must push 'em through faster than a fast four-in-hand. If a chap minds all this, he won't be paying taxes on rawhide, or ever spend his time polishing a ball and chain with his ankles. Now the fact is, master's

---

[1] For when a slave's slaving it like I am for a master who is in love, if he sees his master's heart is running away with him, it's the slave's duty, in my opinion, to hold him in and save him and not hurry him on the way he's headed. It's like boys learning to swim: they lie on a rush float so as not to have to work so hard and so as to swim more easily and use their arms. In the same way I hold that a slave ought to be his master's float, if his master's in love, so as to support him and not let him go to the bottom like—

nunc erus meus amat filiam huius Euclionis pauperis;
eam ero nunc renuntiatum est nuptum huic Mega-
doro dari.

is speculatum huc misit me, ut quae fierent fieret
particeps.

nunc sine omni suspicione in ara hic adsidam sacra;
hinc ego et huc et illuc potero quid agant arbitrarier.

IV. 2.

Eucl. Tu modo cave quoiquam indicassis aurum meum
esse istic, Fides:

non metuo ne quisquam inveniat, ita probe in late-
bris situmst.

edepol ne illic pulchram praedam agat, si quis
illam invenerit   610

aulam onustam auri; verum id te quaeso ut prohi-
bessis, Fides.

nunc lavabo, ut rem divinam faciam, ne affinem morer

quin ubi accersat meam extemplo filiam ducat
domum.

vide, Fides, etiam atque etiam nunc, salvam ut
aulam abs te auferam:

tuae fide concredidi aurum, in tuo loco et fano est
situm.

Strob. Di immortales, quod ego hunc hominem facinus
audivi loqui:

se aulam onustam auri abstrusisse hic intus in fano
Fide.

cave tu illi fidelis, quaeso, potius fueris, quam mihi.

atque hic pater est, ut ego opinor, huius erus
quam amat, virginis.

ibo hinc intro, perscrutabor fanum, si inveniam
uspiam   620

aurum, dum hic est occupatus. sed si repperero,
o Fides,

in love with the daughter of poor old Euclio here; and he's just got word she's going to be married to Megadorus there. So he's sent me over to keep my eyes peeled and report on operations. I'll just settle down alongside this sacred altar (*does so*) and no one'll suspect me. I can inspect proceedings at both houses from here.

ene 2.

ENTER *Euclio* WITHOUT SEEING *Strobilus.*

ucl. (*plaintively*) Only be sure you don't let anyone know my gold is there, Faith: no fear of anyone finding it, not after the lovely way I tucked it in that dark nook. (*pauses*) Oh my God, what a beautiful haul he would get, if anyone should find it—a pot just crammed with gold! For mercy's sake, though, Faith, don't let him! (*walks slowly toward house*) Now I'll have a bath, so that I may sacrifice and not hinder my prospective son-in-law from marrying my girl the moment he claims her. (*looking down street toward temple*) Take care now, Faith, do, do, do take care I get my pot back from you safe. I've trusted my gold to your good faith, laid it away in your grove and shrine.

[EXIT *Euclio* INTO HOUSE.

rob. (*jumping up*) Ye immortal gods! What's all this I heard the fellow tell of! A pot just crammed with gold hidden in the shrine of Faith here! For the love of heaven, Faith, don't be more faithful to him than to me. Yes, and he's the father of the girl that is master's sweetheart, or I'm mistaken. I'm going in there: I'll search that shrine from top to bottom and see if I can't find the gold somewhere while he's busy here. But if I come across it—oh, Faith, I'll pour you out a

mulsi congialem plenam faciam tibi fideliam.

id adeo tibi faciam; verum ego mihi bibam, ubi id
fecero.

IV. 3.

Eucl. Non temere est quod corvos cantat mihi nunc ab
laeva manu;

semul radebat pedibus terram et voce croccibat sua:

continuo meum cor coepit artem facere ludicram

atque in pectus emicare. sed ego cesso currere?

IV. 4.

Eucl. I foras, lumbrice, qui sub terra erepsisti modo,

qui modo nusquam comparebas, nunc, cum compa-
res, peris.

ego pol te, praestrigiator, miseris iam accipiam
modis.   630

Strob. Quae te mala crux agitat? quid tibi mecum est
commerci, senex?

quid me adflictas? quid me raptas? qua me causa
verberas?

Eucl. Verberabilissime, etiam rogitas, non fur, sed trifur?

Strob. Quid tibi surrupui?

Eucl.   Redde huc sis.

Strob.   Quid tibi vis reddam?

Eucl.   Rogas?

Strob. Nil equidem tibi abstuli.

298

THE POT OF GOLD

five pint pot of wine and honey! There now! that's what I'll do for you; and when I've done that for you, why, I'll drink it up for myself.

[EXIT TO TEMPLE AT A RUN.

Scene 3.

RE-ENTER *Euclio* FROM HOUSE.

Eucl. (*excitedly*) It means something—that raven cawing on my left just now! And all the time a-clawing the ground, croaking away, croaking away! The minute I heard him my heart began to dance a jig and jumped up into my throat. But I must run, run! [EXIT TO TEMPLE.

Scene 4.

A FEW MOMENTS ELAPSE. THEN THE SOUND OF A SCUFFLE DOWN THE STREET. RE-ENTER *Euclio* DRAGGING *Strobilus*.

Eucl. Come! out, you worm! crawling up from underground just now! A minute ago you weren't to be found anywhere, and (*grimly*) now you're found you're finished! Oh-h-h-h, you felon! I'm going to give it to you, this very instant! (*beats him*)

Strob. What the devil's got into you? What business have you got with me, old fellow? What are you pounding me for? What are you jerking me along for? What do you mean by battering me?

Eucl. (*still pummelling him*) Mean, eh? You batterissimo. You're not a thief: you're three thieves.

Strob. What did I steal from you?

Eucl. (*threateningly*) You kindly give it back.

Strob. Back? What back?

Eucl. A nice question!

Strob. I didn't take a thing from you, honestly.

299

Eucl.	At illud quod tibi abstuleras cedo.
	ecquid agis?
Strob.	Quid agam?
Eucl.	Auferre non potes.
Strob.	Quid vis tibi?
Eucl.	Pone.
Strob.	Id quidem pol te datare credo consuetum, senex.
Eucl.	Pone hoc sis, aufer cavillam, non ego nunc nugas
	ago.
Strob.	Quid ego ponam? quin tu eloquere quidquid est
	suo nomine.
	non hercle equidem quicquam sumpsi nec tetigi.
Eucl.	Ostende huc manus. 640
Strob.	Em tibi, ostendi, eccas.
Eucl.	Video. age ostende etiam tertiam.
Strob.	Laruae hunc atque intemperiae insaniaeque agitant
	senem.
	facisne iniuriam mihi?
Eucl.	Fateor, quia non pendes, maximam.
	atque id quoque iam fiet, nisi fatere.
Strob.	Quid fatear tibi?
Eucl.	Quid abstulisti hinc?
Strob.	Di me perdant, si ego tui quicquam abstuli
	nive adeo abstulisse vellem.
Eucl.	Agedum, excutedum pallium.
Strob.	Tuo arbitratu.
Eucl.	Ne inter tunicas habeas.
Strob.	Tempta qua lubet.

Eucl. Well, what you took dishonestly, then! Hand it over! Come, come, will you!

Strob. Come, come, what?

Eucl. You shan't get away with it.

Strob. What is it you want?

Eucl. Down with it!

Strob. Down with it, eh! Looks as if you'd downed too much of it yourself already, old boy.

Eucl. Down with it, I tell you! None of your repartee! I'm not in the humour for trifling now.

Strob. Down with what? Come along, speak out and give it its name, whatever it is. Hang it all, I never took a thing nor touched a thing, and that's flat.

Eucl. Show me your hands.

Strob. (*stretching them out*) All right—there they are: have a look.

Eucl. (*dryly*) I see. Come now, the third one: out with it.

Strob. (*aside*) He's got 'em! The old chap's mad, stark, staring mad! (*to Euclio, virtuously*) Now aren't you doing me an injury?

Eucl. I am, a hideous injury—in not hanging you. And I'll soon do that, too, if you don't confess.

Strob. Confess what?

Eucl. What did you carry off from here? (*pointing toward temple*)

Strob. (*solemnly*) May I be damned, if I carried off a thing of yours. (*aside*) Likewise if I didn't want to.

Eucl. Come on, shake out your cloak.

Strob. (*doing so*) Anything you say.

Eucl. Um! probably under your tunic.

Strob. (*cheerfully*) Feel anywhere you please.

L

Eucl. Vah, scelestus quam benigne : ut ne abstulisse intellegam.

novi sycophantias.   age rusum ostende huc manum dexteram.

Strob.   Em.

Eucl.   Nunc laevam ostende.

Strob.   Quin equidem ambas profero. 65

Eucl. Iam scrutari mitto.   redde huc.

Strob.   Quid reddam ?

Eucl.   A, nugas agis, certe habes.

Strob.   Habeo ego ?   quid habeo ?

Eucl.   Non dico, audire expetis. id meum, quidquid habes, redde.

Strob.   Insanis : perscrutatus es tuo arbitratu, neque tui me quicquam invenisti penes.

Eucl. Mane, mane.   quis illic est ?   quis hic intus alter erat tecum simul ?

perii hercle : ille nunc intus turbat, hunc si amitto hic abierit.

postremo hunc iam perscrutavi, hic nihil habet. abi quo lubet.

Strob. Iuppiter te dique perdant.

Eucl.   Haud male egit gratias. ibo intro atque illi socienno tuo iam interstringam gulam.

fugin hinc ab oculis ?   abin an non.

Strob.   Abeo.

Eucl.   Cave sis [1] te videam. 66

---

[1] Corrupt (Leo) : *revideam* Bothe.

eucl.   Ugh! you rascal! How obliging you are! That I may think you didn't take it! I'm up to your dodges. (*searches him*) Once more now—out with your hand, the right one.

ob.   (*obeying*) There you are.

eucl.   Now the left one.

ob.   (*obeying*) Why, certainly: here's the both of 'em.

eucl.   Enough of this searching. Now give it here.

ob.   What?

eucl.   Oh-h! Bosh! You must have it!

ob.   I have it? Have what?

eucl.   I won't say: you're too anxious to know. Anything of mine you've got, hand it over.

ob.   Crazy! You went all through me as much as you liked without finding a solitary thing of yours on me.

eucl.   (*excitedly*) Wait, wait! (*turns toward temple and listens*) Who's in there? Who was that other fellow in there along with you? (*aside*) My Lord! this is awful, awful! There's another one at work in there all this time. And if I let go of this one, he'll skip off. (*pauses*) But then I've searched him already: he hasn't anything. (*aloud*) Off with you, anywhere! (*releases him with a final cuff*)

ob.   (*from a safe distance*) You be everlastingly damned!

eucl.   (*aside, dryly*) Nice way he has of showing his gratitude. (*aloud, sternly*) I'll go in there, and that accomplice of yours—I'll strangle him on the spot. Are you going to vanish? Are you going to get out, or not? (*advances*)

ob.   (*retreating*) I am, I am!

eucl.   And kindly see I don't set eyes on you again.

[EXIT *Euclio* TOWARD TEMPLE.

IV. 5.

Strob. Emortuom ego me mavelim leto malo
quam non ego illi dem hodie insidias seni.
nam hic iam non audebit aurum abstrudere:
credo ecferet iam secum et mutabit locum.
attat, foris crepuit. senex eccum aurum ecfert
     foras.
tantisper huc ego ad ianuam concessero.

IV. 6.

Eucl. Fide censebam maxumam multo fidem
esse, ea sublevit os mihi paenissume:
ni subvenisset corvos, periissem miser.
nimis hercle ego illum corvom ad me veniat velim.   670
qui indicium fecit, ut ego illi aliquid boni
dicam; nam quod edit tam duim quam perduim.
nunc hoc ubi abstrudam cogito solum locum.
Silvani lucus extra murum est avius,
crebro salicto oppletus. ibi sumam locum.
certumst, Silvano potius credam quam Fide.

Strob. Euge, euge, di me salvom et servatum volunt.
iam ego illuc praecurram atque inscendam aliquam
     in arborem
indeque observabo, aurum ubi abstrudat senex.
quamquam hic manere me erus sese iusserat;   680
certum est, malam rem potius quaeram cum lucro.

IV. 7.

Lyc.   Dixi tibi, mater, iuxta rem mecum tenes,
super Euclionis filia. nunc te obsecro

ne 5.

ob. I'd sooner be tortured to death than not give that old fellow a surprise to-day. (*reflecting*) Well, after this he won't dare hide his gold here. What he'll most likely do is bring it out with him and put it somewhere else. (*listening*) Hm-m-m! There goes the door! Aha! the old boy's coming out with it. I'll just back up by the doorway for a while. (*hides by Megadorus's house*)

ne 6.   RE-ENTER *Euclio* WITH POT.

cl. I used to fancy Faith, of all deities, was absolutely faithful, and here she's just missed making a downright ass of me. If that raven hadn't stood by me, I'd be a poor, poor ruined man. By heavens, I'd just like that raven to come and see me, the one that warned me, I certainly should, so that I might pay him a handsome—compliment. As for tossing him a bite to eat, why, that would amount to throwing it away. (*meditating*) Let me think now; where is some lonely spot to hide this in? (*after a moment*) There's that grove of Silvanus outside the wall, solitary, willow thickets all around. There's where I'll pick my place. I'd sooner trust Silvanus than Faith, and that's settled.   [EXIT *Euclio.*

ob. Good! Good! The gods are with me: I'm a made man! Now I'll run on ahead and climb some tree there so as to sight the place where the old fellow hides it. What if master did tell me to wait here! I'd sooner look for a thrashing along with the cash, and that's settled.   [EXIT *Strobilus.*

ne 7.   ENTER *Lyconides* AND *Eunomia.*

c. That's the whole story, mother: you see how it is with me and Euclio's daughter as well as I do.

305

       resecroque, mater, quod dudum obsecraveram:
       fac mentionem cum avonculo, mater mea.

Eun.   Scis tute facta velle me quae tu velis,
       et istuc confido a fratre me impetrassere;
       et causa iusta est, siquidem ita est ut praedicas,
       te eam compressisse vinulentum virginem.

Lyc.   Egone ut te advorsum mentiar, mater mea?   690

Phaed. Perii, mea nutrix.   obsecro te, uterum dolet.
       Iuno Lucina, tuam fidem!

Lyc.   Em, mater mea,
       tibi rem potiorem verbo: clamat, parturit.

Eun.   Ei hac intro mecum, gnate mi, ad fratrem meum,
       ut istuc quod me oras impetratum ab eo auferam.

Lyc.   I, iam sequar te, mater.   sed servom meum
       Strobilum miror ubi sit, quem ego me iusseram
       hic opperiri.   nunc ego mecum cogito:
       si mihi dat operam, me illi irasci iniurium est.
       ibo intro, ubi de capite meo sunt comitia.   700

IV. 8.

Strob. Picis divitiis, qui aureos montes colunt,
       ego solus supero.   nam istos reges ceteros
       memorare nolo, hominum mendicabula:
       ego sum ille rex Philippus.   o lepidum diem.
       nam ut dudum hinc abii, multo illo adveni prior
       multoque prius me conlocavi in arborem
       indeque spectabam aurum ubi abstrudebat senex.

And now, mother, I beg you, beg you again and again, as I did before: do tell my uncle about it, mother dear.

u. Your wishes are mine, dear; you know that yourself: and I feel sure your uncle will not refuse me. It's a perfectly reasonable request, too, if it's all as you say and you actually did get intoxicated and treat the poor girl so.

e. Is it like me to look you in the face and lie, my dear mother?

ued. (*within Euclio's house*) Oh—oh! Nurse! Nurse dear! Oh, God help me! The pain!

. There, mother! There's better proof than words gives. Her cries! The child!

u. (*agitated*) Come, darling, come in to your uncle with me, so that I may persuade him to let it be as you urge.

. You go, mother: I'll follow you in a moment.

[EXIT *Eunomia* INTO *Megadorus's* HOUSE.
I wonder (*looking around*) where that fellow Strobilus of mine is that I told to wait for me here. (*pauses*) Well, on thinking it over, if he's doing something for me, it's all wrong my finding fault with him. (*turning toward Megadorus's door*) Now for the session that decides my fate.   [EXIT.

ne 8.   ENTER *Strobilus* WITH POT.

ob. (*elated*) Woodpeckers that haunt the Hills of Gold, eh! I can buy 'em up my own single self. As for the rest of your big kings—not worth mentioning, poor beggarlets! I am the great King Philip. Oh, this is a grand day! Why, after I left here a while ago I got there long before him and was up in a tree long before he came: and from there I spotted where the old chap hid

307

    ubi ille abiit, ego me dorsum duco de arbore,
    exfodio aulam auri plenam.   inde ex eo loco
    video recipere se senem; ille me non videt,   710
    nam ego declinavi paululum me extra viam.
    attat, eccum ipsum. ibo ut hoc condam domum.

IV. 9.
Eucl.   Perii interii occidi.   quo curram? quo non curram?
    tene, tene.   quem? quis?
    nescio, nil video, caecus eo atque equidem quo eam
      aut ubi sim aut qui sim
    nequeo cum animo certum investigare. obsecro
      vos ego, mi auxilio,
    oro obtestor, sitis et hominem demonstretis, quis
      eam abstulerit.
    quid est? quid ridetis? novi omnes, scio fures esse
      hic complures,
    qui vestitu et creta occultant sese atque sedent
      quasi sint frugi.
    quid ais tu? tibi credere certum est, nam esse
      bonum ex voltu cognosco.
    hem, nemo habet horum? occidisti. dic igitur,
      quis habet? nescis?   720
         heu me miserum, misere perii,
         male perditus, pessime ornatus eo:
         tantum gemiti et mali maestitiaeque
         hic dies mi optulit, famem et pauperiem.
         perditissimus ego sum omnium in terra;
         nam quid mi opust vita, qui tantum auri
         perdidi, quod concustodivi
         sedulo? egomet me defraudavi
         animumque meum geniumque meum;
         nunc eo alii laetificantur
            meo malo et damno. pati nequeo.

the stuff. After he'd gone I scrabbled down, dug up the pot full of gold! Then I saw him coming back from the place; he didn't see me, though. I slipped off a bit to one side of the road. (*looking down street*) Aha! there he comes! I'll home and tuck this out of sight. [EXIT *Strobilus.*

Scene 9.

ENTER *Euclio* FRANTIC.

Eucl. (*running wildly back and forth*) I'm ruined, I'm killed, I'm murdered! Where shall I run? Where shan't I run? Stop thief! Stop thief! What thief? Who? I don't know! I can't see! I'm all in the dark! Yes, yes, and where I'm going, or where I am, or who I am—oh, I can't tell, I can't think! (*to audience*) Help, help, for heaven's sake, I beg you, I implore you! Show the man that took it. Eh, what's that? What are you grinning for? I know you, the whole lot of you! I know there are thieves here, plenty of 'em, that cover themselves up in dapper clothes and sit still as if they were honest men. (*to a spectator*) You, sir, what do you say? I'll trust you, I will, I will. Yes, you're a worthy gentleman; I can tell it from your face. Ha! none of them has it? Oh, you've killed me! Tell me, who has got it, then? You don't know? Oh dear, oh dear, oh dear! I'm a ruined man! I'm lost, lost! Oh, what a plight! Oh, such a cruel, disastrous, dismal day—it's made a starveling of me, a pauper! I'm the forlornest wretch on earth! Ah, what is there in life for me when I've lost all that gold I guarded, oh, so carefully! I've denied myself, denied my own self comforts and pleasures; yes, and now others are making merry over my misery and loss! Oh, it's unendurable!

Lyc. Quinam homo hic ante aedis nostras eiulans con-
 queritur maerens?
 atque hic quidem Euclio est, ut opinor. oppido
 ego interii: palamst res,
 scit peperisse iam, ut ego opinor, filiam suam.
 nunc mi incertumst
 abeam an maneam, an adeam an fugiam quid
 agam edepol nescio. 730

IV. 10

Eucl. Quis homo hic loquitur?

Lyc. Ego sum miser.

Eucl. Immo ego sum, et misere perditus,
 cui tanta mala maestitudoque optigit.

Lyc. Animo bono es.

Eucl. Quo, obsecro, pacto esse possum?

Lyc. Quia istuc facinus, quod tuom
 sollicitat animum, id ego feci et fateor.

Eucl. Quid ego ex te audio

Lyc. Id quod verumst.

Eucl. Quid ego de te commerui, adulescens, mali,
 quam ob rem ita faceres meque meosque perditum
 ires liberos?

Lyc. Deus impulsor mihi fuit, is me ad illam inlexit

Eucl. Quo modo?

Lyc. Fateor peccavisse et me culpam commeritum
 scio;
 id adeo te oratum advenio ut animo aequo ignoscas
 mihi.

Eucl. Cur id ausu's facere, ut id quod non tuom esset
 tangeres? 740

Lyc. Quid vis fieri? factum est illud: fieri infectum non
 potest.
 deos credo voluisse; nam ni vellent, non fieret, scio.

310

ENTER *Lyconides* FROM HOUSE OF *Megadorus*.

yc.   Who in the world is raising all this howling, groaning hullabaloo before our house here? (*looking round*) Upon my word, it's Euclio, I do believe. (*drawing back*) My time has certainly come: it's all out. He's just learned about his daughter's child, I suppose. Now I can't decide whether to leave or stay, advance or retreat. By Jove, I don't know what to do!

Scene 10.

ucl.   (*hearing sound of voice only*) Who's that talking here?

yc.   (*stepping forward*) I'm the poor wretch, sir.

ucl.   No, no, I'm the poor wretch, a poor ruined wretch, with all this trouble and tribulation.

yc.   Keep your courage up, sir.

ucl.   For heaven's sake how can I?

yc.   Well, sir, that outrage that distresses you—(*hesitantly*) I'm to blame, and I confess it, sir.

ucl.   Hey? What's that?

yc.   The truth.

ucl.   How have I ever harmed you, young man, for you to act like this and try to ruin me and my children?

yc.   It was some demon got hold of me, sir, and led me on.

ucl.   How is this?

yc.   I admit I've done wrong, sir; I deserve your reproaches, and I know it; more than that, I've come to beg you to be patient and forgive me.

ucl.   How did you dare do it, dare touch what didn't belong to you?

yc.   (*penitently*) Well, well, sir,—it's done, and it can't be undone. I think it must have been fated; otherwise it wouldn't have happened, I'm sure of that.

311

Eucl. At ego deos credo voluisse ut apud me te in nervo
enicem.

Lyc. Ne istuc dixis.

Eucl.   Quid tibi ergo meam me invito tactiost?

Lyc. Quia vini vitio atque amoris feci.

Eucl.   Homo audacissime,
cum istacin te oratione huc ad me adire ausum, im-
pudens!
nam si istuc ius est ut tu istuc excusare possies,
luci claro deripiamus aurum matronis palam,
post id si prehensi simus, excusemus ebrios
nos fecisse amoris causa. nimis vilest vinum atque
amor,   750
si ebrio atque amanti impune facere quod lubeat licet.

Lyc. Quin tibi ultro supplicatum venio ob stultitiam meam.

Eucl. Non mi homines placent qui quando male fecerunt
purigant.
tu illam scibas non tuam esse: non attactamoportuit.

Lyc. Ergo quia sum tangere ausus, haud causificor quin
eam
ego habeam potissimum.

Eucl.   Tun habeas me invito meam?

Lyc. Haud te invito postulo; sed meam esse oportere
arbitror.
quin tu iam invenies, inquam, meam illam esse
oportere, Euclio.

Eucl. Iam quidem hercle te ad praetorem rapiam et tibi
scribam dicam,
nisi refers.

Lyc.   Quid tibi ego referam?

Eucl.   Quod surripuisti meum. 760

Lyc. Surripui ego tuom? unde? aut quid id est?

Eucl.   Ita te amabit Iuppiter
ut tu nescis.

Eucl.   Yes, and I think it must have been fated that I'm to shackle you at my house and murder you!

Lyc.   Don't say that, sir.

Eucl.   Then why did you lay hands on what was mine, without my permission?

Lyc.   It was all because of drink . . . and . . . love, sir.

Eucl.   The colossal impudence of it! To dare to come to me with a tale like that, you shameless rascal! Why, if it's legal to clear yourself that way, we should be stripping ladies of their jewellery on the public highways in broad daylight! And then when we were caught we'd excuse ourselves on the score that we were drunk and did it out of love. Drink and love are altogether too cheap, if your drunken lover can do what he likes and not suffer for it.

Lyc.   Yes, but I've come of my own accord, sir, to entreat you to pardon my madness.

Eucl.   I have no patience with men who do wrong and then try to explain it away. You knew you had no right to act so: you should have kept hands off.

Lyc.   Well, now that I did venture to act so, I have no objection to holding to it, sir,—I ask nothing better.

Eucl.   (*more angry*) Hold to it? Against my will?

Lyc.   I won't insist on it against your will, sir; but I do think my claim is just. Why, you'll soon come to realize the justice of it yourself, sir, I assure you.

Eucl.   I'll march you off to court and sue you, by heaven I will, this minute, unless you bring it back.

Lyc.   I? Bring what back?

Eucl.   What you stole from me.

Lyc.   I stole something of yours? Where from? What?

Eucl.   (*ironically*) God bless your innocence—you don't know!

313

Lyc.   Nisi quidem tu mihi quid quaeras dixeris.

Eucl. Aulam auri, inquam, te resposco, quam tu confes-
su's mihi
te abstulisse.

Lyc.   Neque edepol ego dixi neque feci.

Eucl.   Negas ?

Lyc. Pernego immo. nam neque ego aurum neque
istaec aula quae siet
scio nec novi.

Eucl.   Illam, ex Silvani luco quam abstuleras, cedo.
i, refer. dimidiam tecum potius partem dividam.
tam etsi fur mihi es, molestus non ero. i vero,
refer.

Lyc. Sanus tu non es qui furem me voces. ego te,
Euclio,
de alia re rescivisse censui, quod ad me attinet ;   770
¹magna est res quam ego tecum otiose, si otium
est, cupio loqui.

Eucl. Dic bona fide : tu id aurum non surripuisti ?

Lyc.   Bona.

Eucl. Neque eum scis qui abstulerit ?

Lyc.   Istuc quoque bona.

Eucl.   Atque id si scies
qui abstulerit, mihi indicabis ?

Lyc.   Faciam.

Eucl.   Neque partem tibi
ab eo qui habet indipisces neque furem excipies ?

Lyc.   Ita.

Eucl. Quid si fallis ?

Lyc.   Tum me faciat quod volt magnus Iuppiter.

Eucl. Sat habeo. age nunc loquere quid vis.

---

¹ Corrupt (Leo) : *res* excised by Hare.

THE POT OF GOLD

Lyc. Not unless you say what you're looking for.

Eucl. The pot of gold, I tell you; I want back the pot of gold you owned up to taking.

Lyc. Great heavens, man! I never said that or did it, either.

Eucl. You deny it?

Lyc. Deny it? Absolutely. Why, I don't know, haven't any idea, about your gold, or what that pot is.

Eucl. The one you took from the grove of Silvanus—give it me. Go, bring it back. (*pleadingly*) You can have half of it, yes, yes, I'll divide. Even though you are such a thief, I won't make any trouble for you. Do, do go and bring it back, oh do!

Lyc. Man alive, you're out of your senses, calling me a thief. I supposed you had found out about something else that does concern me, Euclio. There's an important matter I'm anxious to talk over quietly with you, sir, if you're at leisure.

Eucl. Give me your word of honour: you didn't steal that gold?

Lyc. (*shaking his head*) On my honour.

Eucl. And you don't know the man that did take it?

Lyc. Nor that, either, on my honour.

Eucl. And if you learn who took it, you'll inform me?

Lyc. I will.

Eucl. And you won't go shares with the man that has it, or shield the thief?

Lyc. No.

Eucl. What if you deceive me?

Lyc. Then, sir, may I be dealt with as great God sees fit.

Eucl. That will suffice. All right now, say what you want.

Lyc.   Si me novisti minus,
    genere quo sim gnatus: hic mihi est Megadorus
        avonculus,
    meus pater fuit Antimachus, ego vocor Lyconides,
    mater est Eunomia.

Eucl.   Novi genus. nunc quid vis? id volo   780
    noscere.

Lyc.   Filiam ex te tu habes.

Eucl.   Immo eccillam domi.

Lyc. Eam tu despondisti, opinor, meo avonculo?

Eucl.   Omnem rem tenes.

Lyc. Is me nunc renuntiare repudium iussit tibi.

Eucl. Repudium rebus paratis, exornatis nuptiis?
    ut illum di immortales omnes deaeque quantum est
        perduint,
    quem propter hodie auri tantum perdidi infelix,
        miser.

Lyc. Bono animo es, bene dice. nunc quae res tibi et
        gnatae tuae
    bene feliciterque vortat—ita di faxint, inquito.

Eucl. Ita di faciant.

Lyc.   Et mihi ita di faciant. audi nunciam.
    qui homo culpam admisit in se, nullust tam parvi
        preti,   790
    quom pudeat, quin purget sese. nunc te obtestor,
        Euclio,
    ut si quid ego erga te imprudens peccavi aut gna-
        tam tuam,
    ut mi ignoscas eamque uxorem mihi des, ut leges
        iubent.
    ego me iniuriam fecisse filiae fateor tuae,
    Cereris vigiliis, per vinum atque impulsu adule
        scentiae.

Eucl. Ei mihi, quod ego facinus ex te audio?

316

THE POT OF GOLD

yc.   In case you're not acquainted with my family connections, sir,—Megadorus here is my uncle: my father was Antimachus, and my own name is Lyconides: Eunomia is my mother.

ucl.   I know who you are. Now what do you want? That's what I wish to know.

yc.   You have a daughter.

ucl.   Yes, yes, at home there!

yc.   You have betrothed her to my uncle, I understand.

ucl.   Precisely, precisely.

yc.   He has asked me to inform you now that he breaks the engagement.

ucl.   (*furious*) Breaks the engagement, with everything ready, the wedding prepared for? May all the everlasting powers above consume that villain that's to blame for my losing my gold, all that gold, poor God-forsaken creature that I am!

yc.   Brace up, sir: don't curse. And now for something that I pray will turn out well and happily for yourself and your daughter—" God grant it may! " Say that.

ucl.   (*doubtfully*) God grant it may!

yc.   And God grant it may for me, too! Now listen, sir. There isn't a man alive so worthless but what he wants to clear himself when he's done wrong and is ashamed. Now, sir, if I've injured you or your daughter without realizing what I was doing, I implore you to forgive me and let me marry her as I'm legally bound to. (*nervously*) It was the night of Ceres' festival . . . and what with wine and . . . a young fellow's natural impulses together . . . I wronged her, I confess it.

ucl.   Oh, oh, my God! What villainy am I hearing of?

317

Lyc.   Cur eiulas,
quem ego avom feci iam ut esses filiai nuptiis ?
nam tua gnata peperit, decumo mense post : nume-
    rum cape ;
ea re repudium remisit avonculus causa mea.
i intro, exquaere, sitne ita ut ego praedico.

Eucl.   Perii oppido,   800
ita mihi ad malum malae res plurimae se adgluti-
    nant.
ibo intro, ut quid huius verum sit sciam.

Lyc.   Iam te sequor.
haec propemodum iam esse in vado salutis res
    videtur.
nunc servom esse ubi dicam meum Strobilum non
    reperio ;
nisi etiam hic opperiar tamen paulisper ; postea
    intro
hunc subsequar. nunc interim spatium ei dabo
    exquirendi
meum factum ex gnatae pedisequa nutrice anu :
    ea rem novit.

ACTVS V

Strob. Di immortales, quibus et quantis me donatis gau-
          diis.
          quadrilibrem aulam auro onustam habeo. quis me
          est ditior ?
          quis me Athenis nunc magis quisquam est homo
          cui di sint propitii ?   810

Lyc.   Certo enim ego vocem hic loquentis modo mi
          audire visus sum.

Strob.   Hem,
          erumne ego aspicio meum ?

318

Lyc. (*patting his shoulder*) Lamenting, sir, lamenting, when you're a grandfather, and this your daughter's wedding day? You see it's the tenth month since the festival—reckon it up—and we have a child, sir. This explains my uncle's breaking the engagement: he did it for my sake. Go in and inquire if it isn't just as I tell you.

Eucl. Oh, my life is wrecked, wrecked! The way calamities swarm down and settle on me one after another! Go in I will, and have the truth of it!

[EXIT INTO HIS HOUSE.

Lyc. (*as he disappears*) I'll soon be with you, sir. (*after a pause, contentedly*) It does look as if we were pretty nearly safe in the shallows now. (*looking around*) Where in the world my fellow Strobilus is I can't imagine. Well, the only thing to do is to wait here a bit longer; then I'll join father-in-law inside. Meanwhile I'll let him have an opportunity to inquire into the case from the old nurse that's been his daughter's maid: she knows about it all. (*waits in doorway*)

ACT V

ENTER *Strobilus.*

Strob. Ye immortal gods, what joy, what bliss, ye bless me with! I have a four pound pot of gold, chock full of gold! Show me a man that's richer! Who's the chap in all Athens now that Heaven's kinder to than me?

Lyc. Why, it surely seemed as if I heard some one's voice just then. (*catches a glimpse of Strobilus's face, the latter wheeling around as he sees Lyconides*)

Strob. (*aside*) Hm! Is that master there?

319

Lyc.	Videon ego hunc servom meum?
Strob.	Ipsus est.
Lyc.	Haud alius est.
Strob.	Congrediar.
Lyc.	Contollam gradum.

credo ego illum, ut iussi, eampse anum adiisse,
    huius nutricem virginis.

Strob. Quin ego illi me invenisse dico hanc praedam[1]?
igitur orabo ut manu me emittat. ibo atque elo-
    quar.
repperi—

Lyc.	Quid repperisti?
Strob.	Non quod pueri clamitant

in faba se repperisse.

Lyc.	Iamne autem, ut soles? deludis.
Strob.	Ere, mane, eloquar iam, ausculta.
Lyc.	Age ergo loquere.
Strob.	Repperi hodie, 820

ere, divitias nimias.

Lyc.	Ubinam?
Strob.	Quadrilibrem, inquam,

aulam auri plenam.

Lyc. Quod ego facinus audio ex te? Euclioni hic seni
    subripuit.
ubi id est aurum?

Strob.   In arca apud me. nunc volo me emitti manu.

Lyc.   Egone te emittam manu,
    scelerum cumulatissume?

Strob.   Abi, ere, scio quam rem geras.
lepide hercle animum tuom temptavi. iam ut eri-
    peres apparabas:
quid faceres, si repperissem?

---

[1] *praedam atque eloquar* MSS: Leo brackets *atque
eloquar.*

Lyc. (*aside*) My servant, is it?

Strob. (*aside, after a quick glance*) It's the governor.

Lyc. (*aside*) Himself.

Strob. (*aside*) Here goes. (*moves toward Lyconides*)

Lyc. (*aside*) I'll go meet him. No doubt he's followed instructions and been to see that old woman I mentioned, my girl's nurse.

Strob. (*aside*) Why not tell him I've found this prize? Then I'll beg him to set me free. I'll up and let him have the whole story. (*to Lyconides, as they meet*) I've found——

Lyc. (*scoffingly*) Found what?

Strob. No such trifle as youngsters hurrah over finding in a bean.[1]

Lyc. At your old tricks? You're chaffing. (*pretends to be about to leave*)

Strob. Hold on, sir: I'll tell you all about it this minute. Listen.

Lyc. Well, well, then, tell away.

Strob. Sir, to-day I've found—boundless riches!

Lyc. (*interested*) You have? Where?

Strob. A four pound pot, sir, I tell you, a four pound pot just full of gold!

Lyc. What's all this you've done? He's the man that robbed old Euclio. Where is this gold?

Strob. In a box at home. Now I want you to set me free.

Lyc. (*angrily*) I set you free, you, you great lump of iniquity?

Strob. (*crestfallen, then laughing heartily*) Go along with you, sir! I know what you're after. Gad! that was clever of me, testing you in that way! And you were just getting ready to drop on it! Now what would you be doing, if I really had found it?

---

[1] It is uncertain what they did find.

Lyc.   Non potes probasse nugas.
i, redde aurum.

Strob.   Reddam ego aurum?

Lyc.   Redde, inquam, ut huic reddatur.

Strob.   Unde?

Lyc.   Quod modo fassu's esse in arca.

Strob.   Soleo hercle ego garrire nugas.   830

Lyc.[1]

Strob.   Ita loquor.

Lyc.   At scin quomodo?[2]

Strob.   Vel hercle enica,
numquam hinc feres a me

FRAGMENTA

pro illis corcotis, strophiis, sumptu uxorio   I

ut admemordit hominem   II

Eucl.   ego ecfodiebam in die denos scrobes.   III

Eucl.   nec noctu nec diu   IV

quietus umquam servabam eam : nunc dormiam.

qui mi holera cruda ponunt, hallec adduint.   V

---

[1] Leo notes lacuna here : *Non te habere dicis aurum* Leo.
[2] Leo notes lacuna here : *Verberibus caedere donec reddideris* Leo.

yc.   No, no, that won't pass. Off with you: hand over the gold.

rob.   Hand over the gold? I?

yc.   Yes, hand it over, so that it may be handed over to Euclio.

rob.   Gold? Where from?

yc.   The gold you just admitted was in the box.

rob.   Bless your heart, sir, my tongue's all the time running on foolish-like.

yc.

rob.   That's what I say.

yc.   (*seizing him*) See here, do you know what you'll get?

rob.   By heaven, sir, you can even kill me, but you won't have it from me, never——

The rest of the play is lost, save for a few fragments. Apparently Lyconides, on returning the pot of gold, was given permission to marry Euclio's daughter ; and Euclio, having a change of heart, or influenced by his Household God, gave it to the young couple as a wedding present.

FRAGMENTS

Instead of those fine saffron dresses, girdles, trousseau outlay
How he fleeced the man

1 *Eucl.* I used to be digging ten ditches a day.

Eucl. I never had a bit of rest day or night watching it: now I shall sleep.

People that serve me raw vegetables ought to add some sauce.

BACCHIDES

OR

THE TWO BACCHISES

PERSONAE

PISTOCLERVS ADVLESCENS	MNESILOCHVS ADVLESCENS
BACCHIS ⎫	PHILOXENVS SENEX
BACCHIS ⎭ SORORES MERETRICES	PARASITVS
LYDVS PAEDAGOGVS	PVER
CHRYSALVS SERVVS	ARTAMO LORARIVS
NICOBVLVS SENEX	CLEOMACHVS MILES

DRAMATIS PERSONAE

PISTOCLERUS, *son of Philoxenus.*
BACCHIS OF ATHENS
BACCHIS OF SAMOS, *her sister* } *courtesans.*
LYDUS, *slave of Philoxenus and tutor of Pistoclerus.*
CHRYSALUS, *slave of Nicobulus and Mnesilochus.*
NICOBULUS, *an old gentleman of Athens.*
MNESILOCHUS, *his son.*
PHILOXENUS, *an old gentleman of Athens.*
A PARASITE, *a retainer of the Captain's.*
A PAGE *in the service of the Captain.*
ARTAMO, *Nicobulus's slave overseer.*
CLEOMACHUS, *a Captain.*

Scene :—Athens. A street with the houses of Bacchis and Nicobulus side by side.

The first part of the play is lost, save for a few fragments, together with the last part of THE POT OF GOLD : *Leo's summary of it follows :*

Pistoclerus has received a letter from his friend Mnesilochus at Ephesus asking for help in his love affair. He has been captivated by a girl there named Bacchis, who has been hired for a year by a certain Captain Cleomachus and taken by him to Athens. Mnesilochus wishes his friend to find Bacchis and obtain her release from the Captain. A servant of Bacchis of Athens has gone down to the harbour and comes back to her mistress with the report that her sister Bacchis has arrived. In charge of a slave of the Captain's this sister appears. The sisters meet with Pistoclerus, who is in search of his friend's sweetheart, and determine to make him useful.

TITUS MACCIUS PLAUTUS

FRAGMENTA

quibus ingenium in animo utibilest, modicum et
    sine vernilitate   I (IV G)
vincla, virgae, molae: saevitudo mala fit peior   II (V)
converrite [1] scopis, agite strenue   III (VI)
                               ecquis evocat   IV (VII)
cum nassiterna et cum aqua istum impurissimum?
sicut lacte lactis similest   V (VIII)

Bacch. illa mi cognominis fuit   VI (III)

latro suam qui auro vitam venditat   VII (IX)
scio spiritum eius maiorem esse multo   VIII (X)
quam folles taurini habent, cum liquescunt
petrae, ferrum ubi fit.
                  Cuiatis tibi visust?
Praenestinum opino esse, ita erat gloriosus.
neque id haud subditiva gloria oppidum arbitror. IX (XI)

Puer ne a quoquam acciperes alio mercedem annuam, X (XVII)
nisi ab sese, nec cum quiquam limares caput.
limaces viri   XI (XVIII)
cor meum, spes mea,   XII (XIII)
mel meum, suavitudo, cibus, gaudium.
sine te amem   XIII (XIV)
Cupidon tecum saevust anne Amor?   XIV (XIX)
Vlixem audivi fuisse aerumnosissimum,   XV (I)
qui annis viginti errans a patria afuit;
verum hic adulescens multo Vlixem anteit [2]
qui ilico errat intra muros civicos.
quidquid est nomen sibi   XVI (II)

---

[1] Leo notes lacuna here: *aedis* Ritschl.
[2] Leo notes lacuna here: *fide* Leo.

THE TWO BACCHISES

FRAGMENTS

I   Those with a mental make-up of the right sort, modest and civil

II   Shackles, whips, work in the mill: frightful cruelty gets to be more frightful

III   Sweep (it) up with your brooms: come, be lively

IV   Some one call out that vile wretch with a big pail and some water.

V   As much alike as two drops of milk are.

Bacch.   She had the same name as myself

VI

VII   A mercenary who sells his life for gold.
I'm sure his breathing's much louder than the puffs from a bull's-hide bellows when they're melting rocks at the iron-works.
Where does he come from, do you think?
Praeneste, probably, to judge from his boasting.

X   I don't think the town's fame is at all supposititious.

Page   Not to let you take a yearly fee from anyone

X   else but him, or rub heads with anyone.

XI   Slugs of men.

XII   My heart, my hope, my honey, sweetness, food delight.

XIII   Do let me love you

XIV   Is it Cupid, or Love, raging within you?

XV   They say Ulysses had an awfully hard time of it, away from home as he was for twenty years, wandering round. But this young gentleman is a long way ahead of Ulysses with his wandering round here inside the city walls.

XVI   Whatever her (his) name is

331

Pistoc.	quae sodalem atque me exercitos habet	**xvii** (xii)
	nam credo cuivis excantare cor potes.	**xviii** (xx)
	sin lenocinium forte collibitum est tibi,	**xix** (xvi)
	videas mercedis quid tibi est aecum dari,	
	ne istac aetate me sectere gratiis.	30
	Arabus.	**xx** (xv)

Bacch. Quid si hoc potis est ut tu taceas, ego loquar?

Soror   Lepide, licet.

Bacch. Ubi me fugiet memoria, ibi tu facito ut subvenias, soror.

Soror Pol magis metuo, ne defuerit mi in monendo oratio.

Bacch. Pol ego metuo, lusciniolae ne defuerit cantio. sequere hac.

Pistoc. Quid agunt duae germanae meretrices cognomines? quid in consilio consuluistis?

Bacch.   Bene.

Pistoc.   Pol haud meretricium est.   40

Bacch. Miserius nihil est quam mulier.

Pistoc.   Quid esse dices dignius?

Bacch. Haec ita me orat, sibi qui caveat aliquem ut hominem reperiam,

       ut istunc militem—ut, ubi emeritum sibi sit, se revehat domum.

       id, amabo te, huic caveas.

33²

istoc.	A girl that has been keeping my chum and me
vii	exercised
viii	For I do believe you can witch the heart out of anyone you please.
ix	But if pandering happens to have caught your fancy, you should consider what price ought to be paid you, that you may not run after me at that time of life for nothing.
x	Arabian

> *Bacchis* AND HER SISTER ARE STANDING TOGETHER TALKING, *Pistoclerus* APART.

acch. How about your keeping a quiet tongue yourself, if possible, and my doing the talking?

ister Charming! By all means.

Bacch. In case my memory deserts me, see you come to the rescue, sister.

ister Goodness me! I'm more afraid of sage suggestions failing myself.

Bacch. (*laughing*) Goodness me! And I'm afraid of song failing the little nightingale. Come on. (*leads the way toward Pistoclerus*)

Pistoc. (*aside, nervously*) What are those two up to, those harlot sisters with the same name? (*aloud, trying to assume the air of a man of the world*) What have you girls settled on in that session?

Bacch. Something nice.

Pistoc. By Jove! Unusual in the profession!

Bacch. (*in apparent dejection*) Oh, there's nothing more miserable than a woman!

Pistoc. And what ought to be more so, in your opinion?

Bacch. My sister here is imploring me to find some one to stand by her, so that our Captain—so that he may carry her back home when she's served her time. Do stand by her in this, there's a dear.

M

Pistoc. Quid isti caveam?
Bacch. Ut revehatur domum,
ubi ei dediderit operas, ne hanc ille habeat pro
ancilla sibi;
nam si haec habeat aurum quod illi renumeret,
faciat lubens.
Pistoc. Ubi nunc is homost?
Bacch. Iam hic credo aderit. sed hoc idem apud nos rectius
poteris agere; atque is dum veniat, sedens ibi op-
peribere.
eadem biberis, eadem dedero tibi, ubi biberis, savium.
Pistoc. Viscus merus vostrast blanditia.
Bacch. Quid iam?
Pistoc. Quia enim intellego, 50
duae unum expetitis palumbem,[1] perii harundo
alas verberat.
non ego istuc facinus mihi, mulier, conducibile esse
arbitror.
Bacch. Qui, amabo?
Pistoc. Quia, Bacchis, bacchas metuo et bacchanal tuom.
Bacch. Quid est? quid metuis? ne tibi lectus malitiam
apud me suadeat?
Pistoc. Magis illectum tuom quam lectum metuo. mala
tu es bestia.
nam huic aetati non conducit, mulier, latebrosus locus.
Bacch. Egomet, apud me si quid stulte facere cupias, pro-
hibeam.
sed ego apud me te esse ob eam rem, miles cum
veniat, volo,
quia, cum tu aderis, huic mihique haud faciet quisquam iniuriam:
tu prohibebis, et eadem opera tuo sodali operam
dabis; 60

---

[1] Corrupt (Leo): *perii* MSS: *prope* Ritschl.

Pistoc. Stand by her? How?

Bacch. To have her carried back home when she's finished her service, so that he mayn't keep her for his maid servant. Why, if she only had the money to pay him back, she'd be glad to do it.

Pistoc. Where is this man at present?

Bacch. He'll be here soon, I suppose. But this is a matter you can manage better at our house; yes, you sit down and wait there till he comes. (*coaxingly*) You shall have something to drink, too, and after that I'll give you just the nicest sort of kiss, too.

Pistoc. Nothing but birdlime, these honeyed words.

Bacch. Oh now, why?

Pistoc. Well, because here you are, the pair of you, after one lone pigeon. (*aside*) Damnation! The limed twigs are brushing my wings! (*aloud, stiffly*) Madam, I consider this an unprofitable business for me to be in.

Bacch. Bless your heart, why so?

Pistoc. Well, Bacchis, I'm afraid of Bacchantes and your Bacchante resort.

Bacch. How's that? What are you afraid of? The couch's tempting you to be naughty with me?

Pistoc. It's not so much the couch as the couch's alluring occupant I'm afraid of. You're a dangerous animal. Why, dens of darkness don't become a young fellow like me.

Bacch. (*quite artless*) If you felt like doing anything silly there with me, I'd stop you my own self. But this is why I want you to be at my house when the Captain comes—because no one will do her (*pointing to sister*) or me any harm when you're by. You'll prevent it, and be helping along your chum at the same time; and when that military man

335

et ille adveniens tuam med esse amicam suspicabitur.
quid, amabo, opticuisti?

Pistoc.   Quia istaec lepida sunt memoratui:
eadem in usu atque ubi periclum facias, aculeata sunt,
animum fodicant, bona distimulant, facta et famam
    sauciant.

Soror   Quid ab hac metuis?

Pistoc.   Quid ego metuam rogitas? adulescens homo
penetrem me huius modi in palaestram, ubi damnis
    desudascitur? [1]

Bacch.   Lepide memoras.

Pistoc.   Ubi ego capiam pro machaera turturem,[2]
pro galea scaphium, pro insigni sit corolla plectilis,   70
pro hasta talos, pro lorica malacum capiam pallium,
ubi mihi pro equo lectus detur, scortum pro scuto
    accubet?
apage a me, apage.

Bacch.   Ah, nimium ferus es.

Pistoc.   Mihi sum.

Bacch.   Malacissandus es.
equidem tibi do hanc operam.

Pistoc.   Ah, nimium pretiosa es operaria.

Bacch.   Simulato me amare.

Pistoc.   Utrum ego istuc iocon adsimulem an serio?

Bacch.   Heia, hoc agere meliust. miles quom huc adveniat,
te volo
me amplexari.

Pistoc.   Quid eo mi opus est?

Bacch.   Ut ille te videat volo.
scio quid ago.

---

[1] Leo brackets following v., 67: *ubi pro disco damnum capiam, pro cursura dedecus?*

[2] Leo brackets following v., 69: *ubique imponat in manum alius mihi pro cestu cantharum.*

	arrives, he'll take me for your sweetheart. Now, now, my dearie,—why so silent?
stoc.	Because those words of yours have a pretty sound: but when a fellow takes 'em up and tries 'em they're barbed—they pink a heart, run a fortune through, disable a character and reputation.
ster	Why are you afraid of her?
istoc.	Why am I afraid of her, eh? A young fellow like me to enter a physical training school of this sort (*pointing to Bacchis's house*) where a man only sweats himself to insolvency?
acch.	(*with pretended admiration*) You do say such clever things!
istoc.	Where my sword would be a turtle dove, my helmet a wine bowl, my plume a woven chaplet, my spear a dice box, my corselet a downy robe; where I'd be given a couch for a horse, with a bad bad girl beside me for a buckler? Hence! Avaunt!
acch.	Ah, you're too hard on us!
istoc.	I am hard on myself.
acch.	We'll have to soften you. Yes indeed, I'll take you in hand myself—(*fondling him*) this way.
istoc.	(*submitting reluctantly*) Ah, your handiwork is too expensive.
acch.	Do make believe you love me.
istoc.	(*smiling*) Make believe in fun, or as if I meant business?
acch.	(*reprovingly*) Now, now! here's what we'd better do. When the Captain arrives I want you to hug me.
istoc.	What's the use of my doing that?
acch.	I want him to see you. I know what I'm doing.

337

Pistoc.   Et pol ego scio quid metuo. sed quid ais?

Bacch.   Quid est?

Pistoc. Quid si apud te eveniat desubito prandium aut
            potatio

forte aut cena, ut solet in istis fieri conciliabulis,   80

ubi ego tum accumbam?

Bacch.   Apud me, mi anime, ut lepidus cum lepida
            accubet.

locus hic apud nos, quamvis subito venias, semper
    liber est.

ubi tu lepide voles esse tibi " mea rosa," mihi dicito

" dato qui bene sit ": ego ubi bene sit tibi locum
    lepidum dabo.

Pistoc. Rapidus fluvius est hic, non hac temere transiri
            potest.

Bacch. Atque ecastor apud hunc fluvium aliquid perdun-
            dumst tibi.

manum da et sequere.

Pistoc.   Aha, minime.

Bacch.   Quid ita?

Pistoc.   Quia istoc inlecebrosius

fieri nil potest: nox mulier vinum homini adule-
    scentulo.

Bacch. Age igitur, equidem pol nihili facio nisi causa tua.

ille quidem hanc abducet; tu nullus adfueris, si
    non lubet.   90

Pistoc. Sumne autem nihili, qui nequeam ingenio moderari
            meo?

Bacch. Quid est quod metuas?

Pistoc.   Nihil est, nugae. mulier, tibi me emancupo:

tuos sum, tibi dedo operam.

stoc. Gad! And I know what I'm fearing. But, I say.

cch. Well?

stoc. What if there should happen to be an impromptu luncheon or drinking party at your house, or a dinner party, perhaps the ordinary thing at resorts like yours—where would my place be then?

cch. Next to me, darling; a nice boy and a nice girl side by side. This place at my house is your very own always, no matter how unexpectedly you come. Whenever you want to have a nice time just say, "Give me a comfy place, rosey dear," and I'll give you a nice place to be comfy in.

stoc. (*half to himself*) This is a rapid stream: dangerous crossing here!

cch. (*aside*) My conscience, yes! And a stream you're bound to lose something in, young man! (*aloud*) Give me your hand and come along. (*tries to take it*)

stoc. (*drawing back*) Oh no, not a bit of it!

cch. Why not?

stoc. Because a young fellow couldn't be offered a more enticing combination than that—wine, woman, and evening hours.

cch. All right then. Dear me, I don't mind at all except for your sake, indeed I don't. To be sure he'll carry her off; but don't you come near me if you don't like to. (*looks at him sadly and appealingly*)

stoc. (*half aside*) So I've no mind at all, eh—no power to control myself?

cch. What is it you're afraid of?

stoc. (*pauses, then ardently*) Nothing! Bagatelles! I surrender myself to you, my lady: I'm all your own; command me.

Bacch.   Lepidu's. nunc ego te facere hoc volo.
ego sorori meae cenam hodie dare volo viaticam :
eo tibi argentum iubebo iam intus ecferri foras ;
tu facito opsonatum nobis sit opulentum opsonium.

Pistoc. Ego opsonabo, nam id flagitium meum sit, mea te
  gratia
et operam dare mi et ad eam operam facere sumptum
  de tuo.

Bacch. At ego nolo dare te quicquam.

Pistoc.   Sine.

Bacch.   Sino equidem, si lubet.
propera, amabo.

Pistoc.   Prius hic adero quam te amare desinam. 100

Soror Bene me accipies advenientem, mea soror.

Bacch.   Quid ita, obsecro ?

Soror Quia piscatus meo quidem animo hic tibi hodie
  evenit bonus.

Bacch. Meus ille quidemst. tibi nunc operam dabo de
  Mnesilocho, soror,
ut hic accipias potius aurum, quam hinc eas cum
  milite.

Soror Cupio.

Bacch.   Dabitur opera. aqua calet : eamus hinc
  intro, ut laves.
nam uti navi vecta es, credo timida es.

Soror   Aliquantum, soror.[1]

Bacch. Sequere hac igitur me intro in lectum, ut sedes
  lassitudinem.

---

[1] Leo brackets following v., 107 : *simul huic nescio cui,
turbare qui huc it, decedamus.*

acch. That's a nice boy! (*petting him*) Now this is what
I want you to do. I want to give my sister a
dinner to-day to celebrate her coming. I'll tell
them to bring you out some money at once, and
you're to see to provisioning us in perfectly splendid
style. (*turns to call to servant within*)

istoc. (*eagerly*) I'll stand the provisioning myself: why,
it wouldn't be decent of me to let you give me
a good time, in your kindness, and pay the bills
for it too.

acch. (*glancing slyly at her sister*) But I don't want it to
cost you anything.

istoc. Do let me.

acch. Oh, very well, if you really want to. Hurry along,
there's a dear.

istoc. (*fondly*) I'll be back before I've stopped loving you.
[EXIT *Pistoclerus.*

ster You're going to entertain me finely on my arrival,
sister mine.

acch. Indeed? Why do you say that?

ster Well, that's something fine in the fish line (*with a
smile toward the retreating figure of Pistoclerus*) you've
landed to-day, at least I think so.

acch. Oh yes, I've caught him all right. Now I must
help you out in regard to Mnesilochus, my dear,
so that you may pick up some money here rather
than go trooping off with the Captain.

ster I do so wish you would.

acch. We'll see to it. (*going toward house*) The water's
hot: let's go inside so that you may bathe. For after
that sea trip of yours I dare say you're feeling shaky.

ster More or less, sister.

acch. Come on in with me then, so as to lie down and
get rested. [EXEUNT.

TITUS MACCIUS PLAUTUS

I. 2.

Lydus Iam dudum, Pistoclere, tacitus te sequor,
expectans quas tu res hoc ornatu geras.   110
namque ita me di ament, ut Lycurgus mihi quidem
videtur posse hic ad nequitiam adducier.
quo nunc capessis ted hinc adversa via
cum tanta pompa?

Pistoc.   Huc.

Lydus   Quid huc? quis istic habet?

Pistoc. Amor, Voluptas, Venus, Venustas, Gaudium,
Iocus, Ludus, Sermo, Suavisaviatio.

Lydus Quid tibi commercist cum dis damnosissimis?

Pistoc. Mali sunt homines, qui bonis dicunt male;
tu dis nec recte dicis: non aequom facis.

Lydus An deus est ullus Sauvisaviatio?   120

Pistoc. An non putasti esse umquam? o Lyde, es barbarus;
quem ego sapere nimio censui plus quam Thalem,
is stultior es barbaro poticio,
qui tantus natu deorum nescis nomina.

Lydus Non hic placet mi ornatus.

Pistoc.   Nemo ergo tibi
haec apparavit: mihi paratum est quoi placet.

Lydus Etiam me advorsus exordire argutias?
qui si decem habeas linguas, mutum esse addecet.

342

THE TWO BACCHISES

Scene 2.   (*An hour has elapsed.*)

ENTER *Pistoclerus* PRECEDED BY SLAVES CARRYING PROVISIONS, FLOWERS, ETC. *Lydus* FOLLOWS.

Lydus (*magisterially*) I have been following you in silence for some time, Pistoclerus, waiting to see what you were about with this gear. (*pointing to slaves and their hampers*) Why, Lord love me, I do believe Lycurgus [1] himself could be led astray here. Where are you betaking yourself now, going away up the street with such a train?

Pistoc. (*pointing to Bacchis's door*) Here.

Lydus What do you mean by " here "? Who lives there?

Pistoc. (*rapturously*) Love, Delight, Venus, Grace, Joy, Jest, Jollity, Chitchat, Kissykissysweetkins!

Lydus (*shocked*) What commerce have you with such pernicious, pernicious deities?

Pistoc. It takes a bad man to say bad things of the good; you're blaspheming the gods: it's wrong.

Lydus You mean to say there is a god Kissykissysweet kins?

Pistoc. You mean to say you didn't ever suppose there was? Oh, Lydus, you are a barbarian! I fancied you were ever so much wiser than Thales and here you are, sillier than a barbarian babe in arms—your age, and not knowing the names of the gods!

Lydus I do not like this paraphernalia.

Pistoc. Well, nobody got it together for you: it was got for me, and I do like it.

Lydus Are you actually commencing to make smart replies to me? You whom it befits to be mute, even if you had ten tongues?

The Spartan reformer.

343

Pistoc. Non omnis aetas, Lyde, ludo convenit.

magis unum in mentemst mihi nunc, satis ut com- 130
mode

pro dignitate opsoni haec concuret cocus.

Lydus Iam perdidisti te atque me atque operam meam,

qui tibi nequiquam saepe monstravi bene.

Pistoc. Ibidem ego meam operam perdidi, ubi tu tuam :

tua disciplina nec mihi prodest nec tibi.

Lydus O praeligatum pectus.

Pistoc.   Odiosus mihi es.

tace atque sequere, Lyde, me.

Lydus   Illuc sis vide,

non paedagogum iam me, sed Lydum vocat.

Pistoc. Non par videtur neque sit consentaneum,

cum haec qui emit intus sit et cum amica accubet 140

cumque osculetur et convivae alii accubent,

praesentibus illis paedagogus una ut siet.

Lydus An hoc ad eas res opsonatumst, obsecro ?

Pistoc. Sperat quidem animus : quo evenat dis in manust.

Lydus Tu amicam habebis ?

Pistoc.   Cum videbis, tum scies.

Lydus Immo neque habebis neque sinam ; i prorsum
domum.

Pistoc. Omitte, Lyde, ac cave malo.

Lydus   Quid ? cave malo ?

Pistoc. Iam excessit mi aetas ex magisterio tuo.

Lydus O barathrum, ubi nunc es ? ut ego te usurpem
lubens.[1]

149

---

[1] Leo brackets following **v.**, 150 : *video nimio iam multo
plus quam volueram.*

istoc. We aren't schoolboys for ever, Lydus. The one thing uppermost in my mind just now is that the cook may do as creditable a job on these edibles as their excellence calls for.

ydus Ah, now you have thrown yourself away, and me, and my labour,—me, who many a time gave you good advice, all in vain!

istoc. I threw away my own labour at the same place you did yours: your system of instruction is no good to either of us.

ydus Oh, what an obdurate breast!

istoc. You're a bore! Keep still and come along, Lydus.

ydus Now kindly look at that! He no longer calls me " Tutor," merely Lydus.

istoc. It's not the proper thing, it would be out of place, when the man who bought all this is inside there, and on a couch with his mistress, kissing her—and other guests about—to have his " Tutor " there in their presence.

ydus (*horrified*) In the name of heaven! These provisions bought for such an orgy?

istoc. (*flippantly*) Well, of course man proposes and God disposes.

ydus You to have a mistress, you?

istoc (*enthusiastically*) Once you see her, then you'll know!

ydus Never! You shall not have one; I will not allow it. (*taking Pistoclerus by the arm and trying to lead him back*) Go home this instant.

istoc. (*pulling away*) Leave me alone, Lydus, and (*threateningly*) look out for trouble.

ydus What? " Look out for trouble? "

istoc. I'm too old for you to play the teacher these days.

ydus (*tragically*) Oh, pit, where art thou now? How

TITUS MACCIUS PLAUTUS

	vixisse nimio satiust iam quam vivere.	
	magistron quemquam discipulum minitarier? [1]	
Pistoc.	Fiam, ut ego opinor, Hercules, tu autem Linus.	
Lydus	Pol metuo magis, ne Phoenix tuis factis fuam	
	teque ad patrem esse mortuom renuntiem.	
Pistoc.	Satis historiarumst.	
Lydus	Hic vereri perdidit.	
	compendium edepol haud aetati optabile	
	fecisti, cum istanc nactu's inpudentiam.	160
	occisus hic homo est. ecquid in mentem est tibi	
	patrem tibi esse?	
Pistoc.	Tibi ego an tu mihi servos es?	
Lydus	Peior magister te istaec docuit, non ego.	
	nimio es tu ad istas res discipulus docilior,	
	quam ad illa quae te docui, ubi operam perdidi.[2]	
Pistoc.	Istactenus tibi, Lyde, libertas datast	
	orationis. satis est. sequere hac me ac tace.	

ACTVS II

Chrys.	Erilis patria, salve, quam ego biennio,	170
	postquam hinc in Ephesum abii conspicio lubens.	
	saluto te, vicine Apollo, qui aedibus	

---

[1] Leo brackets following v., 153, 154 :
nil moror discipulos mihi iam plenos sanguinis.
valens afflictat me vacivom virium.

I have no liking for these full-blooded pupils : the sturdy
youngster is bullying me, destitute of strength as I am.

[2] Leo brackets following v., 166, 167 :
edepol fecisti furtum in aetatem malum
cum istaec flagitia me celavisti et patrem.

Good heavens ! Such villainy in a lad of your age,
concealing such atrocities from me and from your father !

346

gladly would I take thee for mine own! Far
better that I had died than lived for this! A pupil
to threaten his teacher?

Pistoc. It's a Hercules I'll be, I'm thinking, and you a
Linus.[1]

Lydus Great heavens! I have more fear of your actions
forcing me to be a Phoenix [2] and to convey to
your father the news of your death.

Pistoc. (*impatiently*) Enough of your tales!

Lydus He is lost to shame! Great heavens! You gained
nothing that does credit to your years in acquiring
this impudence. The creature is past redemption!
Does it ever occur to you that you have a father?

Pistoc. Am I your servant, or you mine?

Lydus It was a wicked, wicked teacher gave you these
lessons, not I! You are a much apter pupil in
matters of this sort than in the subjects I lost my
labour teaching you.

Pistoc. (*coolly*) I've let you rant to your heart's content,
so far, Lydus. Now drop it. Follow me this way
and keep your mouth shut.

[EXEUNT INTO THE HOUSE OF *Bacchus*, *Lydus*
RELUCTANTLY.

ACT II

ENTER *Chrysalus.*

Chrys. (*jauntily*) Greetings, land of my—master! Land
that I behold with joy after departing hence to
Ephesus two years agone! (*turning toward altar of
Apollo in front of house*) Thee I greet, neighbour

---

[1] Linus was killed by his pupil, Hercules.
[2] Phoenix, Achilles' preceptor, informed Peleus, Achilles'
father, of his son's death.

347

propinquos nostris accolis, veneroque te,
ne Nicobulum me sinas nostrum senem
prius convenire quam sodalem viderim
Mnesilochi Pistoclerum, quem ad epistulam
Mnesilochus misit super amica Bacchide.

II. 2.

Pistoc. Mirumst me ut redeam te opere tanto quaesere,
qui abire hinc nullo pacto possim, si velim :
ita me vadatum amore vinctumque adtines.　　　180

Chrys. Pro di immortales, Pistoclerum conspicor.
o Pistoclere, salve.

Pistoc.　　　　　　Salve, Chrysale.

Chrys. Compendi verba multa iam faciam tibi.
venire tu me gaudes : ego credo tibi ;
hospitium et cenam pollicere, ut convenit
peregre advenienti : ego autem venturum adnuc.
salutem tibi ab sodali solidam nuntio :
rogabis me ubi sit : vivit.

Pistoc.　　　　　　Nempe recte valet ?

Chrys. Istuc volebam ego ex te percontarier.

Pistoc. Qui scire possum ?

Chrys.　　　　Nullus plus:

Pistoc.　　　　　　Quemnam ad modum ?　190

Chrys. Quia si illa inventa est, quam ille amat, recte valet ;
si non inventa est, minus valet moribundusque est.
animast amica amanti : si abest, nullus est ;
si adest, res nullast : ipsus est—nequam et miser.
sed tu quid factitasti mandatis super ?

Pistoc. Egon ut, quod ab illoc attigisset nuntius,
non impetratum id advenienti ei redderem ?
regiones colere mavellem Acherunticas.

348

THE TWO BACCHISES

Apollo, who dost dwell adjacent to our house, and I do implore thee not to let our old man Nicobulus fall in with me ere I see Pistoclerus, the chum of Mnesilochus, to whom Mnesilochus hath sent a letter about his mistress, Bacchis.

Scene 2.   ENTER *Pistoclerus* FROM HOUSE OF *Bacchis.*

Pistoc. (*to Bacchis within*) It seems curious, your begging me so hard to come back, when I couldn't possibly leave you if I wanted, when you've got me so bound over to you, held fast in the fetters of love.

Chrys. Ye everlasting gods! It's Pistoclerus. What ho, sir! How are you?

Pistoc. And yourself, Chrysalus?

Chrys. Here's for saving you the trouble of a long speech, sir. You're glad I've come: I believe you. You promise to do the honours and dine me, the stranger from afar, and so you should: for my part, I accept. I bring you cordial greetings from your chum. You'll ask me where he is: alive.

Pistoc. (*eagerly*) And well, well, of course?

Chrys. That's what I wanted to ask you.

Pistoc. How can I know?

Chrys. None better.

Pistoc. Why, how so?

Chrys. Because if his ladylove has been discovered, he's perfectly well: if she's not discovered, he's not so well; he's at death's door. His love is life to a lover: if she's away, he's lost; if she's there, his cash is lost, he himself being—a poor good-for-nothing fool. But you—what have you been doing about his commission?

Pistoc. I? Am I the man to let him arrive and find the request his messenger mentioned unattended to? I'd sooner pass my days in the lower regions.

349

Chrys. Eho, an invenisti Bacchidem?

Pistoc.   Samiam quidem.   199, 200

Chrys. Vide quaeso, ne quis tractet illam indiligens;
scis tu ut confringi vas cito Samium solet.

Pistoc. Iamne ut soles?

Chrys.   Dic ubi ea nunc est, obsecro.

Pistoc. Hic, exeuntem me unde aspexisti modo.

Chrys. Ut istuc est lepidum: proximae viciniae
habitat. ecquidnam meminit Mnesilochi?

Pistoc.   Rogas?
immo unice unum plurimi pendit.

Chrys.   Papae.

Pistoc. Immo ut eam credis? misera amans desiderat.

Chrys. Scitum istuc.

Pistoc.   Immo, Chrysale, em, non tantulum
umquam intermittit tempus quin eum nominet.   210

Chrys. Tanto hercle melior.

Pistoc.   Immo—

Chrys.   Immo hercle abiero
potius.

Pistoc.   Num invitus rem bene gestam audis eri?

Chrys. Non res, sed actor mihi cor odio sauciat.
etiam Epidicum, quam ego fabulam aeque ac me
   ipsum amo,
nullam aeque invitus specto, si agit Pellio.
sed Bacchis etiam fortis tibi visast?

350

THE TWO BACCHISES

Chrys. Hullo! You haven't found Bacchis?

Pistoc. Yes, the Samian one.

Chrys. (*affecting terror*) Heavens! do see that no one handles that one carelessly; you know that Samian [1] ware, how precious brittle it is.

Pistoc. The same old wag, eh?

Chrys. Tell me where she is now, for heaven's sake.

Pistoc. Here in the house you just saw me coming out of.

Chrys. Here's a go! Residing in the immediate neighbourhood! Well, well! does she remember Mnesilochus?

Pistoc. Remember him? More than that, she thinks he's the one and only man on earth.

Chrys. Oh pshaw!

Pistoc. More than that, what do you suppose her feelings are? The poor affectionate thing is dying for him.

Chrys. Quite charming!

Pistoc. More than that, Chrysalus—look!—she doesn't let even so much (*illustrating*) time pass without mentioning his name.

Chrys. Humph! So much the better of her.

Pistoc. More than that——

Chrys. (*bored*) More than that, by gad, I'd rather get out of range!

Pistoc. You don't object to hearing that your master is in a prosperous situation, do you?

Chrys. It's not the situations that make me sick unto death; it's your confounding acting. Even the *Epidicus* [2]—a comedy I love as well as my own self—well, there's not a one I so object to seeing, if Pellio's playing in it. But you really consider Bacchis a fine lively one, do you?

---

[1] A fragile and (*The Captives* 291) cheap kind of pottery.
[2] One of Plautus's plays.

Pistoc.   Rogas?
ni nanctus Venerem essem, hanc Iunonem dicerem.
Chrys.   Edepol, Mnesiloche, ut hanc rem natam intellego,
quod ames paratumst: quod des inventost opus.
nam istic fortasse auro est opus.
Pistoc.   Philippeo quidem.   220
Chrys.   Atque eo fortasse iam opust.
Pistoc.   Immo etiam prius:
nam iam huc adveniet miles.
Chrys.   Et miles quidem?
Pistoc.   Qui de amittenda Bacchide aurum hic exiget.
Chrys.   Veniat quando volt, atque ita ne mihi sit morae.
domist: non metuo nec ego quoiquam supplico,
dum quidem hoc valebit pectus perfidia meum.
abi intro, ego hic curabo.   tu intus dicito
Mnesilochum adesse Bacchidi.
Pistoc.   Faciam ut iubes.
Chrys.   Negotium hoc ad me adtinet aurarium.
mille et ducentos Philippum attulimus aureos   230
Epheso, quos hospes debuit nostro seni.
inde ego hodie aliquam machinabor machinam,
unde aurum efficiam amanti erili filio.
sed foris concrepuit nostra: quinam exit foras?

II. 3.

Nic.   Ibo in Piraeum, visam ecquae advenerit
in portum ex Epheso navis mercatoria.
nam meus formidat animus, nostrum tam diu
ibi desidere neque redire filium.

352

Pistoc. Do you ask me that? If [1] I hadn't lighted on Venus myself, I'd call her Juno.

Chrys. (*half aside*) Well, by gad, Mnesilochus, as far as I can understand the present situation, you've got your love: the wherewithal is what you need to find. (*to Pistoclerus*) For I dare say there is need of gold in the affair.

Pistoc. Yes, and good coin of the realm.

Chrys. And furthermore, I dare say it's needed soon.

Pistoc. No, before that, even: for a Captain's due here soon.

Chrys. Indeed? A Captain, too?

Pistoc. Who'll be after money for letting Bacchis go.

Chrys. (*airily*) Let him come when he wants, yes, and let him take care not to keep me waiting. I'm provided: I fear no man and supplicate no man, not I, —at least as long as this heart of mine can prompt a good stiff lie. Inside with you: (*grandly waving Pistoclerus in*) I'll take charge here myself. You tell Bacchis in there that she may expect Mnesilochus at once.

Pistoc. Very well. [EXIT.

Chrys. It's my look out, this business of the exchequer. We've brought twelve hundred sovereigns from Ephesus, money a friend there owed our old man. I'll machinate some machinations to-day for transferring part of said gold to my lovesick young master. (*listening*) But there goes our door! Wonder who's coming out. (*steps aside*)

Scene 3.   ENTER *Nicobulus* FROM HIS HOUSE.

Nic. I'll walk down to the Piraeus and see if any merchantman has come in from Ephesus. It worries me to have my son dilly-dallying there so long and not returning.

---

[1] Venus and Juno not being sisters.

353

Chrys. Extexam ego illum pulchre iam, si di volunt.
    haud dormitandumst : opus est chryso Chrysalo.   240
    adibo hunc, quem quidem ego hodie faciam hic
       arietem
    Phrixi, itaque tondebo auro usque ad vivam cutem.
    servos salutat Nicobulum Chrysalus.

Nic. Pro di immortales, Chrysale, ubi mist filius ?

Chrys. Quin tu salutem primum reddis quam dedi ?

Nic. Salve. sed ubinamst Mnesilochus ?

Chrys.   Vivit, valet.

Nic. Venitne ?

Chrys.   Venit.

Nic.   Euax, aspersisti aquam.
    benene usque valuit ?

Chrys.   Pancratice atque athletice.

Nic. Quid hoc ?   qua causa eum in Ephesum miseram,
    accepitne aurum ab hospite Archidemide ?   250

Chrys. Heu, cor meum et cerebrum, Nicobule, finditur,
    istius hominis ubi fit quomque mentio.
    tun hospitem illum nominas hostem tuom ?

Nic. Quid ita, obsecro hercle ?

Chrys.   Quia edepol certo scio,
    Volcanus, Luna, Sol, Dies, dei quattuor,
    scelestiorem nullum inluxere alterum.

Nic. Quamne Archidemidem ?

Chrys.   Quam, inquam, Archidemidem

Nic. Quid fecit ?

Chrys.   Quid non fecit ?   quin tu id me rogas ?
    primumdum infitias ire coepit filio,

THE TWO BACCHISES

hrys.   (*aside*) I'll unravel him handsomely now, God willing. No sleepyheadedness allowed: Chrysalus, you must be a golden chrysalis! Here's at him— the man I'll certainly make a [1]Phrixus's ram here to-day, and by the same token shear off his gold right down to the quick! (*aloud, ceremoniously*) Greetings to Nicobulus from servant Chrysalus, sir.

ic.   Chrysalus! for the love of heaven where is my son?

hrys.   (*affecting pique*) Why don't you return my greeting first, sir?

ic.   How d'ye do. (*more animatedly*) But where on earth is Mnesilochus?

hrys.   Alive and well.

ic.   Has he come?

hrys.   He has.

ic.   (*fervently*) Oh, good, good! That news is like a dash of water! Has he been well all this time?

hrys.   In fighting trim, a perfect athlete.

ic.   How about it? The business I sent him to Ephesus for? Did he get the gold from my friend Archidemides?

hrys.   (*disgustedly*) Ugh! My heart and head fairly split, sir, whenever I hear that fellow mentioned. Call that friend of yours fiend, won't you?

ic.   Bless my soul! Why, for heaven's sake?

hrys.   Good Lord! Because I'm positive the four gods, Fire, Moon, Sun, and Day, never shone on a more abandoned villain.

ic.   Than Archidemides?

hrys.   Yes, than Archidemides.

ic.   What has he done?

hrys.   What hasn't he done? Why don't you ask me that? Well, in the first place he began lying to

---

[1] The owner of the ram with the golden fleece.

negare se debere tibi triobolum. 260
continuo antiquom hospitem nostrum sibi
Mnesilochus advocavit, Pelagonem senem;
eo praesente homini extemplo ostendit symbolum,
quem tute dederas, ad eum ut ferret, filio.

Nic. Quid ubi ei ostendit symbolum?

Chrys. Infit dicere
adulterinum et non eum esse symbolum.
quotque innocenti ei dixit contumelias!
adulterare eum aibat rebus ceteris.

Nic. Habetin aurum? id mihi dici volo.

Chrys. Postquam quidem praetor recuperatores dedit, 270
damnatus demum, vi coactus reddidit
ducentos et mille Philippum.

Nic. Tantum debuit.

Chrys. Porro etiam ausculta pugnam quam voluit dare.

Nic. Etiamnest quid porro?

Chrys. Em, accipitrina haec nunc erit.

Nic. Deceptus sum, Autolyco hospiti aurum credidi.

Chrys. Quin tu audi.

Nic. Immo ingenium avidi haud pernoram hospitis.

Chrys. Postquam aurum abstulimus, in navem conscen-
dimus,
domi cupientes. forte ut adsedi in stega,
dum circumspecto, atque ego lembum conspicor
longum, strigorem maleficum exornarier. 280

Nic. Perii hercle, lembus ille mihi laedit latus.

your son and disclaimed owing you a single six-pence. Immediately Mnesilochus summoned that old gentleman, Pelagon, that's been our friend so long; in his presence he promptly shows the fellow the token, the one you gave your son yourself to carry to him.

Nic. (*anxiously*) And what when he showed him the token?

Chrys. (*indignantly*) He cries out it's a counterfeit and not the right token at all. And how he did heap insults on your innocent boy! Said he was an old hand at counterfeiting.

Nic. Have you got the money? Do tell me that.

Chrys. To be sure, after the judge had appointed arbitrators, he was finally convicted, and, under compulsion, he handed over twelve hundred pounds.

Nic. (*with a sigh of relief*) That was all he owed.

Chrys. There's more still, sir,—listen how he wanted to knock us out.

Nic. More still?

Chrys. Now then! (*aside*) This'll be a regular hawk swoop.

Nic. (*hotly*) I've been deceived! I've trusted my gold to an Autolycus [1] of a friend!

Chrys. Come, come, listen.

Nic. Ah, no, I didn't fathom his greedy soul.

Chrys. After we got the gold we embarked, eager for home. I was sitting on deck, and while I was looking around, my eye just happened to fall on a long, staunch, wicked-looking galley being fitted out for sea.

Nic. Hell and fury! That galley is ramming me amid-ships!

---

[1] A noted thief, the grandfather of Ulysses.

357

Chrys. Is erat communis cum hospite et praedonibus.
Nic. Adeon me fuisse fungum, ut qui illi crederem,
cum mi ipsum nomen eius Archidemides
clamaret dempturum esse, si quid crederem?
Chrys. Is lembus nostrae navi insidias dabat.
occepi ego observare eos quam rem gerant.
interea e portu nostra navis solvitur.
ubi portu eximus, homines remigio sequi,
neque aves neque venti citius. quoniam sentio   290
quae res gereretur, navem extemplo statuimus.
quoniam vident nos stare, occeperunt ratem
tardare [1] in portu.
Nic.   Edepol mortalis malos.
quid denique agitis?
Chrys.   Rursum in portum recipimus.
Nic. Sapienter factum a vobis. quid illi postea?
Chrys. Revorsionem ad terram faciunt vesperi.
Nic. Aurum hercle auferre voluere: ei rei operam
dabant.
Chrys. Non me fefellit, sensi, eo exanimatus fui.
quoniam videmus auro insidias fieri,
capimus consilium continuo; postridie   300
auferimus aurum omne illis praesentibus
palam atque aperte, ut illi id factum sciscerent.
Nic. Scite hercle. cedo quid illi?
Chrys.   Tristes ilico,
quom extemplo a portu ire nos cum auro vident,
subducunt lembum capitibus quassantibus.
nos apud Theotimum omne aurum deposivimus,
qui illic sacerdos est Dianae Ephesiae.

          [1] *Tardare* Hauptius : *turbare* MSS.

hrys.   (*with emphasis*) It was owned between your friend and some pirates.

ic.   (*agonized*) Could I have been such an imbecile as to trust the fellow when his very name, Archidemides, fairly bawled out that I'd be damnéd easy, if I did trust him with anything?

hrys.   (*warming up*) This galley was lying in wait for our ship. I began to keep an eye on their operations aboard her. Meanwhile our ship weighs anchor and moves out of the harbour. When we get outside they row after us fast as a bird, fast as the wind. Now that I noticed what was up, we brought to at once. Now that they saw us lying to they began to slow down there in the harbour.

ic.   God bless me, what rascals! What did you do then?

hrys.   We put back to the harbour.

ic.   That was wise. What did they do after that?

hrys.   Toward evening they went ashore.

ic.   By the Lord! They wanted to make off with the gold: that was their aim!

hrys.   I knew that well enough: I saw through it. That drove me frantic. Now that we perceived that they had designs on the gold, we laid our plans at once; the next day we carried it all ashore publicly and openly while they were by, to let them know it was done.

ic.   By Jove, a neat idea! Come, come, what did they do?

hrys.   Looked doleful on the spot, and as soon as they see us go away from the harbour with the gold there's a shaking of heads and they beach their galley. As for us, we deposited all the gold with Theotimus, the priest of Diana there at Ephesus.

359

Nic.	Quis istic Theotimust?
Chrys.	Megalobuli filius,
	qui nunc in Ephesost Ephesiis carissimus.
Nic.	Ne ille hercle mihi sit multo tanto carior, 310
	si me illo auro tanto circumduxerit.
Chrys.	Quin in eapse aede Dianai conditumst.
	ibidem publicitus servant.
Nic.	Occidistis me;
	nimio hic privatim servaretur rectius.
	sed nilne attulistis inde auri domum?
Chrys.	Immo etiam. verum quantum attulerit nescio.
Nic.	Quid? nescis?
Chrys.	Quia Mnesilochus noctu clanculum
	devenit ad Theotimum, nec mihi credere
	nec cuiquam in navi voluit: eo ego nescio
	quantillum attulerit; verum haud permultum
	attulit. 320
Nic.	Etiam dimidium censes?
Chrys.	Non edepol scio;
	verum haud opinor.
Nic.	Fertne partem tertiam?
Chrys.	Non hercle opinor; verum verum nescio.
	profecto de auro nil scio nisi nescio.
	nunc tibimet illuc navi capiundumst iter,
	ut illud reportes aurum ab Theotimo domum.
	atque heus tu.
Nic.	Quid vis?
Chrys.	Anulum gnati tui
	facito ut memineris ferre.
Nic.	Quid opust anulo?
Chrys.	Quia id signumst cum Theotimo, qui eum illi adferet,
	ei aurum ut reddat.
Nic.	Meminero, et recte mones. 330
	sed divesne est istic Theotimus?

360

THE TWO BACCHISES

ic. (*suspiciously*) Who is that Theotimus?

hrys. (*reassuringly*) Megalobulus's son, sir, and quite the dearest man in all Ephesus to the Ephesians.

ic. Good Lord! He certainly would be a very very much dearer man to me, if he should swindle me out of so much gold.

hrys. Oh, but it's stored in the temple of Diana itself. It's in public keeping there.

ic. Yes, worse luck! It would be a great deal safer in private keeping here. But you didn't bring any of it home, not any?

hrys. To be sure, we did. Just how much we brought, though, I don't know.

ic. What? Don't know?

hrys. You see Mnesilochus visited Theotimus on the sly, by night, and he didn't care to confide in me or anyone else aboard: so I don't know just what trifle he did bring along; not very much, though.

ic. As much as half, do you think?

hrys. Upon my soul, I don't know; but I don't believe so.

ic. A third. eh?

hrys. Bless my soul, I don't believe so; however, I don't know. In fact, all I know about the money is that I don't know. Now you'll have to make a voyage there yourself, sir, so as to get it from Theotimus and bring it back home. And, oh, I say!

ic. Well?

hrys. See you remember to take your son's ring along.

ic. Ring? What for?

hrys. Because we arranged with Theotimus that he's to give the gold to the man that brings him that ring.

ic. I shall remember; well you mentioned it, too. But is that Theotimus wealthy?

Chrys.   Etiam rogas?
quin auro habeat soccis subpactum solum?

Nic.   Cur ita fastidit?

Chrys.   Tantas divitias habet;
nescit quid faciat auro.

Nic.   Mihi dederit velim.
sed qui praesente id aurum Theotimo datumst?

Chrys.   Populo praesente: nullust Ephesi quin sciat.

Nic.   Istuc sapienter saltem fecit filius,
cum diviti homini id aurum servandum dedit;
ab eo licebit quamvis subito sumere.

Chrys.   Immo em tantisper numquam te morabitur   340
quin habeas illud quo die illuc veneris.

Nic.   Censebam me effugisse a vita marituma,
ne navigarem tandem hoc aetatis senex;
id mi haud, utrum velim, licere intellego:
ita bellus hospes fecit Archidemides.
ubi nunc est ergo meus Mnesilochus filius?

Chrys.   Deos atque amicos iit salutatum ad forum.

Nic.   At ego hinc eo ad illum, ut convenam quantum
    potest.

Chrys.   Ille est oneratus recte et plus iusto vehit.
exorsa haec tela non male omnino mihi est: 350
ut amantem erilem copem facerem filium,
ita feci, ut auri quantum vellet sumeret,
quantum autem lubeat reddere ut reddat patri.
senex in Ephesum ibit aurum arcessere,
hic nostra agetur aetas in malacum modum,
siquidem hic relinquet neque secum abducet senex
med et Mnesilochum. quas ego hic turbas dabo!

Chrys.	Wealthy, eh? Wealthy? And he with gold soles on his shoes!
Nic.	What makes him so high and mighty?
Chrys.	He's so rich; he doesn't know what to do with gold.
Nic.	(*sighing*) Wish he'd give it to me! But who was there when this money was given to Theotimus?
Chrys.	The whole population, sir: there's not a soul in Ephesus but knows about it.
Nic.	My son showed sense in that, at any rate,—giving it to a wealthy man to keep for him. You can get it from such a man at a moment's notice.
Chrys.	Oh no, he'll never keep you waiting, not—see here—(*illustrating*) not so long: he'll let you have it the day you arrive.
Nic.	I thought I had escaped from the seafaring life, that an old man of my age might really be done with voyaging. But no choice is left me, I perceive, in this case—thanks to the tactics of my charming friend Archidemides. Where is my son Mnesilochus at present, then?
Chrys.	Gone to the forum to pay his respects to the gods and his friends.
Nic.	Well, I shall go and try to find him as soon as possible. [EXIT TO FORUM.
Chrys.	(*gleefully*) He's nicely freighted, he is, in fact, overfreighted. Not a half bad sort of web I've woven here! To set up the young master in funds for his love affair, I've fixed things so that he can take as much of the gold as he wants himself, yes, and pass on to his father as much as he likes to pass on. The old man will go to Ephesus to fetch the gold and we'll be living a downy life of it here, that is, if the old chap leaves us here and doesn't drag me and Mnesilochus along with him. Oh, won't

TITUS MACCIUS PLAUTUS

sed quid futurumst, cum hoc senex resciverit,
cum se excucurisse illuc frustra sciverit
nosque aurum abusos?   quid mihi fiet postea?   360
credo hercle adveniens nomen mutabit mihi
facietque extemplo Crucisalum me ex Chrysalo.
aufugero hercle, si magis usus venerit.
si ero reprehensus, macto ego illum infortunio:
si illi sunt virgae ruri, at mihi tergum domist.
nunc ibo, erili filio hanc fabricam dabo
super auro amicaque eius inventa Bacchide.

ACTVS III

Lydus Pandite atque aperite propere ianuam hanc Orci,
      obsecro.
    nam equidem haud aliter esse duco, quippe quo
      nemo advenit,
    nisi quem spes reliquere omnes, esse ut frugi possiet.   370
    Bacchides non Bacchides, sed bacchae sunt acer-
      rumae.
    apage istas a me sorores, quae hominum sorbent
      sanguinem.
    omnis ad perniciem instructa domus opime atque
      opipare—
    quae ut aspexi, me continuo contuli protinam in pedes.
    egone ut haec conclusa gestem clanculum? ut
      celem patrem,
    Pistoclere, tua flagitia aut damna aut desidiabula?[1]
    neque mei neque te tui intus puditumst factis quae
      facis,

[1] Leo brackets following v., 377–378.
*quibus patrem et me teque amicosque omnes affectas tuos
ad probrum, damnum, flagitium appellere una et perdere.*
You are doing your best by such conduct to bring igno-
miny, loss, disgrace, upon every one of us, your father
and me and yourself and all your friends, and ruin us.

364

I turn things upside down here! (*pauses*) But
what'll happen when the old man discovers it?
When he finds out he's gone on a wild goose chase
and we've used up the cash? What will happen
to me then? Gad! I suppose he'll change my
name for me the minute he gets back, and transform me from Chrysalus to Crossalus on the spot.
Oh, well, I'll run for it, if it looks advisable. If
I am caught, he'll have his fill of discomfort: if
he's got rods on the farm, well, I've got a back on
my person. Now I'll be off and let the young
master know about this gold trick and his mistress Bacchis being found.   [EXIT *Chrysalus.*

ACT III

ydus   (*wildly, inside Bacchis's house*) Quick, quick, open
up, I beseech you, unclose this door of hell!
          ENTER *Lydus* HURRIEDLY.
For I verily believe it is nothing else, a place
where no man enters save him who has lost all
hopes of his capacity for good. Bacchises! No
Bacchises these, but the wildest of Bacchantes.
Avaunt, avaunt, ye sisters who suck the blood of
men! Their whole abode is tricked out as a gilded,
gorgeous lure to ruin—as soon as I perceived the
nature of my surroundings I fled, fled forthwith.
(*violently to those within*) Am I the man to carry
this shut up within me, to keep it secret? To
conceal from your father, Pistoclerus, your enormities, your extravagances, your horrid resorts?
Neither in my sight, nor your own, did you feel
any shame at your actions, actions, you infamous

N   365

quibus tuom patrem meque una, amicos, adfinis tuos   380
tua infamia fecisti gerulifigulos flagiti.[1]
de me hanc culpam demolibor iam et seni faciam
    palam,
ut eum ex lutulento caeno propere hinc eliciat foras.

III. 2.

Mnes.   Multimodis meditatus egomet mecum sum, et ita
    esse arbitror :
homini amico, qui est amicus ita uti nomen possidet,
nisi deos ei nil praestare ; id opera expertus sum
    esse ita.
nam ut in Ephesum hinc abii—hoc factumst ferme
    abhinc biennium—
ex Epheso huc ad Pistoclerum meum sodalem
    litteras
misi, amicam ut mi inveniret Bacchidem. illum
    intellego   390
invenisse, ut servos meus mi nuntiavit Chrysalus.
condigne is quam techinam de auro advorsum
    meum fecit patrem,
ut mi amanti copia esset.[2]
nam pol quidem meo animo ingrato homine nihil
    inpensiust ;
malefactorem amitti satius quam relinqui beneficum ;
nimio inpendiosum praestat te quam ingratum dicier ;
illum laudabunt boni, hunc etiam ipsi culpabunt mali.
qua me causa magis cum cura esse aecum, obvigi-
    latost opus.
nunc, Mnesiloche, specimen specitur, nunc certa-
    men cernitur,
sisne necne ut esse oportet, malus, bonus quoivis modi,   400

---

[1] Leo brackets following v., 382 : *nunc prius quam
malum istoc addis, certumst iam dicam patri.*
[2] *sed eccum video incedere* follows in MSS : Leo brackets.

creature, that make your father, and me too, and your friends and relatives accessories to your disgrace. (*making off*) I am going to clear myself of blame in the matter this very minute and inform his poor old father of it all, so that he may hurry and draw him forth from this filthy slough.

Scene 2.

ENTER *Mnesilochus*, FOLLOWED AT SOME DISTANCE BY SLAVES CARRYING HIS LUGGAGE.

Mnes. I've given the question careful consideration, and what I believe is this: nothing but Heaven itself excels a friend who is a friend in the full sense of the term; I've found this is so from my own experience. After I went away from here to Ephesus—almost two years ago, that was—I sent a letter from there to my chum Pistoclerus asking him to find my mistress, Bacchis, for me. And find her he did, it seems, according to that fellow Chrysalus of mine. (*pauses*) Quite worthy of Chrysalus, that scheme of his against my father to get the money, so that my amorous self might have supplies. (*pauses*) Well, well, to my own mind there's nothing more expensive than being an ingrate. Letting a malefactor off is better than turning your back on a benefactor. The name of being too extravagant is a great deal better for you than that of being ungrateful. Good men will speak well of the first sort of fellow: even rascals themselves will blame the second. I must take all the more care, then, how I act and keep my eyes open. Here's where you show a sample of yourself, Mnesilochus; here's where you're put to the test whether you're the man you should be or not—bad or good, whatever you

367

iustus iniustus, malignus largus, comis incommodus.
cave sis te superare servom siris faciundo bene.
utut eris, moneo, haud celabis. sed eccos video incedere
patrem sodalis et magistrum. hinc auscultabo
    quam rem agant.

III. 3.

Lydus Nunc experiar, sitne aceto tibi cor acre in pectore.
sequere.

Phil.   Quo sequar?   quo ducis nunc me?

Lydus   Ad illam quae tuom
perdidit, pessum dedit tibi filium unice unicum.

Phil. Heia, Lyde, leniter qui saeviunt sapiunt magis.
minus mirandumst, illaec aetas si quid illorum facit,
quam si non faciat.   feci ego istaec itidem in adulescentia.

Lydus Ei mihi, ei mihi, istaec illum perdidit assentatio.
nam absque te esset, ego illum haberem rectum
    ad ingenium bonum:
nunc propter te tuamque pravos factus est fiduciam
Pistoclerus.

Mnes.   Di immortales, meum sodalem hic nominat.
quid hoc negoti est, Pistoclerum Lydus quod erum
    tam ciet?

Phil. Paulisper, Lyde, est libido homini suo animo obsequi;
iam aderit tempus, cum sese etiam ipse oderit.
    morem geras;
dum caveatur, praeter aequom ne quid delinquat,
    sine.

410

368

are—just or unjust—mean or generous—gentleman
or cad. Mind you look out not to let your servant
be your better in doing the kindly thing. No
matter what you'll be, I warn you you can't conceal it. (*looking down street*) Hullo, though! Here
come my chum's father and tutor ambling along.
I'll listen to what they're up to from over here.
(*withdraws*)

Scene 3.   ENTER *Lydus* AND *Philoxenus*.

Lydus (*struggling to control himself*) Now we shall see
whether or no you have a heart of fiery feeling
within you. Follow me!

Phil. (*calmly*) Follow you where? Where are you taking
me to now?

Lydus To the woman who has depraved, destroyed your
one and only son!

Phil. Gently, gently, Lydus! " Ire restrained is wisdom
gained." It's less surprising to have a youngster
up to something of that kind than not. I've done
the same sort of thing myself in my younger
days.

Lydus Oh-h-h dear, oh dear! It is that very tolerance
that has been his undoing. Why, but for you, I
should have made a good moral man of him: as it
is, you and your support have made a debauchee
of Pistoclerus.

Mnes. (*aside*) Good God! My chum's name! What
does this mean—Lydus running down his master
Pistoclerus so?

Phil. A man's eager to have his fling for a little while,
Lydus; the time will soon come when he'll actually
loathe himself for it. Give him rein; so long as
he's careful not to go too far in his indiscretions,
why, let him be.

Lydus Non sino, neque equidem illum me vivo corrumpi
    sinam.

sed tu, qui pro tam corrupto dicis causam filio,   420

eademne erat haec disciplina tibi, cum tu adules-
    cens eras?

nego tibi hoc annis viginti fuisse primis copiae,

digitum longe a paedagogo pedem ut efferres
    aedibus.

ante solem exorientem nisi in palaestram veneras,

gymnasi praefecto haud mediocris poenas penderes.

id quom optigerat, hoc etiam ad malum accerse-
    batur malum:

et discipulus et magister perhibebantur improbi.

ibi cursu luctando hasta disco pugilatu pila

saliendo sese exercebant magis quam scorto aut
    saviis:

ibi suam aetatem extendebant, non in latebrosis
    locis.   430

inde de hippodromo et palaestra ubi revenisses
    domum,

cincticulo praecinctus in sella apud magistrum ad-
    sideres

cum libro: cum legeres, si unam peccavisses sylla-
    bam,

fieret corium tam maculosum quam est nutricis
    pallium.

Mnes. Propter me haec nunc meo sodali dici discrucior
    miser;

innocens suspicionem hanc sustinet causa mea.

Phil. Alii, Lyde, nunc sunt mores.

Lydus   Id equidem ego certo scio.

nam olim populi prius honorem capiebat suffragio,

quam magistro desinebat esse dicto oboediens;

ydus I will not let him be, no, nor let him be corrupted
and live to see it, never! But you—with your
pleas for a son so corrupted—was your own train-
ing of this same sort when you were a young
man? I say no, I say you never had a chance
during the first twenty years of your life to stir a
single finger's breadth from the house without your
tutor. Unless you had arrived at the athletic
grounds before sunrise, it was no slight penalty
the Gymnasium Director imposed on you. When
this had happened, this further trouble was added,
that pupil and teacher too were held to be disgraced. There it was by running, wrestling, throwing the spear and discus, boxing, ball, jumping,
they used to get their exercise, rather than by
means of wenches, or kisses: it was there they
used to spend their lives, not in dark dens of
vice. Then when you had returned home from
the track and field, all neat and trim you would
sit on your chair before your teacher with your
book: and while you were reading, if you had
missed a single syllable, your hide would be made
as spotted as a nurse's gown.

Mnes. (*aside*) It's torment, hang it, to have my chum
coming in for all this on my account; it's for my
sake he's shouldering this suspicion, poor innocent.

Phil. (*soothingly*) The customs of to-day are different,
Lydus.

ydus Indeed they are! I realize the truth of that.
Why, in the old days a young man would be
holding office, by popular vote, before he had
ceased to hearken to his teacher's precepts. But
nowadays, before a youngster is seven years old, if
you lay a finger on him, he promptly takes his

371

at nunc, prius quam septuennis est, si attingas eum
   manu,   440
extemplo puer paedagogo tabula disrumpit caput.
cum patrem adeas postulatum, puero sic dicit pater:
" noster esto, dum te poteris defensare iniuria."
provocatur paedagogus: " eho senex minimi preti,
ne attigas puerum istac causa, quando fecit
   strenue." [1]
itur illinc iure dicto. hocine hic pacto potest
inhibere imperium magister, si ipsus primus vapulet?

Mnes. Acris postulatio haec est. cum huius dicta intellego,
mira sunt ni Pistoclerus Lydum pugnis contudit.   450

Lydus Sed quis hic est, quem astantem video ante ostium?
   o Philoxene,
deos propitios me videre quam illum haud mavel-
   lem mihi.

Phil. Quis illic est?

Lydus   Mnesilochus, gnati tui sodalis.[2]
haud consimili ingenio atque ille est qui in lupa-
   nari accubat.
fortunatum Nicobulum, qui illum produxit sibi.

Phil. Salvos sis, Mnesiloche, salvom te advenire gaudeo.

Mnes. Di te ament, Philoxene.

Lydus   Hic enim rite productust patri:
in mare it, rem familiarem curat, custodit domum,
obsequens oboediensque est mori atque imperiis
   patris.
hic sodalis Pistoclero iam puer puero fuit;   460
triduom non interest aetatis uter maior siet:
verum ingenium plus triginta annis maiust quam
   alteri.

---

[1] Leo brackets following v., 446: *it magister quasi lucerna uncto expretus linteo.*
[2] *Pistocleri* follows in MSS: Leo brackets.

writing tablet and smashes his tutor's head with it. When you go to his father with a protest, he talks to the youngster in this strain: (*mimicking*) "You're father's own boy so long as you can defend yourself against abuse." Then the tutor is summoned: "Hey, you worthless old baggage, don't you touch my boy merely for acting like a lad of spirit!" Judgment pronounced, the court adjourns. Can a teacher exert authority here under such conditions, if he is beaten first himself?

Ines. (*aside*) Here's a warm protest! Judging from his remarks, it's a wonder if Pistoclerus hasn't been punching Lydus's head.

ydus (*looking in the direction of Mnesilochus*) But who is this I see standing in front of the door? (*recognizing him*) Ah, Philoxenus, that is a man whose support I should value no less than that of the gods!

hil. Who is it?

ydus Mnesilochus, your son's chum. And a youth so, so different from the one lolling in that vile house! (*pointing to Bacchis's*) Happy, happy Nicobulus to have brought up such a lad!

hil. (*stepping forward*) How are you, Mnesilochus? I'm glad to see you safely back.

Ines. (*heartily shaking hands*) God bless you, Philoxenus!

ydus Ah, yes, here is a son to rejoice a father's heart: goes to sea, attends to family affairs, is the bulwark of the home, observes and obeys his father's every wish and word. He was Pistoclerus's chum even when they were boys—not three days' difference between them so far as age is concerned, but this lad is more than thirty years his senior in native sense.

Phil.   Cave malo et compesce in illum dicere iniuste.

Lydus   Tace,
stultus es qui illi male aegre patere dici qui facit.[1]

Mnes.   Quid sodalem meum castigas, Lyde, discipulum
       tuom?

Lydus   Periit tibi sodalis.

Mnes.   Ne di sirint.

Lydus   Sic est ut loquor.
quin ego cum peribat vidi, non ex audito arguo.

Mnes.   Quid factum est?

Lydus   Meretricem indigne deperit.

Mnes.   Non tu taces?   470

Lydus   Atque acerrume aestuosam: absorbet ubi quemque
       attigit.

Mnes.   Ubi ea mulier habitat?

Lydus   Hic.

Mnes.   Unde esse eam aiunt?

Lydus   Ex Samo.

Mnes.   Quae vocatur?

Lydus   Bacchis.

Mnes.   Erras, Lyde: ego omnem rem scio
quem ad modumst. tu Pistoclerum falso atque in-
       sontem arguis.
nam ille amico et benevolenti suo sodali sedulo
rem mandatam exsequitur. ipsus neque amat nec
       tu creduas.

---

[1] Leo brackets following v., 465, 466:
nam illum meum malum promptare malim quam peculium.

Phil.   *Quidem?*

Lydus   *Quia, malum si promptet, in dies faciat minus.*
Yes, yes, I should rather have him administer my punishment than my money.

Phil.   Why so?

Lydus   Because if he administered my punishment, there would
soon be none left.

il.   (*angrily*) Look out for yourself, and stop speaking about the lad unfairly!

dus   Peace! fool that you are to be pained at hearing him badly spoken of, when he is bad!

nes.   (*innocently*) Why are you finding fault with my chum, Lydus, your own pupil?

dus   (*tragically*) Your chum has perished!

nes.   God forbid!

dus   It's just as I tell you. Ah yes, I myself beheld him in the act: I am not accusing him on hearsay.

nes.   What has happened?

dus   He is shockingly infatuated with a courtesan.

nes.   (*apparently scandalized*) Oh, don't say such a thing!

dus   Yes, and a perfect maelstrom of a woman: she sucks down every man who comes within her reach.

nes.   Where does this woman live?

dus   (*pointing*) Here.

nes.   Where do they say she is from?

dus   Samos.

nes.   What is her name?

dus   Bacchis.

nes.   (*with an air of relief*) You're mistaken, Lydus: I know all about the matter, just how it stands. That's a false charge of yours, and Pistoclerus is innocent. Why, he's fulfilling a commission for a friend and well-wisher of his, a chum, and doing it zealously. He doesn't love her himself, and you mustn't think he does.

Lydus	Itane oportet rem mandatam gerere amici sedulo,
	ut ipsus in gremio osculantem mulierem teneat
	sedens?
	nullo pacto res mandata potest agi, nisi identidem
	manus ferat ei ad papillas, labra a labris nusquam

auferat?   480

nam alia memorare quae illum facere vidi dispudet:
cum manum sub vestimenta ad corpus tetulit
   Bacchidi
me praesente, neque pudere quicquam.   quid verbis
   opust?
mihi discipulus, tibi sodalis periit, huic filius;
nam ego illum periisse dico quoi quidem periit
   pudor.[1]

Mnes.   Perdidisti me, sodalis.   egone ut illam mulierem
capitis non perdam? perire me malis malim modis.   490
satin ut quem tu habeas fidelem tibi aut cui credas
   nescias?

Lydus   Viden ut aegre patitur gnatum esse corruptum
   tuom,
suom sodalem, ut ipsus sese cruciat aegritudine?

Phil.   Mnesiloche, hoc tecum oro, ut illius animum
   atque ingenium regas;
serva tibi sodalem et mihi filium.

Mnes.   Factum volo.

Lydus   Melius esset, me quoque una si cum illo relinqueres.

Phil.   Adfatim est.

---

[1] Leo brackets following v., 486–488:
quid opust verbis? si opperiri vellem paulisper modo,
ut opinor, illius inspectandi mi esset maior copia,
plus viderem quam deceret, quam me atque illo aequom foret.
Why say more? If I had wished to remain but a little
longer, I should have had further opportunity to observe
his conduct, I suppose, and I should have seen more
than was proper, more than became me and him.

ydus (*sharply*) Does executing this commission for his friend, and doing it zealously, call for his sitting down and holding the girl in his lap while she kisses him? Is there no way of his carrying out this commission save by his embracing her time and again in unseemly fashion and never taking his lips an inch from hers? Why, I feel ashamed to mention other things I saw him do, dreadful, dreadful things, in my presence—and never a trace of shame about him. Why say more? My pupil, your chum, this father's son, has perished; for perished I say he has, when his sense of shame has perished.

Ines. You've wrecked my life, (*with special acrimony*) chum! Oh, won't I wreck that woman's! I'd rather die a dog's death than not get even with her! Can it really be you don't know whom to think loyal to you, whom to trust?

ydus (*to Philoxenus*) Do you see how he suffers at your son, his chum, being corrupted; how his very soul is tormented?

hil. Mnesilochus, try to control the lad's impulses and disposition, I beg you. Save your chum for yourself and my son for me.

Ines. (*vehemently*) I wish I might!

ydus (*to Philoxenus*) It would be better for you to leave me with him, too.

hil. No, no, he'll manage.

377

Lydus Mnesiloche, cura, ei, concastiga hominem probe,
        qui dedecorat te, me amicosque alios flagitiis suis.
Phil.   In te ego hoc onus omne impono.   Lyde, sequere
        hac me.
Lydus   Sequor.
III. 4.
Mnes. Inimiciorem nunc utrum credam magis   500
        sodalemne esse an Bacchidem, incertum admodumst.
        illum exoptavit potius ? habeat.   optumest.
        ne illa illud hercle cum malo fecit suo ;
        nam mihi divini numquam quisquam creduat,
        ni ego illam exemplis plurumis planeque—amo.
        ego faxo hau dicet nactam quem derideat.
        nam iam domum ibo atque—aliquid surrupiam patri.
        id isti dabo.   ego istanc multis ulciscar modis.
        adeo ego illam cogam usque ut mendicet—meus
          pater.
        sed satine ego animum mente sincera gero,
        qui ad hunc modum haec hic quae futura fabulor ? 510
        amo hercle opinor, ut pote quod pro certo sciam.
        verum quam illa umquam de mea pecunia
        ramenta fiat plumea propensior,
        mendicum malim mendicando vincere.
        numquam edepol viva me inridebit. nam mihi
        decretumst renumerare iam omne aurum patri.
        igitur mi inani atque inopi subblandibitur
        tum quom blandiri nihilo pluris referet
        quam si ad sepulcrum mortuo narres logos.[1]
        profecto stabilest me patri aurum reddere.   520

---

[1] Leo brackets the following v., 519ᵃ–519ᶜ :
sed autem quam illa umquam meis opulentiis
ramenta fiat gravior aut propensior,
mori me malim excruciatum inopia.
  However, rather than have my money make her a
fraction the weightier or heavier, I'd prefer to perish in
the pangs of want.

Lydus Mnesilochus, take charge of him! Go, rate him well—for degrading you, and me and his other friends with his enormities.

Phil. I put the whole load on your shoulders. (*turns to go*) This way, Lydus; come.

Lydus (*gloomily*) Very well.

[EXEUNT *Philoxenus* AND *Lydus*.

Scene 4.

Mnes. (*tempestuously*) I absolutely can't tell which is my worse enemy now, my chum or Bacchis. Hankered for him instead of me, did she? Let her have him! All right, all right! By heaven, she'll certainly pay for this; for may no one ever believe my sacred word again, if I don't thoroughly and utterly— (*wryly*) love her. She shan't say she's lighted on a man she can laugh to scorn, I promise you. For I'll home this minute, and—steal something from my father and give it to her. I'll be revenged on her in all sorts of ways. Yes indeed, I'll bring her to such a pass that—my father will have to beg his bread. But can I really be in possession of my senses, babbling here in this fashion about these futurities? Good Lord! I do believe I love her— seeing I know it for certain. But sooner than let any cash of mine make her a fraction of a feather- weight the heavier, I'd outbeggar a beggar. By gad, she shan't give me the laugh in this world, never! My mind's made up—I'll count out every bit of that gold to my father this moment. Then let her try her pretty wiles on me when I'm poverty stricken and penniless, when it won't do any more good to coax than if you were to prattle to a dead man at his tomb. The money goes to my father, that's final, absolutely final. At the same time I'll

379

eadem exorabo, Chrysalo causa mea
pater ne noceat, neu quid ei suscenseat
mea causa de auro quod eum ludificatus est;
nam illi aequomst me consulere, qui causa mea
mendacium ei dixit. vos me sequimini.

III. 5.

Pistoc. Rebus aliis antevortar, Bacchis, quae mandas mihi:
Mnesilochum ut requiram atque ut eum mecum ad
    te adducam simul.
nam illud animus meus miratur, si a me tetigit
    nuntius,
quid remoretur.   ibo ut visam huc ad eum, si forte
    est domi.

III. 6.

Mnes. Reddidi patri omne aurum. nunc ego illam me
    velim   530
convenire, postquam inanis sum, contemptricem
    meam.
sed veniam mihi quam gravate pater dedit de
    Chrysalo;
verum postremo impetravi, ut ne quid ei suscenseat.

Pistoc. Estne hic meus sodalis?

Mnes.   Estne hic hostis, quem aspicio, meus?

Pistoc. Certe is est.

Mnes.   Is est.

Pistoc.   Adibo contra et contollam gradum.
salvos sis, Mnesiloche.

Mnes.   Salve.

Pistoc.   Salvos quom peregre advenis,
cena detur.

Mnes.   Non placet mi cena quae bilem movet.

Pistoc. Numquae advenienti aegritudo obiecta est?

Mnes.   Atque acerruma.

380

persuade him to let Chrysalus off for my sake and not to be at all angry with him on account of his fooling him, for my sake, about the gold. Yes, it is only right I should look out for the fellow that lied to him for my sake. (*to slaves with luggage*) Follow me, you. [EXEUNT INTO HOUSE OF *Nicobulus*.

Scene 5. (*Fifteen minutes have elapsed.*)
ENTER *Pistoclerus* FROM *Bacchis's* HOUSE.

Pistoc. (*to Bacchis within*) Everything else shall come second to your commission, Bacchis,—to hunt up Mnesilochus and bring him back with me. Why, I don't know what to make of his delay, if my message reached him. I'll go look him up at the house here, in case he happens to be at home.

Scene 6. ENTER *Mnesilochus* FROM HOUSE.

Mnes. I've handed over the whole sum to my father. Now's the time I should like her to meet me, now that I haven't a sou—my Lady Disdain! (*pausing*) But how father did hate to pardon Chrysalus for me! However, I finally induced him to swallow his wrath.

Pistoc. (*approaching Nicobulus's house*) Isn't that my chum?

Mnes. Isn't that my enemy I see?

Pistoc. (*beaming*) It certainly is.

Mnes. (*glowering*) It is.

Pistoc. I'll step up and meet him. (*hurries to him*) Mnesilochus! bless you!

Mnes. (*gruffly*) Same to you.

Pistoc. (*enthusiastically*) We must have a dinner, now you're safe back from abroad.

Mnes. I have no desire for a dinner that stirs my bile.

Pistoc. (*wonderingly*) You haven't met with any trouble on your return, have you?

Mnes. Yes, of the worst sort.

381

Pistoc. Unde?

Mnes.   Ab homine quem mi amicum esse arbitratus
    sum antidhac.

Pistoc. Multi more isto atque exemplo vivont, quos cum
    censeas   540
    esse amicos, reperiuntur falsi falsimoniis,
    lingua factiosi, inertes opera, sublesta fide.
    nullus est quoi non invideant rem secundam optin-
        gere;
    sibi ne invideatur, ipsi ignavia recte cavent.

Mnes. Edepol ne tu illorum mores perquam meditate tenes.
    sed etiam unum hoc: ex ingenio malo malum in-
        veniunt suo:
    nulli amici sunt, inimicos ipsi in sese omnis habent.
    ei se cum frustrantur, frustrari alios stolidi existu-
        mant.
    sicut est hic, quem esse amicum ratus sum atque
        ipsus sum mihi:
    ille, quod in se fuit, accuratum habuit quod posset
        mali   550
    faceret in me, inconciliaret copias omnis meas.

Pistoc. Improbum istunc esse oportet hominem.

Mnes.   Ego ita esse arbitror.

Pistoc. Obsecro hercle loquere, quis is est?

                  Benevolens vivit tibi.
    nam ni ita esset, tecum orarem ut ei quod posses
        mali
    facere faceres.

Pistoc.   Dic modo hominem qui sit: si non fecero
    ei male aliquo pacto, me esse dicito ignavissimum.

Mnes. Nequam homost, verum hercle amicus est tibi.

Pistoc.   Tanto magis
    dic quis est; nequam hominis ego parvi pendo
    gratiam.

Pistoc. What caused it?

Mnes. A man I always took for a friend till now.

Pistoc. (*indignantly*) There are plenty of fellows amongst us of that character and description, fellows you regard as friends only to find 'em treacherous traitors—energetic talkers, lazy doers, and ready deserters. There's no one they don't envy his good luck. As for themselves, they take proper care no one envies them—their own inertness looks out for that.

Mnes. (*dryly*) Well, well! You certainly have a very intimate acquaintance with their characteristics. But there's this one thing to add: they're cursed by their own cursed dispositions: friends to no man as they are, they themselves have foes in all men. When they're deceiving themselves the fools fancy they are deceiving others. That's the way with this man I thought was as good a friend to me as I am to myself: as far as in him lay he took pains to do me all the harm he could, to defraud me of all I had.

Pistoc. The fellow must be a perfect villain!

Mnes. Precisely my own opinion.

Pistoc. (*more indignantly*) By Jove, now! Who is he? Tell me, tell me.

Mnes. A man on good terms with you. Yes, but for that, I'd beg you to do him any damage you could.

Pistoc. Only tell me who the fellow is: if I don't damage him somehow, you can call me the most spiritless wretch on earth.

Mnes. He's a scoundrel, but good Lord, he is a friend of yours!

Pistoc. All the more reason for telling me who he is; it's little I care for the favour of a scoundrel.

Mnes. Video non potesse quin tibi eius nomen eloquar.
Pistoclere, perdidisti me sodalem funditus.   560

Pistoc. Quid istuc est?

Mnes.   Quid est? misine ego ad te ex Epheso epistulam
super amica, ut mi invenires?

Pistoc.   Fateor factum, et repperi.

Mnes. Quid? tibi non erat meretricum aliarum Athenis
  copia
quibuscum haberes rem, nisi cum illa quam ego
  mandassem tibi
occiperes tute [1] amare et mi ires consultum male?

Pistoc. Sanun es?

Mnes.   Rem repperi omnem ex tuo magistro.   ne nega.
perdidisti me.

Pistoc.   Etiamne ultro tuis me prolectas probris?

Mnes. Quid? amas Bacchidem?

Pistoc.   Duas ergo hic intus eccas Bacchides.

Mnes. Quid? duas?

Pistoc.   Atque ambas sorores.

Mnes.   Loqueris nunc nugas sciens.

Pistoc. Postremo, si pergis parvam mihi fidem arbitrarier,   570
tollam ego ted in collum atque intro hinc auferam.

Mnes.   Immo ibo, mane.

Pistoc. Non maneo, neque tu me habebis falso suspectum.

Mnes.   Sequor.

ACTVS IV

Par. Parasitus ego sum hominis nequam atque improbi,

---

[1] Corrupt (Leo): *tute* (*etiam*) Seyffert: *tute* (*eam*)
Lindsay.

384

Mnes. I see there is nothing for me to do but give you his name. Pistoclerus, (*bitterly*) you have ruined me, your chum, ruined me utterly.

Pistoc. (*aghast*) Eh? What's that?

Mnes. What's that? Didn't I send you a letter from Ephesus about my mistress, asking you to find her for me?

Pistoc. To be sure you did—and I did find her.

Mnes. What? Weren't there enough other women in Athens for you to philander with, without beginning to make love to her, the girl I had entrusted to you, and trying this underhand trick on me?

Pistoc. Are you sane?

Mnes. I have the whole story from your tutor. You needn't deny it. You have ruined me.

Pistoc. (*getting irritated*) Can it be you're bent on provoking me with this uncalled for abuse of yours?

Mnes. Eh? You do love Bacchis?

Pistoc. Well, but look you, there are two Bacchises in here.

Mnes. (*astonished*) What? Two?

Pistoc. And sisters, too.

Mnes. Now you're talking rot, and you know it.

Pistoc. See here now, if you go on making light of my word, I'll perch you up on my neck and carry you off inside. (*seizes him*)

Mnes. No, no, I'll go: wait.

Pistoc. I won't wait, and I won't have you suspecting me falsely, either. (*pulls him toward door*)

Mnes. I'm coming.   [EXEUNT INTO HOUSE.

ACT IV

ENTER *Parasite* WITH *Cleomachus's* PAGE.

Par. The parasite of a worthless reprobate is what I am, the parasite of the Captain that carried the wench

385

militis, qui amicam secum avexit ex Samo.
nunc me ire iussit ad eam et percontarier,
utrum aurum reddat anne eat secum semul.
tu dudum, puere, cum illac usque isti semul:
quae harum sunt aedes, pulta. adi actutum ad fores.
recede hinc dierecte. ut pulsat propudium!
comesse panem tris pedes latum potes,   580
fores pultare nescis. ecquis in aedibust?
heus, ecquis hic est? ecquis hoc aperit ostium?
ecquis exit?

IV. 2.

Pistoc.   Quid istuc? quae istaec est pulsatio?
[1] quae te mala crux agitat, qui ad istunc modum
alieno viris tuas extentes ostio?
fores paene exfregisti. quid nunc vis tibi?

Par.   Adulescens, salve.

Pistoc.   Salve. sed quem quaeritas?

Par.   Bacchidem.

Pistoc.   Utram ergo?

Par.   Nil scio nisi Bacchidem.
paucis: me misit miles ad eam Cleomachus,
vel ut ducentos Philippos reddat aureos   590
vel ut hinc in Elatiam hodie eat secum semul.

Pistoc.   Non it. negat se ituram. abi et renuntia.
alium illa amat, non illum. duc te ab aedibus.

Par.   Nimis iracunde.

Pistoc.   At scin quam iracundus siem?
ne tibi hercle haud longe est os ab infortunio,
ita dentifrangibula haec meis manibus gestiunt.

---

[1] Leo notes lacuna here. *Quae te (male) mala* Lindsay.

386

off from Samos with him. Now he has ordered me to call on her and inquire whether she intends to pay him back his money, or go along with him. (*scanning the houses*) Boy, you came along to the place with her a short time ago: whichever house it is here, knock. Up to the door with you directly: (*page obeys, knocking timidly*) Get out and be hanged to you! How the imp knocks! You can devour a loaf of bread three feet wide: as for knocking at a door, you don't know how. (*pounds vigorously himself, and shouts*) Anyone at home? Hi! Anyone here? Anyone minding this door? Anyone coming?

Scene 2.   ENTER *Pistoclerus* INTO DOORWAY.

Pistoc. (*angrily*) What's all this? What do you mean by pounding so? What the devil ails you, to test your strength on other people's doors this way? You've nearly smashed it off. Now what are you after?

Par. (*somewhat cowed*) Good day, young gentleman.

Pistoc. Good day. But who is it you're looking for?

Par. Bacchis.

Pistoc. Well, which?

Par. Bacchis—that's all I know. Briefly: Captain Cleomachus sent me to say she must either pay him back two hundred golden sovereigns, or else go along with him to-day to Elatea.

Pistoc. She is not going. She refuses to go. Away with you and report! It's another man she loves, not him. March yourself off!

Par. (*soothingly*) You're too irritable.

Pistoc. (*roaring*) But d'ye know how irritable? By the Lord, that face of yours is precious close to a calamity, the way these (*shaking his fists at parasite, who retreats*) tooth-crackers here are itching!

Par.   Cum ego huius verba interpretor, mihi cautiost,
      ne nucifrangibula excussit ex malis meis.
      tuo ego istaec igitur dicam illi periculo.
Pistoc. Quid ais tu?
Par.   Ego istuc illi dicam.
Pistoc.   Dic mihi,   600
      quis tu es?
Par.   Illius sum integumentum corporis.
Pistoc. Nequam esse oportet cui tu integumentum im-
        probu's.
Par.   Sufflatus ille huc veniet.
Pistoc.   Dirrumptum velim.
Par.   Numquid vis?
Pistoc.   Abeas.   celeriter factost opus.
Par.   Vale, dentifrangibule.
Pistoc.   Et tu, integumentum, vale.
      in eum nunc haec res venit locum, ut quid consili
      dem meo sodali super amica nesciam,
      qui iratus renumeravit omne aurum patri,
      neque nummus ullust qui reddatur militi.
      sed huc concedam, nam concrepuerunt fores.   610
      Mnesilochus eccum maestus progreditur foras.
IV. 3.
Mnes. Petulans, protervo iracundo animo, indomito inco-
      gitato,
      sine modo et modestia sum, sine bono iure atque
      honore,
      incredibilis imposque animi, inamabilis inlepidus vivo,
      malevolente ingenio natus. postremo id mi est
      quod volo
          ego esse aliis. credibile hoc est?
        nequior nemost neque indignior quoi
       di bene faciant neque quem quisquam
        homo aut amet aut adeat.

Par.   (*aside, wryly*) To judge from his remarks, I must take care he doesn't knock the nutcrackers out of my jaws. (*aloud*) All right, I'll tell him about this, and it will be at your risk. (*turns to go*)

Pistoc.   See here! (*advancing*)

Par.   (*backing away*) I'll tell him what you say.

Pistoc.   Tell me this, who are you?

Par.   (*impressively*) I am the Captain's corporal integument.

Pistoc.   A sorry specimen he must be to have a rascal like you for an integument!

Par.   He'll be coming here swelling with rage.

Pistoc.   I hope he bursts.

Par.   (*going*) Anything more I can do?

Pistoc.   Yes, get out! And you need to be quick about it. (*advancing*)

Par.   (*running*) Farewell, Sir Toothcracker.

Pistoc.   The same to yourself, Sir Integument. [EXIT *Parasite.*] Now matters have come to the point where I don't know how to advise my chum about his mistress, what with his getting angry and counting out all the gold to his father, and not a penny left to pay the Captain. (*listening*) But I'll step aside here: (*does so*) the door creaked. Ah, there's our woebegone Mnesilochus coming out.

Scene 3.   ENTER *Mnesilochus* FROM *Bacchis's* HOUSE.

Mnes.   A hasty fool, a reckless, passionate, uncontrollable, unthinking fool without method and moderation, that's what I am—a creature without any sense of right and honour, distrustful, hotheaded, loveless, graceless, crabbed and born crabbed! Yes, yes, I'm everything that I wish some one else was! Is this credible? There's not a viler man alive, a man more unworthy of heaven's kindness, of having

389

       inimicos quam amicos aequomst med habere,
       malos quam bonos par magis me iuvare.
         omnibus probris, quae improbis viris   620
       dignia sunt, dignior nullus est homo;

qui patri reddidi omne aurum amans, mihi
quod fuit prae manu. sumne ego homo miser?
perdidi me simulque operam Chrysali.

Pistoc. Consolandus hic mist, ibo ad eum.
       Mnesiloche, quid fit?
Mnes.   Perii.
Pistoc. Di melius faciant.
Mnes.   Perii.
Pistoc. Non taces, insipiens?
Mnes.   Taceam?
Pistoc. Sanus satis non est.
Mnes.   Perii.
       multa mala mi in pectore nunc acria atque acerba
         eveniunt.
       criminin me habuisse fidem? immerito tibi iratus
         fui.
Pistoc. Heia, bonum habe animum.
Mnes.   Unde habeam? mortuos pluris pretist 630
       quam ego sum.
Pistoc.   Militis parasitus venerat modo aurum
         petere hinc,
       eum ego meis dictis malis his foribus atque hac
         platea abegi;
       reppuli, reieci hominem.
Mnes.   Quid mi id prodest? quom ipse veniet,
       quid faciam? nil habeo miser. ille quidem hanc
         abducet, scio.
Pistoc. Si mihi sit, non pollicear.

a mortal soul love him or come near him! Enemies
are what I ought to have, not friends; rascals are
the right people to help me, not honest men. Not
a man on earth has a better title to all the infamy
of an infamous scoundrel! I to give all that gold to
my father, and I in love—gold I had in hand! If
I'm not a poor, poor fool! I've thrown away
my own life together with all Chrysalus did
for me.

istoc. (*aside*) I must console him: I'll up to him. (*aloud,
approaching*) How are things, Mnesilochus?

Ines. I'm done for.

istoc. God forbid!

Ines. (*still more dejectedly*) I'm done for.

istoc. Won't you shut up, you silly fellow?

Ines. Shut up?

istoc. You've lost your wits.

Ines. I'm done for. Oh, the confounded thoughts that
crowd in on me now, exasperating, excruciating!
To have credited that accusation! I had no reason
to be angry with you.

istoc. Oh well, cheer up.

Ines. Where can I get cheer? A corpse is worth more
than I am.

istoc. (*encouragingly*) The Captain's parasite has just been
here after the money: I let him have a volley of
abuse and drove him away up the street here. I
fought him off, flung him back.

Ines. (*disconsolate*) What's the good of that to me?
When he comes himself, what shall I do? I
haven't a penny, wretch that I am! Of course
he'll carry her off, I know that.

istoc. If I had any money myself, I wouldn't promise it
to you.

Mnes.   Scio, dares, novi tuom.
    sed nisi ames, non habeam tibi fidem tantam; eo
      quod amas tamen
    nunc agitas sat tute tuarum rerum; sin liber sies
    egone ut opem mi ferre posse putem inopem te?
      non potest.
Pistoc. Tace modo: deus respiciet nos aliquis.
Mnes.   Nugae.   vale.
Pistoc. Mane.
Mnes.   Quid est?
Pistoc.   Tuam copiam eccam Chrysalum video.   tace.
IV. 4.
Cyhrs. Hunc hominem decet auro expendi, huic decet
    statuam statui ex auro;   640
    nam duplex hodie facinus feci, duplicibus spoliis
      sum adfectus.
      erum maiorem meum ut ego hodie lusi lepide,
      ut ludificatust.
        callidum senem callidis dolis
      compuli et perpuli, mi omnia ut crederet.
        nunc amanti ero filio senis,
          quicum ego bibo, quicum edo et amo,
        regias copias aureasque optuli,
        ut domo sumeret neu foris quaereret.
        non mihi isti placent Parmenones, Syri,
        qui duas aut tris minas auferunt eris.   650
    nequius nil est quam egens consili servos, nisi
        habet multipotens pectus:

Ines. I know, you'd give it to me: I know your way. If you weren't in love yourself, though, I shouldn't have such confidence in you. Being in love, however, you have troubles enough of your own as it is. But even if you were fancy free, could I think you able to supply me, unsupplied as you are yourself? Impossible!

'istoc. Oh, do shut up: some god will look out for us.

Ines. Rubbish! (*despairingly, moving off*) Farewell!

'istoc. (*looking down street*) Wait.

Ines. What's the matter?

'istoc. (*pointing*) Look! I see your supply station, Chrysalus. Sh—h! (*they withdraw*).

cene 4.   ENTER *Chrysalus* IN HIGH SPIRITS.

'hrys. Here is a man (*patting his chest*) that is worth his weight in gold: here is a man who ought to have a gold statue set up for him. Why, I've done a double deed to-day, been graced with double spoils. The old master—how cleverly I did take him in to-day, how he was fooled! Wily as the old chap is, my wily arts impelled him and compelled him to believe me in everything. And now the young master that's in love, the old one's son, that I drink with and eat with and go a-courting with—I've furnished him out with regal supplies, golden supplies, so that he can go to himself for cash and not look for it outside. I haven't any use for those Parmenos,[1] those Syruses [1] that do their masters out of two or three gold pieces. There's nothing more worthless than a servant without brains: he's got to have a precious powerful intellect: whenever a scheme is needed,

---

[1] Rascally slaves in Greek comedies.

ubicumque usus siet, pectore expromat suo.
   nullus frugi esse potest homo,
   nisi qui et bene et male facere tenet.
improbis cum improbus sit, harpaget furibus
      furetur quod queat,
    vorsipellem frugi convenit esse hominem,
    pectus quoi sapit : bonus sit bonis, malus sit malis ; 659–
    utcumque res sit, ita animum habeat.   660
      sed lubet scire quantum aurum erus sibi
      dempsit et quid suo reddidit patri.
      si frugi est, Herculem fecit ex patre :
      decimam partem ei dedit, sibi novem abstulit.
      sed quem quaero optume eccum obviam mihi
        est.
    num qui nummi exciderunt, ere, tibi,
      quod sic terram optuere ?
quid vos maestos tam tristesque esse conspicor ?
non placet nec temere est etiam. quin mihi re-
    spondetis ?   670

Mnes. Chrysale, occidi.
Chrys.   Fortassis tu auri dempsisti parum ?
Mnes. Quam, malum, parum ? immo vero nimio minus
    multo parum.
Chrys. Quid igitur, stulte ? an tu, quoniam occasio ad eam
    rem fuit
    mea virtute parta, ut quantum velles tantum
    sumeres,
    sic hoc digitulis duobus sumebas primoribus ?
    an nescibas quam eius modi homini raro tempus se
    daret ?
Mnes. Erras.
Chrys.   At quidem tute errasti, cum parum immersti
ampliter.

let him produce it from his own intellect. Not a soul can be worth anything, unless he knows how to be good and bad both. He must be a rascal among rascals, rob robbers, steal what he can. A chap that's worth anything, a chap with a fine intellect, has to be able to change his skin. He must be good with the good and bad with the bad; whatever the situation calls for, that he's got to be. (*pausing*) But I should like to know how much money master took for himself and what he passed on to his father. If he is worth anything, he has let his father play Hercules—given him a tithe and made off with nine parts for his own use. (*sees Mnesilochus and Pistoclerus*) Hullo, though! Here's a lucky meeting with the man I'm looking for! (*to Mnesilochus*) You haven't dropped any of the coin, have you, sir,—gazing at the ground that way? (*waits for answer*) What makes you two look so sad and gloomy? (*waits again*) I don't like it: no indeed, it's not for nothing. (*waits again*) Why don't you answer me?

Mnes. Chrysalus, I'm a lost man.

Chrys. You took too little of the gold, perhaps?

Mnes. Too little, eh, curse it! No indeed,—much too much less than too little!

Chrys. Well, how's that, you blockhead? After my ability won you this opportunity to help yourself to just as much as you pleased, you surely didn't pick it up this way (*illustrating*) with a couple of finger tips? Didn't you know how seldom a man is offered such a chance?

Mnes. You're making a mistake.

Chrys. Well, you made another yourself, by not dipping into it deep enough.

Mnes.   Pol tu quam nunc med accuses magis, si magis rem
      noveris.
      occidi.

Chrys.   Animus iam istoc dicto plus praesagitur mali.

Mnes.   Perii.

Chrys.   Quid ita?

Mnes.   Quia patri omne cum ramento reddidi.   680

Chrys.   Reddidisti?

Mnes.   Reddidi.

Chrys.   Omnene?

Mnes.   Oppido.

Chrys.   Occisi sumus.
      qui in mentem venit tibi istuc facinus facere tam
        malum?

Mnes.   Bacchidem atque hunc suspicabar propter crimen,
        Chrysale,
      mi male consuluisse: ob eam rem omne aurum,
        iratus reddidi
      meo patri.

Chrys.   Quid, ubi reddebas aurum, dixisti patri?

Mnes.   Me id aurum accepisse extemplo ab hospite Archi-
        demide.

Chrys.   Em,
      istoc dicto dedisti hodie in cruciatum Chrysalum;
      nam ubi me aspiciet, ad carnuficem rapiet continuo
        senex.

Mnes.   Ego patrem exoravi.

Chrys.   Nempe ergo hoc ut faceret quod loquor?

Mnes.   Immo tibi ne noceat neu quid ob eam rem suscen-
        seat;   690
      atque aegre impetravi.   nunc hoc tibi curandumst,
        Chrysale.

nes. (*moodily*) Good Lord! You'd lecture me more than you do now, if you knew more of the facts. I'm a lost man!

hrys. Now I foresee more trouble coming, after that remark.

nes. I'm done for.

hrys. Why so?

nes. Because I've handed over every scrap of it to my father.

hrys. (*dumbfounded*) Handed it over?

nes. Handed it over.

hrys. Every bit?

nes. Absolutely.

hrys. We're both lost men! What made it enter your head to do such a thing, such an awful thing?

nes. (*awkwardly*) I heard a charge made, Chrysalus, and suspected Bacchis and Pistoclerus here of plotting against me: so I got angry and handed all the money over to my father.

hrys. What did you tell your father when you handed it over?

nes. That I had received it on demand from his friend Archidemides.

hrys. (*grimly*) Aha! And gave Chrysalus over to torment by the statement; for when he sets eyes on me the old man will promptly hale me off to the public torturer.

nes. (*hurriedly*) I persuaded him.

hrys. (*dryly*) Indeed? To do what I'm saying, I take it?

nes. No, no, not to harm you, or be at all angry with you for what you did; and a hard time I had getting it out of him, too. (*pauses, then in flattering manner*) Here's what you must see to now, Chrysalus.

O

Chrys. Quid vis curem?

Mnes.   Ut ad senem etiam alteram facias viam.
compara, fabricare finge quod lubet, conglutina,
ut senem hodie doctum docte fallas aurumque
    auferas.

Chrys. Vix videtur fieri posse.

Mnes.   Perge, ac facile ecfeceris.

Chrys. Quam, malum, facile, quem mendaci prendit manu-
    festo modo?
quem si orem ut mihi nil credat, id non ausit cre-
    dere.

Mnes. Immo si audias quae dicta dixit me adversum tibi.

Chrys. Quid dixit?

Mnes.   Si tu illum solem sibi solem esse diceres,
se illum lunam credere esse et noctem qui nunc
    est dies.

Chrys. Emungam hercle hominem probe hodie, ne id
    nequiquam dixerit.

Mnes. Nunc quid nos vis facere?

Chrys.   Enim nil nisi ut ametis impero.
ceterum quantum lubet me poscitote aurum: ego
    dabo.
quid mihi refert Chrysalo esse nomen, nisi factis
    probo?
sed nunc quantillum usust auri tibi, Mnesiloche?
    dic mihi.

Mnes. Militi nummis ducentis iam usus est pro Bacchide.

Chrys. Ego dabo.

Mnes.   Tum nobis opus est sumptu.

700

Chrys. *(sourly)* What do you want me to see to?

Mnes. To making another march still against the old man. Use your ideas, your devices, your craft, any way you please, stick together some clever scheme to fool the clever old fellow to-day and get away with the gold.

Chrys. It hardly looks possible to me.

Mnes. You go ahead, and you'll carry it through easily.

Chrys. Easily, eh, curse it? A man that has caught me in a barefaced lie? A man that, if I should beg him not to believe me in a thing, wouldn't dare to believe even that!

Mnes. *(smiling feebly)* Worse still—if you had only heard what he said to me about you.

Chrys. What did he say?

Mnes. That if you told him the sun there was the sun, he'd believe it was the moon, and that it was night now, not day.

Chrys. *(thinking a moment, then jubilantly)* By Jupiter! I'll clean the man up in glorious shape to-day, that he mayn't say that for nothing!

Mnes. What do you want us to do now?

Chrys. Oh, make love—that's all I order. But just apply to me for gold, as much as you like: I'm your man. What's the advantage of my being named Chrysalus, unless I live up to it? Well now, Mnesilochus, what's the paltry sum you need? Tell me.

Mnes. *(eagerly)* I need two hundred pounds at once to pay the Captain for Bacchis.

Chrys. I'm your man.

Mnes. Then we must have something for running expenses.

Chrys.   Ah, placide volo
unum quidque agamus : hoc ubi egero, tum istuc
    agam.
de ducentis nummis primum intendam ballistam in
    senem ;
ea ballista si pervortam turrim et propugnacula,   710
recta porta invadam extemplo in oppidum anticum
    et vetus :
si id capso, geritote amicis vostris aurum corbibus,
sicut animus sperat.

Pistoc.   Apud test animus noster, Chrysale.
Chrys. Nunc tu abi intro, Pistoclere, ad Bacchidem, atque
    ecfer cito
Pistoc. Quid?
Chrys.   Stilum, ceram et tabellas, linum.
Pistoc.   Iam faxo hic erunt.
Mnes. Quid nunc es facturus? id mihi dice.
Chrys.   Coctumst prandium?
vos duo eritis atque amica tua erit tecum tertia?
Mnes. Sicut dicis.
Chrys.   Pistoclero nulla amica est?
Mnes.   Immo adest.
alteram ille amat sororem, ego alteram, ambas
    Bacchides.
Chrys. Quid tu loquere?
Mnes.   Hoc, ut futuri sumus.
Chrys.   Ubist biclinium   720
vobis stratum?
Mnes.   Quid id exquaeris?
Chrys.   Res itast, dici volo.
nescis quid ego acturus sim nec facinus quantum
    exordiar.
Mnes. Cedo manum ac subsequere propius me ad fores.
    intro inspice.

Chrys. Oh, I say, let's go gently and attend to things one by one : after I've attended to this, then I'll attend to that. I'll train my catapult on the old fellow for the two hundred first. If I shatter the tower and outworks with the said catapult, the next minute I'll plunge straight through the gate into the ancient and time-worn town : in case I capture it, you two can carry off gold to your lady friends by the basketful, and gratify the hope of your soul.

Pistoc. Our soul is in your keeping, Chrysalus.

Chrys. (*obviously the manager*) Now, Pistoclerus, inside with you to Bacchis and hurry back with——

Pistoc. With what?

Chrys. ——a stylus, wax and tablets, some tape.

Pistoc. I'll have them here at once. [EXIT INTO HOUSE.

Mnes. What are you going to do now? Tell me that.

Chrys. Is lunch cooked? You two, and your girl with you for a third,—is that the plan?

Mnes. Just so.

Chrys. No girl for Pistoclerus?

Mnes. Oh, yes there is! He loves one sister and I the other, both of them Bacchises.

Chrys. (*surprised*) What's that you tell me?

Mnes. Merely our arrangements.

Chrys. Where is this duplex dining-couch of yours set?

Mnes. What do you ask that for?

Chrys. The case calls for it : I want to be told. You don't know what I'm up to, what a monster of a scheme I'm going to get under way.

Mnes. (*slyly*) Give me your hand and follow me closer to the door. (*leads Chrysalus to the house of Bacchis and pushes the door open*) Cast your eyes in there!

401

Chrys. Euax, nimis bellus atque ut esse maxume optabam
locus.

Pistoc. Quae imperavisti. imperatum bene bonis factum
ilicost.

Chrys. Quid parasti?

Pistoc.   Quae parari tu iussisti omnia.

Chrys. Cape stilum propere et tabellas tu has tibi.

Mnes.   Quid postea?

Chrys. Quod iubebo scribito istic. nam propterea te volo
scribere, ut pater cognoscat litteras quando legat.   730
scribe.

Mnes.   Quid scribam?

Chrys.   Salutem tuo patri verbis tuis.

Pistoc. Quid si potius morbum mortem scribat? id erit
rectius.

Chrys. Ne interturba.

Mnes.   Iam imperatum in cera inest.

Chrys.   Dic quem ad modum.

Mnes. " Mnesilochus salutem dicit suo patri."

Chrys.   Adscribe hoc cito:
" Chrysalus mihi usque quaque loquitur nec recte,
pater,

quia tibi aurum reddidi et quia non te fraudave-
rim."

Pistoc. Mane dum scribit.

Chrys.   Celerem oportet esse amatoris manum.

Pistoc. [1] At quidem hercle est ad perdundum magis quam
ad scribundum cita.

Mnes. Loquere. hoc scriptumst.

Chrys.   " Nunc, pater mi, proin tu ab eo ut caveas
tibi,

---

[1] Corrupt (Leo). *At quidem hercle est ad perdundum
magis quam ad scribundum cita* Camerarius: various
readings MSS.

402

hrys. (*looking in*) Hurray! Perfectly delicious, yes, just the sort of place I longed for it to be!

RE-ENTER *Pistoclerus.*

istoc. (*to Chrysalus, with mock deference*) Orders followed, sir! Good orders to good men instantly executed.

hrys. What have you got?

istoc. Everything your mandate called for. (*showing writing materials*)

hrys. (*to Mnesilochus*) Quick! Take the stylus and these tablets, you.

nes. (*obeying*) And then?

hrys. Write down there what I dictate. I want you to do the writing, you see, so that your father will recognize your hand when he reads it. Write.

nes. Write what?

hrys. Oh, some wish—use your own words—for your father's health. (*Mnesilochus writes*)

istoc. Hadn't he better write sickness and death? That will be more to the point.

hrys. (*to Pistoclerus*) Don't muddle him.

nes. That's down now according to orders.

hrys. Let's hear how you've put it.

nes. (*reading*) " Mnesilochus sends best wishes to his father."

hrys. Hurry up, add this: " Chrysalus keeps talking away at me everywhere, father, and talking harshly, because I handed the gold over to you and did not defraud you."

istoc. Give him time to write.

hrys. A lover's hand ought to be nimble.

istoc. Gad, yes! but it makes shorter work of cash than correspondence.

nes. Go on. That's written.

hrys. " Now then, father dear, do be on your guard

403

	sycophantias componit, aurum ut abs ted auferat;	740
	et profecto se ablaturum dixit.'' plane adscribito.	
Mnes.	Dic modo.	
Chrys.	"Atque id pollicetur se daturum aurum mihi,	

Mnes. Dic modo.

Chrys.　　"Atque id pollicetur se daturum aurum mihi,
quod dem scortis quodque in lustris comedim con-
　　graecem, pater.
sed, pater, vide ne tibi hodie verba det: quaeso
　　cave.''

Mnes. Loquere porro.

Chrys.　　　　Adscribe dum etiam—

Mnes.　　　　　　　　Loquere quid scribam modo.

Chrys. "Sed, pater, quod promisisti mihi, te quaeso ut
　　memineris,
ne illum verberes; verum apud te vinctum adser-
　　vato domi.''
cedo tu ceram ac linum actutum. age obliga,
　　obsigna cito.

Mnes. Obsecro, quid istis ad istunc usust conscriptis mo-
　　dum,
ut tibi ne quid credat atque ut vinctum te adservet
　　domi?　　　　　　　　　　　　　　　　　　　　750

Chrys. Quia mi ita lubet.　potin ut cures te atque ut ne
　　parcas mihi?
mea fiducia opus conduxi et meo periclo rem
　　gero.

Mnes. Aequom dicis.

Chrys.　　　　Cedo tabellas.

Mnes.　　　　　　　　Accipe.

Chrys.　　　　　　　　　　Animum advortite.
Mnesiloche et tu, Pistoclere, iam facite in biclinio
cum amica sua uterque accubitum eatis, ita nego-
　　tiumst,
atque ibidem ubi nunc sunt lecti strati potetis
　　cito.

against him—he is laying a rascally scheme to take
the gold from you; and he vows he will take it."
Write that down plain.

nes. (*after a moment*) Yes, yes, go on.

hrys. "And besides, he promises he will give it to me
to spend on women and to squander in riotous
living in low resorts, father. But, father, do see
that he doesn't impose upon you to-day: for
mercy's sake, take care."

nes. (*finishing*) All right, some more.

hrys. Just go on and add—(*thinking*)

nes. Well, say what.

hrys. "However, I beg you to remember what you
promised me, father: don't beat him; but tie him
up and keep watch on him at home." (*to Pistoclerus*)
The wax and tape, you, look sharp! (*Pistoclerus
obeys. To Mnesilochus*) Come on, fasten it, seal it,
quick!

nes. (*obeying*) For heaven's sake, what's the use of a
document like this, telling him not to believe you at
all, to tie you up and keep watch on you at home?

hrys. Because it suits me. Can't you mind your own
business and not bother about me? (*arrogantly*) I
was relying on myself when I contracted for this
job, and I'll take the risk myself in doing it.

nes. Fairly spoken.

hrys. Hand over the tablets.

nes. (*doing so*) Here they are.

hrys. Attention now! Mnesilochus, and you too, Pistoclerus, go at once and take your places on your
duplex dining-couch, each of you beside his girl—
that's the thing to do—and right there where the
couches are set at present you hurry up and begin
drinking.

405

Pistoc. Numquid aliud?

Chrys. Hoc, atque etiam : ubi erit accubitum semel,
ne quoquam exsurgatis, donec a me erit signum
datum.

Pistoc. O imperatorem probum!

Chrys. Iam bis bibisse oportuit.

Mnes. Fugimus.

IV. 5.

Chrys. Vos vostrum curate officium, ego efficiam meum.   760
insanum magnum molior negotium,
metuoque ut hodie possiem emolirier.
sed nunc truculento mi atque saevo usus senest ;
nam non conducit huic sycophantiae
senem tranquillum esse ubi me aspexerit.
versabo ego illum hodie, si vivo, probe.
tam frictum ego illum reddam quam frictum est cicer.
adambulabo ad ostium, ut, quando exeat,
extemplo advenienti ei tabellas dem in manum.

IV. 6.

Nic. Nimium illaec res est magnae dividiae mihi,   770
supterfugisse sic mihi hodie Chrysalum.

Chrys. Salvos sum, iratus est senex. nunc est mihi
adeundi ad hominem tempus.

Nic. Quis loquitur prope?
atque hic quidem, opinor, Chrysalust.

Chrys. Accessero.

Nic. Bone serve, salve. quid fit? quam mox navigo
in Ephesum, ut aurum repetam ab Theotimo domum?

406

stoc. (*turning to go*) Nothing else?

rys. Just this—and one thing more: when you've once taken your places, don't move an inch off the couches until you get the signal from me.

stoc. O peerless leader!

rys. (*bustling them off*) You should have put down two drinks already.

nes. (*in mock terror*) We're running away.

rys. (*grinning*) You two do your duty and I'll attend to mine.

EXEUNT Pistoclerus AND Mnesilochus INTO HOUSE OF

ene 5.   Bacchis.

rys. (*doubtfully*) It's some wild, wild work I've got in hand, and what I'm afraid of is that I can't carry it out. (*pauses*) But now I must make the old man feel fierce and savage. For it won't suit this swindle of mine, to have him peaceful when he sets eyes on me. I'll turn him other end up to-day, handsomely, on my life, I will. I'll see he's roasted like a roasted pea. I'll saunter up to the door so that when he comes out I can hand him the letter the minute he appears. (*withdraws as door opens*)

ene 6.   ENTER Nicobulus FROM HOUSE.

c. Ugh! how it does rankle to have let Chrysalus get out of my reach as he has to-day.

rys. (*in low tone*) Saved! The old fellow's angry. Now is the time to approach him.

c. (*aside*) Who's that speaking near here? (*seeing Chrysalus*) Yes, it's actually Chrysalus, I do believe.

rys. (*aside*) At him now! (*approaches*)

c. Ah! my good servant, how goes it? How soon shall I sail to Ephesus to bring home the gold from

taces? per omnis deos adiuro, ut ni meum
gnatum tam amem atque ei facta cupiam quae is
   velit,
ut tua iam virgis latera lacerentur probe   779–780
ferratusque in pistrino aetatem conteras.
omnia rescivi scelera ex Mnesilocho tua.

Chrys. Men criminatust? optimest: ego sum malus,
ego sum sacer, scelestus. specta rem modo;
ego verbum faciam nullum.

Nic.   Etiam, carnufex,
minitare?

Chrys.   Nosces tu illum actutum qualis sit.
nunc has tabellas ferre me iussit tibi.
orabat, quod istic esset scriptum ut fieret.

Nic. Cedo.

Chrys.   Nosce signum.

Nic.   Novi. ubi ipse est?

Chrys.   Nescio.
nil iam me oportet scire. oblitus sum omnia.   790
scio me esse servom. nescio etiam id quod scio.
nunc ab trasenna hic turdus lumbricum petit;
pendebit hodie pulcre, ita intendi tenus.

Nic. Mane dum parumper; iam exeo ad te, Chrysale

Chrys. Ut verba mihi dat, ut nescio quam rem gerat.
servos arcessit intus qui me vinciant.
bene navis agitatur, pulcre haec confertur ratis.
sed conticiscam, nam audio aperiri fores.

Theotimus? Silent, eh? (*more savagely*) I swear
to heaven if I didn't love my son so, if I wasn't
anxious to gratify his wishes, those flanks of yours
would be torn to ribbons with rods this instant
and you should wear out your days in fetters in the
mill. I have heard about your rascality from
Mnesilochus—everything.

hrys. (*affecting indignation*) He's accused me, me? Very
fine indeed! I'm the one that's bad, I'm the cursed
criminal! (*significantly*) You just keep your eyes
open; that's all I have to say.

ic. What? Threatening, you hangdog?

hrys. You'll shortly know what sort he is. He ordered
me to bring this letter to you now. Begged you
to do what's written there.

ic. Give it here.

hrys. (*obeying*) Take notice of the seal.

ic. (*seeing it is intact*) Yes, yes. Where is my son
himself?

hrys. (*surlily*) Don't know. The proper thing for me now
is to know nothing. I've forgotten everything. I
know I'm a slave. I don't even know what I
do know. (*aside*) Now our thrush here is after the
worm in my trap; he'll soon be hung up handsomely, the way I've set the noose.

ic. (*having read letter*) Just wait a moment; (*goes
toward house*) I'll soon be back with you, Chrysalus.

[EXIT INTO HOUSE.

hrys. (*elated*) Oh, isn't he bluffing me! Oh, isn't it mysterious what he's at! He's fetching servants from
inside to tie me up. A lovely shake-up the galleon
there is getting: the little bark here is putting up
a fine fight! (*listening*) But not a word! I hear
the door opening.

409

IV. 7.

Nic. Constringe tu illi, Artamo, actutum manus.

Chrys. Quid feci?

Nic.   Impinge pugnum, si muttiverit.   800
quid hae locuntur litterae?

Chrys.   Quid me rogas?
ut ab illo accepi, ad te obsignatas attuli.

Nic. Eho tu,[1] loquitatusne es gnato meo
male per sermonem, quia mi id aurum reddidit,
et te dixisti id aurum ablaturum tamen
per sycophantiam?

Chrys.   Egone istuc dixi?

Nic.   Ita.

Chrys. Quis homost qui dicat me dixisse istuc?

Nic.   Tace,
nullus homo dicit: hae tabellae te arguont,
quas tu attulisti. em hae te vinciri iubent.

Chrys. Aha, Bellorophontem tuos me fecit filius: 810
egomet tabellas tetuli ut vincirer. sine.

Nic. Propterea hoc facio, ut suadeas gnato meo
ut pergraecetur tecum, tervenefice.

Chrys. O stulte, stulte, nescis nunc venire te;
atque in eopse adstas lapide, ut praeco praedicat.

Nic. Responde: quis me vendit?

Chrys.   Quem di diligunt
adulescens moritur, dum valet sentit sapit.
hunc si ullus deus amaret, plus annis decem,
plus iam viginti mortuom esse oportuit:

---

[1] Leo notes. acuna here: *tu (scelus)* Ritschl.

410

THE TWO BACCHISES

Scene 7. ENTER *Nicobulus* BRINGING SLAVE OVERSEER AND OTHER SLAVES.

Nic. *(to overseer)* Quick, Artamo, fasten his hands there!

Chrys. *(as Artamo obeys)* What have I done?

Nic. *(to Artamo)* Plant your fists in his face, if he breathes a word. *(to Chrysalus)* What does this letter say?

Chrys. What are you asking me for? I took it from him and brought it to you just as it was, all sealed.

Nic. Oho, you! So you have been giving my son the rough side of your tongue, because he handed over that gold to me? Said you'd take it from me just the same by some rascally scheme, eh?

Chrys. I said that, I?

Nic. Just so.

Chrys. Who's the man says I said that?

Nic. Silence! No man says it: this letter indicts you, the one you brought yourself. *(showing it)* There! This orders you to be tied up.

Chrys. *(resignedly)* Aha! Your son has made a Bellerophon [1] of me: I myself brought the letter to have myself tied up. *(dangerously)* Very well!

Nic. *(ironically)* I do this merely to make you persuade my son to join you in riotous living, you soulless villain.

Chrys. Oh, you poor poor fool, you don't know you're being sold this moment; and here you are standing on the very block with the crier crying you!

Nic. *(mystified)* Answer! Who is selling me?

Chrys. *(sneeringly)* He whom the gods love dies young, while he has his strength and senses and wits. If any god loved this fellow, *(indicating Nicobulus)*

---

[1] Who carried a letter which was to be his own death warrant.

terrai odium ambulat, iam nil sapit   820
nec sentit, tantist quantist fungus putidus.

Nic. Tun terrae me odium esse autumas? abducite hunc
intro atque adstringite ad columnam fortiter.
numquam auferes hinc aurum.

Chrys.   At qui iam dabis.

Nic. Dabo?

Chrys.   Atque orabis me quidem ultro ut auferam,
cum illum rescisces criminatorem meum
quanto in periclo et quanta in pernicie siet.
tum libertatem Chrysalo largibere;
ego adeo numquam accipiam.

Nic.   Dic, scelerum caput,
dic, quo in periclo est meus Mnesilochus filius?   830

Chrys. Sequere hac me, faxo iam scies.

Nic.   Quo gentium?

Chrys. Tres unos passus.

Nic.   Vel decem.

Chrys.   Agedum tu, Artamo,
forem hanc pauxillum aperi; placide, ne crepa;
sat est. accede huc tu. viden convivium?

Nic. Video exadvorsum Pistoclerum et Bacchidem.

Chrys. Qui sunt in lecto illo altero?

Nic.   Interii miser.

Chrys. Novistine hominem?

412

      it's more than ten years, more than twenty years
ago, he ought to have died. He ambles along
encumbering the earth, absolutely witless and
senseless already, worth about as much as a mush-
room—a rotten one.

Nic. (*furious*) So I encumber the earth, do I, according
to you? (*to Artamo and slaves*) March him off
inside! yes, and tie him to a pillar—tight! (*to
Chrysalus*) You shall never take that gold away
from me.

Chrys. (*mysteriously*) However, you'll soon give it away.

Nic. I give it away?

Chrys. Yes, and beg me, beg me of your own accord, to
take it away, when you learn about that accuser of
mine and what danger, what deadly danger, he's
in. Then you'll be all for liberating Chrysalus;
but not for me, I won't be liberated.

Nic. Speak, you fount of iniquity, speak—what danger
is my son Mnesilochus in?

Chrys. (*going toward Bacchis's house*) This way; follow me:
I'll soon let you know.

Nic. (*following*) Where on earth are you taking me?

Chrys. Three steps merely.

Nic. Ten, for that matter.

Chrys. Come on now, you, Artamo; open this door a tiny
bit; easy, don't make it creak. (*Artamo obeys*)
That will do. (*to Nicobulus*) Step up here, you.
See that jovial party? (*pointing inside*)

Nic. (*peeking in*) I see Pistoclerus and Bacchis right
opposite.

Chrys. Who are on that other couch?

Nic. (*peeking again, then with a start*) Death and damnation!

Chrys. Do you recognize the gentleman?

413

Nic.   Novi.

Chrys.   Dic sodes mihi,
bellan videtur specie mulier?

Nic.   Admodum.

Chrys. Quid illam, meretricemne esse censes?

Nic.   Quippini?

Chrys. Frustra es.

Nic.   Quis igitur obsecrost?

Chrys.   Inveneris.   840
ex me quidem hodie numquam fies certior.

IV. 8.

Cleom. Meamne hic Mnesilochus, Nicobuli filius,
per vim ut retineat mulierem? quae haec factiost?

Nic. Quis illest?

Chrys.   Per tempus hic venit miles mihi.

Cleom. Non me arbitratur militem, sed mulierem,
qui me meosque non queam defendere.
nam neque Bellona mi umquam neque Mars cre-
    duat,
ni illum exanimalem faxo, si convenero,
nive exheredem fecero vitae suae.

Nic. Chrysale, quis ille est qui minitatur filio?   850

Chrys. Vir hic est illius mulieris quacum accubat.

Nic. Quid, vir?

Chrys.   Vir, inquam.

Nic.   Nuptanest illa, obsecro?

Chrys. Scies haud multo post.

Nic.   Oppido interii miser.

THE TWO BACCHISES

Nic.   I do.

Chrys. Kindly give me your opinion—good-looking female, eh?

Nic.   (*angrily*) Quite so!

Chrys. Well, do you think she's a harlot?

Nic.   Naturally.

Chrys. You're mistaken.

Nic.   For heaven's sake, who is she, then?

Chrys. (*again mysterious*) You'll soon discover. But you'll never get the information from me to-day.

ENTER *Cleomachus*, APPARENTLY NOT SEEING GROUP AT
Scene 8.   DOORWAY.

Cleom. (*blustering*) Mnesilochus, Nicobulus's son, keep her here by force—my woman? What sort of conduct is this?

Nic.   Who is that?

Chrys. (*aside*) The Captain has come just in the nick of time for me. (*draws Nicobulus farther away*)

Cleom. He takes me for a woman, not a soldier, a woman unable to defend myself and mine! Now never may Bellona [1] and Mars trust me more, unless I extinguish his vital spark, once I come upon him, and unless I disinherit him of his existence!

Nic.   (*anxiously*) Chrysalus! who's that threatening my son?

Chrys. (*coolly*) He is the husband of that woman beside your son on the couch.

Nic.   (*in terror*) What? The husband?

Chrys. That is what I say, the husband.

Nic.   For heaven's sake, is she married?

Chrys. You'll see a little later.

Nic.   Oh! This is perfectly agonizing!

---

[1] The goddess of war.

415

Chrys. Quid nunc? scelestus tibi videtur Chrysalus?
age nunc vincito me, auscultato filio.
dixin tibi ego illum inventurum te qualis sit?

Nic. Quid nunc ego faciam?

Chrys.   Iube sis me exsolvi cito;
nam ni ego exsolvor, iam manufesto hominem op-
    primet.

Cleom. Nihil est lucri quod me hodie facere mavelim,
quam illum cubantem cum illa opprimere, ambo
    ut necem.   860

Chrys. Audin quae loquitur? quin tu me exsolvi iubes?

Nic. Exsolvite istum. perii, pertimui miser.

Cleom. Tum illam, quae corpus publicat volgo suom,
faxo se haud dicat nactam quem derideat.

Chrys. Pacisci cum illo paulula pecunia
potes.

Nic.   Pacisce ergo, obsecro, quid tibi lubet,
dum ne manifesto hominem opprimat neve enicet.

Cleom. Nunc nisi ducenti Philippi redduntur mihi,
iam illorum ego animam amborum exsorbebo op-
    pido.

Nic. Em illuc pacisce, si potes; perge obsecro,   870
pacisce quid vis.

Chrys.   Ibo et faciam sedulo.
quid clamas?

Cleom.   Ubi erus tuos est?

Chrys.   Nusquam. nescio
vis tibi ducentos nummos iam promittier,
ut ne clamorem hic facias neu convicium?

Cleom. Nihil est quod malim.

Chrys. What now? Do you think Chrysalus is the criminal?
Go ahead now, tie me up and listen to your son.
Didn't I tell you you'd find out what sort he is?

Nic. What shall I do now?

Chrys. Kindly have me loosed, and quickly; for if I'm not
loosed, he'll soon be surprising our gentleman
red-handed.

Cleom. There is no amount of money I had rather make
to-day than surprise him with her in his arms, so
that I may slay them both!

Chrys. You hear what he's saying? Why don't you have
me loosed?

Nic. (*to slaves*) Loose him. (*they obey*) This is awful!
Dear, dear, I'm frightened through and through!

Cleom. Then that woman who makes a common prostitute
of herself—I warrant she'll not say she has lit on
a man she can laugh to scorn!

Chrys. You can buy him off for a bit of cash.

Nic. (*beside himself*) Buy him off, then, for heaven's
sake—anything you like—if only he doesn't surprise the lad red-handed and slay him!

Cleom. Unless two hundred pounds are given me at once,
I'll drain them dry, the both of them, of the
breath of life this moment.

Nic. There! Buy him off for that, if you can. At him,
for heaven's sake: buy him off at any price.

Chrys. I'll go and do my best. (*approaching Cleomachus*)
What are you bawling at?

Cleom. Where is your master?

Chrys. (*loudly*) Nowhere. I don't know. (*gets him farther
from Nicobulus*) Do you want to have two hundred
pounds promised you instantly, on condition you
don't come bawling or bellowing here?

Cleom. (*calming down*) Nothing I should like better.

417

Chrys.   Atque ut tibi mala multa ingeram?

Cleom. Tuo arbitratu.

Nic.   Ut subblanditur carnufex.

Chrys. Pater hic Mnesilochi est; sequere, is promittet tibi.

tu aurum rogato; ceterum verbum sat est.

Nic. Quid fit?

Chrys.   Ducentis Philippis rem pepigi.

Nic.   Ah, salus

mea, servavisti me. quam mox dico " dabo "?   880

Chrys. Roga hunc tu, tu promitte huic.

Nic.   Promitto, roga.

Cleom. Ducentos nummos aureos Philippos probos

dabin?

Chrys.   " Dabuntur " inque. responde.

Nic.   Dabo.

Chrys. Quid nunc, impure? numquid debetur tibi?

quid illi molestu's? quid illum morte territas?

et ego te et ille mactamus infortunio.

si tibi est machaera, at nobis veruinast domi:

qua quidem te faciam, si tu me inritaveris,

confossiorem soricina nenia.

iam dudum hercle equidem sentio, suspicio   890

quae te sollicitet: eum esse cum illa muliere.

Cleom. Immo est quoque.

Chrys.   Ita me Iuppiter Iuno Ceres

Minerva [1] Latona Spes Opis Virtus Venus

---

[1] Corrupt (Leo). *Latona Spes* MSS: *Luna Spes* Bergk: *Lato Spes* Ussing.

418

THE TWO BACCHISES

Chrys. (*in low tone*) Yes, and on condition you take plenty of hard words from me?

Cleom. At your own discretion.

Nic. (*hearing only last words*) How the hangdog is wheedling him!

Chrys. Here is (*pointing*) Mnesilochus's father; come on; he'll promise it to you. You ask for the money; (*meaningly*) as for the rest, a word will suffice. (*Cleomachus nods his understanding: they join Nicobulus*)

Nic. Well? Well?

Chrys. I've settled for two hundred pounds.

Nic. (*ecstatic*) Ah, my salvation! you've saved me! How long before I say " I'll pay "?

Chrys. (*to Cleomachus*) You make your demand of him: (*to Nicobulus*) you promise him.

Nic. (*eagerly*) I promise: make your demand.

Cleom. Will you pay me two hundred good honest gold sovereigns?

Chrys. (*to Nicobulus*) " I will ": say that. Answer him.

Nic. I will.

Chrys. (*to Cleomachus*) What now, you beast? Is anything owed you? What are you annoying that gentleman for? What are you scaring him with murderous threats for? We'll give you a horrible time of it, he and I together. You may have a sword, but we've got a little spit at home: if you get me roused, I'll up with it and stick you fuller of holes than a squealing shrewmouse. Good Lord! Why, I saw it all long ago—how you're suffering from the suspicion that he's with the lady there.

Cleom. Suspicion? He is there, too.

Chrys. (*with unction*) So help me Jupiter, Juno, Ceres, Minerva, Latona, Spes, Ops, Virtus, Venus, Castor,

419

TITUS MACCIUS PLAUTUS

       Castor Polluces Mars Mercurius Hercules
       Summanus Sol Saturnus dique omnes ament,
       ut ille cum illa neque cubat neque ambulat
       neque osculatur neque illud quod dici solet.

Nic.   Ut iurat! servat me ille suis periuriis.

Cleom. Ubi nunc Mnesilochus ergost?

Chrys.   Rus misit pater.   900
       illa autem in arcem abiit aedem visere
       Minervae. nunc apertast. i, vise estne ibi.

Cleom. Abeo ad forum igitur.

Chrys.   Vel hercle in malam crucem.

Cleom. Hodie exigam aurum hoc?

Chrys.   Exige, ac suspende te:
       ne supplicare hunc censeas tibi, nihili homo.
       ille est amotus. sine me—per te, ere, opsecro
       deos immortales—ire huc intro ad filium.

Nic.   Quid eo intro ibis?

Chrys.   Ut eum dictis plurumis
       castigem, cum haec sic facta ad hunc faciat modum.

Nic.   Immo oro ut facias, Chrysale, et ted opsecro,
       cave parsis in eum dicere.

Chrys.   Etiam me mones?   910
       satin est si plura ex me audiet hodie mala,
       quam audivit umquam Clinia ex Demetrio?

Nic.   Lippi illic oculi servos est simillimus:
       si non est, nolis esse neque desideres;
       si est, abstinere quin attingas non queas.
       nam ni illic hodie forte fortuna hic foret,

Pollux, Mars, Mercury, Hercules, Summanus, Sol,
Saturn, and all the gods, he is neither lying with
her, nor walking with her, nor kissing her, nor
anything else he has the name of doing.

Nic. (*aside*) What an oath! The man is saving me by
perjuring himself.

Cleom. Where is Mnesilochus at present, then?

Chrys. His father has sent him out to the farm. As for
the lady, she has gone to the Acropolis to visit
Minerva's temple. It's open now. Go and see if
she isn't there.

Cleom. In that case, I'll be off to the forum.

Chrys. Or to blazes, if you like, by gad!

Cleom. Shall I get the money out of him to-day?

Chrys. Get it, and be hanged to you! You needn't think
he will sue for favours from you, you riffraff. [EXIT
Cleomachus] He's sent packing. (*fervently*) In the
name of heaven, sir, do let me go in here and see
your son, I beseech you.

Nic. Go in this house? Why?

Chrys. So that I may reprove him roundly for acting in
such a way as this.

Nic. Let you? I beg you to, Chrysalus, and I beseech
you, don't spare him in the slightest!

Chrys. (*virtuously indignant*) D'ye warn me of that, me? Is
it enough, if he hears more hard words from me
this day than ever Clinia [1] heard from Demetrius? [1]

[EXIT *Chrysalus* INTO HOUSE OF *Bacchis*.

Nic. (*ruefully*) That servant of mine is very much like a
sore eye: if you haven't got one, you don't want
one and don't miss it; if you have, you can't keep
your hands off it. Why, if he hadn't happened by
good luck to be here to-day, the Captain would

---

[1] Characters in some familiar play.

miles Mnesilochum cum uxore opprimeret sua
atque obtruncaret moechum manufestarium.
nunc quasi decentis Philippis emi filium,
quos dare promisi militi : quos non dabo 920
temere etiam prius quam filium convenero.
numquam edepol quicquam temere credam
    Chrysalo ;
verum lubet etiam ni has perlegere denuo :
aequomst tabellis consignatis credere.

IV. 9.

Chrys. Atridae duo frates cluent fecisse facinus maxumum,
    quom Priami patriam Pergamum divina moenitum
      manu
armis, equis, exercitu atque eximiis bellatoribus
mille cum numero navium decumo anno post sube-
    gerunt.
non pedibus termento fuit praeut ego erum ex-
    pugnabo meum
sine classe sineque exercitu et tanto numero militum.[1] 930
nunc prius quam huc senex venit, libet lamentari
    dum exeat.
o Troia, o patria, o Pergamum, o Priame periisti senex,
qui misere male mulcabere quadringentis Philippis
    aureis.
nam ego has tabellas obsignatas consignatas quas fero
non sunt tabellae, sed equos quem misere Achivi
    ligneum.[2]

---

[1] Leo brackets the following v., 931 :
cepi expugnavi amanti erili filio aurum ab suo patre.
[2] Leo brackets the following v., 937–940 :
*Epiust Pistoclerus : ab eo haec sumptae ; Mnesilochus Sino est
relictus, ellum non in busto Achilli, sed in lecto accubat ;
Bacchidem habet secum : ille olim habuit ignem qui sig-
    num daret,
hunc ipsum exurit ; ego sum Vlixes, cuius consilio haec gerunt.*

have surprised Mnesilochus with his wife and cut him to pieces for an adulterer caught in the act. As it is, I have bought my son, so to speak, for the two hundred pounds I promised to pay the Captain —two hundred I won't be rash enough to pay him yet, before I have met the boy. I'll put no rash confidence in Chrysalus, never, by heaven! But I've a mind to read this over (*looking at letter*) once more still: a man ought to have confidence in a sealed letter. [EXIT INTO HOUSE.

cene 9. (*Fifteen minutes have elapsed.*)

ENTER Chrysalus FROM Bacchis's HOUSE.

Chrys. (*bumptiously*) The two sons of Atreus have the name of having done a mighty deed when Priam's paternal city, Pergamum, "fortified by hand divine," was laid low by 'em after ten years, and they with weapons, horses, and army and warriors of renown and a thousand ships to help 'em. That wasn't enough to raise a blister on their feet, compared with the way I'll take my master by storm, without a fleet and without an army and all that host of soldiers. Now before the old chap appears, I feel like raising a dirge for him till he comes out. (*wailing*) O Troy, O paternal city, O Pergamum! O ancient Priam, thy day is past! Thou shalt be badly, badly beaten—out of four hundred golden sovereigns. Ah yes, these tablets here, (*showing them*) sealed and signed, which I bear, are no tablets, but a horse sent by the Greeks—a wooden horse.[1]

---

[1] Our Epius is Pistoclerus: from his hands were they taken. Mnesilochus is Sinon the abandoned. Behold him! not lying at Achilles' tomb, but on a couch; he has a Bacchis with him; that one of old had a fire, to give the signal,—but this Sinon is burning himself. I am Ulysses whose counsel directs it all.

423

tum quae hic sunt scriptae litterae, hoc in equo
    insunt milites   941
armati atque animati probe. ita res successit mi
    usque adhuc.
atque hic equos non in arcem, verum in arcam
    faciet impetum;
exitium excidium exlecebra fiet hic equos hodie auro
    senis.
nostro seni huic stolido, ei profecto nomen facio
    ego Ilio;
miles Menelaust, ego Agamemno, idem Vlixes
    Lartius,
Mnesilochust Alexander, qui erit exitio rei patriae
    suae;
is Helenam avexit, cuia causa nunc facio obsidium
    Ilio.
nam illi itidem Vlixem audivi, ut ego sum, fuisse
    et audacem et malum:
in dolis ego prensus sum, ille mendicans paene in-
        ventus interiit,   950
    dum ibi exquirit fata Iliorum; adsimiliter mi
        hodie optigit.
    vinctus sum, sed dolis me exemi: item se ille
        servavit dolis.
Ilio tria fuisse audivi fata quae illi forent exitio:
signum ex arce si periisset; alterum etiamst Troili
    mors;
tertium, cum portae Phrygiae limen superum scin-
    deretur:
paria item tria eis tribus sunt fata nostro huic Ilio.
nam dudum primo ut dixeram nostro seni men-
    dacium
et de hospite et de auro et de lembo, ibi signum
    ex arce iam abstuli.

Moreover, the words herein inscribed are the soldiers within this horse, soldiers armed to the teeth and full of fight. Thus has my scheme progressed up till now. Aye, and this horse will proceed to assail not a stronghold, but a strongbox. The wreck, ruin, and rape of the old man's gold will this horse prove to-day. This silly old man of ours—I dub him Ilium, I certainly do. The Captain is Menelaus, I Agamemnon: I am likewise Laertian Ulysses: Mnesilochus is Alexander,[1] who will be the destruction of his native city; he is the one that carried off Helen, on account of whom I now besiege Ilium. At that Ilium Ulysses, so they say, was a bold, bad man, just as I am now. I was caught in my wiles; he was found begging and almost perished, while he was seeking to learn there the destinies of the Ilians. What befell me to-day was quite similar. I was bound, but released myself by wiles: by wiles he likewise saved himself. In the case of that Ilium, so they say, there were three fateful events which would prove her downfall: if the image [2] disappeared from the citadel; still a second, the death of Troilus [3]; the third, when the upper lintel of the Phrygian gate should be torn away. Counterparts of these three are three fateful events, too, in the case of this Ilium of ours. For a little while ago when I first told our old man that lie about his friend and the gold and the galley, I there and then stole the image from the citadel.

---

[1] Paris.
[2] The Palladium, a statue of Pallas.
[3] A son of Priam, slain by Achilles.

iam duo restabant fata tunc, nec magis id ceperam
   oppidum.
post ubi tabellas ad senem detuli, ibi occidi Troilum,   960
cum censuit Mnesilochum cum uxore esse dudum
   militis.[1]
post cum magnifico milite, urbes verbis qui inermus
   capit,
conflixi atque hominem reppuli; dein pugnam
   conserui seni:
eum ego adeo uno mendacio devici, uno ictu extempulo
cepi spolia. is nunc ducentos nummos Philippos
   militi,
     quos dare se promisit, dabit,   970
nunc alteris etiam ducentis usus est, qui dispen-
   sentur
   Ilio capto, ut sit mulsum qui triumphent milites.[2]
sed Priamum adstantem eccum ante portam video.
   adibo atque adloquar.

---

[1] Leo brackets the following v., 962–965:
ibi vix me exsolvi: id periclum adsimilo, Vlixem ut prae-
*   dicant*
cognitum ab Helena esse proditum Hecubae; sed ut olim
*   ille se*
blanditiis exemit et persuasit se ut amitteret,
item ego dolis me illo extuli e periclo et decepi senem.

[2] Leo brackets the following v., 973–977:
sed Priamus hic multo illi praestat: non quinquaginta
*   modo,*
quadringentos filios habet atque equidem omnis lectos sine
*   probro:*
eos ego hodie omnis contruncabo duobus solis ictibus.
nunc Priamo nostro si est quis emptor, comptionalem
*   senem*
vendam ego, venalem quem habeo, extemplo ubi oppidum
*   expugnavero.*

Even then two fateful events were yet to come,
and the town was still untaken.   Later, on carrying the letter to the old man, I then slew my
Troilus, when he thought Mnesilochus a short time
ago was with the Captain's wife.[1]   Still later I
closed with the noble Captain—who captures cities
with no weapon save his mighty tongue—and
hurled him back.   Next I joined battle with the
old man: aye, and him I struck down with a
single lie; a single blow, and the spoils were
mine.   He now will give the Captain the two
hundred pounds he promised him.   And now
there is need of another two hundred still, to be
disbursed, on Ilium's capture, that the soldiery
may have wine and honey to celebrate their
victory.[2]   [ENTER *Nicobulus* FROM HIS HOUSE.]   Aha,
though!   I see Priam standing before the gate.
I'll up and address him.

[1] Then it was I just managed to get free: this danger
I liken to that they tell of when Ulysses was recognized
by Helen and betrayed to Hecuba.   But as he, in former
days, got away by means of his honeyed words and persuaded her to let him go, so also I, by means of my wiles,
got out of danger and deceived the old man.

[2] But this Priam is far superior to that one: not a mere
fifty sons has he; he has four hundred, yes, and every
one is unquestionably a choice and flawless specimen.
This day I will annihilate 'em all with just two blows.
Now, if there is anyone who cares to buy our Priam, I
will sell off the old gentleman I have on sale, as a job
lot, the moment I have taken the town by storm.

Nic. Quoianam vox prope me sonat?
Chrys.   O Nicobule.
Nic.   Quid fit?
    quid quod te misi, ecquid egisti?
Chrys.   Rogas? congredere.
Nic.   Gradior.   980
Chrys. Optumus sum orator. ad lacrumas coegi homi-
    nem castigando
  maleque dictis, quae quidem quivi comminisci.
Nic.   Quid ait?
Chrys.   Verbum
  nullum fecit: lacrumans tacitus auscultabat quae
    ego loquebar;
        tacitus conscripsit tabellas, obsignatas mi has
        dedit.
    tibi me iussit dare, sed metuo, ne idem cantent
    quod priores.
        nosce signum. estne eius?
Nic.   Novi. libet perlegere has.
Chrys.   Perlege.
  nunc superum limen scinditur, nunc adest exi-
    tium Ilio,
  turbat equos lepide ligneus.
Nic.   Chrysale, ades, dum ego has perlego.
Chrys. Quid me tibi adesse opus est?
Nic.   Volo,[1]
  ut scias quae hic scripta sient.
Chrys. Nil moror neque scire volo.
Nic. Tamen ades.
Chrys.   Quid opust?
Nic.   Taceas:
  quod iubeo id facias.
Chrys.   Adero.   990A

---

[1] *ut quod iubeo facias* follows in MSS : Leo brackets.

428

Nic. (*looking round*) Whose voice is that I hear near me?

Chrys. (*approaching*) Oh, sir!

Nic. (*eagerly*) How goes it? What about your mission —have you accomplished anything?

Chrys. Do you ask that? Come here, close.

Nic. (*doing so*) I am.

Chrys. (*enthusiastic*) I'm the orator for you! I fairly brought our man to tears, by saying all the harsh, bitter things I could think of.

Nic. What did he say?

Chrys. Not a word: just wept in silence and paid attention to what I was telling him. Still silent, he wrote a letter, sealed it, and gave it to me. He ordered me to give it to you. But I'm afraid it sings the same song as the other one. (*hands tablets to Nicobulus*) Take notice of the seal. Is it his?

Nic. (*examining seal*) Yes, yes. I'm anxious to read this over.

Chrys. Do. (*aside*) Now the upper lintel is being torn away; now Ilium's fall is nigh. The wooden horse is making a beautiful mess of things.

Nic. Chrysalus, stay here while I read this over.

Chrys. What's the use of my staying with you?

Nic. I wish it, so that you may know what is written here.

Chrys. Not for me—I don't wish to know.

Nic. Never mind; stay here.

Chrys. What's the use?

Nic. (*angry*) Silence! do what I tell you.

Chrys. (*apparently reluctant*) Stay I will.

Nic. Euge litteras minutas.

Chrys.   Qui quidem videat parum;
verum, qui satis videat, grandes satis sunt.

Nic.   Animum advortito igitur.

Chrys. Nolo inquam.

Nic.   At volo inquam.

Chrys.   Quid opust?

Nic. At enim id quod te iubeo facias.

Chrys. Iustumst ut tuos tibi servos tuo arbitratu serviat.

Nic. Hoc age sis nunciam.

Chrys.   Ubi lubet, recita: aurium operam tibi dico.

Nic. Cerae quidem haud parsit neque stilo;
sed quidquid est, pellegere certumst.
"Pater, ducentos Philippos quaeso Chrysalo
da, si esse salvom vis me aut vitalem tibi."
malum quidem hercle magnum.

Chrys.   Tibi dico.

Nic.   Quid est?

Chrys. Non prius salutem scripsit?

Nic.   Nusquam sentio. 1000

Chrys. Non dabis, si sapies; verum si das maxume,
ne ille alium gerulum quaerat, si sapiet, sibi:
nam ego non laturus sum, si iubeas maxume.
sat sic suspectus sum, cum careo noxia.

Nic. Ausculta porro, dum hoc quod scriptumst perlego.

Chrys. Inde a principio iam inpudens epistula est.

430

.   (*opening tablets*) Well, well! What tiny letters.

-ys. (*innocently*) Yes, for a man with poor eyes;
      they're big enough, if your sight is good enough,
      though.

.   Well then, pay attention.

-ys. I don't want to, I tell you.

.   But I want you to, I tell you.

-ys. What's the use?

.   See here now, you do what I order.

-ys. (*after reflection, impartially*) It's right for your own
      servant to serve you as you see fit, sir.

.   Now kindly attend to this at once.

-ys. Read when you like, sir: I promise you my ears.

.   (*looking tablets over with a sigh*) He hasn't been
      sparing of wax or stylus, it seems. But whatever
      it is, I'm resolved to read it through. (*reading*)
      " Father, do for mercy's sake give Chrysalus two
      hundred pounds, if you wish to have your son safe,
      or alive." Give him a good sound thrashing, by
      heaven!

-ys. I say.

.   Well?

-ys. Didn't he write a word of greeting first?

.   (*looking*) Not a sign of it.

-ys. (*indignant*) You won't do it, if you're wise; but no
      matter how much you do do it, let him look up
      another porter, if he's wise: for I won't carry it,
      no matter how much you order me. I am sus-
      pected enough as it is, when I'm perfectly blame-
      less.

.   Listen, further, while I read through what is
      written here.

-ys. That's an impudent letter, impudent from the very
      beginning!

431

Nic. " Pudet prodire me ad te in conspectum, pater:
tantum flagitium te scire audivi meum,
quod cum peregrini cubui uxore militis."
pol haud derides; nam ducentis aureis   1010
Philippis redemi vitam ex flagitio tuam.

Chrys. Nihil est illorum quin ego illi dixerim.

Nic. "Stulte fecisse fateor.   sed quaeso, pater,
ne me, in stultitia si deliqui, deseras.
ego animo cupido atque oculis indomitis fui;
persuasumst facere quoius me nunc facti pudet."
prius te cavisse ergo quam pudere aequom fuit.

Chrys. Eadem istaec verba dudum illi dixi omnia.

Nic. " Quaeso ut sat habeas id, pater, quod Chrysalus
me obiurigavit plurumis verbis malis,   1020
et me meliorem fecit praeceptis suis,
ut te ei habere gratiam aequom sit bonam."

Chrys. Estne istuc istic scriptum?

Nic.   Em specta, tum scies.

Chrys. Ut qui deliquit supplex est ultro omnibus.

Nic. " Nunc si me fas est obsecrare abs te, pater,
da mihi ducentos nummos Philippos, te obsecro."

Chrys. Ne unum quidem hercle, si sapis.

Nic.   Sine perlegam.
ego ius iurandum verbis conceptis dedi,
daturum id me hodie mulieri ante vesperum,
prius quam a me abiret.   nunc, pater, ne peri-
erem   1030
cura atque abduce me hinc ab hac quantum potest,

432

ic. (*continuing*) " I'm ashamed to come into your sight,
father: I have heard that you know of my wicked
intrigue with the foreign Captain's wife." Gad!
That is no joke! Two hundred golden sovereigns
it cost me to save your life after that piece of
wickedness!

rys. There's nothing of that I didn't say to him, sir.

ic. " I admit that I acted foolishly. But for mercy's
sake, father, don't desert me, if I have done wrong
in my folly. Wanton desires possessed me, and I
couldn't control my eyes; I was induced to do
what I am now ashamed of doing." Well, pru
dence then, rather than shame now, would have
been the proper thing for you!

rys. Just the very same words I said to him a while
ago, sir.

ic. " Do, please, consider it enough, father, that
Chrysalus has scolded me very very harshly and
has made me a better man by his precepts, so that
you ought to be deeply grateful to him."

rys. Is that written there?

ic. (*showing him the place*) There! look, then you'll
know.

rys. (*piously*) How the wrongdoer does bend the knee
to every one, of his own accord!

ic. " Now if I have a moral right to beseech you,
father, I do beseech you to give me two hundred
pounds."

rys. Not even one, by heaven, if you're wise!

ic. Let me read it through. " I took an oath in express terms to give the woman this sum before
evening comes and she leaves me. Now, father,
do see to it that I don't forswear myself, and do
rescue me just as soon as you can from this creature

433

       quam propter tantum damni feci et flagiti.

       cave tibi ducenti nummi dividiae fuant;

       sescenta tanta reddam, si vivo, tibi.

       vale atque haec cura." quid nunc censes, Chrysale?

Chrys.   Nihil ego tibi hodie consili quicquam dabo,

       neque ego haud committam ut, si quid peccatum siet,

       fecisse dicas de mea sententia.

       verum, ut ego opinor, si ego in istoc sim loco,

       dem potius aurum quam illum corrumpi sinam.   1040

       duae condiciones sunt: utram tu accipias vide:

       vel ut aurum perdas vel ut amator perieret.

       ego neque te iubeo neque veto, neque suadeo.

Nic.   Miseret me illius.

Chrys.   Tuos est, non mirum facis.

       si plus perdundum sit, periisse suaviust,

       quam illud flagitium volgo dispalescere.

Nic.   Ne ille edepol Ephesi multo mavellem foret,

       dum salvos esset, quam revenisset domum.

       quid ego istic? quod perdundumst properem perdere.

       binos ducentos Philippos iam intus ecferam.   1050

       et militi quos dudum promisi miser

       et istos. mane istic, iam exeo ad te, Chrysale.

Chrys.   Fit vasta Troia. scindunt proceres Pergamum.

       scivi ego iam dudum fore me exitio Pergamo.

on account of whom I have been so wasteful and wicked. See you don't let a matter of two hundred pounds vex you; I will pay it back to you a thousand times over, if I live. Good-bye and do look out for this." What do you recommend now, Chrysalus?

Chrys. (*vehemently*) Never a bit of advice will I give you this day! I'll take no chance of your saying, if anything goes wrong, that you did it at my suggestion. However, in my opinion, if I was in your place, I should rather give up the money than let him be debauched. There are two alternatives: see for yourself which to choose: you must either lose the money, or let our lover be forsworn. I do not order you, or forbid you, or urge you, either, not I.

Nic. (*earnestly*) I'm sorry for the lad.

Chrys. Nothing strange in that, your own flesh and blood as he is. (*casually*) If more must be lost, that's pleasanter than having such a piece of wickedness come to be the common talk.

Nic. Good Lord! I should certainly much rather have him at Ephesus, provided he was safe, than back home. (*pauses*) What am I to do in the matter? (*another pause, then irritably*) Let me hurry up and lose what has to be lost. I'll go in and get four hundred pounds at once—the two hundred I promised the Captain a while ago, poor wretch that I am, and this last. Wait where you are: I'll be with you again in a moment, Chrysalus.

[EXIT INTO HOUSE.

Chrys. (*hilarious*). Troy is being made a waste; the chieftains are laying Pergamum low! I knew long ago I'd be the downfall of Pergamum! By gad, the

435

       edepol qui me esse dicat cruciatu malo
       dignum, ne ego cum illo pignus haud ausim dare;
       tantas turbellas facio.   sed crepuit foris :
       ecfertur praeda ex Troia.   taceam nunciam.

Nic.   Cape hoc tibi aurum, Chrysale, i, fer filio.
       ego ad forum autem hinc ibo, ut solvam militi.   1060

Chrys. Non equidem accipiam.   proin tu quaeras qui
         ferat.
       nolo ego mihi credi.

Nic.   Cape vero, odiose facis.

Chrys. Non equidem capiam.

Nic.   At quaeso.

Chrys.   Dico ut res se habet.

Nic.   Morare.

Chrys.   Nolo, inquam, aurum concredi mihi.
       vel da aliquem qui servet me.

                   Ohe, odiose facis.

Chrys. Cedo, si necesse est.

Nic.   Cura hoc.   iam ego huc revenero.

Chrys. Curatum est—esse te senem miserrumum.
       hoc est incepta efficere pulcre : bellule
       mi evenit, ut ovans praeda onustus incederem;
       salute nostra atque urbe capta per dolum   1070
       domum reduco integrum omnem exercitum.
       sed, spectatores, vos nunc ne miremini
       quod non triumpho : pervolgatum est, nil moror;
       verum tamen accipientur mulso milites.

man that says I deserve to be punished damnably
—I surely wouldn't dare bet him I don't. Oh,
the lovely rumpus I'm raising! (*listening*) But the
door creaked: the booty is being carried out from
Troy. Time for me to keep still!

RE-ENTER *Nicobulus* WITH TWO BAGS OF GOLD.

ic. Take this money, Chrysalus: go, carry it to my
son. As for me, I am going to the forum to settle
with the Captain.

hrys. (*drawing back*) No indeed, I won't take it. So you
can look further for some one to carry it. I don't
want it trusted to me.

ic. Come, come, now, take it: you annoy me.

hrys. Indeed I won't take it.

ic. But I beg you.

hrys. (*firmly*) I tell you just how I stand.

ic. (*impatiently*) You're delaying me.

hrys. I don't want money put in my charge, I say.
(*pause*) At least, appoint some one to watch me.

ic. Pshaw! You annoy me.

hrys. (*reluctant*) Give it here, if I must.

ic. (*handing him bag of gold*) Look out for this. I shall
be back here soon.   [EXIT TOWARD FORUM.

hrys. (*as Nicobulus disappears*) It has been looked out for
—your being the poorest old wretch alive. Here's
the way to carry out your attempts in style! Ah,
this is beautiful luck—to be marching along in
jubilation, laden with booty. Safe myself, the
city captured by guile, I am leading my whole
army back home intact. But, spectators, don't be
surprised now that I don't have a triumph: they're
too common: none of them for me. But the
soldiers shall be entertained with wine and honey
just the same. (*turning toward Bacchis's door*) Now

437

nunc hanc praedam omnem iam ad quaestorem
    deferam.

IV. 10.

Phil. Quam magis in pectore meo foveo quas meus filius
        turbas turbet,
    quam se ad vitam et quos ad mores praecipitem
        inscitus capessat,
magis curae est magisque adformido, ne is pereat
    neu corrumpatur.
    scio, fui ego illa aetate et feci illa omnia, sed
        more modesto;
    neque placitant mores quibus video volgo in gnatos
        esse parentes : [1]   1080
ego dare me meo gnato institui, ut animo obse-
    quium sumere possit;
    aequom esse puto, sed nimis nolo desidiae ei dare
        ludum.
            nunc Mnesilochum, quod mandavi,
            viso ecquid eum ad virtutem aut ad
            frugem opera sua compulerit, sic
            ut eum, si convenit, scio fe-
                cisse : eost ingenio natus.

ACTVS V

Nic. Quicumque ubi ubi sunt, qui fuerunt quique futuri
        sunt posthac
    stulti, stolidi, fatui, fungi, bardi, blenni, buccones,
        solus ego omnis longe antideo
        stultitia et moribus indoctis.
        perii, pudet : hocine me aetatis
        ludos bis factum esse indigne ?   1090
        magis quam id reputo, tam magis uror
            quae meus filius turbavit.

────────

[1] Leo brackets the following v., 1081 :
duxi, habui scortum, potavi, dedi, donavi, sed enim id raro.

I'll convey all this booty to the quartermaster-general at once. [EXIT INTO HOUSE.

Scene 10. (*Half an hour has elapsed*)

ENTER *Philoxenus.*

Phil. The more I ponder over the capers my son is cutting, and the life and habits the thoughtless lad is plunging headlong into, the more worried, and the more fearful I get at the danger of his becoming an irreclaimable rake. I know, I was young once myself, and did all those things, but I showed some self-restraint. The attitude I see in the general run of parents toward their sons doesn't suit me. I've made a practice of being liberal to my son, so that he may follow his inclinations; I think it's the fair way; at the same time, I don't want to give too much play to his dawdling. Now I'm going to see Mnesilochus about that commission of mine, and find out if he has driven the boy over to the path of virtue and sobriety by his efforts—as I know he has, if he found occasion: that is his natural disposition. (*goes toward Bacchis's door*)

ACT V

ENTER *Nicobulus* IN A RAGE. WITHOUT SEEING *Philoxenus.*

Nic. Of all the silly, stupid, fatuous, fungus-grown, doddering, drivelling dolts anywhere, past or future, I alone am far and away ahead of the whole lot of 'em in silliness and absurd behaviour! Damnation! I'm ashamed! The idea of my being made a fool of twice at my time of life in this outrageous fashion! The more I think it over, the hotter I get at my son's devilry! I'm

439

perditus sum atque eradicatus
sum, omnibus exemplis excrucior.
omnia me mala consectantur,
omnibus exitiis interii.
Chrysalus med hodie laceravit,
Chrysalus me miserum spoliavit:
is me scelus auro usque attondit
dolis doctis indoctum, ut lubitumst.
ita miles memorat meretricem esse
eam quam ille uxorem esse aiebat,
omniaque ut quidque actum est memoravit,
    eam sibi hunc annum conductam,
relicuom id auri factum quod ego ei
stultissimus homo promisissem : hoc,
    hoc est quo cor peracescit :
hoc est demum quod percrucior,
me hoc aetatis ludificari,[1]
cano capite atque alba barba
    miserum me auro esse emunctum.   1101

perii, hoc servom meum non nauci facere esse
    ausum! atque ego, si alibi
plus perdiderim, minus aegre habeam minusque id
    mihi damno ducam.

Phil.   Certo hic prope me mihi nescio quis loqui visust;
        sed quem video?
        hic quidemst pater Mnesilochi.
Nic.   Euge, socium aerumnae et mei mali video.
        Philoxene, salve.
Phil.   Et tu.   unde agis?
Nic.   Unde homo miser atque infortunatus.
Phil.   At pol ego ibi sum, esse ubi miserum hominem
        decet atque infortunatum.

[1] Leo brackets the following v., 1100 :
        immo edepol sic ludos factum

ruined, eradicated, tortured every way! Every kind of trouble is upon me: I've died every kind of death! I've been mangled to-day by Chrysalus, stripped, poor wretch, by Chrysalus! He has sheared me clean of my gold, the villain, sheared me to suit his taste by his wily arts, artless innocent that I am! The Captain tells me that the woman that rascal said was his wife is a courtesan, and he's given me the full history of the case—how he'd hired her for this year, how the money I'd promised him, like an utter idiot, was the sum due him for the months yet to run. This, this, is what galls me; this is the crowning torment—for me to be gulled at my time of life, for me, poor fool, with my hoary hairs and white beard to be cleaned out of my gold! Oh, damnation! My own servant dares to hold me cheaper than dirt in this fashion! Yes, yes, if I lost more money some other way, I should mind it less and regard the loss as less.

Phil.   It surely seemed as if some one was speaking here near me. (*sees Nicobulus*) But who's this I see? Mnesilochus's father, upon my word! (*approaches*)

Nic.   (*grimly*) Splendid! I see my partner in toil and woe. Good day to you, Philoxenus.

Phil.   And to you. Where are you coming from?

Nic.   Where a wretched, unlucky man should come from.

Phil.   Gad! but I'm on the very spot where a wretched, unlucky man should be.

Nic.	Igitur pari fortuna, aetate ut sumus, utimur.
Phil.	Sic est. sed tu, quid tibist?
Nic.	Pol mihi par, idem est quod tibi.
Phil.	Numquid nam ad filium haec aegritudo attinet? 1110
Nic.	Admodum.
Phil.	Idem mihi morbus in pectorest.
Nic.	At mhi Chrysalus optumus homo perdidit filium, me atque rem omnem meam.
Phil.	Quid tibi ex filio nam, obsecro, aegrest?
Nic.	Scies: id, perit cum tuo: ambo aeque amicas habent
Phil.	Qui scis?
Nic.	Vidi.
Phil.	Ei mihi. disperii.
Nic.	Quid dubitamus pultare atque huc evocare ambos foras?
Phil.	Haud moror.
Nic.	Heus Bacchis, iube sic actutum aperiri fores. nisi mavoltis fores et postes comminui securibus.

V. 2.

Bacch.	Quis sonitu ac tumultu tanto nominat me atque pultat aedes? 1120
Nic.	Ego atque hic.
Bacch.	Quid hoc est negoti nam, amabo? quis has huc ovis adegit?
Nic.	Ovis nos vocant pessumae.

Nic. Then we're alike in luck as we are in years.

Phil. So it seems. But you—what is your trouble?

Nic. Good Lord! The same as yours.

Phil. This dolefulness of yours has something to do with your son, eh?

Nic. (*morosely*) Rather!

Phil. The same ailment is worrying me.

Nic. Well, but Chrysalus—that pattern of excellence— has ruined my boy and me and all that's mine!

Phil. What in the world has your son done to vex you, pray?

Nic. You shall know: this—he's going to the dogs along with yours: the both of them alike have mistresses.

Phil. How do you know?

Nic. I saw.

Phil. (*with apparent conviction*) Oh dear me! Terrible, terrible!

Nic. Why don't we go straight up and knock; and call them both out here?

Phil. (*lukewarm*) I have no objection.

Nic. (*pounding on Bacchis's door*) Hi! Bacchis! Be so good as to have the door opened this instant, unless you prefer to have door and doorposts smashed in with axes!

Scene 2.

Bacch. (*within*) Who's raising such a din and uproar, calling me and beating on the house?

ENTER THE TWO *Bacchises* INTO DOORWAY.

Nic. This gentleman and I.

Bacch. (*to sister after surveying them*) Mercy me, dear, what does this mean? Who drove these sheep here?

Nic. (*to Philoxenus*) They're calling us sheep, the sluts!

443

Soror   Pastor harum
dormit, quom haec eunt sic a pecu balitantes.
Bacch. At pol nitent, haud sordidae videntur ambae.
Soror Attonsae hae quidem ambae usque sunt.
Phil.   Ut videntur
deridere nos.
Nic.   Sine suo usque arbitratu.
Bacch. Rerin ter in anno tu has tonsitari?
Soror Pol hodie altera iam bis detonsa certo est.
Bacch. Vetulae sunt minae ambae.[1]
Soror   At bonas fuisse credo.
Bacch. Viden limulis, obsecro, ut intuentur?   1130
Soror Ecastor sine omni arbitror malitia esse.
Phil. Merito hoc nobis fit, qui quidem huc venerimus.
Bacch. Cogantur quidem intro.
Soror   Haud scio quid eo opus sit,
quae nec lac nec lanam ullam habent. sic sine astent.
exsolvere quanti fuere, omnis fructus
iam illis decidit.   non vides, ut palantes
                 solae liberae
grassentur? quin aetate credo esse mutas:
ne balant quidem, quom a pecu cetero absunt.
                 stultae atque haud malae videntur.
revortamur intro, soror.
Nic.   Ilico ambae   1140
manete: haec oves volunt vos.
Soror Prodigium hoc quidemst: humana nos voce appel-
     lant oves.

---

[1] *Minae ambae* Colerus : *thimiame* MSS.

444

THE TWO BACCHISES

Sister   Their shepherd must be taking a nap, to let them straggle off from the flock this way, bleating.

Bacch.   My goodness, though! They are sleek! they seem to be quite spick and span, both of them.

Sister   Yes, you see they've both been ever so well shorn.

Phil.   (*to Nicobulus*) Hm! They seem to be making fun of us.

Nic.   (*sourly*) Let them go as far as they like.

Bacch.   Do you suppose they are generally sheared three times a year?

Sister   Goodness me! that other one (*indicating Nicobulus*) has been shorn twice this very day for certain.

Bacch.   They're both rather woolless old—(*with a sly glance at her sister*) customers.

Sister   But they used to be good ones, I do believe.

Bacch.   For heaven's sake, do you see the little sidelong glances they're casting at us?

Sister   Oh well, I don't think they mean anything naughty by it.

Phil.   (*to Nicobulus*) This serves us right for coming here!

Bacch.   They really ought to be pushed inside.

Sister   I don't see any use in that; they haven't any milk, or wool either. Let them stand still as they are. They've been worked to their full value: all the fruit has dropped off of them already. Don't you see how they straggle along aimlessly, alone, untended? Why, I do believe they're dumb with age: they don't even bleat at being away from the rest of the flock. They seem perfectly harmless—just silly. Let's go back inside, sister.

Nic.   Stay where you are, both of you: these sheep want you.

Sister   Dear, dear, miraculous! The sheep are addressing us, quite as if they were human!

Nic. Haec oves vobis malam rem magnam, quam debent,
dabunt.

Bacch. Si quam debes, te condono: tibi habe, numquam
abs te petam.

sed quid est quapropter nobis vos malum minita-
mini?

Phil. Quia nostros agnos conclusos istic esse aiunt duos.

Nic. Et praeter eos agnos meus est istic clam mordax
canis:

qui nisi nobis producuntur iam atque emittuntur
foras,

arietes truces nos erimus, iam in vos incursabimus.

Bacch. Soror, est quod te volo secreto.

Soror. Eho, amabo.

Nic. Quo illaec abeunt?

Bacch. Senem illum tibi dedo ulteriorem, lepide ut lenitum
reddas;   1150

ego ad hunc iratum adgrediar, si possumus nos hos
intro inlicere huc.

Soror Meum pensum ego lepide accurabo, quamquam
odiost mortem amplexari.

Bacch. Facito ut facias.

Soror Taceas. tu tuom facito: ego quod dixi haud mutabo.

Nic. Quid illaec illic in consilio duae secreto consultant?

Phil. Quid ais tu, homo?

Nic. Quid me vis?

Phil. Pudet dicere me tibi quiddam.

Nic. Quid est quod pudeat?

Phil. Sed amico homini tibi quod volo credere certumst.
nihili sum.

446

ic   These sheep are going to give you all the trouble they owe you.

acch. If you owe anything, I'll forgive it you: keep it yourself—I'll never come to you for it. But what's the reason for your threatening us with trouble?

hil. Because they say our lambs are shut up in there, (*pointing to house*) two of them.

ic. And besides those lambs, there's a dog of mine, a biter, skulking in there: unless these beasts are produced for us immediately and let out of doors, we'll turn into ferocious rams, and immediately butt you.

acch. Sister, I want a word with you in private. (*takes her aside*)

ister (*inquiringly*) Well, well, there's a dear!

ic. Where are they off to?

acch. I give that further old fellow (*pointing to Philoxenus*) over to you to get nicely pacified; I'll make up to this bear, (*indicating Nicobulus*) and we'll see if we can't lure them inside here.

ister (*without enthusiasm*) I'll take care of my stint nicely enough, even though it is sickening to hug a death's-head.

acch. See you do it.

ister Hush! You do your share, and I won't fail to keep my word.

ic. What are they scheming, those two, in that secret session?

hil. (*awkwardly*) I say, old fellow.

ic. What do you want?

hil. There's something I'm ashamed to tell you.

ic. What is it you are ashamed of?

hil. But to a good friend like you—yes, I'm going to own up to what I want. (*pauses*) I'm an ass.

447

Nic. Istuc iam pridem scio. sed qui nihili es ? id memora.

Phil. Tactus sum vehementer visco ;
cor stimulo foditur.

Nic. Pol tibi multo aequius est coxendicem.
sed quid istuc est ? etsi iam ego ipsus quid sit
probe scire puto me ; 1160
verum audire etiam ex te studeo.

Phil. Viden hanc ?

Nic. Video.

Phil. Haud mala est mulier.

Nic. Pol vero ista mala et tu nihili.

Phil. Quid multa ? ego amo.

Nic. An amas ?

Phil. ναὶ γάρ.

Nic. Tun, homo putide, amator istac fieri aetate audes ?

Phil. Qui non ?

Nic. Quia flagitium est.

Phil. Quid opust verbis ? meo filio non sum iratus,
neque te tuost aequom esse iratum : si amant,
sapienter faciunt.

Bacch. Sequere hac.

Nic. Eunt eccas tandem
probri perlecebrae et persuastrices.
quid nunc ? etiam redditis nobis
filios et servom ? an ego experior
tecum vim maiorem ?

Phil. Abin hinc ?
non homo tu quidem es, qui istoc pacto tam lepidam
inlepide appelles.

Bacch. Senex optime quantumst in terra, sine me hoc
exorare abs te, 1170

Nic.   I have known that for some time. But why are you an ass? Explain that.

Phil.   (*with a wry smile*) I'm most confoundedly caught in bird-lime; my heart's pierced by a goad.

Nic.   Jove! much more to the point, if it were your nether portions! But what do you mean? And yet I think I have a pretty fair notion myself what it is already; however, I'm anxious to have it from your own lips.

Phil.   Do you see this girl? (*pointing to the Sister*)

Nic.   I do.

Phil.   (*approvingly*) Not a bad one!

Nic.   (*indignantly*) Good Lord! She certainly is a bad one, and you are an ass.

Phil.   (*not listening*) In short, I'm in love with her.

Nic.   You in love?

Phil.   *Bien sûr!*

Nic.   You, you disgusting creature? You venture to turn lover at your age?

Phil.   Why not?

Nic.   Because it's infamous.

Phil.   (*gathering courage rapidly*) Tut, tut! I'm not angry at my son, and you oughtn't to be angry at yours: if they're in love, they're acting wisely.

Bacch.   (*to sister*) Come along.

Nic.   Ah, there they come at last, the seductive, persuasive pests! (*to sisters*) Well now? See here, are you going to give us back our sons and servant? Or shall I try more vigorous measures with you?

Phil.   (*to Nicobulus, protestingly*) Get out, will you? There's no red blood in you, addressing a sweet little girl (*leering at Bacchis*) in that sour fashion.

Bacch.   (*to Nicobulus, as she tries to fondle him*) You nicest old man in all the world, do let me persuade you

449

        ut istuc delictum desistas tanto opere ire oppug-
           natum.

Nic.   Ni abeas, quamquam tu bella es,
        malum tibi magnum dabo iam.

Bacch.   Patiar,
           non metuo, ne quid mihi doleat
             quod ferias.

Nic.   Ut blandiloquast!
        ei mihi, metuo.

Soror   Hic magis tranquillust.

Bacch.   I hac mecum intro atque ibi, si quid vis,
        filium concastigato.

Nic. Abin a me, scelus?

Bacch.   Sine, mea pietas, te exorem.

Nic.   Exores tu me?

Soror Ego quidem ab hoc certe exorabo.

Phil.   Immo ego te oro, ut me intro abducas.

Soror Lepidum te.

Phil.   At scin quo pacto me ad te intro abducas?

Soror   Mecum ut sis.

Phil.   Omnia quae cupio commemoras.

Nic.   Vidi ego nequam homines, verum te
        neminem deteriorem.

Phil.   Ita sum.   1180

Bacch. I hac mecum intro, ubi tibi sit lepide victibus, vino
        atque unguentis.

Nic.   Satis, satis iam vostrist convivi:
        me nil paenitet ut sim acceptus:
        quadringentis Philippis filius me et

	not to be so awfully opposed to your son's naughtiness.
Nic.	(*struggling to be very stern*) Unless you get away from me—no matter if you are pretty—I'll give you a good sound slap this minute.
Bacch.	(*softly, still fondling him*) I'll take it. I'm not afraid of your striking me so as to hurt at all.
Nic.	(*aside*) What a coaxer she is! Oh, dear me! I'm afraid!
Sister	(*caressing Philoxenus to his high satisfaction*) This one is more peaceful.
Bacch.	Do come inside here with me: yes, and punish your son ever so, in there, if you like.
Nic.	Get away from me, you hussy!
Bacch.	Let me persuade you, that's a love! (*tries to draw him toward house*)
Nic.	You persuade me?
Sister	I'll certainly persuade my man, at any rate.
Phil.	(*returning her embrace with vigour*) No you won't: I myself beg you to take me inside.
Sister	Oh, you delightful man!
Phil.	But do you know on what condition you can take me inside.
Sister	Yes, your being with me.
Phil.	The sum total of my desires!
Nic.	(*pulling himself together*) I have seen worthless men, but never a worse one than you.
Phil.	(*cheerfully*) So I am.
Bacch.	(*to Nicobulus*) Do come along inside with me: you'll have a lovely time—things to eat, and wine and perfumes.
Nic.	Enough, enough of your banqueting already—it makes no difference to me how I'm entertained! Four hundred pounds I've been tricked out of by

451

TITUS MACCIUS PLAUTUS

	Chrysalus circumduxerunt.	
	quem quidem ego ut non excruciem,	
	alterum tantum auri non meream.	
Bacch.	Quid tandem, si dimidium auri	
	redditur, in hac mecum intro? atque ut	
	eis delicta ignoscas.	
Phil.	Faciet.	
Nic.	Minime, nolo. nil moror, sine sic.	
	malo illos ulcisci ambo.	

Phil. Etiam tu, homo nihili? quod di dant boni cave
    culpa tua amissis:
  dimidium auri datur: accipias, potesque et scortum
    accumbas.

Nic. Egon ubi filius corrumpatur meus, ibi potem?

Phil.   Potandumst. 1190

Nic. Age iam, id ut ut est, etsi est dedecori patiar, fa-
    cere inducam animum:
  egon, cum haec cum illo accubet, inspectem?

Bacch.   Immo equidem pol tecum accumbam,
    te amabo et te amplexabor.

Nic. Caput prurit, perii, vix negito.

Bacch. Non tibi venit in mentem, amabo,
    si dum vivas tibi bene facias
    tam pol id quidem esse haud perlonginquom,
    neque, si hoc hodie amissis, post in
    morte eventurum esse umquam?

Nic. Quid ago?

452

my son and Chrysalus. And I wouldn't forgo
making that slave bleed for it, not for another
four hundred.

Bacch. Well, but supposing half of it is given back, won't
you come in with me, then? Yes, and pardon their
offences?

Phil. He'll do it.

Nic. (*with all his remaining resolution*) Not a bit of it: I
don't want to. None of this for me: leave me
alone. I prefer to take vengeance on that pair.

Phil. (*aside to Nicobulus*) See here, you—ass! Look out
you don't lose the blessings the gods give you, and
have yourself to blame for it. Here's half the
money given you: take it, and drink and have a
good time with the wench.

Nic. (*very feebly*) I drink in the house where my son is
being debauched?

Phil. (*clapping him on the shoulder*) Drink you must.

Nic. (*giving way temporarily*) Come on then, no matter
what it is, disgraceful though it be, I'll stand it,
I'll bring myself to it. (*after a pause, doubtfully*)
Am I to look on while she's on the couch beside
him?

Bacch. Goodness me, no indeed! I'll be on the couch beside you, loving you and hugging you. (*snuggles
up to him*)

Nic. (*aside*) My head does itch! Dear, dear, dear! It
is hard to keep on saying no!

Bacch. My dear man, doesn't it occur to you that, supposing you do enjoy yourself all your life, this life is
very, very short, after all,—good gracious, yes!—
and that if you let this chance slip, it won't come
again when you're dead, ever?

Nic. (*nearly helpless*) What am I to do?

453

Phil.   Quid agas ? rogitas etiam ?

Nic.   Libet et metuo.

Bacch.   Quid metuis ?

Nic. Ne obnoxius filio sim et servo.

Bacch.   Mel meum, amabo, etsi haec fiunt,
tuost : unde illum sumere censes, nisi quod tute illi
     dederis ?
hanc veniam illis sine te exorem.

Nic.   Ut terebrat ! satin offirmatum
quod mihi erat, id me exorat ?   1200
tua sum opera et propter te improbior.

Bacch.   Ne tis [1] quam mea mavellem.
satin ego istuc habeo firmatum ?

Nic.   Quod semel dixi haud mutabo

Bacch. It dies, ite intro accubitum,
filii vos exspectant intus.

Nic.   Quam quidem actutum emoriamur.

Soror Vesper hic est, sequimini.

Nic.   Ducite nos quo lubet tamquam quidem addictos.

Bacch. Lepide ipsi hi sunt capti, suis qui filiis fecere insi-
     dias.

                [1] *tis* Schroeder : *is* MSS.

THE TWO BACCHISES

Phil. To do? The idea of asking that!

Nic. I long to, and—I'm afraid.

Bacch. Afraid of what?

Nic. Of humbling myself before my son and servant.

Bacch. Oh, honey, there's a dear, now! Even if it's all so, he's your own boy: where do you think he's to get money, except from your own generous self? Do let me persuade you to forgive them.

Nic. (*half aside*) How she does drill through a man! Is she actually persuading me against my fixed intention? (*giving up the struggle and yielding to Bacchis's caresses*) I'm a reprobate now, and all because of you and your efforts.

Bacch. (*softly and tenderly*) Oh, I do wish it had been your efforts rather than (*giving her sister a dreary smile*) mine. So I'm actually to take that as your fixed intention?

Nic. What I have once said I won't change.

Bacch. The day is going: go inside and take your places on the couches. Your sons are within waiting for you.

Nic. (*dryly*) Yes, waiting for us to breathe our last with clerity.

Sister. It's evening: come along.

Nic. Take us where you please, just as if we were your veritable bond servants.

Bacch. (*aside to spectators*) Here they are, prettily caught themselves—after laying traps for their sons.

[EXEUNT OMNES INTO HOUSE OF *Bacchis*.

GREX

Hi senes nisi fuissent nihili iam inde ab adulescentia,
non hodie hoc tantum flagitium facerent canis
capitibus;
neque adeo haec faceremus, ni antehac vidissemus
fieri,
ut apud lenones rivales filiis fierent patres.   1210
spectatores, vos valere volumus et clare adplaudere.

EPILOGUE

SPOKEN BY THE COMPANY.

Unless these old men had been worthless from their very youth, they would not be guilty of such an enormity as this to-day when their heads are hoary; nor, indeed, would we have presented such a comedy, unless we had seen before now how fathers become their sons' rivals at places of unsavoury repute. Spectators, we wish you health and—your loud applause.

THE CAPTIVES

ARGVMENTVM

Captust in pugna Hegionis filius;
Alium quadrimum fugiens servus vendidit.
Pater captivos commercatur Aleos,
Tantum studens ut natum captum recuperet;
Et inibi emit olim amissum filium.
Is suo cum domino veste versa ac nomine
Vt amittatur fecit: ipsus plectitur;
Et is reduxit captum, et fugitivum simul,
Indicio cuius alium agnoscit filium.

PERSONAE

ERGASILVS PARASITUS
HEGIO SENEX
LORARIVS
PHILOCRATES ADULESCENS
TYNDARVS SERVUS
ARISTOPHONTES ADULESCENS
PVER
PHILOPOLEMVS ADULESCENS
STALAGMVS SERVUS

ARGUMENT OF THE PLAY

One of Hegio's sons has been taken prisoner in a battle with the Eleans; the other was stolen by a runaway slave and sold when he was four years old. The father, in his great anxiety to recover the captured boy, bought up Elean prisoners of war; and among those that he purchased was the son he had lost many years before   This son, having exchanged clothes and names with his Elean master, secured the latter's release, taking the consequences himself.   This master of his returned, bringing Hegio's captive son, and along with him that runaway slave, whose disclosures led to the recognition of the other son.

DRAMATIS PERSONAE

ERGASILUS, *a parasite.*
HEGIO, *an old gentleman.*
SLAVE OVERSEER, *belonging to Hegio.*
PHILOCRATES, *a young Elean captive.*
TYNDARUS, *his slave, captured with him.*
ARISTOPHONTES, *a young Elean captive.*
A PAGE, *in the service of Hegio.*
PHILOPOLEMUS, *Hegio's son.*
STALAGMUS, *Hegio's slave.*

PROLOGVS

Hos quos videtis stare hic captivos duos,
illi qui astant,[1] hi stant ambo, non sedent;
hoc vos mihi testes estis me verum loqui.
senex qui hic habitat Hegio est huius pater.
sed is quo pacto serviat suo sibi patri,
id ego hic apud vos proloquar, si operam datis.
seni huic fuerunt filii nati duo;
alterum quadrimum puerum servos surpuit
eumque hinc profugiens vendidit in Alide
patri huius.   iam hoc tenetis?[2] optume est.   10
negat hercle ille ultimus.   accedito.
si non ubi sedeas locus est, est ubi ambules,
quando histrionem cogis mendicarier.
ego me tua causa, ne erres, non rupturus sum.
vos qui potestis ope vestra censerier,
accipite relicuom: alieno uti nil moror.
fugitivos ille, ut dixeram ante, huius patri

---

[1] Corrupt (Leo): *vincti quia astant* Fleckeisen.
[2] Leo notes lacuna here : *(cette), iam hoc tenetis* Schoell.

Scene:—A city in Aetolia. A street on which stands Hegio's house.

PROLOGUE

Tyndarus AND *Philocrates* ARE CHAINED, IN AN UN-COMFORTABLE POSITION, TO A PILLAR IN FRONT OF *Hegio's* HOUSE.

These two prisoners you see standing here, well, both of those bystanders are men who are—standing, not sitting down. (*Prologue laughs uproariously at his pleasantry*) I leave it to you if so much is not true. The old man that lives yonder—(*pointing to Hegio's house*) Hegio, by name—is this man's (*pointing to Tyndarus*) father. But how it happens that he is the slave of his own father I shall (*jauntily*) here in your midst proclaim, with your kind attention. This old gentleman had two sons. One of them, when he was four years old, was stolen by a slave who took to his heels and sold the boy in Elis to the father of this worthy (*pointing to Philocrates*) here. Now you take me? Very good! Bless my soul! That gentleman at the back says he does not. Let him step this way. (*no move in audience*) In case there is no opportunity to take a seat, sir, you can take a (*pointing to an exit*) stroll, seeing you insist on making an actor turn beggar. I have no intention of bursting myself, merely to keep you from misunderstanding the plot. (*to rest of audience*) As for you gentlemen who do own enough property to pay taxes on, let me discharge my debt: none of the credit system for me. That runaway slave, as I

463

domo quem profugiens dominum abstulerat vendidit.
is postquam hunc emit, dedit eum huic gnato suo
peculiarem, quia quasi una aetas erat.   20
hic nunc domi servit suo patri, nec scit pater;
enim vero di nos quasi pilas homines habent.
rationem habetis, quo modo unum amiserit.
postquam belligerant Aetoli cum Aleis,
ut fit in bello, capitur alter filius:
medicus Menarchus emit ibidem in Alide.
coepit captivos commercari hic Aleos,
si quem reperire possit qui mutet suom,
illum captivom: hunc suom esse nescit, qui domist.
et quoniam heri indaudivit, de summo loco   30
summoque genere captum esse equitem Aleum,
nil pretio parsit, filio dum parceret:
reconciliare ut facilius posset domum,
emit hosce e praeda ambos de quaestoribus.
hisce autem inter sese hunc confinxerunt dolum,
quo pacto hic servos suom erum hinc amittat domum.
itaque inter se commutant vestem et nomina;
illic vocatur Philocrates, hic Tyndarus:
huius illic, hic illius hodie fert imaginem.
et hic hodie expediet hanc docte fallaciam,   40
et suom erum faciet libertatis compotem,

said before, stole his young master when he de-
camped and sold him to this (*indicating Philocrates*)
man's father. This gentleman, on buying the boy,
gave him to this son of his for his very own, the
two being of about the same age. Now here he
is, back home, his own father's slave without his
father knowing it. Ah yes, the gods use us
mortals as footballs! Well, you comprehend the
way in which he lost one son. Later, when war
broke out between the Aetolians and Eleans, the
other son was taken prisoner—a common occur-
rence in times of war—and a doctor, Menarchus,
in that same Elis, bought the young man. Hegio
then began to buy up Elean captives, hoping to
get hold of one that he could exchange for his son
—the captive son, that is: for he has no idea that
this man at his home is his own child. And inasmuch as he heard it rumoured yesterday that an
Elean knight of the very highest rank and family
connections had been captured, he had no thought
of saving money if only he could save his son. So
in the hope of getting that son back home more
readily he bought both of these prisoners from the
commissioners who were disposing of the spoils.
These same prisoners, however, have got together
and laid a scheme, as you can see, to the end that
the slave here (*indicating Tyndarus*) may send his
master off home. Accordingly, they have exchanged
clothes and names with each other. That one
(*indicating Tyndarus*) is calling himself Philocrates,
and this one (*indicating Philocrates*) Tyndarus: each
is posing as the other for the time being. And
Tyndarus here is going to work out this trick to-day
like an artist, and set his master at liberty. By so

465

eodemque pacto fratrem servabit suom
reducemque faciet liberum in patriam ad patrem,
imprudens : itidem ut saepe iam in multis locis
plus insciens quis fecit quam prudens boni.
sed inscientes sua sibi fallacia
ita compararunt et confinxerunt dolum
itaque hi commenti, de sua sententia
ut in servitute hic ad suom maneat patrem :
ita nunc ignorans suo sibi servit patri ;   50
homunculi quanti sunt, quom recogito !
haec res agetur nobis, vobis fabula.
sed etiam est, paucis vos quod monitos voluerim.
profecto expediet fabulae huic operam dare.
non pertractate facta est neque item ut ceterae :
neque spurcidici insunt versus, immemorabiles ;
hic neque periurus leno est nec meretrix mala
neque miles gloriosus ; ne vereamini,
quia bellum Aetolis esse dixi cum Aleis :
foris illic extra scaenam fient proelia.   60
nam hoc paene iniquomst, comico choragio
conari desubito agere nos tragoediam.
proin si quis pugnam expectat, litis contrahat :
valentiorem nactus adversarium
si erit, ego faciam ut pugnam inspectet non bonam,
adeo ut spectare postea omnis oderit.
abeo.   valete, iudices iustissimi
domi duellique duellatores optumi.

doing he will rescue his own brother, too, and enable him to return home to his father a free man, all quite unwittingly,—as in so many cases before now a man has often done more good unconsciously than wittingly. But all unconsciously, in their trickery, they have so planned and contrived and schemed, acting upon their own ideas, that Tyndarus will stay here as his own father's slave. So now it is his father he is serving unawares. What helpless creatures we mortals be, when I stop to reflect! All this will be fact on the boards, fiction for the benches. About one thing more, though, I should like to offer a word or two of suggestion. It will undeniably be to your profit to pay attention to this play. It is not composed in the hackneyed style, is quite unlike other plays; nor does it contain filthy lines that one must not repeat. In this comedy you will meet no perjured pimp, or unprincipled courtesan, or braggart captain. Let not my statement that the Aetolians and Eleans are at war alarm you: engagements will take place off the stage yonder. It would almost amount to imposition, you know, for us, in our comedy get-up, to try to present a tragedy all of a sudden. So if anyone is looking for a battle scene, let him pick a quarrel: if he gets a good strong opponent, I promise him a glimpse of a battle scene so unpleasant that hereafter he will hate the very sight of one. (*turning to go*) And so good-bye to you, most just of judges here at home and doughtiest of fighters in the field.

[EXEUNT *Prologue* AND *Captives*.

467

TITUS MACCIUS PLAUTUS

ACTVS I

Erg. Iuventus nomen indidit Scorto mihi,
eo quia invocatus soleo esse in convivio.   70
scio absurde dictum hoc derisores dicere,
at ego aio recte.   nam scortum in convivio
sibi amator, talos quom iacit, scortum invocat.
estne invocatum an non est?   est planissume;
verum hercle vero nos parasiti planius,
quos numquam quisquam neque vocat neque in-
    vocat.
quasi mures semper edimus alienum cibum;
ubi res prolatae sunt, quom rus homines eunt,
simul prolatae res sunt nostris dentibus.
quasi, cum caletur, cocleae in occulto latent,   80
suo sibi suco vivont, ros si non cadit,
item parasiti rebus prolatis latent
in occulto miseri victitant suco suo,
dum ruri rurant homines quos ligurriant.
prolatis rebus parasiti venatici
sumus, quando res redierunt, molossici
odiosicique et multum incommodestici.
et hic quidem hercle, nisi qui colaphos perpeti
potest parasitus frangique aulas in caput,
[1] ire extra portam Trigeminam ad saccum licet.   90
quod mihi ne eveniat, non nullum periculum est.

---

[1] *vel* precedes in MSS : Leo brackets.

468

THE CAPTIVES

ACT I

ENTER *Ergasilus* LOOKING HUNGRY AND FORLORN.

Erg. The young fellows have dubbed me Missy, on the gound that whenever they're at their banquets I feel called upon to be with 'em. To be sure, the professional wags say it is an absurd nickname, but I protest it's a good one. For at banquets when the young sparks are playing dice they call upon their missies, yes, their missies, to be with 'em as they make a throw. Does missy feel called upon to be with 'em, or not? Most unmistakably. But by heaven, I tell you we parasites feel the call more unmistakably still, for no one else ever feels for us or calls us, either. Like mice, we're forever nibbling at some one else's food. When the holidays come, and men hie 'em to their country estates, our grinders take a holiday, too. It's the same as snails hiding in their holes during the dog days and living on their own juices when there's no dew falling: that's the way with parasites during the holidays—hide in their holes, poor devils, and subsist on their own juices while the people they could get pickings from are in the rural regions ruralizing. So long as the holidays last we parasites are greyhounds: when they're over we are wolf-hounds and dear-hounds and bore-hounds, very much so. And, by gad, in this town, at least, if a parasite objects to being banged about and having crockery smashed on his cranium, he can betake himself to the far side of Three Arch Gate and a porter's bag. (*ruefully*) Which is precious likely to be my own fate. For

469

nam postquam meus rex est potitus hostium—
ita nunc belligerant Aetoli cum Aleis;
nam Aetolia haec est, illic est captus in Alide,
Philopolemus, huius Hegionis filius
senis, qui hic habitat, quae aedes lamentariae
mihi sunt, quas quotienscumque conspicio fleo;
nunc hic occepit quaestum hunc fili gratia
inhonestum et maxime alienum ingenio suo:
homines captivos commercatur, si queat   100
aliquem invenire, suom qui mutet filium.
quod quidem ego nimis quam cupio [1] ut impetret:
nam ni illum recipit, nihil est quo me recipiam.
nam nulla est spes iuventutis, sese omnis amant;
ille demum antiquis est adulescens moribus,
cuius numquam voltum tranquillavi gratiis.
condigne pater est eius moratus moribus.
nunc ad eum pergam.   sed aperitur ostium,
unde saturitate saepe ego exii ebrius.

I. 2.

Hegio Advorte animum sis tu: istos captivos duos,   110
heri quos emi de praeda a quaestoribus,
eis indito catenas singularias
istas, maiores, quibus sunt iuncti, demito;
sinito ambulare, si foris si intus volent,
sed uti adserventur magna diligentia.
liber captivos avis ferae consimilis est:
semel fugiendi si data est occasio,
satis est, numquam postilla possis prendere.

---

[1] Leo notes lacuna here: *cupio (fieri)* Schoell.

after my patron fell in with the enemy—the Aetolians, you see, are at war now with the Eleans; this is Aetolia, you understand, and it's there in Elis that Philopolemus is a captive, Philopolemus being the son of Hegio here, the old gentleman that lives in (*pointing*) that house (and a lamentatious house it is! every time I look at it, it makes me weep!)—well, now Hegio has taken up his present business, all for his son's sake, ungentlemanly business as it is, and quite beneath a man of his type. He's buying up prisoners of war, to see if he can't come across one to exchange for his boy. And Lord! how I do yearn for him to succeed! You see, it's a matter of his coming home, or my going hungry. For our young fellows are absolutely unpromising—egoists, the whole lot of 'em! But he is a young gentleman of the old school, that lad: I never smoothed the wrinkles out of his brow without getting more than a thankye for it. His father is just such another perfect gentleman. Now for a call on him. (*moves toward Hegio's house*) But there goes his door, out of which I've often come so full of food I was fairly tipsy. (*withdraws*)

Scene 2.   ENTER *Hegio* WITH *Slave Overseer*.

Hegio   Attention, please, my man. Those two captives that I bought yesterday from the commissioners in charge of the spoils—put the light irons on them and take off the heavy ones they're coupled with. Let them walk out here or inside, whichever they please; but look after them sharp, mind you. A captive free is a regular wild bird: once given a chance to flit, that is enough—you can never get hold of him again.

Lor. Omnes profecto liberi lubentius
sumus quam servimus.

Hegio.   Non videre ita tu quidem.   120

Lor. Si non est quod dem, mene vis dem ipse—in
pedes?

Hegio Si dederis, erit extemplo mihi quod dem tibi.

Lor. Avis me ferae consimilem faciam, ut praedicas.

Hegio Ita ut dicis: nam si faxis, te in caveam dabo.
sed satis verborumst.   cura quae iussi atque abi.
ego ibo ad fratrem ad alios captivos meos,
visam ne nocte hac quippiam turbaverint.
inde me continuo recipiam rursum domum.

Erg. Aegre est mi, hunc facere quaestum carcerarium
propter sui gnati miseriam miserum senem.   130
sed si ullo pacto ille huc conciliari potest,
vel carnificinam hunc facere possum perpeti.

Hegio Quis hic loquitur?

Erg.   Ego, qui tuo maerore maceror,
macesco, consenesco et tabesco miser;
ossa atque pellis sum miser a macritudine;
neque umquam quicquam me iuvat quod edo domi:
foris aliquantillum etiam quod gusto, id beat.

Hegio Ergasile, salve.

Erg.   Di te bene ament, Hegio.

Hegio Ne fle

Erg.   Egone illum non fleam? egon non defleam
talem adulescentem?

Over. Well, of course sir, we'd all rather be free than slaves.

Hegio That seems untrue of you at any rate.[1]

Over. In case I haven't anything else to give you, how about my giving you—the slip?

Hegio Give me that, and I shall shortly have something to give you.

Over. I'll copy that wild bird you speak of.

Hegio Exactly—for then I'll cage you. But enough of this. Mind my orders and be off with you. I'll drop in at my brother's for a look at my other prisoners, and see if they made any disturbance last night. Then I'll return home again at once.

                           [EXIT *Overseer* INTO HOUSE.

Erg. (*with a loud sigh*) It does grieve me to see the poor old gentleman at this gaoler's job for his poor son's sake. (*in lower tone*) However, if he only manages to get the lad back here somehow, let him turn hangman, too,—I can stand it.

Hegio (*looking round*) Who is that speaking here?

Erg. (*stepping forward*) I—a man that am all worn out by your woe, that am getting thin, growing old, pining away in sorrow; I'm nothing but skin and bones, I feel for you so. Nothing I eat—at home—ever does me any good. (*aside*) But how I do relish the merest morsel when I'm dining out!

Hegio Ah, good day, Ergasilus.

Erg. God bless you, Hegio, bless you bounteously! (*grasps Hegio's hand fervently and bursts into tears*)

Hegio Don't cry.

Erg. I not cry for him? I not cry my eyes out for such a youth?

    [1] Implying that he had not tried to save money to buy his liberty.

473

Hegio	Semper sensi, filio	140

meo te esse amicum, et illum intellexi tibi.

Erg. Tum denique homines nostra intellegimus bona,

quom quae in potestate habuimus, ea amisimus.

ego, postquam gnatus tuos potitust hostium,

expertus quanti fuerit nunc desidero.

Hegio Alienus cum eius incommodum tam aegre feras,

quid me patrem par facerest, cui ille est unicus?

Erg. Alienus ego? alienus illi? aha, Hegio,

numquam istuc dixis neque animum induxis tuom;

tibi ille unicust, mi etiam unico magis unicus.   150

Hegio Laudo, malum cum amici tuom ducis malum.

nunc habe bonum animum.

Erg.   Eheu, huic illud dolet,

quia nunc remissus est edendi exercitus.

Hegio Nullumne interea nactu's, qui posset tibi

remissum quem dixti imperare exercitum?

Erg. Quid credis? fugitant omnes hanc provinciam,

quoi optigerat postquam captust Philopolemus

tuos.

Hegio Non pol mirandum est fugitare hanc provinciam.

multis et multigeneribus opus est tibi

militibus: primumdum opus est Pistorensibus: 160

THE CAPTIVES

Hegio (*somewhat moved*) I always did feel that you were a friend to my son, and I realized that he regarded you as one.

Erg. Ah, we mortals realize the value of our blessings only when we have lost them. Myself now—after your son fell in with the enemy, I have come to understand how much he meant to me, and now I long for him.

Hegio When an outsider like you takes his misfortune so bitterly, how must I feel, his father, and he my only son?

Erg. (*choking*) An outsider? I? An outsider to that boy? Oh-h-h, Hegio! don't say a thing like that, don't let such a thought enter your mind, ever! Your only son, yes,—but he was even more than that to me: he was my only only! (*sobs violently*)

Hegio I appreciate this, that you consider your friend's disaster your own. (*patting him on the back*) Come now, take heart.

Erg. Oh, dear! oh, dear! here's (*rubbing his stomach*) where it hurts: my whole commissary department has been disbanded now, you see.

Hegio (*smiling*) And meantime haven't you hit upon any-one that could reorganize the department you say is disbanded?

Erg. Would you believe it? Every one keeps fighting shy of the office ever since your Philopolemus, its duly elected occupant, was captured.

Hegio Bless my soul! no wonder they fight shy of it. You need many recruits, of many sorts, too: why, in the first place you need Pad-u-ans;[1] and there

---

[1] Here, as in the lines 880–883, the translator craves pardon for distorting the ages and spoiling the climes in his efforts to secure something of the effect of the original puns.

475

eorum sunt aliquot genera Pistorensium:
opus Paniceis est, opus Placentinis quoque;
opus Turdetanis, opust Ficedulensibus;
iam maritumi omnes milites opus sunt tibi.

Erg. Ut saepe summa ingenia in occulto latent;
hic qualis imperator nunc privatus est.

Hegio Habe modo bonum animum, nam illum confido domum
in his diebus me reconciliassere.
nam eccum hic captivom adulescentem intus
  Aleum,
prognatum genere summo et summis ditiis: 170
hoc illum me mutare confido pote.

Erg. Ita di deaeque faxint. sed num quo foras
vocatus es ad cenam?

Hegio   Nusquam, quod sciam.
sed quid tu id quaeris?

Erg.   Quia mi est natalis dies;
propterea te vocari ad te ad cenam volo.

Hegio Facete dictum. sed si pauxillo potes
contentus esse.

Erg.   Ne perpauxillum modo,
nam istoc me assiduo victu delecto domi;
age sis, roga emptum: nisi qui meliorem adferet
quae mi atque amicis placeat condicio magis, 180
quasi fundum vendam, meis me addicam legibus.

Hegio Profundum vendis tu quidem, haud fundum, mihi.
sed si venturu's, temperi.

Erg.   Em, vel iam otium est.

are several kinds of Paduans: you need the support of Bologna, and you need Frankfurters too;
you need Leghorners and you need Pis-ans, and
furthermore you need every fighter in fin land.

Erg. (*appreciatively*) How often it does happen that the
greatest talents are shrouded in obscurity! This
man now—what a generalissimo, and here he is
only a private citizen!

Hegio Well, well, now, take heart. As a matter of fact, I
trust we shall have the boy back with us in a few
days. For, look you (*pointing to house*) I have a
young Elean prisoner inside here—splendid family,
quantities of money: I count on being able to exchange him for my son.

Erg. (*heartily*) The gods and goddesses be with you! I
say, though,—you haven't been invited out to
dinner anywhere?

Hegio (*cautiously*) Nowhere, to my knowledge. But why
do you ask?

Erg. Well, to-day is my birthday: so consider yourself
invited to take dinner at—your house.

Hegio (*laughing*) Well put! But only on condition you
can be content with very little.

Erg. Yes, only don't make it very, very, very little, for
that is what I regale myself on constantly at
home. Come on, come on, do please say " Done! "
(*after a pause, formally*) In the event of no party
making a better offer, more satisfactory to myself
and associates, I'll knock myself down to you—on
my own terms—just as if I was selling an estate
by auction.

Hegio An estate indeed! You mean an empty state.
But if you intend to come, come in season.

Erg. Oho! I'm at leisure this minute, for that matter.

Hegio	I modo, venare leporem: nunc irim tenes;
	nam meus scruposam victus commetat viam.
Erg.	Numquam istoc vinces me, Hegio, ne postules:
	cum calceatis dentibus veniam tamen.
Hegio	Asper meus victus sane est.
Erg.	Sentisne essitas?
Hegio	Terrestris cena est.
Erg.	Sus terrestris bestia est.
Hegio	Multis holeribus.
Erg.	Curato aegrotos domi.

190

numquid vis?

Hegio	Venias temperi.
Erg.	Memorem mones.
Hegio	Ibo intro atque intus subducam ratiunculam,
	quantillum argenti mi apud trapezitam siet.
	ad fratrem, quo ire dixeram, mox ivero.

ACTVS II

Lor. Si di immortales id voluerunt, vos hanc aerumnam
          exsequi,
        decet id pati animo aequo: si id facietis, levior
          labos erit.
              domi fuistis, credo, liberi:
        nunc servitus si evenit, ei vos morigerari mos bo-
          nust
        et erili imperio eamque ingeniis vostris lenem
          reddere.
              indigna digna habenda sunt, erus quae facit.   200

478

Hegio No, no, go hunt your hare : you've got only a hedge-hog so far. For it is a rocky road my table travels.

Erg. You'll never down me that way, Hegio, and don't you think to do it : I'll be with you just the same—with my teeth shod.

Hegio My meals are perfect terrors, really.

Erg. Tearers? Do you eat brambles?

Hegio Well, things that root in the earth.

Erg. A porker does that.

Hegio Mostly vegetables, I mean.

Erg. Open a sanitarium, then. (*turning to go*) Anything else I can do for you?

Hegio Come in season.

Erg. (*cheerfully*) The suggestion is superfluous. [EXIT.

Hegio (*sighing as he looks at the back of his prospective guest*) I must go in and reckon up my bit of a bank balance, and see how low it is. Then to my brother's, where I spoke of going before.

[EXIT INTO HOUSE.

ACT II

ENTER FROM *Hegio's* HOUSE Overseers AND *Slaves* WITH *Philocrates* AND *Tyndarus* IN FETTERS : THE TWO HAVE EXCHANGED CLOTHES

Over. (*to captives, patronizingly*) Seeing it's the will of Heaven you're in this box, the thing for you to do is to take it calmly : do that, and you won't have such a hard time of it. At home you were free men, I suppose : since you happen to be slaves at present, it's a good idea to accept the situation and a master's orders gracefully, and make things easy to bear by taking 'em the proper way. Any-thing a master does is right, no matter how wrong it is.

479

Captivi   Oh oh oh.

Lor.   Eiulatione haud opus est, oculis haud [1] lacrimanti-
          bus :
          in re mala animo si bono utare, adiuvat.

Tynd.   At nos pudet, quia cum catenis sumus.

Lor.   At pigeat postea
          nostrum erum, si vos eximat vinculis,
          aut solutos sinat, quos argento emerit.

Tynd.   Quid a nobis metuit ? scimus nos
          nostrum officium quod est, si solutos sinat.

Lor.   At fugam fingitis : sentio quam rem agitis.

Philocr. Nos fugiamus ? quo fugiamus ?

Lor.   In patriam.

Philocr.   Apage, haud nos id deceat.
          fugitivos imitari.

Lor.   Immo edepol, si erit occasio, haud dehortor.   210

Tynd.   Unum exorare vos sinite nos.

Lor.   Quidnam id est ?

Tynd.   Ut sine hisce arbitris
          atque vobis nobis detis locum loquendi.

Lor.   Fiat.   abscedite hinc : nos concedamus huc.
          sed brevem orationem incipisse.

Tynd.   Em istuc mihi certum erat.   concede huc.

Lor.   Abite ab istis.

Tynd.   Obnoxii ambo
          vobis sumus propter hanc rem, quom quae volumus
             nos
          copia est ; ea [2] facitis nos compotes.

Philocr. Secede huc nunciam, si videtur, procul,

---

[1] Leo's correction of *multa miraclitis* of the MSS.
[2] Corrupt (Leo) : *ea* MSS : *consili* Schoell.

Captive (*protestingly*) Oh-h-h-h!

Over. There's no need of howling or crying. It helps to take bad things well.

Tynd. But to be in chains—we feel disgraced!

Over. But it's disgusted our master would feel later on, if he took the chains off, or let you loose, when he's paid money for you.

Tynd. What has he to fear from us? We realise what our duty is, if he should let us loose.

Over. Ah yes, you're planning to run for it! I see what's afoot.

Philocr. Run—we? Where should we run to?

Over. Home.

Philocr. Get out! The idea of our acting like runaway slaves!

Over. Lord! why not? I'm not saying you shouldn't, if you get the chance.

Tynd. (*with dignity*) Be good enough to grant us one request.

Over. Well, what is it?

Tynd. Merely this—give us an opportunity to talk together without being overheard by these good fellows (*pointing to slaves*) and yourselves.

Over. All right. (*to slaves*) Away with you! (*to other overseer*) Let's drop back here. (*to captives*) Make it short, though.

Tynd. Oh yes, that was my intention. (*to Philocrates, drawing him farther from slaves*) Come this way.

Over. (*to slaves still hanging about*) Get out and leave 'em alone. (*slaves obey*)

Tynd. (*to overseers*) We are much obliged to you, both of us, for the privilege of doing as we wish; we owe it to you.

Philocr. (*to Tyndarus*) Step over here now, if you please,

ne arbitri dicta nostra arbitrari queant 220
neu permanet palam haec nostra fallacia.
nam doli non doli sunt, nisi astu colas,
sed malum maxumum, si id palam provenit.
nam si erus mihi es tu atque ego me tuom esse
    servom assimulo,
tamen viso opust, cauto est opus, ut hoc sobrie
    sineque arbitris
accurate agatur, docte et diligenter;
tanta incepta res est: haud somniculose hoc
    agendum est.

Tynd.   Ero ut me voles esse.
Philocr.   Spero.
Tynd. Nam tu nunc vides pro tuo caro capite
carum offerre me meum caput vilitati. 230
Philocr. Scio.
Tynd.   At scire memento, quando id quod voles habebis;
nam fere maxima pars morem hunc homines ha-
    bent; quod sibi volunt,
      dum id impetrant, boni sunt;
      sed id ubi iam penes sese habent,
ex bonis pessimi et fraudulentissimi
fiunt: nunc ut mihi te volo esse autumo.[1]
Philocr. Pol ego si te audeam, meum patrem nominem:
nam secundum patrem tu es pater proximus.
Tynd. Audio.
Philocr.   Et propterea saepius te uti memineris moneo: 240
non ego erus tibi, sed servos sum; nunc obsecro te
    hoc unum—

---

[1] Leo brackets the following v., 237:
    quod tibi suadeam, suadeam meo patri.

come over, so that no one may catch what we say and leave us with a scheme that has leaked out. (*they move still farther from the overseers*) Shrewd management is what makes a trick a trick, you know : once it gets out, it becomes an instrument of torture. No matter if you are passing as my master and I as your slave, even so we've got to be wary, we've got to be cautious, so that our plan may be worked out in a clear-headed way, quietly and carefully, with discretion and diligence. It's a big job we've got in hand : we can't go to sleep over it.

Tynd. I will be all you wish me to be, sir.

Philocr. I hope so.

Tynd. For that matter, sir, you already see that to save a man I love, I am holding my own life cheap, much as I love it.

Philocr. I realize it.

Tynd. But remember to realize it when you get what you want. For, generally speaking, men have a habit of being fine fellows so long as they are seeking some favour; but when they have obtained it there's a change, and your fine fellows turn into villainous cheats of the worst description. In all this, sir, I'm telling you how I wish you to act toward me.

Philocr. By heaven, I might call you my father, if I chose : for next to my real father you are the best one I have.

Tynd. I know, I know.

Philocr. And that's just why I keep reminding you the oftener to remember what the situation calls for : I'm not your master, I'm a slave. Now I beg this one thing of you—since we have unmistak-

quoniam nobis di immortales animum ostenderunt
    suom,
ut qui erum me tibi fuisse atque esse conservom
    velint,
quom antehac pro iure imperitabam meo, nunc te
    oro per precem—
per fortunam incertam et per mei te erga bonita-
    tem patris,
perque conservitium commune, quod hostica evenit
    manu,
ne me secus honore honestes quam quom servibas
    mihi,
atque ut qui fueris et qui nunc sis meminisse ut
    memineris.

Tynd.   Scio quidem me te esse nunc et te esse me.
Philocr. Em istuc si potes
    memoriter meminisse, inest spes nobis in hac   250
    astutia.

II. 2.
Hegio   Iam ego revertar intro, si ex his quae volo exquisivero.
    ubi sunt isti quos ante aedis iussi huc produci foras?
Philocr. Edepol tibi ne in quaestione essemus cautum intel-
    lego,
    ita vinclis custodiisque circum moeniti sumus.
Hegio   Qui cavet ne decipiatur, vix cavet, cum etiam cavet;
    etiam cum cavisse ratus est, saepe is cautor captus
    est.
    an vero non iusta causa est, ut vos servem sedulo,
    quos tam grandi sim mercatus praesenti pecunia?
Philocr. Neque pol tibi nos, quia nos servas, aequomst vitio
    vortere,
    neque te nobis, si abeamus hinc, si fuat occasio.   260
Hegio   Ut vos hic, itidem illic apud vos meus servatur filius.
Philocr. Captus est?

484

able proof that it's Heaven's will I should no
longer be your master but your fellow slave, I, who
used to have the right to command you, now implore and entreat you—by the common peril in
which we stand and by my father's kindness to
you and by the captivity which the chances of war
have brought upon us both, don't feel less respect
for my wishes than you did when you were my
slave, and remember, remember carefully, both
who you were and who you are now.

Tynd. Yes, yes, I know that I am you for the time being
and that you are I.

Philocr. There! manage to remember to keep that in mind,
and this scheme of ours looks likely.

Scene 2.   ENTER *Hegio* FROM HOUSE.

Hegio (*to those within*) I shall be back directly, if I find out
what I want to know from these fellows. (*to overseers*) Where are those prisoners I had brought out
in front of the house here?

Philocr. (*advancing, pertly*) Gad! You guarded against having
to look for us far, I perceive,—see how we're barri-
caded with chains and watchmen.

Hegio The man on his guard against being deceived is
hardly on his guard even when he is on his guard;
even when he supposed he was on his guard, your
guarder has often enough been gulled. Really
though, haven't I good reason to take pains to keep
you, when I paid so high for you, cash down?

Philocr. Bless your heart, sir, we haven't any right to find
fault with you for trying to keep us, or you with
us, if we clear out—if we get a chance.

Hegio My son is kept prisoner there in your country just
as you are here.

Philocr. Captured?

485

TITUS MACCIUS PLAUTUS

Hegio   Ita.

Philocr.   Non igitur nos soli ignavi fuimus.

Hegio Secede huc. nam sunt quae ex te solo scitari volo.
   quarum rerum te falsilocum mi esse nolo.

Philocr.   Non ero
   quod sciam. si quid nescibo, id nescium tradam tibi.

Tynd. Nunc senex est in tostrina, nunc iam cultros attinet.
   ne id quidem, involucrum inicere, voluit, vestem ut
    ne inquinet.
   sed utrum strictimne adtonsurum dicam esse an per
    pectinem,
   nescio ; verum, si frugist, usque admutilabit probe.

Hegio Quid tu ? servosne esse an liber mavelis, memora   270
   mihi.

Philocr. Proxumum quod sit bono quodque a malo longis-
    sume,
   id volo ; quamquam non multum fuit molesta
    servitus,
   nec mihi secus erat quam si essem familiaris filius.

Tynd. Eugepae, Thalem talento non emam Milesium,
   nam ad sapientiam huius [1] nimius nugator fuit.
   ut facete orationem ad servitutem contulit.

Hegio.   Quo de genere natust illic Philocrates ?

Philocr.   Polyplusio :
   quod genus illi est unum pollens atque honoratis-
    sumum.

Hegio Quid ipsus hic ? quo honore est illic ?

Philocr.   Summo, atque ab summis viris.[2]   279

Hegio Quid divitiae, suntne opimae ?

Philocr.   Unde excoquat sebum senex.

Hegio Quid pater, vivitne ?

---

[1] Leo notes lacuna here : *huius (ille)* Camerar us.
[2] Leo brackets the following v., 280 :

Hegio   *Tum igitur ei cum in Aleis tanta gratia est, ut praedicas.*

486

Hegio Yes.

Philocr. Then other folks besides us have been cowards.

Hegio (*leading him farther from Tyndarus*) Step over here. There are some matters I wish to ask you about in private. No lying about them, mind.

Philocr. Not I, sir, not if I know. If I don't know about a thing, I'll (*innocently*) tell you what I don't know.

Tynd. (*aside, cheerfully*) Now the old fellow is in the barber's chair, yes, now we have the clippers on him. And master not even willing to throw a towel over him to keep his clothes clean! Is it going to be a close crop, I wonder, or just a trim?— that's the question. If he knows his business, though, he'll dock him handsomely.

Hegio See here, would you prefer to be a slave or a free man, tell me that?

Philocr. The maximum of pleasure and the minimum of pain, that's my preference, sir; but being a slave hasn't bothered me much, though: I wasn't treated any differently than if I'd been a son of the house.

Tynd. (*aside*) Well done my boy! I wouldn't buy Milesian Thales at a thousand thalers: why, he was nothing but the veriest amateur of a wise man compared with master here. How cleverly he's dropped into the servant jargon!

Hegio Who are Philocrates' people there in Elis?

Philocr. The Goldfields, sir,—the most influential and respected family in those parts easily.

Hegio And the young man himself? How does he stand?

Philocr. Very high indeed, sir,—belongs to the highest circles.

Hegio How about his property? Pretty fat one, eh?

Philocr. Fat? Old Goldfields could get dripping out of it.

Hegio What about his father? Is he living?

Philocr.   Vivom, cum inde abimus, liquimus;
nunc vivatne necne, id Orcum scire oportet scilicet.

Tynd.   Salva res est, philosophatur quoque iam, non men-
          dax modo est.

Hegio   Quid erat ei nomen?

Philocr.   Thensaurochrysonicochrysides.

Hegio   Videlicet propter divitias inditum id nomen quasi
          est.

Philocr. Immo edepol propter avaritiam ipsius atque
          audaciam.[1]

Hegio   Quid tu ais? tenaxne pater est eius?

Philocr.   Immo edepol pertinax;
quin etiam ut magis noscas: Genio suo ubi quando
          sacruficat,   290
ad rem divinam quibus est opus, Samiis vasis utitur,
ne ipse Genius surripiat: proinde aliis ut credat vide.

Hegio   Sequere hac me igitur. eadem ego ex hoc quae
          volo exquaesivero.
          Philocrates, hic fecit, hominem frugi ut facere
          oportuit.
          nam ego ex hoc quo genere gnatus sis scio, hic
          fassust mihi;
          haec tu eadem si confiteri vis, tua ex re feceris:
          quae tamen scio scire me ex hoc.

Tynd.   Fecit officium hic suom,
cum tibi est confessus verum, quamquam volui
          sedulo
meam nobilitatem occultare et genus et divitias
          meas,
Hegio; nunc quando patriam et libertatem perdidi,   300
non ego istunc me potius quam te metuere aequom
          censeo.

────────

[1] Leo brackets the following v., 288:
nam ille quidem Theodoromedes fuit germano nomine.

Philocr. He was when we left home; whether he's alive now or not, of course you had better inquire below as to that, sir.

Tynd. (*aside*) The situation is saved! Now he not only lies but moralizes.

Hegio What was his name?

Philocr. Ducatsdoubloonsandpiecesofeightson.

Hegio A sort of name applied to him on account of his money, I take it.

Philocr. (*apparently struck by a new idea*) Lord, no! on account of his being so greedy and grasping, sir.

Hegio What's that? His father's rather close, is he?

Philocr. Close? My word, sir! he's adhesive! Why, really,—just so as to give you a better notion of him—whenever he sacrifices to his own Guardian Spirit he won't use any dishes needed in the service except ones made of Samian earthenware, for fear his very Guardian Spirit may steal 'em. You can see from this what a confiding character he is in general.

Hegio Well, well, come this way with me. (*aside, as they join Tyndarus*) I'll soon get the information I want out of the master here at the same time. (*to Tyndarus*) Philocrates, your servant has acted as a worthy fellow ought to act. Yes, I know from him about your family: he has admitted everything. If you choose to be equally open with me, it will be to your advantage: however, I have been completely informed already by him.

Tynd. (*with dignified melancholy*) He has done his duty in admitting the truth to you, much as I did wish to keep you in the dark, Hegio, about my rank and birth and wealth; now that I am a man without a country, a prisoner, I suppose it is not to be

489

vis hostilis cum istoc fecit meas opes aequabiles;
memini, cum dicto haud audebat: facto nunc
   laedat licet.
sed viden? fortuna humana fingit artatque ut lubet:
me, qui liber fueram servom fecit, e summo infi-
   mum;
qui imperare insueram, nunc alterius imperio ob-
   sequor.
et quidem si, proinde ut ipse fui imperator familiae,
habeam dominum, non verear ne iniuste aut graviter
   mi imperet.
Hegio, hoc te monitum, nisi forte ipse non vis,
   voluerim.

Hegio Loquere audacter.

Tynd.   Tam ego fui ante liber quam gnatus tuos, 310
tam mihi quam illi libertatem hostilis eripuit manus,
tam ille apud nos servit, quam ego nunc hic apud
   te servio.
est profecto deus, qui quae nos gerimus auditque
   et videt:
is, uti tu me hic habueris, proinde illum illic
   curaverit;
bene merenti bene profuerit, male merenti par erit.
quam tu filium tuom, tam pater me meus desiderat.

Hegio Memini ego istuc. sed faterin eadem quae hic
   fassust mihi?

Tynd. Ego patri meo esse fateor summas divitias domi
meque summo genere gnatum. sed te optestor,
   Hegio,
ne tuom animum avariorem faxint divitiae meae: 320
ne patri, tam etsi sum unicus, decere videatur
   magis,
me saturum servire apud te sumptu et vestitu
   tuo

expected that he should stand more in awe of me than of you. The chances of war have put master and man on an equal footing. I remember the time when he did not venture to offend me by a word: now he is at liberty to do me an actual injury. But you see! fortune moulds us, pinches us, to suit her whims: here am I, the one-time free man, a slave—tossed from the heights to the depths. Accustomed to command, I am now at another's beck and call. And indeed, if I might have such a master as I myself was when I was the head of a household, I should have no fear of being treated unjustly or harshly. There is one thing I should like to impress upon you, Hegio,—unless you object, maybe.

Hegio No, no, speak out.

Tynd. Once I was free as your son; an enemy's success deprived me of my liberty as he was deprived of his; he is a slave in my country as I am here with you. There surely is a God who hears and sees what we do: and according to your treatment of me here, so will he look after your son there. He will reward the deserving and requite the undeserving. Just as you long for your son, so does my father long for me.

Hegio I know all that—but do you admit the truth of what this fellow has told me?

Tynd. I do admit that my father is a very wealthy man at home and that I do come of very good family. But, Hegio, I beseech you, don't let my wealth make your demands too exorbitant: for my father, even though I am his only son, might feel that it was better for me to remain your slave, well fed and clothed at your expense, than to come to

491

potius quam illi, ubi minime honestumst, mendi-
    cantem vivere.[1]

Hegio   Non ego omnino lucrum omne esse utile homini
    existimo :

scio ego, multos iam lucrum lutulentos homines
    reddidit ;

est etiam ubi profecto damnum praestet facere
    quam lucrum.

odi ego aurum : multa multis saepe suasit perperam.

nunc hoc animum advorte, ut ea quae sentio pariter
    scias.

filius meus illic apud vos servit captus Alide :   330

eum si reddis mihi, praeterea unum nummum ne duis

et te et hunc amittam hinc. alio pacto abire non potes.

Tynd.   Optumum atque aequissumum oras optumusque
    hominum es homo.

sed is privatam servitutem servit illi an publicam?

Hegio   Privatam medici Menarchi.

Tynd.   Pol is quidem huius est cliens.

tam hoc quidem tibi in proclivi quam imber est
    quando pluit.

Hegio   Fac is homo ut redimatur.

Tynd.   Faciam. sed te id oro, Hegio—

Hegio   Quid vis, dum ab re ne quid ores, faciam.

Tynd.   Ausculta, tum scies.

ego me amitti, donicum ille huc redierit, non postulo.

verum quaeso ut aestumatum hunc mihi des, quem
    mittam ad patrem,   340

ut is homo redimatur illi.

Hegio   Immo alium potius misero

hinc, ubi erunt indutiae, illuc, tuom qui conveniat
    patrem,

---

[1] Leo brackets the following v., 324 :

Hegio   *Ego virtute deum et maiorum nostrum dives sum satis.*

	beggary there at home where it would disgrace us most.
Hegio	I am not a man who regards each and every acquisition of money as a blessing: plenty of people have been tainted before now by this money getting, I know that. There are even times when it certainly is more profitable to lose money than to make it. Gold! I despise it: it has led many a man into many a wrong course. Now give me your attention: I want you to understand thoroughly what I have in mind. (*slowly and emphatically*) My son is a prisoner in Elis, a slave there among your countrymen: get him back to me, and without your giving me a single penny in addition, I will let you go home, and your servant, too. On no other terms can you get off.
Tynd.	A very fair and reasonable proposition, sir, and you are the very fairest of men. Does he belong to some private person, though, or to the state?
Hegio	To a private person, a doctor named Menarchus.
Tynd.	(*aside*) Jove! why, he's a client of master's! (*aloud*) Why, this will be just as easy for you as rain when it pours.
Hegio	Have him ransomed.
Tynd.	I will. But thus much I beg of you, Hegio,——
Hegio	(*eagerly*) Anything you please, provided my interests don't suffer by it.
Tynd.	Listen, and you can see if they will. I don't ask to be released myself until my servant gets back. But I do urge you to let me have him under a forfeit, to send to father so that your son there can be ransomed.
Hegio	Oh no, I'll send some one else instead when we have an armistice: that will be preferable: he

493

qui tua quae tu iusseris mandata ita ut velis perferat.

Tynd. At nihil est ignotum ad illum mittere : operam luseris.

hunc mitte, hic transactum reddet omne, si illuc venerit.

nec quemquam fideliorem neque cui plus credat potes mittere ad eum nec qui magis sit servos ex sententia, neque adeo cui suom concredat filium hodie audacius. ne vereare, meo periclo huius ego experiar fidem, fretus ingenio eius, quod me esse scit erga se benevolum.   350

Hegio Mittam equidem istunc aestumatum tua fide, si vis.

Tynd.   Volo;

quam citissime potest, tam hoc cedere ad factum volo.

Hegio Num quae causa est quin, si ille huc non redeat, viginti minas

mihi des pro illo?

Tynd.   Optuma immo.

Hegio   Solvite istum nunciam,

atque utrumque.

Tynd.   Di tibi omnis omnia optata offerant,

cum me tanto honore honestas cumque ex vinclis eximis.

hoc quidem haud molestumst, iam quod collus collari caret.

Hegio Quod bonis bene fit beneficium, gratia ea gravida est bonis.

nunc tu illum si illo es missurus, dice monstra praecipe

quae ad patrem vis nuntiari.   vin vocem huc ad te ?

Tynd.   Voca.   360

II. 3.

Hegio   Quae res bene vortat mihi meoque filio
          vobisque, volt te novos erus operam dare

494

shall confer with your father and carry out your
orders to your satisfaction.

ynd. But it's no good sending a stranger to him: you'll
have frittered away your time. Send him: (*pointing
to Philocrates*) he will transact the whole affair,
once he gets there. You can't send him a more
reliable man, one he would trust more, a servant
that's more to his mind; I may go so far as to say
there is no one he would be readier to entrust his
own son to. Never fear: I will be responsible for
his fidelity. I can depend on his goodness of heart;
he appreciates my kindness to him.

legio Very well, I'll send him under a forfeit, on your
guarantee, if you wish.

ynd. I do wish it. And I wish to have all this an
accomplished fact just as quickly as possible.

legio Have you any objection to paying me eighty
pounds for him in case he doesn't return?

ynd. Not the slightest—fair as can be.

legio (*to overseers*) Take the chains off that fellow at
once, off both of them, in fact.

ynd. (*as slaves obey*) God grant your every wish, sir, for
your highly considerate conduct toward me and for
releasing me. (*aside, stretching himself*) I tell you
what, it's no unpleasant sensation, having that
necklet off one's neck.

legio " A good deed done a good man yields a large
return of good." Now if you intend to send that
fellow home, inform him, instruct him, give him
full particulars as to the message he's to carry your
father. Shall I call him over here to you?

ynd. Do.

cene 3.

legio (*going to Philocrates*) God bless us all in this, me,

495

	tuo veteri domino, quod is velit, fideliter.	
	nam ego te aestumatum huic dedi viginti minis,	
	hic autem te ait mittere hinc velle ad patrem,	
	meum ut illic redimat filium, mutatio	
	inter me atque illum ut nostris fiat filiis.	
Philocr.	Utroque vorsum rectumst ingenium meum,	
	ad te atque ad illum; pro rota me uti licet:	
	vel ego huc vel illic vortar, quo imperabitis.	370
Hegio	Tute tibi tuopte ingenio prodes plurumum,	
	cum servitutem ita fers ut ferri decet.	
	sequere. em tibi hominem.	
Tynd.	Gratiam habeo tibi,	
	quom copiam istam mi et potestatem facis,	
	ut ego ad parentes hunc remittam nuntium,	
	qui me quid rerum hic agitem et quid fieri velim	
	patri meo, ordine omnem rem, illuc perferat.	
	nunc ita convenit inter me atque hunc, Tyndare,	
	ut te aestumatum in Alidem mittam ad patrem,	
	si non rebitas huc, ut viginti minas	380
	dem pro te.	
Philocr.	Recte convenisse sentio.	
	nam pater expectat aut me aut aliquem nuntium,	
	qui hinc ad se veniat.	
Tynd.	Ergo animum advortas volo	
	quae nuntiare hinc te volo in patriam ad patrem.	
Philocr.	Philocrates, ut adhuc locorum feci, faciam sedulo,	
	ut potissimum quod in rem recte conducat tuam,	
	id petam idque persequar corde et animo atque	
	viribus.	

and my son, and yourselves! My man, your new master wishes you to do something your old master wishes, and to do it faithfully. The fact is, I have given you over to him, under an eighty pound forfeit, he saying he desires to send you off to his father and let him ransom my son there in Elis, so that he may exchange my boy for his own.

Philocr. I'm quite disposed to do both of you a good turn, sirs, you and him both; you can use me like a wheel, I'll turn your way or his, either way, wherever you like.

Hegio And you are acting very much to your own advantage in being so disposed, and in accepting your slavery as you should. Follow me. (*leading way to Tyndarus*) There's your man.

Tynd. (*sedately*) I thank you, sir, for affording me this opportunity, of making him my messenger to my parents, so that he may carry to my father a full account of me and my situation here, and what I wish him to see to. (*turning to Philocrates*) Tyndarus, this gentleman and I have just arranged that I send you to Elis to father, under a forfeit: if you fail to return, I am to pay him eighty pounds for you.

Philocr. And a good arrangement, too, in my opinion. For the old gentleman's expecting either me or some messenger to come to him from here.

Tynd. Well then, I wish you to pay attention to the message I wish you to take home to him.

Philocr. I'll do the best I can for you, sir, just as I always have: anything that makes for your good, sir, I'll work my hardest for, and follow up with all my heart and soul and strength.

Tynd. Facis ita ut te facere oportet. nunc animum ad-
vortas volo:
omnium primum salutem dicito matri et patri
et cognatis et si quem alium benevolentem videris; 390
me hic valere et servitutem servire huic homini
optumo,
qui me honore honestiorem semper fecit et facit.

Philocr. Istuc ne praecipias, facile memoria memini
tamen.

Tynd. Nam equidem, nisi quod custodem habeo, liberum
me esse arbitror.
dicito patri, quo pacto mihi cum hoc convenerit
de huius filio.

Philocr.   Quae memini, mora mera est monerier.

Tynd. Ut eum redimat et remittat nostrum huc amborum
vicem.

Philocr. Meminero.

Hegio   At quamprimum pote: istuc in rem utriquest
maxime.

Philocr. Non tuom tu magis videre quam ille suom gnatum
cupit.

Hegio Meus mihi, suos cuique est carus.

Philocr.   Numquid aliud vis patri 400
nuntiari?

Tynd.   Me hic valere et—tute audacter dicito,
Tyndare—inter nos fuisse ingenio haud discorda-
bili,
neque te commeruisse culpam—neque me adver-
satum tibi—
beneque ero gessisse morem in tantis aerumnis
tamen;
neque med umquam deseruisse te neque factis
neque fide,
rebus in dubiis egenis. haec pater quando sciet,

498

Tynd. The proper spirit. Now I wish you to pay attention. First of all, remember me to my father and mother and my relatives and anyone else you may see who is interested in my welfare; tell them I am in good health here and a slave of this most estimable gentleman who has always accorded me the (*with emphasis*) very extraordinary consideration which I still enjoy.

Philocr. No instructions needed along that line, sir: I can remember to mind that easily enough, without.

Tynd. For really, aside from the fact that I have a guard, I feel that I am a free man. Tell my father what arrangement this gentleman and I have made regarding his son.

Philocr. Mere waste of time, sir, to remind me of what I remember.

Tynd. That he is to ransom him and send him back here in exchange for us both.

Philocr. I'll remember.

Hegio Yes, but just as quickly as possible: that's of the highest importance to each of us.

Philocr. You don't long to see your son any more than he does his, sir.

Hegio My son is dear to me, as his own son is to every father.

Philocr. No further message for him, eh?

Tynd. (*somewhat at a loss*) Say I am in good health here, and—(*earnestly*) Tyndarus, speak up boldly to him, yourself,—say that we have never been at variance, that I have never had reason to find fault with you (nor you to think me obstinate) and that you have served your master to the full even in such adversity. Say that a treacherous act, a disloyal thought were things undreamed of even in the dark hours of

Tyndare, ut fueris animatus erga suom gnatum
    atque se,
numquam erit tam avarus, quin te gratiis emittat
    manu [1];
et mea opera, si hinc rebito, faciam ut faciat facilius.
nam tua opera et comitate et virtute et sapientia   410
fecisti ut redire liceat ad parentis denuo,
cum apud hunc confessus es et genus et divitias meas:
quo pacto emisisti e vinclis tuom erum tua sapientia.

Philocr. Feci ego ista ut commemoras, et te meminisse
    id gratum est mihi.
merito tibi ea evenerunt a me; nam nunc, Philocrates,
si ego item memorem quae me erga multa fecisti
    bene,
nox diem adimat; nam quasi servos meus esses,
    nihilo setius
tu mihi obsequiosus semper fuisti.

Hegio   Di vostram fidem,
hominum ingenium liberale. ut lacrumas excuti-
    unt mihi.
videas corde amare inter se. quantis lautus laudibus   420
suom erum servos collaudavit.

Tynd.   Pol istic me haud centesimam
partem laudat quam ipse meritust ut laudetur
    laudibus.

Hegio Ergo cum optume fecisti, nunc adest occasio
bene facta cumulare, ut erga hunc rem geras fideliter.

Philocr. Magis non factum possum velle, quam opera expe-
    riar persequi;
id ut scias, Iovem supremum testem laudo, Hegio,
me infidelem non futurum Philocrati

Hegio   Probus es homo.

---

[1] Corrupt (Leo): *quin te gratiis* MSS. *gratiis quin te*
Schoell.

distress. When my father knows of this, Tyndarus,
knows what your spirit toward his son and himself
has been, he will never be so niggardly as not to
set you free at his own expense; and if I return,
I will put forth my own efforts to make him the
more ready to do it. For it is through your efforts
and good will and devotion and wisdom that I have
a chance to go back to my parents once more, inasmuch as you informed this gentleman of my
family and wealth: thanks to your wisdom in
doing so, your master's fetters have been removed.

Philocr. Right you are, sir, so I did, and I'm glad you remember it. You deserve anything I've done for
you, too; why, sir, if I was to go on like that now
and mention how many good turns you've done
me, it would take all day and more; why, it was
just as if you had been my slave, not a bit different,
the deferential way you've always treated me.

Hegio (*half aside*) Bless my soul, what noble natures!
Dear, dear, it brings the tears to my eyes! You
can see they are simply devoted to each other.
The way that splendid slave praised his own
master—a perfect panegyric!

Tynd. Heavens, sir, he doesn't praise me a hundredth
part as much as he deserves to be praised himself.

Hegio (*to Philocrates*) Well then, having been such an
excellent servant, here is an opportunity to crown
your services by carrying through this business for
him faithfully.

Philocr. I'll be just as keen in actually trying to do it as I
can be for wanting it done, sir; and to prove it,
sir, I swear by God Almighty that I'll never be
unfaithful to Philocrates—

Hegio (*heartily*) Worthy fellow!

Philocr. Nec me secus umquam ei facturum quicquam
quam memet mihi.

Tynd. Istaec dicta te experiri et operis et factis volo;
et, quo minus dixi quam volui de te, animum ad-
vortas volo,   430
atque horunc verborum causa caveto mi iratus fuas ;
sed, te quaeso, cogitato hinc mea fide mitti domum
te aestimatum, et meam esse vitam hic pro te po-
sitam pignori,
ne tu me ignores, quom extemplo meo e conspectu
abscesseris,
quom me servom in servitute pro ted hic reliqueris,
tuque te pro libero esse ducas, pignus deseras
neque des operam pro me ut huius reducem facias
filium.[1]
fac fidelis sis fideli, cave fidem fluxam geras :
nam pater, scio, faciet quae illum facere oportet
omnia ;   440
serva tibi in perpetuom amicum me, atque hunc
inventum inveni.
haec per dexteram tuam te dextera retinens manu
opsecro, infidelior mihi ne fuas quam ego sum tibi.
tu hoc age.   tu mihi erus nunc es, tu patronus, tu
pater,
tibi commendo spes opesque meas.

Philocr.   Mandavisti satis
satin habes, mandata quae sunt facta si refero ?

Tynd.   Satis.

Philocr. Et tua et tua huc ornatus reveniam ex sententia.
numquid aliud ?

Tynd.   Ut quam primum possis redeas.

Philocr.   Res monet.

---

[1] Leo brackets the following v., 438 :
scito te hinc minis viginti aestumatum mittier.

Philocr. —or ever act any differently by him than I would
by my own self.

Tynd. (*with increased earnestness*) It is the actual performance, the deed, I wish to test those words
by; and inasmuch as I said less than I wished
about your conduct, I wish you to pay particular
attention,—yes, and be sure not to take offence
at what I say. But I beg you, do bear in mind
the fact that you are being sent off home, sent
home at my risk and under a forfeit, and that I am
staking my life for you here: so don't forget me
the moment you are out of sight, when you have
left me here in servitude, a slave, in your stead;
and don't consider yourself a free man and let
your promise go and fail to save me by bringing
back this gentleman's son. Be faithful, I entreat
you, to one who has shown his faith, and don't falter
in that faithfulness. As for my father, I am sure
he will do everything he should do. For your part,
keep me your friend for ever, and do not lose this
friend (*indicating Hegio*) you have found. This I
beseech you by this hand (*grasping Philocrates'
right hand*), this hand I hold in mine: don't be less
true to me than I am to you. (*after a pause*) Well,
to the work! You are my master now, my pro-
tector, my father, you and you only: to you I
commend my hopes and my welfare.

Philocr. Enough commands, sir. Will you be satisfied, if I
turn your commands to accomplished facts?

Tynd. Yes.

Philocr. I'll come back here equipped to suit you (*to Hegio*)
sir, and you, (*to Tyndarus*) too. Nothing else?

Tynd. Return as soon as you can.

Philocr. Naturally, sir.

503

Hegio   Sequere me, viaticum ut dem a trapezita tibi,
          eadem opera a praetore sumam syngraphum.

Tynd.   Quem syngraphum?   450

Hegio   Quem hic ferat secum ad legionem, hinc ire huic
          ut liceat domum.
          tu intro abi.

Tynd.   Ben ambulato.

Philocr.   Bene vale.

Hegio   Edepol rem meam
          constabilivi, quom illos emi de praeda a quae-
             storibus;
          expedivi ex servitute filium, si dis placet.
          at etiam dubitavi, hos homines emerem an non
             emerem, diu.
          servate istum sultis intus, servi, ne quoquam pedem
          ecferat sine custodela. iam ego apparebo domi;
          ad fratrem modo captivos alios inviso meos,
          eadem percontabor, ecquis hunc adulescentem no-
             verit.
          sequere tu. te ut amittam; ei rei primum prae-
             vorti volo.   460

ACTVS III

Erg.   Miser homo est, qui ipse sibi quod edit quaerit et
          id aegre invenit,
          sed ille est miserior, qui et aegre quaerit et nihil
             invenit;

    504

Hegio   (*to Philocrates*) Follow me. I must go to the banker's and give you some money for travelling expenses: I'll get a passport from the praetor at the same time.

Tynd.   What passport?

Hegio   One to take to the army with him so that he'll be allowed to go off home. As for yourself, you go inside.

Tynd.   (*to Philocrates*) A good journey to you.

Philocr.   Good-bye, sir, good-bye!

                [EXIT *Tyndarus* INTO *Hegio's* HOUSE.

Hegio   (*aside, in high spirits*) Well, well, well, it was the making of me when I bought those two from the commissioners! I've set my son at liberty, God willing! And to think I hesitated for a long time whether to buy them or not! (*to overseers*) Please keep an eye on that prisoner inside there, my lads, and don't let him set a foot out here anywhere without a guard. I shall soon be home myself. I'll just step over to my brother's for a look at my other captives: at the same time I'll inquire if any one of them knows this young gentleman. (*to Philocrates*) Come, my man, so that I may send you off; I want to attend to that first.

                [EXEUNT *Hegio* AND *Philocrates*.

ACT III

(*An hour has elapsed.*)

ENTER *Ergasilus*, MUCH DEPRESSED.

Erg.   It's sad when a man has to spend his time looking for his food and has hard work finding it. It's sadder, though, when he has hard work looking for it and doesn't find it. But it's saddest of all when a

ille miserrimust, qui cum esse cupit, tum quod edit
  non habet.
nam hercle ego huic die, si liceat, oculos effodiam
  libens,
ita malignitate oneravit omnis mortalis mihi ;
neque ieiuniosiorem neque magis ecfertum fame
vidi nec quoi minus procedat quidquid facere
  occeperit,
ita venter gutturque resident esurialis ferias.
ilicet parasiticae arti maximam malam crucem,
ita iuventus iam ridiculos inopesque ab se segregat.   470
nil morantur iam Lacones unisubselli viros,
plagipatidas, quibus sunt verba sine penu et pecunia
eos requirunt, qui libenter, quom ederint, reddant
  domi ;
ipsi obsonant, quae parasitorum ante erat provincia,
ipsi de foro tam aperto capite ad lenones eunt
quam in tribu aperto capite sontes condemnant reos ;
neque ridiculos iam terrunci faciunt, sese omnes
  amant.
nam uti dudum hinc abii, accessi ad adulescentes
  in foro.
"salvete" inquam. "quo imus una" inquam
  "ad prandium?" atque illi tacent.
"quid ait 'hoc' aut quis profitetur?" inquam.
  quasi muti silent,   480
neque me rident. "ubi cenamus?" inquam.
  atque illi abnuont.
dico unum ridiculum dictum de dictis melioribus,
quibus solebam menstruales epulas ante adipiscier :
nemo ridet ; scivi extemplo rem de compecto geri ;
ne canem quidem irritatam voluit quisquam imi-
  tarier,
saltem, si non arriderent, dentes ut restringerent.

man is pining to eat, and no food in range. By gad, if I only could, I'd like to dig the eyes out of this day, it's made every living soul so damnably mean to me! A more hungriful day, a more bulged-out-with-starvation day, a more unprogressive day for every undertaking, I never did see! Such a famine feast as my inside is having! Devil take the parasitical profession! How the young fellows nowadays do sheer off from impecunious wits! Not a bit of use have they nowadays for us Spartans, us valiant benchenders, us descendants of old Takesacuff, whose capital is talk without cash and comestibles. The guests they're after are the ones that enjoy a dinner and then like to return the compliment. They do their marketing themselves, too,—that used to be the parasites' province—and away they go from the forum themselves to interview the pimps, just as barefaced as they are in court when they condemn guilty defendants. They don't care a farthing for wits these days: they're egoists, every one. Why, when I left here a little while ago, I went up to some young fellows in the forum. " Good day," says I. " Where are we going to lunch together? " says I. Sudden silence. " Who says: ' This way '? Who makes a bid? " says I. Dumb as mutes, didn't even give me a smile. " Where do we dine? " says I. A shaking of heads. I told 'em a funny story—one of my best, that used to find me free board for a month. Nobody smiled. I saw in a moment it was a put-up job; not a one of 'em was even willing to act like a cross dog and at least show their teeth, no matter if they wouldn't laugh. I left 'em after I saw I was being made a

abeo ab illis, postquam video me sic ludificarier;
pergo ad alios, venio ad alios, deinde ad alios : una
    res.
omnes de compecto rem agunt, quasi in Velabro
    olearii.
nunc redeo inde, quoniam me ibi video ludificarier.   490
item alii parasiti frustra obambulabant in foro.
nunc barbarica lege certumst ius meum omne per-
    sequi :
qui consilium iniere, quo nos victu et vita prohi-
    beant,
is diem dicam, irrogabo multam, ut mihi cenas
    decem
meo arbitratu dent, cum cara annona sit.   sic egero.
nunc ibo ad portum hinc : est illic mi una spes
    cenatica ;
si ea decolabit, redibo huc ad senem ad cenam
    asperam.

III. 2.

Hegio   Quid est suavius, quam bene rem gerere,
      bono publico, sic ut ego feci heri,
        cum emi hosce homines : ubi quisque vident,   500
      eunt obviam gratulanturque eam rem.
        ita me miserum restitando
        retinendoque lassum reddiderunt :
      vix ex gratulando miser iam eminebam.
        tandem abii ad praetorem ; ibi vix requievi :
      rogo syngraphum, datur mi ilico ; dedi Tyndaro :
      ille abiit domum.
        inde ilico praevortor domum, postquam id
          actum est ;

508

fool of this way; up I went to some others, and
then to others, and to others still,—same story.
They're all in a combination, just like the oil
dealers in the Velabrum.[1] So here I am back
again, seeing I was trifled with there. Some more
parasites were prowling round the forum all for
nothing, too. Now I'm going to have the foreign
law on those chaps and demand my full rights, I
certainly am: it's conspiracy, conspiracy to deprive
us of sustenance and life, and I'm going to summon 'em, fine 'em—make 'em give me ten dinners,
at my discretion, and that will be when food is
dear. That's how I'll catch them. (*turning to go*)
Well, now for the harbour. That's where my
one hope is, gastronomically speaking; if that
oozes away, I'll come back here to the old man's
terror of a meal.

[EXIT *Ergasilus*, LOOKING IN ALL DIRECTIONS FOR A
POSSIBLE HOST.

Scene 2.   ENTER *Hegio* WITH *Aristophontes* AND *Slaves*

Hegio (*highly pleased with himself*) Now what makes you
feel better than managing your affairs properly and
contributing to the common good, just as I did
yesterday in buying these prisoners? Whenever
anyone sees me, up he comes and congratulates
me on it! Dear, dear! I was so worn out with all
their stopping and detaining me, it got to be
frightfully hard work emerging from the flood of
felicitations. At last I escaped to the praetor's.
Barely waiting to catch my breath, I asked for a
passport: got it on the spot; gave it to Tyndarus:
he's off for home. After seeing to that, I first

---

[1] A market district in Rome.

eo protinus ad fratrem, mei ubi sunt alii captivi.
rogo, Philocratem ex Alide ecquis hominum
noverit: tandem hic exclamat, eum sibi esse
    sodalem ;   510
dico eum esse apud me; hic extemplo orat obse-
    cratque,
eum sibi ut liceat videre:
    iussi ilico hunc exsolvi. nunc tu sequere me,
ut quod me oravisti impetres, eum hominem uti
    convenias.

III. 3.
Tynd.   Nunc illud est, cum me fuisse quam esse nimio
        mavelim :
nunc spes opes auxiliaque a me segregant spernunt-
    que se.
hic illest dies, cum nulla vitae meae salus sperabilest,
neque exitium [1] exitio est neque adeo spes, quae
    mi hunc aspellat metum,
nec subdolis mendaciis mihi usquam mantellum
    est meis,[2]   520
neque deprecatio perfidiis meis nec male factis
    fuga est.
nec confidentiae usquam hospitium est nec dever-
    ticulum dolis :
operta quae fuere aperta sunt, patent praestigiae,
    omnis res palam est, neque de hac re negotium est,
quin male occidam oppetamque pestem eri vicem
    meamque.
perdidit me Aristophontes hic qui venit modo intro:[3]

---

[1] Corrupt (Leo): *exitium* Pontanus : *exilium* MSS.
[2] Leo brackets the following v., 521:
nec sycophantiis nec fucis ullum mantellum obviam est.
[3] Corrupt (Leo): *qui venit modo intro* MSS : *modo qui venit intro* Lindsay.

start straight for home. Then I go on to my
brother's where the rest of my prisoners are.
Inquire if any one of 'em knows Philocrates of
Elis. Finally this fellow (*pointing to Aristophontes*)
calls out that Philocrates is a particular friend of
his. I tell him he's at my house; the next instant
he's begging and beseeching me for a chance to
see him. I had him unfettered at once. (*to Aristophontes*) Now, sir, come this way, so as to obtain
your request and meet your friend.

[EXEUNT INTO HOUSE: AS THEY GO IN *Tyndarus*
RUSHES OUT.

Scene 3.

Tynd. (*grimly*) Now's the time when I should infinitely
prefer to be underground than on it! Hope,
resources, help—all deserting, all leaving me in
the lurch now! My day has come: I can never
hope to get out of this alive. Done for, and
nothing to be done for it! There's no prospect of
staving off the danger, either, and not a thing to
drape my crafty lies with. My falsehoods can't
beg themselves off, or my transgressions take to
their heels: no lodgings anywhere for brass: guile
can't find accommodations. The covert's un-
covered, our plot's apparent, everything's out.
There's nothing to do about it: I must drop off
disagreeably, and come to a painful end for master
—also for myself. He's been the ruin of me, this
Aristophontes that just went inside: he knows

511

is me novit, is sodalis Philocrati et cognatus est.
neque iam Salus servare, si volt, me potest, nec
    copia est,
nisi si aliquam corde machinor astutiam.   530
quam, malum?   quid machiner?   quid commini-
    scar? maxumas
nugas ineptus incipisso.   haereo.

III. 4.

Hegio   Quo illum nunc hominem proripuisse foras se di-
    cam ex aedibus?

Tynd.   Nunc enim vero ego occidi: eunt ad te hostes,
    Tyndare.
quid loquar?   quid fabulabor?   quid negabo aut
    quid fatebor?
mihi res omnis in incerto sita est.   quid rebus
    confidam meis?
utinam te di prius perderent. quam periisti e patria
    tua,
Aristophontes, qui ex parata re imparatam omnem
    facis.
occisa est haec res, nisi reperio atrocem mi aliquam
    astutiam.

Hegio   Sequere. em tibi hominem. adi, atque adloquere.
Tynd.   Quis homo est me hominum miserior?   540
Arist.   Quid istuc est quod meos te dicam fugitare oculos,
    Tyndare,
proque ignoto me aspernari, quasi me numquam
    noveris?
equidem tam sum servos quam tu, etsi ego domi
    liber fui,
tu usque a puero servitutem servivisti in Alide.

Hegio   Edepol minime miror, si te fugitat aut oculos tuos,
aut si te odit, qui istum appelles Tyndarum pro
    Philocrate.

me: he's a particular friend of Philocrates, related
to him, too. Salvation herself can't save me now,
if she so desires: there's no chance unless I can
invent some clever scheme. But what, curse it?
What can I invent? What can I devise? (*reflecting, then doubtfully*) Oh, this is awful nonsense I'm
at, poor simpleton! (*disgustedly*) Stuck!

Scene 4.   ENTER *Hegio, Aristophontes,* AND *Slaves.*

Hegio Where did that fellow bolt for out of the house
just now, I wonder?

Tynd. (*aside*) It's all over with me, all over with me now:
the enemy are upon you, Tyndarus! What shall I
say? What story shall I tell? What shall I deny
—or what admit? It's a shaky business for me on
every side! What faith can I put in my luck?
Oh, I wish the gods had made away with you before you made away from home, Aristophontes,—
upsetting my settled plan completely! The game
is up, unless I hit upon some awfully clever
scheme.

Hegio (*to Aristophontes, on seeing Tyndarus*) Come along!
There's your man! Go up and speak to him!

Tynd. (*aside, as Aristophontes approaches*) What mortal
man is in a more confounded hole than this?
(*pretends not to recognize him*)

Arist. I wonder what you mean by this, Tyndarus,—
avoiding my eye and snubbing me as a stranger,
quite as if you never knew me? I'm just as much
of a slave as you are, to be sure, but at home I was
free: as for you, you've been slaving it in Elis
from your boyhood up.

Hegio Bless my soul! I'm not a bit surprised if he avoids
you, or your eye, no, nor if he detests you, when
you call him Tyndarus instead of Philocrates.

513

Tynd. Hegio, hic homo rabiosus habitus est in Alide,
ne tu quod istic fabuletur auris immittas tuas.
nam istis hastis insectatus est domi matrem et
    patrem,
et illic isti qui insputatur morbus interdum venit.   550
proin tu ab istoc procul recedas.

Hegio   Ultro istum a me.

Arist.   Ain, verbero?
me rabiosum atque insectatum esse hastis meum
    memoras patrem,
et eum morbum mi esse, ut qui me opus sit inspu-
    tarier?

Hegio Ne verere, multos iste morbus homines macerat,
quibus insputari saluti fuit atque is profuit.

Arist. Quid tu autem? etiam huic credis?

Hegio   Quid ego credam huic?

Arist.   Insanum esse me?

Tynd. Viden tu hunc, quam inimico voltu intuetur? con-
    cedi optumumst,
Hegio: fit quod tibi ego dixi, gliscit rabies, cave
    tibi.

Hegio Credidi esse insanum extemplo, ubi te appellavit
    Tyndarum.

Tynd. Quin suom ipse interdum ignorat nomen neque
    scit qui siet.   560

Hegio At etiam te suom sodalem esse aibat.

Tynd.   Haud vidi magis.
et quidem Alcumeus atque Orestes et Lycurgus
    postea
una opera mihi sunt sodales qua iste.

THE CAPTIVES

Tynd.   (*dragging Hegio aside*) Hegio, this fellow was looked upon as a raving maniac in Elis, so don't you let him fill your ears with his babble. Why, at home he chased his father and mother about with a spear, and every once in a while he has an attack of the disease that people spit on.[1] So get out of his reach, then,—well away.

Hegio   (*to slaves*) Keep him off! Keep him off!

Arist.   What's that, you rascal? I'm a raving maniac and chased my own father with a spear, you say? I have the disease that calls for my being spat upon?

Hegio   (*cheeringly*) Never you mind! Many a man's consumed by that disease of yours, who's been helped by being spat on, and it's brought him through.

Arist.   (*to Hegio, hotly*) How's this? You, too? Do you actually believe him?

Hegio   Believe him in what?

Arist.   That I'm insane?

Tynd.   (*to Hegio*) Do you see him—that angry glare of his? You'd better leave, Hegio. It's just as I said: a fit's coming on. Look out for yourself!

Hegio   (*hastily moving farther off*) I thought so, I thought he was crazy, from the moment he called you Tyndarus.

Tynd.   Why, at times he positively forgets his own name and doesn't know who he is.

Hegio   But he was even saying you were an intimate friend of his.

Tynd.   (*dryly*) Quite so! And the fact is that Alcumeus,[2] in that case, and Orestes,[2] and Lycurgus [2] too, are intimate friends of mine, just exactly as much.

---

[1] Epilepsy.
[2] Madmen, celebrated in Greek mythology. Alcumeus = Alcmaeon.

515

Arist.   At etiam, furcifer,
male loqui mi audes? non ego te novi?

Hegio   Pol planum id quidem est,
non novisse, qui istum appelles Tyndarum pro
    Philocrate.
quem vides, eum ignoras: illum nominas quem non
    vides.

Arist. Immo iste eum sese ait, qui non est, esse, et qui
    vero est, negat.

Tynd. Tu enim repertu's, Philocratem qui superes veri-
    verbio.

Arist. Pol ego ut rem video, tu inventu's, vera vanitudine
    qui convincas. sed quaeso hercle, agedum aspice
    ad me.

Tynd.   Em.
Arist.   Dic modo: 570
tun negas te Tyndarum esse?

Tynd.   Nego, inquam.
Arist.   Tun te Philocratem
esse ais?

Tynd. Ego, inquam.
Arist.   Tune huic credis?
Hegio   Plus quidem quam tibi aut mihi.
nam ille quidem, quem tu hunc memoras esse,
    hodie hinc abiit Alidem
ad patrem huius.

Arist.   Quem patrem, qui servos est?
Tynd.   Et tu quidem
servos es, liber fuisti, et ego me confido fore,
si huius huc reconciliasso in libertatem filium

Arist. Quid ais, furcifer? tun te gnatum esse memoras
    liberum?

Tynd. Non equidem me Liberum, sed Philocratem esse aio.
Arist.   Quid est?

516

THE CAPTIVES

Arist.   Ha! You scoundrel, do you dare go on maligning
         me? Don't I know you?
Hegio   Good heavens! It's quite plain you don't know
         him—calling him Tyndarus instead of Philocrates!
         The man you see you don't know: you name the
         man you don't see.
Arist.   No, sir! This fellow says he's the man he isn't,
         and says he isn't the man he really is.
Tynd.   (to Aristophontes, meaningly) So you have turned up
         to beat Philocrates in stating facts!
Arist.   Good Lord! As I look at it, you have been un-
         earthed to browbeat facts by stating falsehoods.
         But come now, confound it, look me in the
         eye!
Tynd.   (doing so coolly) Well?
Arist.   Now tell me: do you deny that you are Tyndarus?
Tynd.   I do, certainly.
Arist.   You claim to be Philocrates, you?
Tynd.   I certainly do.
Arist.   (to Hegio, exasperated) Do you believe him?
Hegio   More than I do you, surely,—or myself. For you
         see, the fellow you tell me this man is—he went
         away to Elis to-day to this man's father.
Arist.   (contemptuously) Father! What do you mean, when
         he's a slave?
Tynd.   Well, you, too, are a slave and once were free:
         and (with emphasis) I hope to be so myself, when
         I have restored this gentleman's son to home
         and liberty.
Arist.   What's that, you villain? You tell me you were
         born a freeman?
Tynd.   No indeed, my name is not Freeman, but Philo-
         crates: that's what I say.
Arist.   What's all this? How the rascal's making game

517

ut scelestus, Hegio, nunc iste te ludos facit.

nam is est servos ipse, neque praeter se umquam
ei servos fuit.   580

Tynd. Quia tute ipse eges in patria nec tibi qui vivas
domist,

omnis inveniri similis tui vis ; non mirum facis :

est miserorum, ut malevolentes sint atque invideant
bonis.

Arist. Hegio, vide sis, ne quid tu huic temere insistas
credere.

atque, ut perspicio, profecto iam aliquid pugnae
edidit.

filium tuom quod redimere se ait, id ne utiquam
mihi placet.

Tynd. Scio te id nolle fieri ; efficiam tamen ego id, si di
adiuvant.

illum restituam huic, hic autem in Alidem me meo
patri.

propterea ad patrem hinc amisi Tyndarum.

Arist.   Quin tute is es :

neque praeter te in Alide ullus servos istoc nomin-
est.   590

Tynd. Pergin servom me exprobrare esse, id quod vi
hostili optigit ?

Arist. Enim iam nequeo contineri.

Tynd.   Heus, audin quid ait ? quin fugis ?

iam illic hic nos insectabit lapidibus, nisi illunc
iubes

comprehendi.

Arist.   Crucior.

Tynd.   Ardent oculi : fit opus, Hegio ;

viden tu illi maculari corpus totum maculis
luridis ?

atra bilis agitat hominem.

518

of you, Hegio! Why he's a slave himself—the
only one he ever had.

Tynd. (*superior*) Just because you yourself are poverty-
stricken in your own country, with nothing at
home to live on, you want to have every one else
put in the same list. There is nothing strange in
that: it is characteristic of poor beggars to be ill-
natured, and envy the well-to-do.

Arist. Hegio, I beg you take care not to go on with your
rash confidence in this fellow. And for that matter,
he's certainly given you a fall or two already, I
take it. This talk of his about rescuing your son
doesn't please me at all.

Tynd. (*with an appealing look*) I know you don't want it
done; but I'll bring it about, God helping me.
(*slowly*) I will restore his son to this gentleman,
and then this gentleman will send me back to Elis
to my father. That was why I sent Tyndarus off to
my father.

Arist. Why, you're Tyndarus yourself: and besides you
there's not a slave in Elis of that name.

Tynd. Still taunting me with being a slave, eh? A slave
as it happens, because the enemy were too much
for us!

Arist. (*angrily*) I positively can't control myself any
longer!

Tynd. (*apparently alarmed, to Hegio*) Aha! Hear what
he's saying? Run, why don't you? He'll be
after us with stones in a minute, if you don't have
him seized.

Arist. Oh, this is driving me wild!

Tynd. His eyes are blazing! He's having one, Hegio!
See how his whole body is covered with lurid spots?
It's black fury that's tormenting the fellow!

519

Arist.	At pol te, si hic sapiat senex, pix atra agitet apud carnificem tuoque capiti inluceat.
Tynd.	Iam deliramenta loquitur, laruae stimulant virum. hercle qui, si hunc comprehendi iusseris, sapias magis.
Arist.	Crucior, lapidem non habere me, ut illi mastigiae 600 cerebrum excutiam, qui me insanum verbis concinnat suis.
Tynd.	Audin lapidem quaeritare?
Arist.	Solus te solum volo, Hegio.
Hegio	Instinc loquere, si quid vis, procul. tamen audiam.
Tynd.	Namque edepol si adbites propius, os denasabit tibi mordicus.
Arist.	Neque pol me insanum, Hegio, esse creduis neque fuisse umquam, neque esse morbum quem istic autumat.
	verum si quid metuis a me, iube me vinciri : volo, dum istic itidem vinciatur.
Tynd.	Immo enim vero, Hegio, istic, qui volt, vinciatur.
Arist.	Tace modo. ego te, Philocrates false, faciam ut verus hodie reperiare Tyndarus. 610 quid mi abnutas?
Tynd.	Tibi ego abnuto?
Arist.	Quid agat, si absis longius?
Hegio	Quid ais? quid si adeam hunc insanum?
Tynd.	Nugas. ludificabitur,

Arist. Now, by the Lord, if this old gentleman did the wise thing, it's black pitch that would torment you at the executioner's, and light up that head of yours!

Tynd. Now he's got to the raving point! Evil spirits are hounding the man, Hegio. Heavens! You'd do more wisely to have him seized!

Arist. Oh, damnation! not to have a stone to knock out the brains of this blackguard that's driving me mad with his talk!

Tynd. Hear that—looking for a stone!

Arist. (*struggling to contain himself*) Hegio, I want a word with you all alone.

Hegio (*timorously*) Say it from there, if there's anything you want—from away off there. I shall hear it all the same.

Tynd. That's right, by Jove! for if you go any nearer, he'll bite your nose off.

Arist. Heavens and earth, Hegio! don't believe I'm insane, or that I have, or ever had, the disease he's talking about. However, if you're at all afraid of me, have me tied up. I am willing, provided that fellow is tied up too.

Tynd. No indeed, Hegio, certainly not: tie up the fellow that wants it.

Arist. You keep still, now! I'll soon show you up, you false Philocrates, for the real Tyndarus. (*Tyndarus makes signs to him behind Hegio's back*) What are you shaking your head at me for?

Tynd. I shaking my head at you?

Arist. (*to Hegio*) What would he do, if you were farther off?

Hegio See here, what if I should step up to this lunatic?

Tynd. Ridiculous! He'll make a fool of you, jabbering

521

garriet quoi neque pes umquam neque caput com-
pareat.
ornamenta absunt : Aiacem, hunc cum vides, ipsum
vides.

Hegio Nihili facio. tamen adibo.

Tynd.   Nunc ego omnino occidi,
nunc ego inter sacrum saxumque sto, nec quid
faciam scio.

Hegio Do tibi operam, Aristophontes, si quid est quod
me velis.

Arist. Ex me audibis vera quae nunc falsa opinare, Hegio.
sed hoc primum, me expurigare tibi volo, me insaniam   620
neque tenere neque mi esse ullum morbum, nisi
quod servio.
at ita me rex deorum atque hominum faxit patriae
compotem,
ut istic Philocrates non magis est quam aut ego
aut tu.

Hegio   Eho dic mihi,
quis illic igitur est ?

Arist.   Quem dudum dixi a principio tibi.
hoc si secus reperies, nullam causam dico quin mihi
et parentum et libertatis apud te deliquio siet.

Hegio Quid tu ais ?

Tynd.   Me tuom esse servom et te meum erum.

Hegio   Haud istuc rogo.
fuistin liber ?

Tynd.   Fui.

Arist.   Enim vero non fuit, nugas agit.

Tynd. Qui tu scis ? an tu fortasse fuisti meae matri
obstetrix,
qui id tam audacter dicere audes ?

Arist.   Puerum te vidi puer. 630

something without head or tail to it. Look at this fellow, and you're looking at a regular Ajax [1]—all but the make-up.

Hegio I don't care. I'm going to step up to him just the same. (*approaches Aristophontes hesitantly*)

Tynd. (*aside*) Now I'm done for entirely. Now I'm between the axe and the altar, and what to do I don't know.

Hegio I'm at your service, Aristophontes, if there's anything you want of me.

Arist. I'll show you, Hegio, that all this you take for a lie is the truth. But first I want to clear myself with you, and assure you that I am not insane, and have no affliction except captivity. And now,— (*solemnly*) so may the King of heaven and earth restore me to my native land,—that fellow is no more Philocrates than you or I.

Hegio (*impressed*) Hey? Tell me, who is he then?

Arist. The man I told you he was to begin with, a while ago. If you find it otherwise, I make no objection to forfeiting my parents and my liberty and staying here with you.

Hegio (*to Tyndarus*) And you—what have you to say?

Tynd. (*urbanely*) That I am your servant, and that you are my master.

Hegio (*impatiently*) That isn't what I'm asking about. Were you a freeman?

Tynd. I was.

Arist. He certainly was not. Absurd!

Tynd. (*superciliously*) How do you know? Or were you my mother's midwife, perhaps, that you venture to speak with such assurance on this point?

Arist. I saw you when we were both boys.

---

[1] Another madman of Greek mythology.

523

Tynd.   At ego te video maior maiorem: em rursum tibi.
meam rem non cures, si recte facis. nunc ego curo
    tuam?

Hegio   Fuitne huic pater Thensaurochrysonicochrysides?

Arist.   Non fuit, neque ego istuc nomen umquam audivi
ante hunc diem.
Philocrati Theodoromedes fuit pater.

Tynd.   Pereo probe.
quin quiescis? i dierectum cor meum, ac suspende te.
tu sussultas, ego miser vix asto prae formidine.

Hegio   Satin istuc mihi exquisitum est, fuisse hunc servom
    in Alide
neque esse hunc Philocratem?

Arist.   Tam satis quam numquam hoc invenies secus.
sed ubi is nunc est?

Hegio   Ubi ego minime atque ipsus se volt maxume.
sed vide sis.

Arist.   Quin exploratum dico et provisum hoc tibi.

Hegio   Certon?

Arist.   Quin nihil, inquam. invenies magis hoc certo
certius.
Philocrates iam inde usque amicus fuit mihi a puero
    puer.

Hegio   Tum igitur ego deruncinatus, deartuatus sum miser
huius scelesti techinis, qui me ut lubitum est ducta-
    vit dolis.
sed qua faciest tuos sodalis Philocrates?

Arist.   Dicam tibi:
macilento ore, naso acuto, corpore albo, oculis nigris,
subrufus aliquantum, crispus, cincinnatus.

Hegio   Convenit.

640

Tynd. Well, I see you now we are both grown-ups. There's one for you! You wouldn't meddle with my business, if you behaved decently. I don't meddle with yours, do I?

Hegio Wasn't his father called Ducatsdoubloonsand-piecesofeightson?

Arist. No sir, he was not, and I never heard that name before to-day. The father of Philocrates was Theodoromedes.

Tynd. (*aside, dryly*) I'm jolly well done for. Stop your noise, will you, heart? Go to the deuce, and be hanged to you! Jumping up and down, while I, poor devil, can hardly stand for fear!

Hegio Am I to take it as absolutely clear that this fellow was a slave in Elis, that he is not Philocrates?

Arist. So absolutely that you'll never find it to be any-thing different. But where is Philocrates at present?

Hegio (*savagely*) Where I least want him, and he most wants to be. Do, do, see if there's not some mis-take, though.

Arist. No, I'm sure of my ground and fully informed in what I tell you.

Hegio You're certain?

Arist. You'll never find a deader certainty than this, I assure you. Philocrates has been a friend of mine ever since he was a boy.

Hegio So then, I've been trimmed, torn limb from limb, poor fool, by the arts of this rogue, who's taken me in with his tricks to suit his taste! But what does your friend Philocrates look like?

Arist. I'll tell you: thin face, sharp nose, complexion fair, black eyes, hair a little reddish, waving, and curled.

Hegio That agrees!

s

Tynd. Ut quidem hercle in medium ego hodie pessume
     processerim.
     vae illis virgis miseris, quae hodie in tergo morien-
     tur meo. 650
Hegio Verba mihi data esse video.
Tynd.   Quid cessatis, compedes,
     currere ad me meaque amplecti crura, ut vos cus-
     todiam?
Hegio Satin med illi hodie scelesti capti ceperunt dolo?
     illic servom se assimulabat, hic sese autem liberum.
     nuculeum amisi, retinui pignori putamina.
     ita mihi stolido sursum versum os sublevere offuciis.
     hic quidem me numquam irridebit. Colaphe, Cor-
     dalio, Corax,
     ite istinc, ecferte lora.

III. 5.
Cola.   Num lignatum mittimur?
Hegio Inicite huic manicas [1] mastigiae.
Tynd. Quid hoc est negoti? quid ego deliqui?
Hegio   Rogas. 660
     sator sartorque scelerum, et messor maxume?
Tynd. Non occatorem dicere audebas prius?
     nam semper occant prius quam sariunt rustici.
Hegio At tu confidenter [2] mihi contra astitit.
Tynd. Decet innocentem servom atque innoxium
     confidentem esse, suom apud erum potissimum.
Hegio Adstringite isti sultis vehementer manus.
Tynd. Tuos sum, tu has quidem vel praecidi iube.
     sed quid negoti est, quam ob rem suscenses mihi?

     [1] Leo notes lacuna here : *manicas* (*maxumas*) Spengel.
     [2] Leo notes lacuna here : *ut* (*etiam*) Schoell.

Tynd. (*aside ruefully*) Gad! Indeed it does—with my coming into damned unpleasant prominence this day. Alas for those poor whips that are doomed this day to die upon my back!

Hegio I see I've been duped!

Tynd. (*aside*) Come on, ye shackles, run up and embrace my shanks, so that I may keep you safe!

Hegio Well, haven't those rascal captives taken me in with this day's trickery? The other one pretended he was the slave, while this fellow here played the freeman. I've lost the kernel and kept the shell for surety. That's the way they've daubed my face up for me, ass that I am! (*grimly*) This one shall never have the laugh on me, at any rate. (*stepping to door and calling*) Box! Buffum! Bangs! Come! Out with you! Bring your straps!

Scene 5. [ENTER OVERSEERS, CARRYING HEAVY RAWHIDES.

Box (*merrily cracking a whip*) You don't want us to go and tie up faggots, do you, sir?

Hegio Clap handcuffs on this rogue. (*pointing to Tyndarus*)

Tynd. (*as they obey*) What does this mean? What have I done?

Hegio Done! You sower and hoer of sin—(*more savagely*) and reaper, especially!

Tynd. (*politely*) Couldn't you manage to slip in " harrower "? Why, farmers always harrow before they hoe.

Hegio (*angrily*) Now look at that! the bold way he stands up to me!

Tynd. A guiltless, harmless slave ought to face his own master boldly, his own master, of all men.

Hegio (*to overseers*) Fasten his hands, tight, mind you!

Tynd. I am yours. Have them cut off, even, for that matter. But what does this mean? Why this rage at me?

527

TITUS MACCIUS PLAUTUS

Hegio	Quia me meamque rem, quod in te uno fuit, 670
	tuis scelestis falsidicis fallaciis
	deartuasti dilaceravisti atque opes
	confecisti omnes, res ac rationes meas:
	ita mi exemisti Philocratem fallaciis.
	illum esse servom credidi, te liberum;
	ita vosmet aiebatis itaque nomina
	inter vos permutastis.
Tynd.	Fateor, omnia
	facta esse ita ut tu dicis, et fallaciis
	abiisse eum abs te mea opera atque astutia;
	an, obsecro hercle te, id nunc suscenses mihi? 680
Hegio	At cum cruciatu maxumo id factumst tuo.
Tynd.	Dum ne ob male facta, peream, parvi aestumo.
	si ego hic peribo, ast ille ut dixit non redit,
	at erit mi hoc factum mortuo memorabile,
	me meum erum captum ex servitute atque hostibus
	reducem fecisse liberum in patriam ad patrem,
	meumque potius me caput periculo
	praeoptavisse, quam is periret, ponere.
Hegio	Facito ergo ut Acherunti clueas gloria.
Tynd.	Qui per virtutem, periit, at non interit. 690
Hegio	Quando ego te exemplis pessumis cruciavero
	atque ob sutelas tuas te morti misero,
	vel te interiisse vel periisse praedicent;
	dum pereas, nihil intererit: dicant vivere.

528

THE CAPTIVES

Tegio Because as far as in you lay you've sent me and my hopes to smash, demolished me, with your rascally deceitful dodges, and spoiled all my chances, all my prospects and plans. That's the way you, got Philocrates off—by swindling me! I supposed he was the slave and you the freeman; that's what you said yourselves; that's how you exchanged names.

Tynd. (*coolly*) I admit it: it is all as you say—yes, you were swindled out of him, and it was my support and my scheming that did it. But heavens and earth, that isn't what sets you raging at me, is it?

Tegio You shall pay for doing it, though, pay for it with your own best blood!

Tynd. (*simply*) Provided it is not for wrongdoing, let me die—it matters little. If I myself do die here, and if he does fail to return, as he said he would, what I have done, at least, will be remembered when I am gone—men will tell how I saved my captured master from slavery and from his enemies, restored him, a free man, to his home and his father, and how I chose to put my own life in peril rather than let him die.

Iegio Well then, you can look in the next world for that glorious name of yours.

Tynd. The man that dies in a worthy cause does not perish utterly.

Iegio After I've tortured you in the most excruciating ways possible, and sent you to perdition for the lies you've patched up, let 'em announce that you've perished utterly, or that you've merely died; so long as you're dead, no matter—they can say you're living, for all I care.

Tynd.	Pol si istuc faxis, haud sine poena feceris,
	si ille huc rebitet, sicut confido affore.
Arist.	Pro di immortales, nunc ego teneo, nunc scio
	quid hoc sit negoti. meus sodalis Philocrates
	in libertate est ad patrem in patria. bene est,
	nec quisquam est mihi, aeque melius cui velim. 700
	sed hoc mihi aegre est, me huic dedisse operam
	malam,
	qui nunc propter me meaque verba vinctus est.
Hegio	Votuin te quicquam mi hodie falsum proloqui?
Tynd.	Votuisti.
Hegio	Cur es ausus mentiri mihi?
Tynd.	Quia vera obessent illi quoi operam dabam:
	nunc falsa prosunt.
Hegio	At tibi oberunt.
Tynd.	Optumest.
	at erum servavi, quem servatum gaudeo,
	cui me custodem addiderat erus maior meus.
	sed malene id factum arbitrare?
Hegio	Pessume.
Tynd.	At ego aio recte, qui abs te sorsum sentio. 710
	nam cogitato, si quis hoc gnato tuo
	tuos servos faxit, qualem haberes gratiam?
	emitteresne necne eum servom manu?
	essetne apud te is servos acceptissimus?
	responde.
Hegio	Opinor.
Tynd.	Cur ergo iratus mihi es?
Hegio	Quia illi fuisti quam mihi fidelior.

Tynd. You do that, sir, and I swear it will cost you dear, if my master comes back, as I expect him to do.

Arist. (*aside*) Great God! Now I see it! Now I understand what it all means! My chum Philocrates is free, has gone home to his father. Good! And not a friend have I got that I wish better luck to, either. But I do feel bad about the cursed way I've treated Tyndarus here! He's got me and my tongue to thank for being strapped up at this moment.

Hegio Didn't I tell you not to deceive me in the slightest particular?

Tynd. Yes.

Hegio Then why did you dare lie to me?

Tynd. Because the truth would have harmed the person I was trying to help: as it is, deceit has served his turn.

Hegio It won't serve yours, however.

Tynd. Very well, sir. I saved my master, at any rate, and I'm happy in having saved the man that my older master put in my care. Really now, do you think this was a wrong act?

Hegio Atrocious!

Tynd. Well, sir, I differ with you—I say it was right. Why, just think! if a slave of yours did the same thing for your own son, what would be your feeling toward him? Would you set this slave free, or not? Wouldn't this slave be your favourite? Answer me that.

Hegio (*reluctantly*) I suppose so.

Tynd. Why are you angry at me, then?

Hegio Because you have been more faithful to him than to me.

531

TITUS MACCIUS PLAUTUS

Tynd. Quid? tu una nocte postulavisti et die
recens captum hominem, nuperum novicium,
te perdocere ut melius consulerem tibi,
quam illi, quicum una a puero aetatem exegeram? 720

Hegio Ergo ab eo petito gratiam istam. ducite,
ubi ponderosas crassas capiat compedes.
inde ibis porro in latomias lapidarias.
ibi quom alii octonos lapides effodiunt, nisi
cotidiano sesquiopus confeceris,
Sescentoplago nomen indetur tibi.

Arist. Per deos atque homines ego te obtestor, Hegio,
ne tu istunc hominem perduis.

Hegio Curabitur;
nam noctu nervo vinctus custodibitur,
interdius sub terra lapides eximet: 730
diu ego hunc cruciabo, non uno absolvam die.

Arist. Certumne est tibi istuc?

Hegio Non moriri certius.
abducite istum actutum ad Hippolytum fabrum,
iubete huic crassas compedes impingier;
inde extra portam ad meum libertum Cordalum
in lapicidinas facite deductus siet:
atque hunc me velle dicite ita curarier,
ne qui deterius huic sit quam cui pessume est.

Tynd. Cur ego te invito me esse salvom postulem?
periclum vitae meae tuo stat periculo. 740
post mortem in morte nihil est quod metuam mali.
etsi pervivo usque ad summam aetatem, tamen
breve spatium est perferundi quae minitas mihi.
vale atque salve, etsi aliter ut dicam meres.

532

Tynd. What? Did you expect in a single night and day to teach a man just recently captured, a slave you had hardly bought, to consult your interests more than those of the master I grew up from boyhood with?

Hegio Well then, look to him for your thanks for it. (*to overseers*) Off with him and have him shackled— heavy ones, solid ones! (*to Tyndarus*) After that you shall go straight to the stone quarries. There, while the rest of them are digging out their eight blocks a day, you're to do half as much again, or you'll be dubbed The Cracks-collector.

Arist. Hegio! for God's sake don't let the man be utterly lost!

Hegio Lost? We'll see to that! Why, at night he'll be chained up in a cell and guarded, and in the day-time he'll be under ground hewing out stone. It's agony long drawn out he'll get from me; I won't end it for him all in one day.

Arist. (*distressed*) Is this your fixed intention, sir?

Hegio Fixed as death! (*to overseers*) Quick! March him off to Hippolytus the blacksmith and have some solid irons forged on him; then he's to be escorted outside the city to my freedman Cordalus and the quarries. Yes, and tell Cordalus I want it seen to that he be treated quite as well as the man that's treated (*ferociously*) worst.

Tynd. Why should I ask for mercy when you refuse it? My life is risked at risk to you. After death, there is no evil in death for me to fear. And even if I live on and on to the very limits of human life, it's still only for a short time I shall have to endure what you threaten me with. Farewell, sir, and God bless you, no matter if you do deserve to have me

tu, Aristophontes, de me ut meruisti, ita vale;
nam mihi propter te hoc optigit.

Hegio   Abducite.

Tynd.   At unum hoc quaeso, si huc rebitet Philocrates,
ut mi eius facias conveniundi copiam.

Hegio   Periistis, nisi hunc iam e conspectu abducitis.

Tynd.   Vis haec quidem hercle est, et trahi et trudi simul.   750

Hegio   Illic est abductus recta in phylacam, ut dignus est.
ego illis captivis aliis documentum dabo,
ne tale quisquam facinus incipere audeat.
quod absque hoc esset, qui mihi hoc fecit palam,
usque offrenatum suis me ductarent dolis.
nunc certum est nulli posthac quicquam credere.
satis sum semel deceptus. speravi miser
ex servitute me exemisse filium :
ea spes elapsa est. perdidi unum filium,
puerum quadrimum quem mihi servos surpuit,   760
neque eum servom umquam repperi neque filium ;
maior potitus hostium est. quod hoc est scelus ?
quasi in orbitatem liberos produxerim.
sequere hac. reducam te ubi fuisti. neminis
miserere certum est, quia mei miseret neminem.

Arist.   Exauspicavi ex vinclis. nunc intellego
redauspicandum esse in catenas denuo.

534

	wish you something else. As for you, Aristophontes, fare you well—as well as you deserve of me; for it is all on account of you that this has happened to me.
Hegio	(*to overseers*) Off with him.
Tynd.	But I do ask this one thing of you, sir: if Philocrates comes back, give me a chance to meet him.
Hegio	(*to overseers*) Out of my sight with him this instant, or I'll murder you! (*they seize Tyndarus and hurry him off roughly*)
Tynd.	(*dryly*) Well, well! This is positive violence, being pushed and pulled at the same time.

[EXEUNT.

Hegio   That rascal is bound straight for the prison cell he's entitled to. I'll make an example of him for the benefit of those other prisoners, so that none of them will dare engage in such deviltry. If it hadn't been for this fellow here who disclosed it all, they'd have bitted me and led me along with their tricks till the end of time. Never again do I trust a soul in anything, that's settled. Once cheated is enough. (*pauses, then gloomily*) I hoped, poor fool, that I had ransomed my son from slavery—a hope that's slipped away! I lost one son, a four-year-old boy that a slave kidnapped, and never a trace of slave or son since. And my older boy in the hands of enemies! What curse am I under? As if I'd begotten children so as to be left childless! (*to Aristophontes*) This way, you. (*going toward brother's house*) Back you go where you were before. I am determined to pity no one, since no one pities me.

Arist.   (*wryly*) It seemed a good omen, my getting out of irons. Now I perceive I must omen myself back to chains again. [EXEUNT.

ACTVS IV

Erg.   Iuppiter supreme, servas me measque auges opes,
          maximas opimitates opiparasque offers mihi,
          laudem lucrum, ludum iocum, festivitatem ferias,   770
          pompam penum, potationis saturitatem, gaudium,
          nec cuiquam homini supplicare [1] nunc certum est
              mihi ;
          nam vel prodesse amico possum vel inimicum per-
              dere,
          ita hic me amoenitate amoena amoenus oneravit dies.
          sine sacris hereditatem sum aptus effertissimam.
          nunc ad senem cursum capessam hunc Hegionem,
              cui boni
          tantum affero quantum ipsus a dis optat, atque
              etiam amplius.
          nunc certa res est, eodem pacto ut comici servi
              solent.
          coniciam in collum pallium, primo ex med hanc
              rem ut audiat :
          speroque me ob hunc nuntium aeternum adeptu-
              rum cibum.   780
IV. 2.
Hegio   Quanto in pectore hanc rem meo magis voluto,
          tanto mi aegritudo auctior est in animo.
          ad illum modum sublitum os esse mi hodie !
              neque id perspicere quivi.
          quod cum scibitur, tum per urbem inridebor.
          cum extemplo ad forum advenero, omnes lo-
              quentur :
          " hic illest senex doctus, quoi verba data sunt."
          sed Ergasilus estne hic, procul quem video ?
          conlecto quidem est pallio.   quidnam acturust ?

          ───────────────
          [1] Leo notes lacuna here : *mihi (quod domist)* Schoell.
          536

THE CAPTIVES

ACT IV

(It is to be assumed that several hours only have elapsed.)

ENTER *Ergasilus*, ELATED.

Erg.   Great God on high, thou dost preserve me and prosper me with fatness! Boundless abundance, yea, sublime abundance dost thou bring me! Praise, profit, pleasure, jollity, festivity, feasting, trains of victuals, eatables, drinkables, satiety, joy! Never will I toady to human being more, I now resolve it. Why, I can bless my friend or blast my foe, now that this delightful day has loaded me down with its delightful delightfulness! I've landed a legacy stuffed fit to burst, and not a single encumbrance attached! Now for a race up to old Hegio here: I'm bringing him all the happiness he craves of Heaven, yes, and more, too. I know what I'll do now: like slaves in the comedies, I'll bundle my cloak round my neck and run, so that I'll be the first man he hears this news from: and I hope to get food for ever and ever for my information.

Scene 2.   ENTER *Hegio.*

Hegio   *(soliloquizing moodily)* The more I think it over, the sourer I feel. The idea of their playing upon me in that style to-day! And I couldn't see through it. When it gets known, I shall be the joke of the town. The moment I appear at the forum they'll all be saying: "Here comes that smart old fellow that got humbugged." *(observing Ergasilus)* But isn't that Ergasilus I see over there? With his cloak all tucked up, too! Now what in the world is he going to do? *(steps aside)*

537

Erg.   Move aps te moram atque, Ergasile, age hanc rem.   790
eminor interminorque, ne mi obstiterit obviam
nisi quis satis diu vixisse sese homo arbitrabitur.
nam qui obstiterit, ore sistet.

Hegio   Hic homo pugilatum incipit.

Erg.   Facere certumst. proinde ita omnes itinera in-
sistant sua,
ne quis in hanc plateam negoti conferat quicquam
sui.
nam meus est ballista pugnus, cubitus catapultast
mihi,
umerus aries, tum genu quemque icero ad terram
dabo,
dentilegos omnes mortales faciam, quemque offen-
dero.

Hegio   Quae illaec eminatiost nam? nequeo mirari satis.

Erg.   Faciam ut huius diei locique meique semper me-
minerit.[1]   800

Hegio   Quid hic homo tantum incipissit facere cum tantis
minis?

Erg.   Prius edico, ne quis propter culpam capiatur suam:
continete vos domi, prohibete a vobis vim meam.

Hegio   Mira edepol sunt, ni hic in ventrem sumpsit confi-
dentiam.
vae misero illi, cuius cibo iste factust imperiosior.

Erg.   Tum pistores scrofipasci, qui alunt furfuribus sues,
quarum odore praeterire nemo pistrinum potest:
eorum si quoiusquam scrofam in publico conspexero,
ex ipsis dominis meis pugnis exculcabo furfures.   810

---

[1] Leo brackets the following v., 801:
*Qui mihi in cursu opstiterit, faxo vitae is ex'emplo opsti-
terit suae.*
The man that stands in my path shall forthwith stand in
the way of his own existence.

Erg.   (*with burlesque importance and bustle*) No dawdling now, Ergasilus! At it, my boy, at it! I give you to wit by all the law's pains and penalties that no man stand in my way, unless he thinks he has lived long enough. For the man that does stand in my way shall stand on his head. (*squares off and delivers lusty blows at imaginary passers-by*)

Hegio   (*aside*) The fellow is going in for a boxing match!

Erg.   I'll do it, I'm resolved. So everybody keep where they belong, and don't anyone bring his business into this street! I tell you what, my fist is a siege-gun, and this forearm is my catapult, and my shoulder is a battering ram, yes, and every man I lay my knee into will bite the earth. I'll make every man I meet a tooth-collector.

Hegio   (*aside*) What on earth does all this bluster mean? Quite unaccountable!

Erg.   I'll make him remember this day and this place and me for ever.

Hegio   (*aside*) What giant undertaking is the fellow at, with all this big talk?

Erg.   I give you due notice, that no one may come to grief through his own ignorance of the law: stay at home: keep away from me—I am a violent man.

Hegio   (*aside*) Bless my soul! I'll be sworn he's got some assurance put into his inside. Heaven help the poor wretch whose larder has set him up so!

Erg.   And as for the millers that keep sows, and feed waste stuff to their swine, that raise such a stench nobody can go by the mill,—if I spy a sow of any one of 'em on the public highway, I'll up with my fists and stamp the stuffing out of those sows'—owners.

Hegio   Basilicas edictiones atque imperiosas habet:
         satur homost, habet profecto in ventre confiden-
            tiam.

Erg.   Tum piscatores, qui praebent populo pisces foetidos,
         qui advehuntur quadrupedanti crucianti cantherio,
         quorum odos subbasilicanos omnes abigit in forum,
         eis ego ora verberabo surpiculis piscariis,
         ut sciant, alieno naso quam exhibeant molestiam.
         tum lanii autem, qui concinnant liberis orbas oves,
         qui locant caedundos agnos et duplam agninam
            danunt,
         qui petroni nomen indunt verveci sectario,   820
         eum ego si in via petronem publica conspexero,
         et petronem et dominum reddam mortales miser-
            rumos.

Hegio   Eugepae, edictiones aedilicias hic quidem habet,
         mirumque adeost ni hunc fecere sibi Aetoli agora-
            nomum.

Erg.   Non ego nunc parasitus sum, sed regum rex regalior,
         tantus ventri commeatus meo adest in portu cibus.
         sed ego cesso hunc Hegionem onerare laetitia
            senem,
         quo homine hominum adaeque nemo vivit fortuna-
            tior?

Hegio   Quae illaec est laetitia, quam illic laetus largitur
            mihi?

Erg.   Heus ubi estis? ecquis hic est? ecquis hoc aperit
            ostium?   830

Hegio   Hic homo ad cenam recipit se ad me.
Erg.   Aperite hasce ambas fores
         prius quam pultando assulatim foribus exitium
            adfero.

Hegio   Perlubet hunc hominem colloqui. Ergasile.
Erg.   Ergasilum qui vocat?

THE CAPTIVES

Hegio   (*aside*) Right royal and imperious pronunciamentos.
The man is gorged: he certainly has got some
assurance stowed away inside.

Erg.   Then the fishmongers that travel around on a
jogging, jolting gelding, and offer folk stale fish so
strong it drives every last lounger in the arcade
out into the forum—I'll whack their faces with
their own fish baskets, just to teach 'em what an
abomination they are to the public nose. Yes,
and the butchers, too, that bereave sheep of their
little ones, that engage to sell you lambs fit for
slaughter, and then give you lamb as old as two
lambs, and pass off a tough old ram as a prime
wether—if I spy that ram on a city thoroughfare,
I'll make ram and owner the saddest men alive!

Hegio   (*aside*) Splendid! Why, he is issuing edicts like a
Comptroller of the Victualling: I shouldn't be
surprised if the Aetolians have made him market
inspector.

Erg.   I'm no parasite now, not I! I'm a precious potent
potentate of potentates, with all that invoice at
the harbour for my belly—food, food! But I
must hurry and load old Hegio here with ecstasy.
There's not a luckier man alive than he!

Hegio   (*aside*) What ecstasy is it this ecstatic creature is
going to lavish on me?

Erg.   (*pounding on Hegio's door*) Hi! Where are you?
Anybody here? Anybody going to open this door?

Hegio   (*aside*) The fellow is coming to dine with me.

Erg.   Open this door—both doors—before I knock 'em
to flinders and finish 'em for good and all!

Hegio   (*aside*) I should quite enjoy a word with him.
(*aloud*) Ergasilus!

Erg.   (*still pounding*) Who calls Ergasilus?

541

Hegio   Respice.

Erg.   Fortuna quod tibi nec facit nec faciet, me iubes.
  sed quis est?

Hegio   Respice ad me, Hegio sum.

Erg.   Oh mihi,
  quantum est hominum optumorum optume, in
  tempore advenis.

Hegio   Nescio quem ad portum nactus es ubi cenes, eo
  fastidis.

Erg.   Cedo manum.

Hegio   Manum?

Erg.   Manum, inquam, cedo tuam actutum.

Hegio   Tene.

Erg.   Gaude.

Hegio   Quid ego gaudeam?

Erg.   Quia ego impero, age gaude modo.

Hegio   Pol maerores mi antevortunt gaudiis.[1]   840

Erg.   Iam ego ex corpore exigam omnis maculas mae-
  rorum tibi.
  gaude audacter.

Hegio   Gaudeo, etsi nil scio quod gaudeam.

Erg.   Bene facis.   iube—

Hegio   Quid iubeam?

Erg.   Ignem ingentem fieri.

Hegio   Ignem ingentem?

Erg.   Ita dico, magnus ut sit.

Hegio   Quid?   me, volturi,
  tuan causa aedis incensurum censes?

Erg.   Noli irascier.
  iuben an non iubes astitui aulas, patinas elui,
  [2] laridum atque epulas foveri foculis ferventibus?
  alium pisces praestinatum abire?

---

[1] *Noli irascier* follows in MSS : Leo brackets.
[2] Corrupt (Leo) : *laridum ac pernas* Schoell.

Hegio Vouchsafe me a look, sir.

Erg. (*without turning his head*) Vouchsafe you a look, eh! That is more than Good Luck does for you, or ever will do, either! Who is it, though?

Hegio Look around this way. It's Hegio.

Erg. (*rushing up*) Oh! oh! You best of all the best men that tread the earth, you come just in time!

Hegio You have hit upon some one or other at the harbour to dine with: that's why you are so haughty.

Erg. (*rapturously*) Give me your hand!

Hegio My hand?

Erg. Your hand, I say—give me your hand this instant!

Hegio (*doing so*) Take it. (*Ergasilus shakes it vigorously*)

Erg. Rejoice!

Hegio Rejoice—I? What for?

Erg. Because I bid you to. Come now, rejoice!

Hegio Good Lord, man! grief takes precedence of joy in my case.

Erg. I will remove every grief spot from off your person for you this minute. Rejoice, rejoice boldly!

Hegio Well, I am rejoicing, although I haven't the least idea why I should.

Erg. Much obliged! Order—

Hegio (*suspiciously*) Order what?

Erg. —a fire to be built, an enormous fire.

Hegio An enormous fire?

Erg. That's what I say—make it a big one.

Hegio (*angry*) How's that? Do you think I'm going to burn my house down for your benefit, you vulture?

Erg. Calm yourself, sir. Will you order the pots to be set near the oven, or won't you—and the platters washed—and bacon and lovely things to eat to be warmed up in fire-pans piping hot? And some one to go and lay in fish?

Hegio	Hic vigilans somniat.
Erg.	Alium porcinam atque agninam et pullos gallina- ceos?
Hegio	Scis bene esse, si sit unde.
Erg.	[1] Pernam atque ophthalmiam, 850 horaeum, scombrum et trygonum et cetum, et mol- lem caseum?
Hegio	Nominandi istorum tibi erit magis quam edundi copia hic apud me, Ergasile.
Erg.	Mean me causa hoc censes dicere?
Hegio	Nec nihil hodie nec multo plus tu hic edes, ne frustra sis. proin tu tui cottidiani victi ventrem ad me afferas.
Erg.	Quin ita faciam, ut tute cupias facere sumptum, etsi ego vetem.
Hegio	Egone?
Erg.	Tune.
Hegio	Tum tu mi igitur erus es.
Erg.	Immo benevolens. vin te faciam fortunatum?
Hegio	Malim quam miserum quidem.
Erg.	Cedo manum.
Hegio	Em manum.
Erg.	Di te onmes adiuvant.
Hegio	Nil sentio
Erg.	Non enim es in senticeto, eo non sentis. sed iube 860 vasa tibi pura apparari ad rem divinam cito, atque agnum afferri proprium pinguem.
Hegio	Cur?

[1] Corrupt (Leo): *pern[ul]am* Geppert.

544

Hegio	Day dreams, poor fellow!
Erg.	And some one else to get pork and lamb and spring chicken?
Hegio	You know how to enjoy yourself—given the wherewithal.
Erg.	And ham and river-lamprey and pickled fish, mackerel and sting ray and tunny, and nice soft cheese?
Hegio	You will have more of an opportunity to mention those viands, Ergasilus, than to masticate them here at my house.
Erg.	Do you suppose I'm saying this on my own account?
Hegio	What you get here to-day will be a cross between nothing and next to nothing; make no mistake about that. So bring me a stomach that is ready for your ordinary fare.
Erg.	Why, I'll make you long to squander money, you yourself, even though I should forbid it.
Hegio	Me?
Erg.	Yes, sir, you!
Hegio	Then you are my master, I take it.
Erg.	No, no, your whole-souled friend. Do you want me to make you a fortunate man?
Hegio	Rather than unfortunate, why, yes.
Erg.	Give me your hand.
Hegio	Here it is. (*Ergasilus again shakes it fervently*)
Erg.	The gods are with you!
Hegio	I wouldn't know it.
Erg.	You wouldn't? Well, you're out of the wood; that's why you don't twig it. But see they get the holy vessels ready for worship—quick! Yes, and have a special lamb brought in, a fat one.
Hegio	Why?

545

Erg.   Ut sacrufices.

Hegio   Cui deorum?

Erg.   Mi hercle, nam ego nunc tibi sum summus Iuppiter,
idem ego sum Salus, Fortuna, Lux, Laetitia, Gaudium.

proin tu deum hunc saturitate facias tranquillum tibi.

Hegio   Esurire mihi videre.

Erg.   Mi quidem esurio, non tibi.

Hegio   Tuo arbitratu, facile patior.

Erg.   Credo, consuetu's puer.

Hegio   Iuppiter te dique perdant.

Erg.   Te hercle—mi aequom est gratias
agere ob nuntium; tantum ego nunc porto a portu
tibi boni:

nunc tu mihi places.

Hegio   Abi, stultu's, sero post tempus venis.   870

Erg.   Igitur olim si advenissem, magis tu tum istuc
diceres;

nunc hanc laetitiam accipe a me, quam fero. nam
filium

tuom modo in portu Philopolemum vivom, salvom
et sospitem

vidi in publica celoce, ibidemque illum adulescen-
tulum

Aleum una et tuom Stalagmum servom, qui aufugit
domo,

qui tibi surripuit quadrimum puerum filiolum tuom.

Hegio   Abi in malam rem, ludis me.

Erg.   Ita me amabit sancta Saturitas,
Hegio, itaque suo me semper condecoret cognomine,
ut ego vidi.

Hegio   Meum gnatum?

Erg.   Tuom gnatum et genium meum.

Hegio   Et captivom illum Alidensem?

546

Erg.   So that you may offer sacrifice.

Hegio   To what deity?

Erg.   To me, by gad! For I'm your Jupiter Most High now, myself; and Salvation, Fortune, Light, Gladness, Joy—they're all this identical I! So mind you placate this divinity by stuffing him full.

Hegio   You need food, I fancy.

Erg.   No sir, I need food I fancy, not food you fancy.

Hegio   (*smiling*) Have it your own way: I'm perfectly willing to—crawl.

Erg.   Crawl? I believe you: it's a habit you—fell into —as a child.

Hegio   (*disgusted*) Oh, you be damned, sir!

Erg.   And by Jove, you be—grateful to me, as you ought, for my news. The glorious news from the port I'm just reporting! Now your dinner begins to tempt me.

Hegio   Be off, you idiot: you're behind time, you have come too late.

Erg.   Well, if I had come before, then you'd have had more reason to say that. (*slowly and portentously*) Now, sir, prepare for the ecstasy of which I am the vehicle. A few minutes ago at the harbour your son, your son Philopolemus, alive, safe and sound, —I saw him, saw him in a despatch boat, and along with him that young Elean and your slave Stalagmus that stole your little four year old boy.

Hegio   To the devil with you! You're making fun of me.

Erg.   So help me Holy Stuffing, so may she grace me with her name for evermore—I did see them, Hegio!

Hegio   (*sceptically*) My son?

Erg.   Your son and my guardian angel.

Hegio   And that Elean prisoner?

Erg.	Μὰ τὸν Ἀπόλλω.
Hegio	Et servolum 880

meum Stalagmum, meum qui gnatum surripuit?

Erg.	Ναὶ τὰν Κόραν.
Hegio	Iam credo?
Erg	Ναὶ τὰν Πραινέστην.
Hegio.	Venit?
Erg.	Ναὶ τὰν Σιγνίαν.
Hegio	Certon?
Erg.	Ναὶ τὸν Φρουσινῶνα.
Hegio	Vide sis.
Erg.	Ναὶ τὸν Ἀλάτριον.
Hegio	Quid tu per barbaricas urbes iuras?
Erg.	Quia enim item asperae

sunt ut tuom victum autumabas esse.

Hegio	Vae aetati tuae.
Erg.	Quippe quando mihi nil credis, quod ego dico sedulo.

sed Stalagmus quoius erat tunc nationis, cum hinc
abit?

Hegio	Siculus.
Erg.	At nunc Siculus non est, Boius est, Boiam terit:

liberorum quaerundorum causa ei, credo, uxor
datast.

Hegio	Dic, bonan fide tu mi istaec verba dixisti?
Erg.	Bona. 890
Hegio	Di immortales, iterum gnatus videor, si vera

autumas.

Erg.	Ain tu? dubium habebis etiam, sancte quom ego

iurem tibi?

postremo, Hegio, si parva iuri iurandost fides,
vise ad portum.

548

Erg.   *Oui, par* Hercules!

Hegio   And that miserable slave of mine, Stalagmus, that kidnapped my son?

Erg.   *Oui, par* Hercul-aneum!

Hegio   I'm to believe that?

Erg.   *Oui, par* Pompeii!

Hegio   He's come?

Erg.   *Oui, par* Sorrento!

Hegio   You're sure?

Erg.   *Oui, par* Amalfi!

Hegio   Careful now!

Erg.   *Oui, par* Torre dell'Annunziata!

Hegio   What are you swearing by foreign cities for!

Erg.   Well, because they're the same as you said your meals were—perfect terrors.

Hegio   Plague take you!

Erg.   My sentiments exactly, seeing you don't believe a word I tell you in sober earnest. Stalagmus, though, —what was his nationality when he disappeared?

Hegio   Sicilian.

Erg.   But he's no Sicilian now: he's a Gaul—he's being galled,[1] anyhow, by that thing he's attached to: he's coupled with the article so as to get children, I suppose?

Hegio   See here, have you told me all this in good faith?

Erg.   In good faith.

Hegio   Great heavens! I feel like a new man, if what you say is true.

Erg.   Eh? How's that? You'll still doubt me when I'd give you my sacred word on it? Very well then, Hegio, if my solemn oath is insufficient for you, go down to the harbour and see for yourself.

---

[1] Boia means a woman of the Boii, also a malefactor's collar.

Hegio   Facere certumst. tu intus cura quod opus est.
sume, posce, prome quid vis. te facio cellarium.

Erg.   Nam hercle, nisi mantiscinatus probe ero, fusti
pectito.

Hegio   Aeternum tibi dapinabo victum, si vera autumas.

Erg.   Unde id?

Hegio   A me meoque gnato.

Erg.   Sponden tu istud?

Hegio   Spondeo.

Erg.   At ego tuom tibi advenisse filium respondeo.

Hegio   Cura quam optume potes.

IV. 3

Erg.   Bene ambula et redambula.   900
illic hinc abiit, mihi rem summam credidit cibariam.
di immortales, iam ut ego collos praetruncabo
tegoribus,
quanta pernis pestis veniet, quanta labes larido,
quanta sumini absumedo, quanta callo calamitas,
quanta laniis lassitudo, quanta porcinariis.
nam si alia memorem, quae ad ventris victum con-
ducunt, morast.
nunc ibo, ut pro praefectura mea ius dicam larido,
et quae pendent indemnatae pernae, eis auxilium
ut feram.

IV. 4.

Puer   Diespiter te dique, Ergasile, perdant et ventrem
tuom,

550

Hegio	(*excited*) Precisely what I will do. You go inside and attend to what's needed. Take anything you want, ask for it, get it from the store-room. I make you butler.
Erg.	(*wild with joy*) Now by Jupiter, if I don't do some handsome catering, comb me down with a club!
Hegio	I'll dinner you till doomsday, if it's true.
Erg.	And who's to pay?
Hegio	I and my son.
Erg.	I have your word on that?
Hegio	My word.
Erg.	And for my part, my word to you is—your son has arrived.
Hegio	(*making off toward harbour*) Attend to everything the very best you can.

Scene 3.

Erg.	A pleasant walk and—backwalk—to you. [EXIT *Hegio*] He's gone! And the whole blessed commissariat left to me! Ye immortal gods! how I'll knock necks off backs now! Ah, ham's case is hopeless, and bacon's in a bad, bad way! And sow's udder—done for utterly! Oh, how pork rind will go to pot! Butchers and pig-dealers—won't I bustle 'em! Why, if I should mention all the other things that go to bolster up a belly, it would be a waste of time. I must off this minute to perform my official duties and pass judgment on bacon and help out hams that are still untried and in suspense.

[EXIT INTO HOUSE, HURRIEDLY : UPROAR WITHIN.

Scene 4.   ENTER *Page*, ANGRY AND EXCITED, FROM *Hegio's* HOUSE.

Page	(*shaking his fist at door*) May all the powers of heaven destroy you, Ergasilus, and that belly of

parasitosque omnis, et qui posthac cenam parasitis
    dabit.   910
clades calamitasque, intemperies modo in nostram
    advenit domum.
quasi lupus esuriens ille metui ne in me faceret
    impetum.
ubi [1] voltus esurientis vidi, eius extimescebam
    impetum
nimisque hercle ego illum male formidabam, ita
    frendebat dentibus.
adveniens deturbavit totum cum carne carnarium :
arripuit gladium, praetruncavit tribus tegoribus
    glandia ;
aulas calicesque omnes confregit, nisi quae modiales
    erant.
cocum percontabatur, possentne scriae fervescere.
cellas refregit omnis intus reclusitque armarium.
adservate istunc, sultis, servi. ego ibo, ut conve-
    niam senem.
dicam ut sibi penum alium adornet, siquidem sese
    uti volet ;   920
nam hic quidem, ut adornat, aut iam nihil est aut
    iam nihil erit.

ACTVS V

Hegio   Iovi disque ago gratias merito magnas,
    quom reducem tuo te patri reddiderunt
    quomque ex miseriis plurimis me exemerunt,
    quae adhuc te carens dum hic[2] fui sustentabam,
    quomque hunc conspicor in potestate nostra,
    quomque huius reperta est fides firma nobis.

    [1] *voltus esurientis* (*vidi, eius extimescebam*) Leo : A
reading doubtful : other MSS omit the line.
    [2] Corrupt (Leo): *te carens dum hic* P : *carens dum huc* A.

yours and all parasites and anyone that gives a
parasite a meal hereafter! Disaster, devastation,
a tornado, has just fallen on our house. I was
afraid he'd jump at my throat like a ravening
wolf! As soon as I saw that ravenous look of his
I almost died for fear he'd make a rush at me—
Lord, how he did scare me, how he kept grinding
his teeth! In he came and tugged down the
meat, rack and all—grabbed a knife and lopped
the choice bits off three necks of pork—and smashed
every pot and tureen that didn't hold a peck or
more! Kept asking the cook if he couldn't possibly
use the big pickle vats to boil things in! Broke
into all the cupboards and raided the pantry!
(*shouting to those within*) Hi, boys! watch him, will
you! I'm going to find the old man. I'll tell
him, so that he can get in more victuals for himself, that is if he wants any for his own use: for
to judge from the way this fellow is getting 'em
out here, there's nothing left now, or won't be
long. [EXIT.

ACT V

(*Half an hour has elapsed.*)
ENTER *Hegio, Philopolemus, Philocrates*, AND
Stalagmus.

Hegio (*to Philopolemus*) I thank God with all my heart, as
I ought, for bringing you back to your father, and
for relieving me of the dreadful anguish I've been
enduring as day after day went by, and I still here
without you; yes, and for letting me see this
rascal (*indicating Stalagmus*) in my power, and for
this gentleman's (*indicating Philocrates*) proving himself a man of honour in standing by his promise to us.

553

Philop. Satis iam dolui ex animo, et cura me satis et lacru-
　　mis maceravi,
　　satis iam audivi tuas aerumnas, ad portum mihi
　　quas memorasti.
　　hoc agamus.

Philocr.　　　　　Quid nunc, quoniam tecum servavi fidem　930
　　tibique hunc reducem in libertatem feci?

Hegio　　　　　　　　　　　Fecisti ut tibi,
　　Philocrates, numquam referre gratiam possim satis,
　　proinde ut tu promeritu's de me et filio.

Philop.　　　　　　　　　　　Immo potes,
　　pater, et poteris et ego potero, et di eam potesta-
　　　tem dabunt
　　ut beneficium bene merenti nostro merito muneres;
　　sicut tu huic [1] potes, pater mi, facere merito max-
　　　ume.

Hegio Quid opust verbis? lingua nullast qua negem quid-
　　quid roges.

Philocr. Postulo abs te, ut mi illum reddas servom, quem
　　hic reliqueram
　　pignus pro me, qui mihi melior quam sibi semper fuit,
　　pro bene factis eius ut ei pretium possim reddere.　940

Hegio Quod bene fecisti referetur gratia id quod postulas;
　　et id et aliud, quod me orabis, impetrabis. atque te
　　nolim suscensere quod ego iratus ei feci male.

Philocr. Quid fecisti?

Hegio　　　　　In lapicidinas compeditum condidi,
　　ubi rescivi mihi data esse verba.

　　　　　　　　[1] *tu huic* MSS : *nunc* Leo.

554

Philop. (*seeing Philocrates is getting impatient*) I've had quite enough bitter suffering, and enough of wearing myself out with anxiety and weeping, too, and I've heard quite enough of your distress of which you told me at the harbour, father! So now to the main point. (*turns to Philocrates*)

Philocr. (*to Hegio*) What of me, sir, now that I have kept faith with you and secured the liberty of your son here?

Hegio After the way you have acted, Philocrates, I'm entirely unable to show gratitude enough for your treatment of me and my son.

Philop. No, no, you are able, father, yes, and always will be able, and so shall I be, and Heaven will give you the ability to do a deserved kindness to a man that has been so kind to us. It's just as with this slave here, (*pointing to Stalagmus*) father dear; you're able to give him his full deserts.

Hegio (*to Philocrates*) It's plain enough, sir,—I have no tongue with which to refuse a request of yours.

Philocr. What I ask you to do is to give me back the slave I left here as security for myself—he was always ready to sacrifice himself for me!—so that I can reward him for his kindnesses.

Hegio You have been kind to us, sir, and I shall be glad to do as you ask; both that request, and any other, will be granted. (*embarrassed*) And—and I trust you won't be incensed at me for getting angry and treating him badly.

Philocr. (*anxiously*) What did you do?

Hegio I had him fettered and put down in the stone quarries when I found out I had been imposed upon.

555

Philocr.   Vae misero mihi,
         propter meum caput labores homini evenisse op-
            tumo.

Hegio At ob eam rem mihi libellam pro eo argenti ne
            duis :
         gratiis a me, ut sit liber, ducito.

Philocr.   Edepol, Hegio,
         facis benigne. sed quaeso, hominem ut iubeas
            arcessi.

Hegio   Licet.
         ubi estis vos? ite actutum, Tyndarum huc arces-   950
            site.
         vos ite intro. interibi ego ex hac statua verberea
            volo
         erogitare, meo minore quid sit factum filio.
         vos lavate interibi.

Philop.   Sequere hac, Philocrates, me intro.

Philocr.   Sequor.
V. 2.

Hegio Age tu illuc procede, bone vir, lepidum mancu-
            pium meum.

Stal. Quid me oportet facere, ubi tu talis vir falsum
            autumas ?
         fui ego bellus, lepidus : bonus vir numquam, neque
            frugi bonae,
         neque ero umquam, ne erres : spem ponas me
            bonae frugi fore.

Hegio Propemodum ubi loci fortunae tuae sint facile in-
            tellegis.
         si eris verax, tua ex re, facies ex mala meliusculam
         recte et vera loquere, sed neque vere neque tu   960
            recte adhuc
         fecisti umquam.

556

Philocr. God forgive me! To think of the splendid fellow suffering so, and all for my sake!

Hegio Well, sir, this being so, you needn't give me a single farthing for him: take him from me gratis —he is a free man.

Philocr. Well, well, Hegio, many thanks! But have him sent for, I beg you.

Hegio By all means. *(calling to slaves in house)* Where are you? [ENTER OVERSEERS] Quick! go bring Tyndarus here. [EXEUNT OVERSEERS] *(to Philopolemus and Philocrates)* As for you lads, step inside. Meanwhile I want to inquire of this whipping post here *(pointing to Stalagmus)* what was done with my younger son. You can take a bath meanwhile.

Philop. Come along in with me, Philocrates.

Philocr. Certainly. [EXEUNT.

Scene 2.

Hegio *(to Stalagmus)* Come now, you! Over there with you, *(pointing)* my good sir, my charming piece of property.

Stal. *(sullenly)* What can you look for from me, when a fine gentleman like you tells lies? I've had my day as a dandy, a charmer: a good sir, or good for anything, I never was, and I never will be, make no mistake: don't you build up hopes I will be good for anything.

Hegio You have no difficulty in appreciating your position pretty fairly well. Now be truthful, and you'll be acting to your own advantage and make a bad prospect somewhat better. Out with your story; make it straightforward and honest— virtues you have never displayed hitherto, however-

T

Stal.	Quod ego fatear, credin pudeat cum autumes?
Hegio	At ego faciam ut pudeat, nam in ruborem te totum dabo.
Stal.	Eia, credo ego imperito plagas minitaris mihi.
	tandem ista aufer ac dic quid fers, ut feras hinc quod petis.
Hegio	Satis facundu's. sed iam fieri dicta compendi volo.
Stal.	Ut vis fiat.
Hegio	Bene morigerus fuit puer, nunc non decet.
	hoc agamus. iam animum advorte ac mihi quae dicam edissere.[1]
Stal.	Nugae istaec sunt. non me censes scire quid dignus siem?
Hegio	At ea subterfugere potis es pauca, si non omnia.
Stal.	Pauca effugiam, scio; nam multa evenient, et merito meo,
	quia et fugi et tibi surripui filium et eum vendidi.
Hegio	Cui homini?
Stal.	Theodoromedi in Alide Polyplusio, sex minis.
Hegio	Pro di immortales, is quidem huius est pater Philocrati.
Stal.	Quin melius novi quam tu et vidi saepius.
Hegio	Serva, Iuppiter supreme, et me et meum gnatum mihi.
	Philocrates, per tuom te genium obsecro, exi, te volo.

970 *(marginal line number, opposite* At ea subterfugere...*)*

---

[1] Leo brackets the following v., 968 :
   si eris verax, ex tuis rebus feceris meliusculas.

Stal.   When I'm ready to admit a thing myself d'ye think I should be ashamed of it just because you say it's so?

Hegio   I'll make you ashamed, though: (*savagely*) I tell you what, I'll make one big blush of you.

Stal.   (*ironically*) La! La! I'm promised a whipping, it seems, and I such a novice at it—oh, yes I am! Look here, get done with that talk and say what you've got to propose, so as to get what you're after.

Hegio   Quite a gift of tongue, sir! But oblige me by saving some of it for the moment.

Stal.   Anything you like.

Hegio   (*half aside*) That compliance he showed as a boy hardly becomes him at present. (*aloud*) To business! Now then, pay attention and answer me fully.

Stal.   Rot! Don't you suppose I know what I deserve?

Hegio   Well, you have a chance to escape a little of it, if not all.

Stal.   Little enough I'll escape, I know that; for there'll be plenty coming, and it serves me right, seeing I ran away and kidnapped your son and sold him.

Hegio   To whom?

Stal.   (*drawling*) Theodoromedes Goldfields, in Elis, for twenty-four pounds.

Hegio   God bless my soul! Why, he is the father of Philocrates here!

Stal.   Well, I know him better than you, and I've seen him oftener.

Hegio   God Almighty, save me and save my boy for me! (*running to door and shouting*) Philocrates! Here, here, come, on your life! I want you!

V. 3.

Philocr. Hegio, assum.   si quid me vis, impera.

Hegio   Hic gnatum meum
tuo patri ait se vendidisse sex minis in Alide.

Philocr. Quam diu id factum est?

Stal.   His annus incipit vicensimus.   980

Philocr. Falsa memorat.

Stal.   Aut ego aut tu.   nam tibi quadrimulum
tuos pater peculiarem parvolo puero dedit.

Philocr. Quid erat ei nomen? si vera dicis, memoradum
mihi.

Stal.   Paegnium vocitatust, post vos indidistis Tyndaro.

Philocr. Cur ego te non novi?

Stal.   Quia mos est oblivisci hominibus
neque novisse cuius nihili sit faciunda gratia.

Philocr. Dic mihi, isne istic fuit, quem vendidisti meo patri,
qui mihi peculiaris datus est?

Stal.   Huius filius.

Hegio Vivitne is homo?

Stal.   Argentum accepi, nil curavi ceterum.

Hegio Quid tu ais?

Philocr.   Quin istic ipsust Tyndarus tuos filius,   990
ut quidem hic argumenta loquitur. nam is mecum
  a puero puer
bene pudiceque educatust usque ad adulescentiam.

Hegio Et miser sum et fortunatus, si vos vera dicitis;
eo miser sum quia male illi feci, si gnatust meus.

560

THE CAPTIVES

Scene 3.   [ENTER *Philocrates*.

Philocr. Here I am, Hegio. If I can be of any service, command me.

Hegio (*beside himself*) This fellow says my son—he sold him to your father—for twenty-four pounds—in Elis!

Philocr. How long ago was this?

Stal. Going on for twenty years.

Philocr. He's lying.

Stal. (*indifferent*) One of us is. As a matter of fact, your father gave you a little four year old boy for your own, when you were nothing but a youngster yourself.

Philocr. (*interested*) What was his name? If your story is true, come, tell me that.

Stal. Styled Pettie, he was: later on you folks called him Tyndarus.

Philocr. How is it I don't know you?

Stal. Because it's the regular thing to forget a fellow and cut him, in case his good will can't help you at all.

Philocr. Tell me, was that boy you sold my father the same one that was given me for my own?

Stal. (*with a nod in Hegio's direction*) His son.

Hegio (*eagerly*) Is he alive, this—man?

Stal. I got the money: that's all I bothered about.

Hegio (*to Philocrates*) What do you say?

Philocr. Why, it's Tyndarus himself that is your son, at least according to this fellow's evidence. For Tyndarus has been brought up with me from the time we were boys, and brought up in good honest fashion.

Hegio I feel miserable and happy both, if what you two say is true! Miserable at having been so hard on

T*   561

eheu, quom ego plus minusve feci quam me aequom
  fuit.
quod male feci crucior; modo si infectum fieri
  possiet.
sed eccum incedit huc ornatus haud ex suis virtu-
  tibus.

V. 4.

Tynd. Vidi ego multa saepe picta, quae Acherunti fierent
cruciamenta, verum enim vero nulla adaeque est
  Acheruns
atque ubi ego fui, in lapicidinis. illic ibi de-
  mumst locus,   1000
ubi labore lassitudo est exigunda ex corpore.
nam ubi illo adveni, quasi patriciis pueris aut
  monerulae,
aut anites aut coturnices dantur, quicum lusitent
itidem mi haec advenienti upupa, qui me delectem,
  datast.
sed erus eccum ante ostium, et erus alter eccum
  ex Alide
rediit.

Hegio   Salve, exoptate gnate mi.
Tynd.   Hem, quid gnate mi?
attat, scio cur te patrem adsimules esse et me
  filium:
quia mi item ut parentes lucis das tuendi copiam.
Philocr. Salve, Tyndare.
Tynd.   Et tu, quoius causa hanc aerumnam
  exigo.
Philocr. At nunc liber in divitias faxo venies. nam tibi   1010
pater hic est; hic servos, qui te huic hinc quadrimum surpuit,
vendidit patri meo te sex minis, is te mihi
parvolum peculiarem parvolo puero dedit:

him, if he is my own boy! Dear, dear! how much
more I've done than I ought, or how much less! It's
torment, to think of the horrible thing I've done—
oh, if it could only be undone! (*looking down street*)
Look, though,—there he comes! To be decked
out like that, the noble fellow!

ENTER *Tyndarus* ESCORTED BY OVERSEERS. HE IS

Scene 4. HEAVILY IRONED AND CARRIES A CROWBAR

Tynd. (*dryly*) I have seen a good many pictures whose
subject was torture in Hell: but upon my soul,
there is no hell that can match those stone quarries
where I've been. That place down there is certainly the one where a weary man can be dead
sure of working off his tired feeling. Why, when
I got there it was just like your young scions of
the nobility being given daws or ducks or quails
for playfellows: my own case exactly—the moment I arrived they gave me this crow to have
a lark with. (*looking toward Hegio's house*) But
there's my master in front of the door—and, yes,
my other master back from Elis!

Hegio Oh, how are you, my own longed-for son?

Tynd. Eh? " My son? " How's that? (*pauses, then with
a weary laugh*) Ah, yes, yes, I see the point of your
father and son chaff: just as parents do, you give
me a chance to behold the light of day.

Philocr. God bless you, Tyndarus!

Tynd. And you, sir, for whose sake I'm undergoing this
confounded experience.

Philocr. But now you shall be a free man, Tyndarus, and a
rich one, I promise you. For here is (*indicating
Hegio*) your father; this slave (*indicating Stalagmus*) stole you away from him here when you were
four years old and sold you to my father for

563

illic indicium fecit; nam hunc ex Alide huc re-
duximus.

Tynd. Quid huius filium?

Philocr. Intus eccum fratrem germanum tuom.[1]

Tynd. Nunc edepol demum in memoriam regredior, au-
disse me
quasi per nebulam, Hegionem meum patrem voca-
rier.

Hegio Is ego sum.

Philocr. Compedibus quaeso ut tibi sit levior filius
atque huic gravior servos.

Hegio Certum est principio id praevortier.
eamus intro, ut arcessatur faber, ut istas compedes
tibi adimam, huic dem.

Stal. Quoi peculi nihil est, recte feceris.

---

[1] Leo brackets the following v., 1016–1022:

Tynd. *Quid tu ais? adduxtin illum huius captivom filium?*
Philocr. *Quin, inquam, intus hic est.*
Tynd. *Fecisti edepol et recte et bene.*
Philocr. *Nunc tibi pater hic est: hic fur est tuos, qui parvom hinc
te abstulit.*
Tynd. *At ego hunc grandis grandem natu ob furtum ad carnificem
dabo.*
Philocr. *Meritus est.*
Tynd. *Ergo edepol merito meritam mercedem dabo.* 1020
sed tu dic oro: pater meus tune es?
Hegio *Ego sum, gnate mi.*
Tynd. *Nunc demum in memoriam redeo, cum mecum recogito.*

	twenty-four pounds. And when we were both small boys, father gave you to me for my own. That fellow there has proved it all; you see we brought him back here from Elis.
Tynd.	(*dazed*) What about his son?
Philocr.	Look—inside there—your own brother! [1]
Tynd.	Great heavens! When I think back I do now at last remember hearing—in a cloudy sort of way—my father called Hegio!
Hegio	(*embracing him*) I am that Hegio!
Philocr.	(*to Hegio, pointing to the shackles on Tyndarus*). Those irons, sir,—for mercy's sake get yourself a lighter son, and him a heavier slave. (*indicating Stalagmus*)
Hegio	Yes, yes, I must see to that first of all. Let's go inside and have a blacksmith sent for, so that I may get those irons off of you and make this fellow (*turning to Stalagmus*) a present of them.
Stal.	Thanks awfully—seeing I haven't a thing I can call my own. [EXEUNT OMNES.

---

[1] *Tynd.*	What do you say? Did you bring this gentleman's captive son?
Philocr.	Yes, yes, he's inside, I tell you.
Tynd.	By heaven, sir, you have acted fairly and honourably.
Philocr.	Now here is your father : and here is the thief who stole you away from here when you were small.
Tynd.	But now that we're both big, I'll hand him over to the executioner for that theft.
Philocr.	He deserves it.
Tynd.	Well then, I'll give him his deserved deserts deservedly, by gad! But you, sir, speak, I beseech you. Are you my father?
Hegio	I am, my dear lad.
Tynd.	Now at last I remember—when I think it over.

TITUS MACCIUS PLAUTUS

CATERVA

Spectatores, ad pudicos mores facta haec fabula
  est,
neque in hac subigitationes sunt neque ulla amatio 1030
nec pueri suppositio nec argenti circumductio,
neque ubi amans adulescens scortum liberet clam
  suom patrem.
huius modi paucas poetae reperiunt comoedias,
ubi boni meliores fiant. nunc vos, si vobis placet
et si placuimus neque odio fuimus, signum hoc
  mittite:
qui pudicitiae esse voltis praemium, plausum date.

THE CAPTIVES

EPILOGUE

SPOKEN BY THE COMPANY.

Spectators, this play was composed with due regard to the proprieties: here you have no vicious intrigues, no love affair, no supposititious child, no getting money on false pretences, no young spark setting a wench free without his father's knowledge. Dramatists find few plays such as this which make good men better. Now, if you so please, and if we have pleased you and have not been boring, intimate as much: you who wish virtue to be rewarded, give us your applause.

INDEX OF PROPER NAMES

The index is limited to names of characters in the plays, and of characters, persons, towns, countries and peoples mentioned in the plays.

INDEX

PRINTED IN GREAT BRITAIN
BY THE WINDMILL PRESS LTD
KINGSWOOD, SURREY

THE LOEB CLASSICAL LIBRARY

VOLUMES ALREADY PUBLISHED

Latin Authors

AMMIANUS MARCELLINUS. Translated by J. C. Rolfe. 3 Vols.

APULEIUS: THE GOLDEN ASS (METAMORPHOSES). W. Adlington (1566). Revised by S. Gaselee.

ST. AUGUSTINE: CITY OF GOD. 7 Vols. Vol. I. G. H. McCrackon. Vol. VI. W. C. Greene.

ST. AUGUSTINE, CONFESSIONS OF. W. Watts (1631). 2 Vols.

ST. AUGUSTINE, SELECT LETTERS. J. H. Baxter.

AUSONIUS. H. G. Evelyn White. 2 Vols.

BEDE. J. E. King. 2 Vols.

BOETHIUS: TRACTS and DE CONSOLATIONE PHILOSOPHIAE. Rev. H. F. Stewart and E. K. Rand.

CAESAR: ALEXANDRIAN, AFRICAN and SPANISH WARS. A. G. Way.

CAESAR: CIVIL WARS. A. G. Peskett.

CAESAR: GALLIC WAR. H. J. Edwards.

CATO: DE RE RUSTICA; VARRO: DE RE RUSTICA. H. B. Ash and W. D. Hooper.

CATULLUS. F. W. Cornish; TIBULLUS. J. B. Postgate; PERVIGILIUM VENERIS. J. W. Mackail.

CELSUS: DE MEDICINA. W. G. Spencer. 3 Vols.

CICERO: BRUTUS, and ORATOR. G. L. Hendrickson and H. M. Hubbell.

[CICERO]: AD HERENNIUM. H. Caplan.

CICERO: DE ORATORE, etc. 2 Vols. Vol. I. DE ORATORE, Books I. and II. E. W. Sutton and H. Rackham. Vol. II. DE ORATORE, Book III. De Fato; Paradoxa Stoicorum; De Partitione Oratoria. H. Rackham.

CICERO: DE FINIBUS. H. Rackham.

CICERO: DE INVENTIONE, etc. H. M. Hubbell.

CICERO: DE NATURA DEORUM and ACADEMICA. H. Rackham.

CICERO: DE OFFICIIS. Walter Miller.

CICERO: DE REPUBLICA and DE LEGIBUS; SOMNIUM SCIPIONIS. Clinton W. Keyes.

CICERO: DE SENECTUTE, DE AMICITIA, DE DIVINATIONE. W. A. Falconer.

CICERO: IN CATILINAM, PRO FLACCO, PRO MURENA, PRO SULLA. Louis E. Lord.

CICERO: LETTERS TO ATTICUS. E. O. Winstedt. 3 Vols.

CICERO: LETTERS TO HIS FRIENDS. W. Glynn Williams. 3 Vols.

CICERO: PHILIPPICS. W. C. A. Ker.

CICERO: PRO ARCHIA POST REDITUM, DE DOMO, DE HARUS-PICUM RESPONSIS, PRO PLANCIO. N. H. Watts.

CICERO: PRO CAECINA, PRO LEGE MANILIA, PRO CLUENTIO, PRO RABIRIO. H. Grose Hodge.

CICERO: PRO CAELIO, DE PROVINCIIS CONSULARIBUS, PRO BALBO. R. Gardner.

CICERO: PRO MILONE, IN PISONEM, PRO SCAURO, PRO FONTEIO, PRO RABIRIO POSTUMO, PRO MARCELLO, PRO LIGARIO, PRO REGE DEIOTARO. N. H. Watts.

CICERO: PRO QUINCTIO, PRO ROSCIO AMERINO, PRO ROSCIO COMOEDO, CONTRA RULLUM. J. H. Freese.

CICERO: PRO SESTIO, IN VATINIUM. R. Gardner.

CICERO: TUSCULAN DISPUTATIONS. J. E. King.

CICERO: VERRINE ORATIONS. L. H. G. Greenwood. 2 Vols.

CLAUDIAN. M. Platnauer. 2 Vols.

COLUMELLA: DE RE RUSTICA. DE ARBORIBUS. H. B. Ash, E. S. Forster and E. Heffner. 3 Vols.

CURTIUS, Q.: HISTORY OF ALEXANDER. J. C. Rolfe. 2 Vols.

FLORUS. E. S. Forster; and CORNELIUS NEPOS. J. C. Rolfe.

FRONTINUS: STRATAGEMS and AQUEDUCTS. C. E. Bennett and M. B. McElwain.

FRONTO: CORRESPONDENCE. C. R. Haines. 2 Vols.

GELLIUS, J. C. Rolfe. 3 Vols.

HORACE: ODES and EPODES. C. E. Bennett.

HORACE: SATIRES, EPISTLES, ARS POETICA. H. R. Fairclough.

JEROME: SELECTED LETTERS. F. A. Wright.

JUVENAL and PERSIUS. G. G. Ramsay.

LIVY. B. O. Foster, F. G. Moore, Evan T. Sage, and A. C. Schlesinger and R. M. Geer (General Index). 14 Vols.

LUCAN. J. D. Duff.

LUCRETIUS. W. H. D. Rouse.

MARTIAL. W. C. A. Ker. 2 Vols.

MINOR LATIN POETS: from PUBLILIUS SYRUS TO RUTILIUS NAMATIANUS, including GRATTIUS, CALPURNIUS SICULUS, NEMESIANUS, AVIANUS, and others with "Aetna" and the "Phoenix." J. Wight Duff and Arnold M. Duff.

OVID: THE ART OF LOVE and OTHER POEMS. J. H. Mozley.

2

OVID: FASTI. Sir James G. Frazer.

OVID: HEROIDES and AMORES. Grant Showerman.

OVID: METAMORPHOSES. F. J. Miller. 2 Vols.

OVID: TRISTIA and EX PONTO. A. L. Wheeler.

PERSIUS. Cf. JUVENAL.

PETRONIUS. M. Heseltine; SENECA: APOCOLOCYNTOSIS.
W. H. D. Rouse.

PLAUTUS. Paul Nixon. 5 Vols.

PLINY: LETTERS. Melmoth's Translation revised by W. M. L.
Hutchinson. 2 Vols.

PLINY: NATURAL HISTORY. H. Rackham and W. H. S. Jones.
10 Vols. Vols. I.–V. and IX. H. Rackham. Vols. VI. and
VII. W. H. S. Jones.

PROPERTIUS. H. E. Butler.

PRUDENTIUS. H. J. Thomson. 2 Vols.

QUINTILIAN. H. E. Butler. 4 Vols.

REMAINS OF OLD LATIN. E. H. Warmington. 4 Vols. Vol. I.
(ENNIUS AND CAECILIUS.) Vol. II. (LIVIUS, NAEVIUS,
PACUVIUS, ACCIUS.) Vol. III. (LUCILIUS and LAWS OF XII
TABLES.) (ARCHAIC INSCRIPTIONS.)

SALLUST. J. C. Rolfe.

SCRIPTORES HISTORIAE AUGUSTAE. D. Magie. 3 Vols.

SENECA: APOCOLOCYNTOSIS. Cf. PETRONIUS.

SENECA: EPISTULAE MORALES. R. M. Gummere. 3 Vols.

SENECA: MORAL ESSAYS. J. W. Basore. 3 Vols.

SENECA: TRAGEDIES. F. J. Miller. 2 Vols.

SIDONIUS: POEMS and LETTERS. W. B. Anderson. 2 Vols.

SILIUS ITALICUS. J. D. Duff. 2 Vols.

STATIUS. J. H. Mozley. 2 Vols.

SUETONIUS. J. C. Rolfe. 2 Vols.

TACITUS: DIALOGUES. Sir Wm. Peterson. AGRICOLA and
GERMANIA. Maurice Hutton.

TACITUS: HISTORIES AND ANNALS. C. H. Moore and J. Jackson.
4 Vols.

TERENCE. John Sargeaunt. 2 Vols.

TERTULLIAN: APOLOGIA and DE SPECTACULIS. T. R. Glover.
MINUCIUS FELIX. G. H. Rendall.

VALERIUS FLACCUS. J. H. Mozley.

VARRO: DE LINGUA LATINA. R. G. Kent. 2 Vols.

VELLEIUS PATERCULUS and RES GESTAE DIVI AUGUSTI. F. W.
Shipley.

VIRGIL. H. R. Fairclough. 2 Vols.

VITRUVIUS: DE ARCHITECTURA. F. Granger. 2 Vols.

Greek Authors

ACHILLES TATIUS. S. Gaselee.

AELIAN: ON THE NATURE OF ANIMALS. A. F. Scholfield. 3 Vols.

AENEAS TACTICUS, ASCLEPIODOTUS and ONASANDER. The Illinios Greek Club.

AESCHINES. C. D. Adams.

AESCHYLUS. H. Weir Smyth. 2 Vols.

ALCIPHRON, AELIAN, PHILOSTRATUS: LETTERS. A. R. Benner and F. H. Fobes.

ANDOCIDES, ANTIPHON, Cf. MINOR ATTIC ORATORS.

APOLLODORUS. Sir James G. Frazer. 2 Vols.

APOLLONIUS RHODIUS. R. C. Seaton.

THE APOSTOLIC FATHERS. Kirsopp Lake. 2 Vols.

APPIAN: ROMAN HISTORY. Horace White. 4 Vols.

ARATUS. Cf. CALLIMACHUS.

ARISTOPHANES. Benjamin Bickley Rogers. 3 Vols. Verse trans.

ARISTOTLE: ART OF RHETORIC. J. H. Freese.

ARISTOTLE: ATHENIAN CONSTITUTION, EUDEMIAN ETHICS, VICES AND VIRTUES. H. Rackham.

ARISTOTLE: GENERATION OF ANIMALS. A. L. Peck.

ARISTOTLE: METAPHYSICS. H. Tredennick. 2 Vols.

ARISTOTLE: METEROLOGICA. H. D. P. Lee.

ARISTOTLE: MINOR WORKS. W. S. Hett. On Colours, On Things Heard, On Physiognomies, On Plants, On Marvellous Things Heard, Mechanical Problems, On Indivisible Lines, On Situations and Names of Winds, On Melissus, Xenophanes, and Gorgias.

ARISTOTLE: NICOMACHEAN ETHICS. H. Rackham.

ARISTOTLE: OECONOMICA and MAGNA MORALIA. G. C. Armstrong; (with Metaphysics, Vol. II.).

ARISTOTLE: ON THE HEAVENS. W. K. C. Guthrie.

ARISTOTLE: ON THE SOUL. PARVA NATURALIA. ON BREATH. W. S. Hett.

ARISTOTLE: ORGANON—Categories, On Interpretation, Prior Analytics. H. P. Cooke and H. Tredennick.

ARISTOTLE: ORGANON—Posterior Analytics, Topics. H. Tredennick and E. S. Foster.

ARISTOTLE: ORGANON—On Sophistical Refutations. On Coming to be and Passing Away, On the Cosmos. E. S. Forster and D. J. Furley.

ARISTOTLE: PARTS OF ANIMALS. A. L. Peck; MOTION AND PROGRESSION OF ANIMALS. E. S. Forster.

4

ARISTOTLE: PHYSICS. Rev. P. Wicksteed and F. M. Cornford. 2 Vols.

ARISTOTLE: POETICS and LONGINUS. W. Hamilton Fyfe; DEMETRIUS ON STYLE. W, Rhys Roberts.

ARISTOTLE: POLITICS. H. Rackham.

ARISTOTLE: PROBLEMS. W. S. Hett. 2 Vols.

ARISTOTLE: RHETORICA AD ALEXANDRUM (with PROBLEMS. Vol. II.). H. Rackham.

ARRIAN: HISTORY OF ALEXANDER and INDICA. Rev. E. Iliffe Robson. 2 Vols.

ATHENAEUS: DEIPNOSOPHISTAE. C. B. Gulick. 7 Vols.

ST. BASIL: LETTERS. R. J. Deferrari. 4 Vols.

CALLIMACHUS: FRAGMENTS. C. A. Trypanis.

CALLIMACHUS, Hymns and Epigrams, and LYCOPHRON. A. W. Mair; ARATUS. G. R. Mair.

CLEMENT of ALEXANDRIA. Rev. G. W. Butterworth.

COLLUTHUS. Cf. OPPIAN.

DAPHNIS AND CHLOE. Thornley's Translation revised by J. M. Edmonds; and PARTHENIUS. S. Gaselee.

DEMOSTHENES I.: OLYNTHIACS, PHILIPPICS and MINOR ORATIONS. I.–XVII. AND XX. J. H. Vince.

DEMOSTHENES II.: DE CORONA and DE FALSA LEGATIONE. C. A. Vince and J. H. Vince.

DEMOSTHENES III.: MEIDIAS, ANDROTION, ARISTOCRATES, TIMOCRATES and ARISTOGEITON, I. AND II. J. H. Vince.

DEMOSTHENES IV.–VI.: PRIVATE ORATIONS and IN NEAERAM. A. T. Murray.

DEMOSTHENES VII.: FUNERAL SPEECH, EROTIC ESSAY, EXORDIA and LETTERS. N. W. and N. J. DeWitt.

DIO CASSIUS: ROMAN HISTORY. E. Cary. 9 Vols.

DIO CHRYSOSTOM. J. W. Cohoon and H. Lamar Crosby. 5 Vols.

DIODORUS SICULUS. 12 Vols. Vols. I.–VI. C. H. Oldfather. Vol. VII. C. L. Sherman. Vols. IX. and X. R. M. Geer. Vol. XI. F. Walton.

DIOGENES LAERTIUS. R. D. Hicks. 2 Vols.

DIONYSIUS OF HALICARNASSUS: ROMAN ANTIQUITIES. Spelman's translation revised by E. Cary. 7 Vols.

EPICTETUS. W. A. Oldfather. 2 Vols.

EURIPIDES. A. S. Way. 4 Vols. Verse trans.

EUSEBIUS: ECCLESIASTICAL HISTORY. Kirsopp Lake and J. E. L. Oulton. 2 Vols.

GALEN: ON THE NATURAL FACULTIES. A. J. Brock.

THE GREEK ANTHOLOGY. W. R. Paton. 5 Vols.

GREEK ELEGY AND IAMBUS with the ANACREONTEA. J. M. Edmonds. 2 Vols.

THE GREEK BUCOLIC POETS (THEOCRITUS, BION, MOSCHUS). J. M. Edmonds.

GREEK MATHEMATICAL WORKS. Ivor Thomas. 2 Vols.

HERODES. Cf. THEOPHRASTUS: CHARACTERS.

HERODOTUS. A. D. Godley. 4 Vols.

HESIOD AND THE HOMERIC HYMNS. H. G. Evelyn White.

HIPPOCRATES and the FRAGMENTS OF HERACLEITUS. W. H. S. Jones and E. T. Withington. 4 Vols.

HOMER: ILIAD. A. T. Murray. 2 Vols.

HOMER: ODYSSEY. A. T. Murray. 2 Vols.

ISAEUS. E. W. Forster.

ISOCRATES. George Norlin and LaRue Van Hook. 3 Vols.

ST. JOHN DAMASCENE: BARLAAM AND IOASAPH. Rev. G. R. Woodward and Harold Mattingly.

JOSEPHUS. H. St. J. Thackeray and Ralph Marcus. 9 Vols. Vols. I.–VII.

JULIAN. Wilmer Cave Wright. 3 Vols.

LUCIAN. 8 Vols. Vols. I.–V. A. M. Harmon. Vol. VI. K. Kilburn.

LYCOPHRON. Cf. CALLIMACHUS.

LYRA GRAECA. J. M. Edmonds. 3 Vols.

LYSIAS. W. R. M. Lamb.

MANETHO. W. G. Waddell: PTOLEMY: TETRABIBLOS. F. E. Robbins.

MARCUS AURELIUS. C. R. Haines.

MENANDER. F. G. Allinson.

MINOR ATTIC ORATORS (ANTIPHON, ANDOCIDES, LYCURGUS, DEMADES, DINARCHUS, HYPEREIDES). K. J. Maidment and J. O. Burrt. 2 Vols.

NONNOS: DIONYSIACA. W. H. D. Rouse. 3 Vols.

OPPIAN, COLLUTHUS, TRYPHIODORUS. A. W. Mair.

PAPYRI. NON-LITERARY SELECTIONS. A. S. Hunt and C. C. Edgar. 2 Vols. LITERARY SELECTIONS (Poetry). D. L. Page.

PARTHENIUS. Cf. DAPHNIS AND CHLOE.

PAUSANIAS: DESCRIPTION OF GREECE. W. H. S. Jones. 4 Vols. and Companion Vol. arranged by R. E. Wycherley.

PHILO. 10 Vols. Vols. I.–V.; F. H. Colson and Rev. G. H. Whitaker. Vols. VI.–IX.; F. H. Colson.

PHILO: two supplementary Vols. (*Translation only.*) Ralph Marcus.

PHILOSTRATUS: THE LIFE OF APOLLONIUS OF TYANA. F. C. Conybeare. 2 Vols.

PHILOSTRATUS: IMAGINES; CALLISTRATUS: DESCRIPTIONS. A. Fairbanks.

6

PHILOSTRATUS and EUNAPIUS: LIVES OF THE SOPHISTS. Wilmer Cave Wright.

PINDAR. Sir J. E. Sandys.

PLATO: CHARMIDES, ALCIBIADES, HIPPARCHUS, THE LOVERS, THEAGES, MINOS and EPINOMIS. W. R. M. Lamb.

PLATO: CRATYLUS, PARMENIDES, GREATER HIPPIAS, LESSER HIPPIAS. H. N. Fowler.

PLATO: EUTHYPHRO, APOLOGY, CRITO, PHAEDO, PHAEDRUS. H. N. Fowler.

PLATO: LACHES, PROTAGORAS, MENO, EUTHYDEMUS. W. R. M. Lamb.

PLATO: LAWS. Rev. R. G. Bury. 2 Vols.

PLATO: LYSIS, SYMPOSIUM, GORGIAS. W. R. M. Lamb.

PLATO: REPUBLIC. Paul Shorey. 2 Vols.

PLATO: STATESMAN, PHILEBUS. H. N. Fowler; ION. W. R. M. Lamb.

PLATO: THEAETETUS and SOPHIST. H. N. Fowler.

PLATO: TIMAEUS, CRITIAS, CLITOPHO, MENEXENUS, EPISTULAE. Rev. R. G. Bury.

PLUTARCH: MORALIA. 15 Vols. Vols. I.–V. F. C. Babbitt. Vol. VI. W. C. Helmbold. Vol. VII. P. H. De Lacy and B. Einarson. Vol. IX. E. L. Minar, Jr., F. H. Sandbach, W. C. Helmbold. Vol. X. H. N. Fowler. Vol. XII. H. Cherniss and W. C. Helmbold.

PLUTARCH: THE PARALLEL LIVES. B. Perrin. 11 Vols.

POLYBIUS. W. R. Paton. 6 Vols.

PROCOPIUS: HISTORY OF THE WARS. H. B. Dewing. 7 Vols.

PTOLEMY: TETRABIBLOS. Cf. MANETHO.

QUINTUS SMYRNAEUS. A. S. Way. Verse trans.

SEXTUS EMPIRICUS. Rev. R. G. Bury. 4 Vols.

SOPHOCLES. F. Storr. 2 Vols. Verse trans.

STRABO: GEOGRAPHY. Horace L. Jones. 8 Vols.

THEOPHRASTUS: CHARACTERS. J. M. Edmonds. HERODES, etc. A. D. Knox.

THEOPHRASTUS: ENQUIRY INTO PLANTS. Sir Arthur Hort, Bart. 2 Vols.

THUCYDIDES. C. F. Smith. 4 Vols.

TRYPHIODORUS. Cf. OPPIAN.

XENOPHON: CYROPAEDIA. Walter Miller. 2 Vols.

XENOPHON: HELLENICA, ANABASIS, APOLOGY, and SYMPOSIUM. C. L. Brownson and O. J. Todd. 3 Vols.

XENOPHON: MEMORABILIA and OECONOMICUS. E. C. Marchant.

XENOPHON: SCRIPTA MINORA. E. C. Marchant.

IN PREPARATION

Greek Authors

ARISTOTLE: HISTORY OF ANIMALS.   A. L. Peck.

PLOTINUS: A. H. Armstrong.

Latin Authors

BABRIUS AND PHAEDRUS.   Ben E. Perry.

DESCRIPTIVE PROSPECTUS ON APPLICATION

London   WILLIAM HEINEMANN LTD
Cambridge, Mass.   HARVARD UNIVERSITY PRESS